Landmark Essays

Landmark Essays

on
American
Public Address

Edited by Martin J. Medhurst

Hermagoras Press
1993

Copyright © 1993 Hermagoras Press

Published 1993 by Hermagoras Press,
P.O. Box 1555, Davis, CA 95617

Cover design by Kathi Zamminer

Typesetting and Camera-ready Production
by Graphic Gold, Davis, California
Manufactured in the United States of America
by KNI Inc., Anaheim, California

ISBN 1-880393-04-2

2 3 4 5 6 7 8 9 0

In memory of...

G. P. MOHRMANN
(1925-1985)

We Men, who in our morn of youth defied
The elements, must vanish—be it so!
Enough, if something from our hands have power
To live, and act, and serve the future hour.
*   -Wordsworth*

129916

About the Editor

Martin J. Medhurst is Professor of Speech Communication and Coordinator of the Program in Presidential Rhetoric at Texas A&M University. He is the author or editor of six books, including *Dwight D. Eisenhower: Strategic Communicator, Eisenhower's War of Words: Rhetoric and Leadership,* and *Cold War Rhetoric: Strategy, Metaphor, and Ideology.* He is a frequent contributor to journals in communication studies and has written chapters for several books, including *Texts in Context, American Rhetoric, The Inaugural Addresses of Twentieth-Century American Presidents, Television Studies,* and *The Modern Presidency and Crisis Rhetoric.* A former book review editor for *The Quarterly Journal of Speech,* Medhurst now serves as senior editor for the Michigan State University Press series in Rhetoric and Public Affairs.

Table of Contents

Introduction

Essays

Introduction

The Academic Study of Public Address:
A Tradition in Transition

by Martin J. Medhurst

This volume traces the historical evolution of American academic thought concerning public address—what it is, how it ought to be studied, and what can be learned by engaging rhetorical texts in an analytical fashion. To begin, one must distinguish among three separate but interrelated uses of the term "public address"—as practice, theory, and criticism.

As a practice, public address usually refers to the making and delivery of public speeches, the paradigmatic instance of which was the nineteenth century platform oration. Men such as Webster, Clay, Calhoun, Lincoln, Ingersoll, Phillips, Moody, and Bryan were distinguished, in part, by their oratorical abilities. Such abilities were recognized throughout the nineteenth century and well into the twentieth as central to democratic life and culture in the United States. To be able to articulate a point of view, defend a proposition, attack an evil, or celebrate a set of common values was seen as one of the central ways in which the people retained their freedoms and shaped their society. Training in public speaking or public address was thus understood to be preparation for citizenship in a democratic Republic. It was this sense of the term that motivated the founding, in 1914, of a new scholarly organization called The National Association of Academic Teachers of Public Speaking. As Andrew Weaver has noted:

> For the founders of The National Association of Academic Teachers of Public Speaking every term in that title had special significance. The organization was to be "national" rather than sectional. It was to be composed of "academic teachers" rather than artists and studio coaches. "Public speaking" was designed to make it clear that attention was to be focused on direct, communicative public address rather than on the half-horse-half-alligator antics of the elocutionists. Our founding fathers believed, almost passionately, that unless artificial and extravagant exhibitionism were abandoned, their courses could never win academic acceptance.[1]

---

[1] Andrew Thomas Weaver, "Seventeen Who Made History—The Founders of the Association," *The Quarterly Journal of Speech* 45 (1959): 196.

Thus, from the outset, public address as an academic subject was understood primarily in terms of performance—learning how to give a speech. One way in which to learn the principles of public speaking was to observe and imitate the speech behaviors of others—to study "great" orators with an eye to emulation of their language, style, or delivery. Implicit in such imitation, however, were certain principles of speech making that transcended the individual—principles that were in some sense general or universal. Such principles included ways to discover ideas for speeches, patterns for organizing those ideas, and use of figures of speech such as metaphor, parallelism, or antithesis. To learn these more general principles, teachers of public speaking turned to the classical treatises on human communication—to what the ancients called rhetoric. Foremost among these works was Aristotle's *Rhetoric*, Cicero's *De Inventione* and *De Oratore*, and the anonymous *Rhetorica Ad Herennium*, once thought to have been written by Cicero. Ancient rhetoric, along with such eighteenth and nineteenth century rhetorical works as Hugh Blair's *Lectures on Rhetoric and Belles Lettres* and Richard Whately's *Elements of Rhetoric*, thus came to serve as the theoretical bases of public address. Rhetoric was the theory; public speaking the practice. The goal was to instruct students in the art of public address and thereby produce graduates capable of exerting leadership in government, education, religion, law, and other professions where the ability to speak clearly and convincingly was highly valued.

Since the motive for introducing public address to the academy was primarily pedagogical, scholarship in the area was slow in developing. The earliest issues of *The Quarterly Journal of Public Speaking* (later *The Quarterly Journal of Speech*) were devoted, for the most part, to problems in the teaching or practice of public speaking, debate, theater, and speech correction. Even so, from the very first volume, published in April 1915, there was a recognition that research would have to become a part of the intellectual agenda if the new field was to thrive.[2] Precisely what form that research was to take or what theoretical perspectives or methodological tools were to be employed was not at all clear. Indeed, what constituted the important questions in need of investigation was not clear. Research questions, to the extent that they existed at all, seemed to be driven by pedagogical rather than theoretical concerns. To solve these pedagogical problems, early scholars of public speaking adapted methods derived from the emerging disciplines of psychology and sociology, turned to English and literature for models of scholarship, or mined for theoretical principles in the works of ancient orators and rhetoricians.

Some of the early work, particularly in the area of classical rhetorical

---

[2] See J. A. Winans, "The Need for Research," *The Quarterly Journal of Public Speaking* 1 (1915): 17-23; and, "Research in Public Speaking—The Research Committee," *The Quarterly Journal of Public Speaking* 1 (1915): 24-32.

theory, was quite good. Between 1915 and 1925, scholars such as Hoyt H. Hudson, Everett Lee Hunt, William E. Utterback, Paul Shorey, and Bromley Smith produced essays of lasting value.[3] Others, such as A. Craig Baird, sought to bring the insights of classical rhetoric to bear on the teaching and practice of debate.[4] Classical rhetoric was slowly becoming the theoretical underpinning of public address. Interestingly enough, there was no parallel movement during the first decade of the discipline to establish a critical or analytical framework parallel to that of the theoretical framework provided by ancient rhetoric. Even had such an analytical framework evolved before 1925, there was no clear object, artifact, event, or group to which such a framework might be applied. In short, there was no basic unit of analysis as existed in other fields of humanistic learning. Whereas the scholar of literature could and did study the plays of Shakespeare, or the poetry of Donne, or the novels of Hawthorne, and the scholar of history could specialize in an era or a movement, and the student of philosophy could focus on metaphysics, or ethics, or analytics, there was developed no parallel route for scholarly endeavor in the field of public address. Indeed, a search of the first ten years of *The Quarterly Journal of Public Speaking* reveals only three articles (out of three-hundred and forty-three published) that even hint at a basic unit of analysis.

In 1916, J.H. Doyle published an essay on "The Style of Wendell Phillips"; in 1920, Charles F. Lindsley produced an essay on "Henry Woodfin Grady, Orator"; and, in 1925, Marvin Bauer wrote a short article on "The Influence of Lincoln's Audiences on His Speeches."[5] Each of these three essays suggested a potential answer to the question, "What is the basic unit of analysis in the field of public address?" With Doyle, one could have said that the basic unit was the rhetorical canon of style and that scholars of public address were expert in the analysis and criticism of oratorical style and its manifestation in the delivery of the speech. Or, with Lindsley, one could have taken the individual speaker as the basic unit of analysis. Such an approach would have resulted in character studies that read the life of the

---

[3] See, for example, Everett Lee Hunt, "Plato on Rhetoric and Rhetoricians," *The Quarterly Journal of Speech Education 6* (June, 1920): 35-56; Bromley Smith, "Prodicus of Ceos: The Sire of Synonomy," *The Quarterly Journal of Speech Education 6* (April, 1920): 51-68; Paul Shorey, "What Teachers of Speech May Learn from the Theory and Practice of the Greeks," *The Quarterly Journal of Speech Education 8* (1922): 105-131; Hoyt H. Hudson, "The Field of Rhetoric," *The Quarterly Journal of Speech Education 9* (1923): 167-180; Hoyt H. Hudson, "Rhetoric and Poetry," *The Quarterly Journal of Speech Education 10* (1924): 143-154; William E. Utterback, "Aristotle's Contribution to the Psychology of Argument," *The Quarterly Journal of Speech Edcuation 11* (1925): 218-225.
[4] A. Craig Baird, "Shall American Universities Adopt the British System of Debating?" *The Quarterly Journal of Speech Education 9* (1923): 205-222; A. Craig Baird, "Argumentation as a Humanistic Subject," *The Quarterly Journal of Speech Education 10* (1924): 258-264.
[5] J. H. Doyle, "The Style of Wendell Phillips," *The Quarterly Journal of Public Speaking 2* (1916): 331-339; Charles F. Lindsley, "Henry Woodfin Grady, Orator," *The Quarterly Journal of Speech Education 6* (April, 1920): 27-42; Marvin Bauer, "The Influence of Lincoln's Audiences on His Speeches," *The Quarterly Journal of Speech Education 11* (1925): 225-229.

orator through the lens of his public orations. The basic form of this approach
would then have been the rhetorical biography. Or, with Bauer, one could
have focused not on the speaker but on the audience, seeking to understand
the influence which the audience exerted on speech composition and delivery.
Such an approach, if applied systematically, might have resulted in studies
that revealed the mind of an era.

Any one of the three approaches employed between 1915 and 1925 might
have provided an analytical framework for study of public address had they
been pursued in a systematic manner, yet none did. Indeed, the field was so
young that even the subject matter which properly fell within its domain was
contested. In 1923, faculty members at Cornell University—one of the first
institutions of higher learning in America to offer the doctorate in Speech—
published a list of one hundred and twenty-nine subjects that could, they
believed, profitably be studied by graduate students of public address. These
topics ranged from the *practical* ("Public speakers and their use of outlines")
to the *theoretical* ("Rhetoric and dialectic") to the *historical* ("Comparative
study of Quintilian, Cicero, and Seneca") to the *pedagogical* ("The teaching
of gesture") to the *analytical* ("A rhetorical study of the speeches of certain
individuals or of certain corpora").[6] One might think that this variety of
materials for study could easily lead to numerous divisions or approaches to
scholarship within the field. But that did not happen. Instead, the patterns
established during the first ten years—the focus on classroom pedagogy as it
applied to performance in public speaking, debate, and theatrical production,
the study of classical rhetoric as historical exemplar and theoretical rationale,
and the analysis of "great" orators, more for their ability to serve as
classroom examples than for any artistic merit that might be present in their
orations—constituted the foci of the field from 1915 until well into the
1960s. As A. M. Drummond noted in 1923, "the chief purpose of our graduate study is to influence the class-room."[7] And so it was.

From Wichelns to Black

Public address scholarship in the period 1925-1965 was characterized by
three watershed events: the publication, in 1925, of Herbert A. Wichelns's
now-classic essay "The Literary Criticism of Oratory"; the issuance, in 1943,
of the two-volume set *A History and Criticism of American Public Address*,
edited by William Norwood Brigance; and the release, in 1965, of Edwin
Black's ground-breaking book, *Rhetorical Criticism: A Study in Method.*[8]

---

[6] "Some Subjects For Graduate Study Suggested by Members of the Department of Public Speaking of
Cornell University," *The Quarterly Journal of Speech Education 9* (1923): 147-153.
[7] A. M. Drummond, "Graduate Work in Public Speaking," *The Quarterly Journal of Speech Education
9* (1923): 136.
[8] Herbert A. Wichelns, "The Literary Criticism of Oratory," in *Studies in Rhetoric and Public Speaking
in Honor of James Albert Winans* (New York: The Century Co., 1925), 181-216; [See pp. 1-32, here.]
William Norwood Brigance, ed., *A History and Criticism of American Public Address*, 2 vols. (New
York: McGraw-Hill, 1943); Edwin Black, *Rhetorical Criticism: A Study in Method* (1965; rpt.
Madison: University of Wisconsin Press, 1978).

Although other events and publications were important, these three constituted truly epochal moments in the intellectual development of the field. To understand the effects these works had on how scholarship in rhetoric and public address was conducted is to begin to understand why most of the essays in this volume deal with matters that might at first seem rather basic, if not merely parochial—the relationship of oratory to the other arts, the place of historical investigation in the study of orators and oratory, the proper scope of oratorical studies (individual speakers *versus* social movements *versus* historical epochs), the proper role of the critic (to describe *versus* to interpret *versus* to judge *versus* to evaluate *versus* to appreciate), the relationship of a speaker's ideas to more general cultural trends, the proper critical standards or norms for evaluation (internal artistic standards *versus* external effects standards *versus* universal truth standards), and the role played by values in the processes of speech composition and reception.

Wichelns and Critical Method

No single work had any greater impact on the field of rhetoric and public address than "The Literary Criticism of Oratory," by Herbert A. Wichelns of Cornell University. Originally published as a chapter in a 1925 book honoring the work of James A. Winans, Wichelns's essay has been reprinted numerous times and is still required reading in courses in speech criticism, rhetorical theory, and rhetorical criticism.[9] Wichelns correctly pointed to the lack of "much serious criticism of oratory."[10] His survey of nineteenth century literary critics found few that dealt at all with oratory, fewer still that treated oratory as something qualitatively different than literature, and only a handful of works whose standards of judgment seemed to him appropriate for an activity that was "partly an art, partly a power of making history, and occasionally a branch of literature."[11] This state of affairs he sought to correct. His goal was to put rhetorical studies on a par with literary studies as an area of academic interest and research.

Wichelns's believed that for oratory to be taken seriously as an academic subject, it had to be treated in a serious manner. That meant, among other things, that it had to be subject to criticism and analysis in much the same manner as enduring works of literature. But Wichelns understood that while the tools of literary analysis were necessary—and perhaps even sufficient—for the student of oratory, the ends of great literature and the means of judging imaginative works were insufficient for the analysis of oratory. Because oratory was "intimately associated with statecraft," it could be

---

[9] Wichelns's essay has most recently been reprinted in Edward P. J. Corbett, James L. Golden, and Goodwin F. Berquist, eds., *Essays on the Rhetoric of the Western World* (Dubuque: Kendall/Hunt Publishing Co., 1990), 55-82 and here, pp. 1-32. My references are to this edition of the essay.

[10] Wichelns, 2.

[11] Wichelns, 24.

understood and appreciated "only by the careful student of history."[12] In short, oratory operated in the real world, not the imaginative; it dealt with real people and events, not characters and plots; it had real and sometimes enduring consequences for the lives of people, not merely some momentary flight into fantasy or make believe. While oratory was a language art, it was also more. It was a power used to shape decision making and influence decision makers. It was, as Aristotle had said about rhetoric, part of the ethical branch of politics, the branch concerned with making decisions about the nature of the good in community.

Wichelns had precious little upon which to build. Among nineteenth-century commentators, he found only the work of Chauncey Goodrich to have "critical significance" for the analysis of oratory. Hence his task was to construct a framework within which scholars of public address could subject oratory to the same sort of analysis that literary scholars accorded to works of fiction. Wichelns held that "the man, his works, his times, are the necessary common topics of criticism" and that "no one of them can be wholly disregarded by any critic."[13] Working from this foundational principle, Wichelns sought to distinguish oratorical or rhetorical criticism from its literary counterpart. "Rhetorical criticism," he wrote, "is not concerned with permanence, nor yet with beauty. It is concerned with effect. It regards a speech as a communication to a specific audience, and holds its business to be the analysis and appreciation of the orator's method of imparting his ideas to his hearers."[14] These three sentences, which would become the source of much misunderstanding and misapplication of Wichelns's ideas, became the theoretical stance from which forty years of work in public address criticism flowed. But this was not all that Wichelns offered. He also articulated a fifteen-point scheme for what "a rhetorical study includes." This scheme included:

1. The speaker's personality as a conditioning factor
2. The public character of the man—what he was thought to be
3. A description of the audience
4. The leading ideas with which he plied his hearers
5. The topics he drew upon
6. The motives to which he appealed
7. Proofs offered in his speeches
8. The relation of surviving texts to what was actually uttered
9. The adapatation to two audiences—that which heard and that which read
10. The speaker's mode of arranging ideas
11. The speaker's mode of expression

---

[12]Wichelns, 2.
[13]Wichelns, 3.
[14]Wichelns, 26.

12. The speaker's habits of preparation
13. The manner of delivery from the platform
14. The speaker's style, especially diction and sentence movement
15. The effect of the discourse on its immediate hearers[15]

It is unclear from Wichelns's essay whether he expected every rhetorical study to touch upon all fifteen of these points. What is clear is that he never intended to reduce the study of oratory to the single question of its effect on the immediate audience. Indeed, had there been a systematic development of Wicheln's fifteen points, the practice of oratorical criticism might have evolved in significantly different directions than it did.

From 1925 through 1935 there was little or no advancement in either the theory or practice of rhetorical criticism. While critical studies increased slightly—fourteen articles out of four hundred and three published in *QJS* during this period)—there emerged neither a basic unit of analysis nor a systematic approach to criticism. The few studies that were published tended to deal with the background and preparation of the speaker, the sources from which speakers drew their ideas, or various aspects of style, often reported in statistical form. Of the fourteen articles published, seven focused on either Abraham Lincoln or Woodrow Wilson. In short, from a conceptual or methodological point of view, there was virtually no advancement between criticism as practiced in the first decade of the field's existence and that practiced in the second decade, Wichelns's seminal essay notwithstanding. Much effort was still expended on the identification of orators for study, the construction of basic bibliographies, and the translation of speeches.[16]

Writing in 1933, William Norwood Brigance lamented the current state of scholarship in rhetoric and public address: "I think we ought to recognize that there is a great body of rhetorical or oratorical literature almost untouched by scholars in our field. Of it, I think we might safely say that this literature can do without our scholarship, but that our scholarship cannot do without that literature. Sooner or later we shall be called to the bar to answer for our neglect."[17] He then went on to suggest "one direction, at least, in which our scholarship ought to move next, namely to undertake a *combined historical* and *critical* study of orators and oratorical literature, and to produce thereby a body of oratorical studies and criticisms worthy of the orators and oratory

---

[15]Paraphrased from Wichelns, 28-29.

[16]See, for example, A. Craig Baird, "A Selected Bibliography of American Oratory," *The Quarterly Journal of Speech Education 12* (1926): 352-356; James Milton O'Neill, "A Bibliographical Introduction to Graduate Work in Speech," *The Quarterly Journal of Speech Education 13* (1927): 39-48; Bromley Smith, "A College Oration of John Milton: A Translation," *The Quarterly Journal of Speech 24* (1928): 392-396; J. Fred McGrew, "A Bibliography of the Works on Rhetoric and Related Subjects in England During the 16th and 17th Centuries," *The Quarterly Journal of Speech 15* (1929): 380-412; Dayton D. McKean, "A Bibliography of Debating," *The Quarterly Journal of Speech 19* (1933): 206-210; and, Abraham Tauber, "A Guide to the Literature of Speech Education," *The Quarterly Journal of Speech 20* (1934): 507-524.

[17]William Norwood Brigance, "Whither Research?" *The Quarterly Journal of Speech 19* (1933): 556.

which induced it."[18] Such an undertaking, Brigance argued, "would produce a body of oratorical criticism and understanding that we do not have today."[19]

Brigance's essay was important, not only for the warning it issued but also for what it did not say. Nowhere in Brigance nor anywhere else in the previous nineteen-year history of the field had anyone suggested—at least not in print—that the basic unit of analysis ought to be the single speech text. Much was written about orators (speakers) and oratory (the act of giving a speech), but virtually nothing about the speech itself as an artistically structured message. For a field which by the mid-1930s was calling itself "Speech," it was indeed ironic that no one undertook the serious study of speeches.[20] It was not until 1937—some twenty-three years after the founding of the discipline—that the *Quarterly Journal of Speech* published the first analysis of a single speech text, an examination of Franklin D. Roosevelt's Second Inaugural Address.[21]

The implications of Brigance's warning, as well as of his oversight, are central to understanding the issues that would come to dominate debate among scholars of rhetoric and public address from the mid-1930s until the mid-1960s. The program that Brigance called for in 1933 was pursued in journal articles over the course of the next decade and culminated in the two-volume work titled, appropriately enough, *A History and Criticism of American Public Address* (1943). But even in the midst of this first truly systematic attempt to establish a body of critical writing, there were raised voices of concern. One such voice was that of Donald Cross Bryant.

Writing in 1937, Bryant raised the issue of "The Problem of Scope and Method in Rhetorical Scholarship." The central question, as he saw it, was "What are we about, and how are we to go about it?"[22] Bryant identified the writing of rhetorical history as a central concern of the discipline: "The criticism of oratory, while never ignoring the place and significance which a speech or a man may have at present, independent of his own age, will be mainly and emphatically interested in what that speech and that man were, or more especially what they seemed to be, to their contemporaries in their contemporary settings. Hence it is that rhetorical criticism . . . cannot do

---

[18]Brigance, "Whither," 557.

[19]Brigance, "Whither," 560.

[20]This statement applies only to published research. It is certainly true that during the 1930s several graduate students wrote theses and/or dissertations which focussed on analysis of individual speeches. For some strange reason, such studies never made it into the professional speech journals, thus retarding the intellectual advancement of the field.

[21]Robert D. King, "Franklin D. Roosevelt's Second Inaugural Address," *The Quarterly Journal of Speech 23* (1937): 439-444.

[22]Donald C. Bryant, "Some Problems of Scope and Method in Rhetorical Scholarship," *The Quarterly Journal of Speech 23* (1937): 182. [See p. 33, here.] In a personal letter to the author on 11 August 1993, Carroll C. Arnold noted that "the problem and scope of rhetorical scholarship was a topic both Baird and Wichelns often discussed in convention papers." Bryant had been a student of Wichelns's at Cornell University.

without rhetorical history, and full and accurate history at that."[23] For Bryant, the proper focus of study was the historical public address, understood as an operative force within the history of its own times. Study of oratory thus became a specialized sort of social, cultural, and intellectual history, as his own studies of Edmund Burke were to demonstrate.[24]

Clearly Bryant, like Brigance, was concerned that the study of oratory not be divorced from the historical circumstances which called it forth and imparted to it its peculiar character. He was also concerned that the intellectual trend-setters of the day—"the work of Turner, of Parrington, of the Beards"—not be allowed to subsume the study of individual orators and speeches. "Probably it has been the fault of history in the past, and especially the fault of the history of literature and oratory," wrote Bryant, "to let the study of figures obscure or blot out the study of forces and social movements. A corrective balance unquestionably needs to be established."[25] Nevertheless, Bryant continued to hold that "competent studies of rhetorics and rhetoricians, of speeches and speakers, will be as much the proper scope of our scholarship as heretofore."[26]

While the study of speeches and speakers may have been considered as well within the "proper scope" of the field in 1937, it is an empirical fact that precious little research on either speeches or speakers had been published as of that date. The absolute number of such studies would dramatically increase over the course of the next twenty-five years, but it was the publication of *A History and Criticism of American Public Address* in 1943 that established the basic approach and pattern that those subsequent studies would follow. Without an understanding of the effect those two volumes had on the way rhetoric and public address was studied within the discipline of speech, it is impossible to account for what happened—or, more accurately, what did not happen—over the course of the next twenty years.

---

[23]Bryant, "Scope and Method," 35.
[24]Donald C. Bryant, "Edmund Burke on Oratory," *The Quarterly Journal of Speech 19* (1933): 1-18; Bryant, "Edmund Burke's Opinions of Some Orators of His Day," *The Quarterly Journal of Speech 20* (1934): 241-254; Bryant, "Some Notes on Burke's Speeches and Writings," *The Quarterly Journal of Speech 25* (1939): 406-409; Bryant, "Edmund Burke's Conversation," in *Studies in Speech and Drama in Honor of Alexander M. Drummond* (Ithaca: Cornell University Press, 1944), 354-368; Bryant, "Edmund Burke: New Evidence, Broader View," *The Quarterly Journal of Speech 38* (1952): 435-445; Bryant, "Burke's *Present Discontents*: The Rhetorical Genesis of a Party Testament," *The Quarterly Journal of Speech 42* (1956): 115-126; Bryant, "The Contemporary Reception of Edmund Burke's Speaking," in *Historical Studies of Rhetoric and Rhetoricians*, ed. Raymond F. Howes (Ithaca: Cornell University Press, 1961), 271-293; Bryant, "Edmund Burke: The New Images," *The Quarterly Journal of Speech 52* (1966): 329-336; Bryant, *Rhetorical Dimensions in Criticism* (Baton Rouge: Louisiana State University Press, 1973), esp. chapters 3-5. These books and articles reflect only the work published in speech outlets. Bryant published many other analyses of Burke's rhetoric. He was one of the first members of the field to pursue a sustained and programmatic research agenda over the course of an entire career.
[25]Bryant, "Problem and Scope," 38.
[26]Bryant, "Problem and Scope," 37.

Brigance and A History and Criticism of American Public Address

William Norwood Brigance opens his preface to volume one of *A History and Criticism of American Public Address* with this sentence: "This work deals with the influence of American public address on the flow of history."[27] It is an auspicious—and in many ways accurate—description of what follows. Public address is viewed by most contributors as a force—an influence—on the shaping of history. So stated, the subject matter becomes history, with public address the particular entree to understanding historical events and personages. Brigance admits that "no adequate history of public address in America has yet been written, and the general national histories have given no systematic account of its influence."[28] He suggests that the present volumes will, at least in part, rectify this problem, while noting that "it was not easy to determine which speakers, among the many influential ones in American history, should be selected for special study. To include only the traditional names, those commonly listed in the histories of 'oratory,' would have been to continue the confusion between those who spoke 'eloquently' and those who spoke effectively, for not always did the same persons do both."[29] In order to make such selections, Brigance reports that the editorial board consulted experts in history, religious history, and legal biography. In other words, scholars from other disciplines became central arbiters of what scholars of public address thought they could or should study.

In addition to framing the volumes as contributions to history and relying upon the judgment of historians in the matter of subject selection, Brigance and his editorial board clearly distinguished between what they called "historical studies" and "critical studies." This seems an amazing retreat from the pen of the man who called, in 1933, for studies that were simultaneously historical and critical.[30] Now studies of historical periods were to be separated from study of the orators who operated within those periods. Thus, volume one was divided between "The Historical Background of American Public Address" (chapters 1-5) and studies of "Leaders in American Public Address" (chapters 6-16). That the so-called "critical studies" were really much more historical and biographical than critical or analytical should not obscure the fact that history and criticism were conceived as two related, but

---

[27]William Norwood Brigance, "Preface," in *A History and Criticism of American Public Address I* (New York: McGraw-Hill, 1943), vii.

[28]Brigance, "Preface," vii.

[29]Brigance, "Preface," viii.

[30]In a letter to the author on 11 August 1993, Carroll C. Arnold (Ph.D., Iowa, 1942), a former student of A. Craig Baird's and a former colleague of Herbert A. Wichelns's, noted that "Brigance's historical emphasis was significantly derived from Baird, I believe. Brigance was one of Craig's first two doctoral students —so early that they had trouble setting up a committee for him, I'm told. My personal opinion is that the shape of the essays in the first two volumes of *History and Criticism* was mostly constrained by what hopeful scholars knew what to do. I recall that when the volumes came out the dominant hope in SCA [then SAA] was that *historians* would find them contributory—which they didn't."

substantively different enterprises. In point of fact, the general historical surveys were, on the whole, better scholarship than the "critical" studies of leaders.

One of the central problems of the Brigance volumes is that virtually no progress in critical methodology had been made from the publication of Wichelns's essay in 1925. Brigance admits as much in his preface when, concerning critical methodology, he notes: "Some prefer the pure Aristotelian pattern. Some prefer their Aristotelianism diluted. Others abjure it altogether."[31] However, even a casual reading reveals that Aristotelianism or neo-Aristotelianism dominates both volumes. Worse yet, it is a bastardized form of Aristotelianism that Aristotle, himself, probably would not recognize. In general the contributors reduced Aristotle's *Rhetoric* to commentary on the three types of oratory (deliberative, forensic, and epideictic), the five canons of rhetoric (invention, disposition, style, memory, and delivery) and the three modes of proof (ethos, pathos, and logos), with some historical background on speech training and preparation added for good measure.

The important point to remember about the Brigance volumes is that they were *both a culmination* of work that had gone on during the preceding decade (1934-1943) *and a model* for much of the work that would be undertaken over the course of the following two decades—all the way until 1965. As such, they were in some senses anachronistic even as they appeared. This fact was clearly recognized by several scholars who wrote in the immediate aftermath of publication. Dallas Dickey, for example, noted that "after nine years of sustained effort on the part of nearly fifty scholars and editorial critics, *A History and Criticism of American Public Address* has been completed and published. Those who helped to produce these volumes, however, know that this enterprise has merely begun the neglected study of the tremendous influence that public address has had on the stream of American history."[32] While Dickey did not question the emphasis on influence nor the sense that the real contribution to be made was to American history, he nonetheless recognized that there was much work left to be done. So, too, did Bower Aly, who, while praising the "biographical approach exhibited in *A History and Criticism of American Public Address*"[33] nevertheless recognized the need to expand both the philosophical premises of criticism and its methodological tools. "The canons of criticism of speechmaking need to be rediscovered for a generation that has never known them," wrote Aly. "Wichelns's germinal essay should not be the last of its kind. Other writing, informed with the idea and method of Wichelns's essay, should draw precept

---

[31]Brigance, "Preface," x.
[32]Dallas C. Dickey, "What Directions Should Future Research in American Public Address Take?" *The Quarterly Journal of Speech* 29 (1943): 300.
[33]Bower Aly, "The History of American Public Address as a Research Field," *The Quarterly Journal of Speech* 29 (1943): 312.

and example from American experience. Scholars should be encouraged to develop philosophical foundation and critical framework for histories of public speaking in the United States."[34] Other voices, however, seemed content with oratorical criticism as currently practiced and represented in the Brigance volumes. The volumes represented, after all, "a critical approach and method securely established in recent years in graduate divisions of speech departments and schools of speech."[35] Having become "established," the approach and method, as A. Craig Baird called it, would dominate the field for the next twenty years.

Not everyone was as enamored with the biographical approach or the Aristotelian method of analysis as the contributors to *A History and Criticism of American Public Address*. Two such critics were Loren Reid and Ernest Wrage. Writing in 1944, Reid warned of "The Perils of Rhetorical Criticism." One such peril was the tendency merely to report historical and biographical data rather than to criticize the content of the speeches. "Although the reader needs to know what the speaker *said*," wrote Reid, "he really seeks a critical judgment *about* the ideas of the speech."[36] Such critical judgment was to be based on detailed research of the speaking situation, research "not likely to come from a college history textbook, but from letters, diaries, memoirs, and periodicals, and sometimes from specialized monographs."[37] In short, Reid called for research in primary sources. He also noted that from a methodological point of view "Aristotelian rhetoric cannot be made to cover every aspect of all types of speaking."[38] To produce good critical studies of public discourse was a demanding task. Neither second-hand history nor narrowly circumscribed rhetorical theory could produce the type of critical research needed to establish public address scholarship as significant. Reid closed by noting:

> Rhetorical criticism is an exacting type of research. The critic must know what is commonly called rhetoric, but to know rhetoric is not enough. He must know historical methods, but to know historical methods is not enough. He must have infinite patience in the search for details. . . . He must have the imagination to recreate events and movements long since passed into time. And he must take to heart his primary and inescapable responsibility as a critic: to interpret, to appraise, to evaluate; to say here the speaker missed, here he hit the mark.[39]

---

[34] Aly, 313.

[35] A. Craig Baird, "Opportunities for Research in State and Sectional Public Speaking," *The Quarterly Journal of Speech* 29 (1943): 304.

[36] Loren D. Reid, "The Perils of Rhetorical Criticism," *The Quarterly Journal of Speech* 30 (1944): 417. [See p. 40, here.]

[37] Reid, 41.

[38] Reid, 45.

[39] Reid, 46. In a personal letter to the author on 11 August 1993, Carroll C. Arnold noted: "What Reid (Baird's student) was trying to do, I believe, was shake up the 'cookie-cutter' use of the historical-critical essays that were being put out at the time. Wrage had just taken a year off to do advanced work in social history, and he was trying to thrust things in a fresh direction, too. Wrage's early death kept us from seeing where his thoughts would have led eventually."

While Reid's critique of traditional studies in public address was implicit, Ernest Wrage's, written three years later in 1947, was explicit. Wrage attacked head-on the traditional paradigm of public address studies. "The prevailing approach to the history and criticism of public address appears to consist of a study of individual speakers for their influence upon history," he wrote. "If one may judge from studies available through publication, they fall short of that ambitious goal."[40] Instead of the traditional speaker-centered studies, Wrage argued for an "idea-centered" approach to public address. Such an approach would focus "upon the speech and its content" and yield "knowledge of more general interest in terms of man's cultural strivings and heritage."[41] Wrage's call for the serious study of the content of speeches was the first since Bryant argued, in 1937, that "speeches and speakers" should remain central to the scope of rhetorical studies. While many studied "speakers" between 1937 and 1947, virtually no one studied "speeches," at least not in the professional literature of the field. The pages of *Speech Monographs* and *The Quarterly Journal of Speech* revealed the true story: between 1937 and 1947, only seven articles that examined some facet of speeches appeared in *QJS*; only three in *SM*. Clearly Wrage was correct in his judgment that "the rich vein of literature in speaking has hardly been tapped."[42] His call for "a wide investigation of sermons, lectures, and speeches related to issues, movements, and periods" was not immediately forthcoming. His vision of studies in public address becoming "a kind of anthropological approach to a segment of cultural history"[43] found few disciples before the mid-1960s, in part because the dominant paradigm had, in fact, become established not as a way of doing public address criticism, but as the only way.

In the same year that Wrage issued his call for "idea-centered" criticism, A. Craig Baird and Lester Thonnsen published their article on "Methodology in the Criticism of Public Address." The article was a prelude to the publication, in 1948, of their textbook, *Speech Criticism*—the first, and for many years the only, textbook on the analysis and criticism of public address. In their article, Baird and Thonnsen took an expansive view of the scope of public address criticism:

> The critical judgment may limit itself to a single speech, one that was delivered either last week or last century. Or the critic may enlarge the scope of his inquiry to encompass the entire speaking career of the orator; to evaluate a speaking movement, such as temperance reform; or to interpret a period of the history of public speaking. The problem, in any case, is that of pronouncing judgment.[44]

---

[40]Ernest J. Wrage, "Public Address: A Study in Social and Intellectual History," *The Quarterly Journal of Speech* 33 (1947): 454. [See p. 57, here.]

[41]Wrage, 57.

[42]Wrage, 55.

[43]Wrage, 59.

[44]A. Craig Baird and Lester Thonnsen, "Methodology in the Criticism of Public Address," *The Quarterly Journal of Speech* 33 (1947): 134. [See p. 48, here.]

However not just any kind of judgment was contemplated by Baird and Thonnsen. "The judgment," they wrote, "concerns the effect of the discourse" and "the rhetorical appraisal . . . seeks to gauge the immediate and larger effects of a given oral discourse."[45] Thus while expanding the potential scope of rhetorical studies on one hand, the authors severely restricted the kinds of judgments that could be rendered about those studies. Precisely the same stance was taken in their 1948 textbook. Whether labeled Aristotelianism, neo-Aristotelianism, or neo-Classicism, by 1948 the "correct" way to conduct a rhetorical critique had been firmly established in graduate schools, journal articles, and textbook. No sooner had this methodological monism reached its zenith, however, than it began to crumble. That the edifice would survive until the mid-1960s should not obscure the fact that it was being systematically challenged from the late 1940s until the publication of *Rhetorical Criticism: A Study in Method* in 1965.

Clearly both Reid and Wrage were signposts of discontent with the reigning paradigm. Others soon joined the rebellion. The first pillar of the edifice to be attacked was the almost singular focus on great speakers. Throughout the 1930s various writers, including Bryant, had called for more attention to social movements and intellectual forces in public address studies. Yet it was not until the publication of S. Judson Crandell's article on "The Beginnings of a Methodology for Social Control Studies in Public Address" (1947) that serious thought was given to how such phenomena might be studied by students of rhetoric and oratory. This essay was followed, in 1952, by Leland Griffin's pathbreaking essay, "The Rhetoric of Historical Movements."[46] While Crandell and Griffin led the way into what would blossom, in the 1960s and early 1970s, into a long series of articles on the rhetoric of various movements, Marie Hochmuth was introducing the field to the thought of Kenneth Burke, I. A. Richards, and other practioners of the "New Rhetoric." Thus throughout the 1950s both the traditional focus on individual speakers and the methodological hegemony of so-called Aristotelianism were called into question.

Even the "effects" standard of evaluation, ostensibly erected by Wichelns and practiced faithfully by critics thereafter, came under scrutiny. Wayland Maxfield Parrish, in an introductory essay to *American Speeches* (1954) titled

---

[45]Baird and Thonnsen, 50.
[46]S. Judson Crandell, "The Beginnings of a Methodology for Social Control Studies in Public Address," *The Quarterly Journal of Speech 33* (1947): 36-39; Leland M. Griffin, "The Rhetoric of Historical Movements," *The Quarterly Journal of Speech 38* (1952): 184-188. In a personal letter to the author on 11 August 1993, Carroll C. Arnold noted: "I think few people know that 'movement studies' were promoted by Wichelns (and Henry Ewbank at Wisconsin) well before they became a `fashion.' Ewbank directed studies on the neutrality debates prior to WW II, I remember (and there were others). Wichelns was more insistent on that tack. He directed [Leland] Griffin's study of the Anti-Masonic movement and Arthur Barnes's (later Head of Journalism at Penn State) study of the Civil Service Reform movement —and there were others that I can't now remember. The trouble was that neither Wichelns nor Ewbank *wrote* about this as a mode of research, so when Griffin came along in publication about movement study, one couldn't tell where the notion had really started."

"The Study of Speeches," argued that "rhetoric, strictly speaking, is not concerned with the *effect* of a speech, but with its *quality*, and its quality can be determined quite apart from its effect."[47] Speeches, Parrish held, were to be judged by their artistic qualities, not their external effects. Parrish noted that "many of the great speeches of history have been made in lost causes," and argued that "a speaker's success in achieving a desired response from his audience is not necessarily proof that he has spoken well, or his failure, that he has spoken ill."[48] Public address was an art and as such had to be evaluated by the internal standards of excellence peculiar to the art. That such internal artistic standards were poorly understood in the 1950s was a direct outcome of the failure to analyze systematically individual speech texts. By 1955, forty years after James A. Winans first called for systematic research in the speech arts, scholars had yet to produce even a single published essay on such key texts as Lincoln's "Gettysburg Address," "House Divided," or "Second Inaugural." There were no studies of Webster's "Seventh of March Address," none of Washington's "Farewell" or Henry's "Give Me Liberty, or Give Me Death." There were no studies of Jonathan Edwards's "Sinners in the Hands of an Angry God" nor of any single address by Charles Grandison Finney, Dwight L. Moody, or Washington Gladden. None of Theodore Roosevelt's speeches had been the subject of rhetorical investigation nor had those of William Jennings Bryan been studied, not even the famous "Cross of Gold." The list could be expanded indefinitely inasmuch as *QJS* and *SM* combined published only nine studies of speech texts between 1945 and 1955.

When Marie Hochmuth edited the third volume of *A History and Criticism of American Public Address* in 1955, the field was already in the midst of change. Yet volume three reflected relatively little of that ferment. There were no Burkean or dramatistic studies, nothing informed by general semantics or Richards's theory of metaphor, no studies of social or historical movements, in short, little to distinguish volume three from volumes one and two published more than a decade earlier. This is not to say that all of the critical essays in volume three were bad; they were not. In point of fact, many of the essays were quite good—Carroll C. Arnold's analysis of George William Curtis and Martin Maloney's "mythic" critique of Clarence Darrow's speaking especially stand out.[49] But the essays all deal with individual speakers, most employ some brand of traditional, if not explicitly Aristotelian analysis, and all spend as much or more time on history and biography as in the act of speech criticism.

In her introductory essay to volume III, "The Criticism of Rhetoric,"

---

[47]Wayland Maxfield Parrish, "The Study of Speeches," in *American Speeches*, ed. Wayland Maxfield Parrish and Marie Hochmuth (New York: Longmans, Green and Co., 1954), 7. [See p. 65, here.]

[48]Parrish, 65.

[49]Carroll C. Arnold, "George William Curtis," in *A History and Criticism of American Public Address III*, ed. Marie Kathryn Hochmuth (New York: Russell & Russell, 1955), 133-174; Martin Maloney, "Clarence Darrow," in *A History and Criticism of American Public Address III*, 262-312.

Marie Hochmuth argued that "the critical process . . . involves identification of what is to be evaluated; it recognizes what is to be evaluated as a cultural product of a particular time; it finally involves a judicial act of determining what is better or worse."[50] The essays in the third volume of *A History and Criticism of American Public Address* fulfilled Hochmuth's requirements, but did so in ways that were largely predictable and which focused most centrally on understanding rhetoric as a cultural product of a particular era. As such, the essays were strong on the social, cultural, and historical factors that conditioned both the production and reception of the oratory, but less satisfying when attempting to identify the significant aspects of the rhetoric itself or in erecting standards of judgment by which to evaluate the discourse.

By the middle 1950s, the academic discipline of Speech had established itself at virtually all of the major land-grant universities in the United States, and in many smaller colleges and universities as well. In this sense, the pedagogical emphasis of the early years had paid handsome dividends in the form of institutionalization of degree programs and professionalization of faculty and scholarly associations. As a discipline founded upon the pedagogical impulse, Speech had long prided itself on its sponsorship of such "practical" activities as college debate, theatrical production, the speaker's bureau, educational broadcasting, and other forms of applied speech communication. Instruction in all three aspects of public address dominated the Speech curriculum. As public address theory, students immersed themselves in classical and early modern rhetoric, and were beginning to mine more contemporary sources of theoretical insight; as practice, students learned the practical skills of public speaking, debate, oral interpretation, and sometimes even radio or television speaking; as criticism, the student of public address read "great" speeches and studied the lives of significant orators, applying the traditional paradigm set forth in Thonnsen and Baird's *Speech Criticism* for purposes of analysis and evaluation.

As a teaching field, Speech was on solid ground as illustrated in Karl R. Wallace's 1954 volume on the *History of Speech Education in America*. As a research field, however, Speech still lagged far behind such modern contemporaries as psychology and sociology, not to mention the more established fields of English, literature, history, and philosophy. Part of the problem, as Carroll C. Arnold noted in 1954, was the field's propensity for borrowing theoretical approaches from other disciplines. Teachers of Speech, Arnold wrote,

> have sought to clothe speech in dignity borrowed of other disciplines.
> Irreproachable collateral materials have sometimes been introduced
> into the speech curriculum until speech improvement wears the white
> coat of physiology, speechmaking hides its face between the covers of

---

[50]Marie Hochmuth, "The Criticism of Rhetoric," in *A History and Criticism of American Public Address III*, 4. [See p. 80, here.]

great books or sinks from sight amid the intricacies of general semantics or psychology, and interpretative and dramatic communication masquerades in the costume of literary criticism. . . . These strivings for status among the liberal studies seldom have established speech as a respected independent field of study; for when wearing the raiment of other disciplines, speech conceals its own distinctive substance and character.[51]

To address this defect, Arnold argued that scholars of speech had to be "prepared to expound our subject as a cohesive body of historical, theoretical, and practical knowledge concerning the unique processes and problems which attend Speaking Man's effort to command the understanding of Listening Man."[52] In the middle 1950s, no such cohesive body of knowledge existed. Over the course of the next decade, however, significant progress would be made in the effort to articulate a unique stance from which to theoretize, criticize, and historicize the study of human communication. Scholars of public address led the way in this effort.

Of course, every field of learning has its mythology. One of the central "myths" of public address scholarship is that all was a vast wasteland prior to the 1965 publication of Edwin Black's *Rhetorical Criticism: A Study in Method*. It is an appealing myth because it makes simple a very complex story. In point of fact, one cannot adequately understand the place or influence of Black's study without first understanding the intellectual milieu from which it flowed. The period from 1955 to 1965 was one of great energy and industry in public address scholarship. It was also a period during which many of the great "advances," often credited to the late 1960s and 1970s, actually had their origin. Several currents merit comment.

First, the study of classical rhetorical theory, long an important part of public address education, experienced a renaissance from 1955 to 1965 when scholars such as Ray Nadeau, G.M.A. Grube, James J. Murphy, Lloyd F. Bitzer, and Edwin Black published key analyses and translations of classical texts.[53] There was, at the same time, a corresponding upturn in the study of renaissance and early modern theories of rhetoric, with Karl Wallace,

---

[51]Carroll C. Arnold, "The Case Against Speech: An Examination of Critical Viewpoints," *The Quarterly Journal of Speech 40* (1954): 167-168.

[52]Arnold, "The Case Against Speech," 168.

[53]See, for example, G.M.A. Grube, "Rhetoric and Literary Criticism," *The Quarterly Journal of Speech 42* (1956): 339-344; Edwin Black, "Plato's View of Rhetoric," *The Quarterly Journal of Speech 44* (1958): 361-374; Ray Nadeau, "Hermogenes on 'Stock Issues' in Deliberative Speaking," *Speech Monographs 25* (1958): 59-66; Lloyd F. Bitzer, "Aristotle's Enthymeme Revisited," *The Quarterly Journal of Speech 45* (1959): 399-408; Ray Nadeau, "Some Aristotelian and Stoic Influences on the Theory of Stases," *Speech Monographs 26* (1959): 248-254; James J. Murphy, "Saint Augustine and the Debate about a Christian Rhetoric," *The Quarterly Journal of Speech 46* (1960): 400-410; Ray Nadeau, "Delivery in Ancient Times: Homer to Quintilian," *The Quarterly Journal of Speech 50* (1964): 53-60; Ray Nadeau, "Hermogenes' *On Stases*: A Translation with an Introduction and Notes," *Speech Monographs 31* (1964): 361-424.

Wilbur Samuel Howell, Herman Cohen, Lawrence Flynn, S.J., and Vincent Bevilacqua leading the way.[54]

Second, interest in contemporary rhetorical theory, begun in 1952 when Marie Hochmuth introduced the field to the thought of Kenneth Burke, blossomed in the mid and late-1950s with studies on Richards, Burke, and Toulmin, and original articles by Burke and Susanne K. Langer.[55] In 1959, Daniel Fogarty, S.J. released *Roots for a New Rhetoric*, thus making the thought of Richards, Burke, and the General Semanticists widely available to students in compendia format. Following from this upsurge of interest in classical, early modern, and contemporary rhetorical theories were specialized studies on the role of metaphor in public address, on validity in argumentation, and on the relationship of axiology to rhetorical discourse.[56]

Third, the criticism of public address started to move substantially beyond the boundaries established by volume III of *A History and Criticism of American Public Address*. For the first time, detailed study of rhetorical texts began to appear in the national speech journals. Foremost among these were studies by Laura Crowell on Roosevelt's "Four Freedoms" speech, Donald C. Bryant on Edmund Burke's *Present Discontents*, and Eugene E. White on Cotton Mather's *Manuductio ad Ministerium*. In addition to textual

---

[54]See, for example, Lawrence J. Flynn, S.J., "The DE ARTE RHETORICA of Cyprian Soarez, S.J.," *The Quarterly Journal of Speech 42* (1956): 367-374; Karl R. Wallace, "Aspects of Modern Rhetoric in Francis Bacon," *The Quarterly Journal of Speech 42* (1956): 398-406; Lawrence J. Flynn, S.J., "Sources and Influences of Soarez' De Arte Rhetorica," *The Quarterly Journal of Speech 43* (1957): 257-265; Herman Cohen, "Hugh Blair's Theory of Taste," *The Quarterly Journal of Speech 44* (1958): 265-274; Wilbur Samuel Howell, "Sources of the Elocutionary Movement in England, 1700-1748," *The Quarterly Journal of Speech 45* (1959): 1-18; Lloyd F. Bitzer, "A Re-evaluation of Campbell's Doctrine of Evidence," *The Quarterly Journal of Speech 46* (1960): 135-140; Vincent M. Bevilacqua, "Rhetoric and Human Nature in Kames' *Elements of Criticism*," *The Quarterly Journal of Speech 48* (1962): 46-60; James L. Golden, "James Boswell on Rhetoric and Belles-Lettres," *The Quarterly Journal of Speech 50* (1964): 266-276; Vincent M. Bevilacqua, "Philosophical Origins of George Campbell's *Philosophy of Rhetoric*," *Speech Monographs 32* (1965): 1-12.

[55]See, for example, Marie Hochmuth, "Kenneth Burke and the "New Rhetoric," *The Quarterly Journal of Speech 38* (1952): 133-144; Kenneth Burke, "A Dramatistic View of the Origins of Language: Part One," *The Quarterly Journal of Speech 38* (1952): 251-264; Kenneth Burke, "A Dramatistic View of the Origins of Language: Part Two," *The Quarterly Journal of Speech 38* (1952): 446-460; Kenneth Burke, "A Dramatistic View of the Origins of Language: Part Three," *The Quarterly Journal of Speech 39* (1953): 79-92; Virginia Holland, "Rhetorical Criticism: A Burkeian Method," *The Quarterly Journal of Speech 39* (1953): 444-450; L. Virginia Holland, "Kenneth Burke's Dramatistic Approach in Speech Criticism," *The Quarterly Journal of Speech 41* (1955): 352-358; Marie Hochmuth, "I.A. Richards and the "New Rhetoric," *The Quarterly Journal of Speech 44* (1958): 1-16; Wayne Brockriede and Douglas Ehninger, "Toulmin on Argument: An Interpretation and Application," *The Quarterly Journal of Speech 46* (1960): 44-53; and Susanne K. Langer, "The Origins of Speech and Its Communicative Functions," *The Quarterly Journal of Speech 46* (1960): 121-134.

[56]See, for example, Charles S. Mudd, "The Enthymeme and Logical Validity," *The Quarterly Journal of Speech 45* (1959): 409-414; Leland M. Griffin, "The Edifice Metaphor in Rhetorical Theory," *Speech Monographs 27* (1960): 279-292; Maurice Natanson, "Rhetoric and Philosophical Argumentation," *The Quarterly Journal of Speech 48* (1962): 24-30; Michael M. Osborn and Douglas Ehninger, "The Metaphor in Public Address," *Speech Monographs 29* (1962): 223-234; Ralph T. Eubanks and Virgil L. Baker, "Toward an Axiology of Rhetoric," *The Quarterly Journal of Speech 48* (1962): 157-168; Karl R. Wallace, "The Substance of Rhetoric: Good Reasons," *The Quarterly Journal of Speech 49* (1963): 239-249; Hermann G. Stelzner, "Analysis by Metaphor," *The Quarterly Journal of Speech 51* (1965): 52-61.

studies, 1955-1965 was the germination period for studies in the rhetoric of movements generally and social protest rhetoric particularly, for genre studies of various sorts, and for some preliminary examinations of speakers who were not white, Anglo-Saxon males, long the preferred site of analysis for the "Great Man" school of criticism.[57]

Fourth, the traditional paradigm for conducting a rhetorical critique began to show signs of weakening. In 1956, Thomas R. Nilsen and Albert J. Croft called into question various aspects of the paradigm. For Nilsen, it was not the emphasis on the speech's effect that was problematic, but the related assumption that effect was to be defined only in terms of the speaker's purported purpose or aim. "It is the viewing of the social act, the speech, so predominantly from the point of view of the individual—the speaker and his purposes—rather than from the point of view of society and its purposes," wrote Nilsen, "that has led to much of the conflict and confusion about effects as an object of criticism."[58] Nilsen wanted to retain the effects criterion, but to redefine effect to refer to that which society viewed as good or desirable, not what the individual speaker sought to achieve. He thus offered "criteria for judgment" drawn from "the assumptions upon which our society is based."[59] By relocating the locus of judgment from the individual to the collective and reconfiguring criticism as an essentially ethical act of judgment rather than a pragmatic act, Nilsen sought to establish social effect as the central criterion of speech criticism.

Albert Croft saw matters differently. To him, the problems of the traditional paradigm were considerably more severe than those identified by Nilsen. "Perhaps the chief problem of research in public address," Croft wrote, "is that we have thought of it all as 'criticism' when some is really theory, some is history, and some is criticism which has not evaluated the speeches studied."[60] The theory-criticism relationship was particularly problematic in the traditional paradigm, Croft held, because "criticism cannot alter theory; it can only use the existing forms." Such criticism was static and treated rhetorical theory "as a closed, fixed system."[61] Such a view of the theory-criticism relationship led to a sort of cookie-cutter criticism, with the

---

[57]See, for example, Howard H. Martin, "The Fourth of July Oration," *The Quarterly Journal of Speech 44* (1958): 393-401; Harry P. Kerr, "The Rhetoric of Political Protest," *The Quarterly Journal of Speech 45* (1959): 146-152; Harry P. Kerr, "The Election Sermon: Primer for Revolutionaries," *Speech Monographs 29* (1962): 13-22; Wil A. Linkugel, "The Woman Suffrage Argument of Anna Howard Shaw," *The Quarterly Journal of Speech 49* (1963): 165-174; Leland M. Griffin, "The Rhetorical Structure of the 'New Left' Movement: Part I," *The Quarterly Journal of Speech 50* (1964): 113-135; Mary W. Graham, "Margaret Chase Smith," *The Quarterly Journal of Speech 50* (1964): 390-393; Charles J. Stewart, "The Pulpit in Time of Crisis: 1865 and 1963," *Speech Monographs 32* (1965): 427-434.

[58]Thomas R. Nilsen, "Criticism and Social Consequences," *The Quarterly Journal of Speech 42* (1956): 175.

[59]Nilsen, 177.

[60]Albert J. Croft, "The Functions of Rhetorical Criticism," *The Quarterly Journal of Speech 42* (1956): 284.

[61]Croft, 285.

role of the critic being reduced to "finding illustrations of standard, precon-
ceived forms."[62] As unproductive as the traditional theory-criticism relationship had been, Croft found the interaction of history and criticism even more
delimiting. The problem was to bring history and criticism into proper relationship one to the other so that the central question of "audience adaptation"
could be explored. Croft observed:

> It is not enough to talk separately about the make-up of an audience
> at one point, about the main propositions of the speaker at another
> point, and about the speaker's use of traditional rhetorical techniques
> at still another point. The main function of history and criticism is to
> show how propositions and audiences are *connected*: how a speaker
> uses techniques to adapt his ideas to his audiences.[63]

These criticisms, though ostensibly derived from examination of graduate
theses, were a telling indictment of critical scholarship as practiced in
professional journals and textbooks.

Opposition to the reigning critical paradigm continued when, in 1957,
Ernest Wrage edited a special issue of *Western Speech* on the subject of
"Criticism and Public Address." Essays by Donald C. Bryant, Robert D.
Clark, Marie Hochmuth, W. Charles Redding, and Barnet Baskerville called
into question several dimensions of the traditional paradigm—the focus on
single speakers, the critical standard of effect on the immediate audience, the
separation of pragmatic from ethical judgment, the bowdlerized
Aristotelianism, the lack of symmetry between judgments of internal artistic
integrity and external political results, and other equally problematic areas.
By the end of the 1950s, the traditional paradigm was in deep trouble. Even
though the early 1960s saw two works published that drew heavily from that
tradition—Marie Hochmuth Nichols's *Rhetoric and Criticism* (1963) and
Antislavery and Disunion, 1858-1861, edited by J. Jeffery Auer (1963), the
tradition itself had been mortally wounded. The "situation" of rhetorical
criticism in the early 1960s called for a response fit for the times. It was not
long in coming.

Black's Rhetorical Criticism: A Study in Method

Although Black's *Rhetorical Criticism* carries a copyright date of 1965, it
is important to remember that the book was originally a dissertation
completed at Cornell University in 1962, under the direction of Herbert A.
Wichelns. It thus represents the thinking of the late 1950s and early 1960s, as
revised for publication in 1965. That the book had an immediate—and in
some ways devastating—influence on both the theory and practice of public
address criticism there can be no doubt. Yet it is important to remember that
the disease had already been diagnosed and various prescriptions for cure

---

[62]Croft, 286.
[63]Croft, 286.

offered before the publication of *Rhetorical Criticism: A Study in Method.* In a sense, Black reaped where others had sown. He did so for several reasons. His was the first book-length analysis of (some would say assault on) the tradition. He not only diagnosed the problems, he also offered potential solutions. And he did this in a writing style that was at once incisive, witty, clear, and logically compelling. Newly hooded, Dr. Black took scapel in hand and proceeded to dissect forty years of public address scholarship. That he did this under the influence and guidance of Herbert A. Wichelns is a historical irony of no small note.

Rhetorical Criticism is a small book that carried a large impact. In six brief chapters, Black laid out his definition of criticism, his view of how rhetorical criticism had been practiced traditionally, the relation of rhetoric to criticism, the uses of Aristotle's *Rhetoric* in the practice of criticism, an "alternative" frame of reference, and a final chapter on "The Genre of Argumentation." Black wasted no time in pointing out the faults of what he called "neo-Aristotelianism":

> The neo-Aristotelians ignore the impact of the discourse on rhetorical conventions, its capacity for disposing an audience to expect certain ways of arguing and certain kinds of justifications in later discourses that they encounter, even on different subjects. Similarly, the neo-Aristotelian critics do not account for the influence of the discourse on its author: the future commitments it makes for him, rhetorically and ideologically; the public image it portrays to which he must adjust.[64]

Black went even further, chastising the traditional critics for viewing discourses as discrete entities, for their interest in immediate effects only, for the linearity—from speaker's background to message construction to audience effect—implied in traditional analysis, for the tendency to reduce the realm of rhetoric to oratory only, and for the assumption of audience rationality implicit in the traditional paradigm.

The extent to which the neo-Aristotelian paradigm dominated the field, even as late as 1965, is revealed by Black's attempt to describe two other extant approaches to rhetorical texts—movement criticism and psychological criticism. Movement studies had made some small degree of progress by 1965, due largely to the work of Leland Griffin. The so-called psychological study, however, was barely discernible, even in outline. Black cites but one instance of a "psychological" criticism in the speech literature and even that instance seems, in retrospect, suspect. Nevertheless Black was on to something. He realized that psychological criticism could be a potent tool in the arsenal of the rhetorical critic if it could be made to comment on the "discourse-as-communication" rather than on the "discourse-as-symptom" of some hidden reality. Black noted that there was "no system of analysis or

---

[64]Black, 35. [See p. 116, here.]

body of techniques available to the critic for the reliable psychological examination of argumentative strategies or discursive texture," yet he was convinced that precisely that kind of examination was necessary for "full disclosure"—the goal of all criticism.[65] Previewing what such a system of analysis might look like, Black wrote:

> We are compelled to believe in the existence of relationships between a man's deepest motives and his discourses. Such a conviction is bound up with the very ways we have of talking about human motives. The mystery lies in the identification of those characteristics of discourse which reveal motive, for we know that motive only rarely receives a full and direct expression.[66]

Black would spend the next twenty years working out an approach to rhetorical criticism that revealed "those characteristics of discourse which reveal motive," but in 1965 it was but a vision of a criticism that did not then exist.[67]

Toward Critical Pluralism

The publication of *Rhetorical Criticism: A Study in Method* was, itself, a rhetorical event, and like all such discourses had effects, both intended and unintended. One of the intended effects was to make scholars start to question, in a systematic fashion, the received wisdom of the traditional paradigm. That such questioning had, in fact, already begun before the publication of Black's book helps to explain the rapidity with which the paradigm collapsed between 1965 and 1969. It was brought down by a confluence of forces—intellectual, social, historical, and political. Black's was the chief, though not the only, intellectual force at work. The social and political world was also changing. Women were entering the academy at an ever-increasing rate; the contemporary woman's movement was in full stride; the black civil rights movement was at its height; and protests over the war in Vietnam were just beginning. In short, it was a historical moment of change on many fronts. For public address scholars such changes were reflected in the topics studied, the methods of analysis employed, and the sense of release or freedom from what was increasingly viewed as an anachronistic and intellectually flawed critical tradition.

The pages of *QJS* and *SM* reflect these changes. The topics become more diverse, as studies of nonoratorical discourse and nondidactic literature start

---

[65]Black, 111, 104. "Disclosure" would become a central term for Black as he worked out his program of psychological criticism. It received its fullest treatment in his essay "Secrecy and Disclosure as Rhetorical Forms," *The Quarterly Journal of Speech 74* (1988): 133-150.

[66]Black, 110.

[67]Black brought his program of psychological criticism to a culmination with the publication of *Rhetorical Questions: Studies of Public Discourse* (Chicago: University of Chicago Press, 1992). The book is a collection and expansion of his criticism from the late 1960s to the early 1990s.

to appear. Movement studies become more frequent, and names other than Leland Griffin start to be associated with movement criticism. The rhetoric of contemporary social protest starts to be studied as an academic specialty, with critics such as Franklyn S. Haiman, Parke Burgess, Robert L. Scott, Donald K. Smith, James R. Andrews, and Richard B. Gregg writing major essays during the later 1960s. Of equal importance, the methods of analysis start to change. Spurred on, in 1968, by a wide-ranging essay on "The Anatomy of Critical Discourse" by Lawrence W. Rosenfield and by a clear articulation of "The Rhetorical Situation" by Lloyd F. Bitzer,[68] critics began to find or invent new critical approaches to rhetorical discourse: genre criticism, analog criticism, mythic criticism, phenomenological criticism, psychological criticism, metaphoric and archetypal criticism, stylistic criticism, dramatistic criticism, fantasy theme criticism, model criticism. Suddenly there seemed to be no end to available critical approaches. The point is that the period from 1965-1980 was one of unprecedented growth both in terms of the objects of criticism and in terms of the methods or approaches used by critics to analyze and evaluate those objects. Whereas prior to 1965 it was a most unusual study that was not concerned with either oratory or didactic literature— pamphlets, tracts, broadsides, instruction manuals and the like—after 1965 such studies became commonplace. So rapidly did this change overtake the field that as early as 1970, conferees at the National Developmental Conference on Rhetoric could conclude:

> Rhetorical criticism is to be identified by the kinds of questions posed by the critic. . . . The critic becomes rhetorical to the extent that he studies his subject in terms of its suasory potential or persuasive effect. So identified, rhetorical criticism may be applied to any human act, process, product, or artifact which, in the critic's view, may formulate, sustain, or modify attention, perceptions, attitudes or behavior.[69]

Clearly this view of criticism's scope and responsibilities went far beyond anything contemplated by traditional scholars of public address. Yet it was precisely the limitations imposed by the tradition that motivated the conferees. As they noted in the same report: "Much of our theory has presupposed formal platform speaking and has thereby ignored a multitude of presentational and transactional possibilities."[70] One of the unfortunate—and unintended—consequences of the bifurcation drawn between studies of platform speaking and the other forms of human communication noted by the conferees was the subtle implication that studies of orators and oratory were

---

[68]See Lawrence W. Rosenfield, "The Anatomy of Critical Discourse," *Speech Monographs 35* (1968): 50-69; Lloyd F. Bitzer, "The Rhetorical Situation," *Philosophy & Rhetoric 1* (1968): 1-14.

[69]Thomas O. Sloan, et al., "Report of the Committee on the Advancement and Refinement of Rhetorical Criticism," in *The Prospect of Rhetoric*, ed. Lloyd F. Bitzer and Edwin Black (Englewood Cliffs: Prentice-Hall, 1971), 220.

[70]Sloan, 222.

somehow old-fashioned or of little intellectual worth. This was particularly unfortunate inasmuch as the old paradigm had not, itself, seriously engaged the speech text as a basic unit of analysis. Even in 1970, the study of speeches had not been undertaken in any systematic way by members of the Speech profession. At the very moment when Speech scholars were in the best position to contribute to studies of oratory, they largely abandoned the field in favor of more contemporary concerns—public protest, media analysis, liberation movements, new critical paradigms, and debate over the proper relationship between rhetorical theory and criticism.

The study of public address did not, of course, simply disappear overnight. The 1970s, though a low point in the history of public address scholarship, nonetheless produced some moments of individual brilliance. Ironically enough, one of those moments involved the analysis of a single speech text—President Richard M. Nixon's Vietnamization speech of November 3, 1969. Between 1970 and 1972, no fewer than four rhetorical critics provided detailed analyses of this one speech. Never before had any single address been the subject of such sustained critical interest. Equally important, each of these four critics—Robert P. Newman, Hermann G. Stelzner, Forbes I. Hill, and Karlyn Kohrs Campbell—took a decidedly different view of the rhetorical action instantiated in the text.[71] This event was one source of what would become, in the 1980s, a full scale school of public address criticism based on the "close reading" of oratorical texts. For the early 1970s, four readings of a single speech was an unusual and, to the surprise of many, highly illuminating exercise.[72] But there were other significant moments as well. Edwin Black began to flesh out his notion of a true psychological criticism with a brilliant essay on "The Second Persona."[73] Arthur L. Smith (now Molefi Kete Asante) made the first contribution toward a theoretical understanding of Black oratory, while Karlyn Kohrs Campbell and Brenda Hancock illuminated oratorical features of the woman's liberation movement.[74] Critics such as G.P. Mohrmann and Michael Leff began to

---

[71] See Robert P. Newman, "Under the Veneer: Nixon's Vietnam Speech of November 3, 1969," *The Quarterly Journal of Speech 56* (1970): 168-178; Hermann G. Stelzner, "The Quest Story and Nixon's November 3, 1969 Address," *The Quarterly Journal of Speech 57* (1971): 163-172; Karlyn Kohrs Campbell, "An Exercise in the Rhetoric of Mythical America," in *Critiques of Contemporary Rhetoric* (Belmont, CA: Wadsworth, 1972), 50-57; Forbes I. Hill, "Conventional Wisdom —Traditional Form: The President's Message of November 3, 1969," *The Quarterly Journal of Speech 58* (1972): 373-386. These articles, along with the subsequent debate between Campbell and Hill, are reprinted in James R. Andrews, *The Practice of Rhetorical Criticism* 2nd ed. (New York: Longman, 1990), 100-150.

[72] Interestingly enough, in the twenty years since the multiple examination of Nixon's Vietnamization Address, only one other speech has been subjected to a similar multi-critic scrutiny. This was Lincoln's Second Inaugural Address. See *Communication Reports 1* (1988): 14-37, where James Arnt Aune, Ronald H. Carpenter, Michael Leff, and Martha Solomon provide contrasting readings. This exchange is also reprinted in Andrews, *The Practice of Rhetorical Criticism*, 65-90.

[73] Edwin Black, "The Second Persona," *The Quarterly Journal of Speech 56* (1970): 109-119.

[74] Arthur L. Smith, *Rhetoric of Black Revolution* (Boston: Allyn and Bacon, 1969); Brenda Robinson Hancock, "Affirmation by Negation in the Women's Liberation Movement," *The Quarterly Journal of Speech 58* (1972): 264-271; Karlyn Kohrs Campbell, "The Rhetoric of Women's Liberation: An Oxymoron," *The Quarterly Journal of Speech 59* (1973): 74-86.

sketch the outlines of a new traditionalism, one that merged the insights of classical and contemporary rhetoric in new and interesting ways, and which would become another source of inspiration for the "close reading" of the 1980s.[75] Debate over the role, purpose, and methods of criticism proceeded unhindered as Philip Wander and Steven Jenkins laid the theoretical basis for what would become, in the 1980s, an ideologically driven criticism, and Wayne Brockriede set forth the dimensions of argument as applied to critical endeavor.[76] Significant studies of public address in the older sense of oratory were conducted by Stephen E. Lucas, Richard B. Gregg, and Halford Ross Ryan, and in 1976, Lucas produced a book-length study, *Portents of Rebellion*, that became a model of public address scholarship.[77] Textbooks on critical method continued to proliferate, with Carroll C. Arnold's *Criticism of Oral Rhetoric* (1974) focussing exclusively on public address.[78]

But the very term "public address" was beginning to take on a much broader meaning than it had carried under the old paradigm. Once confined to platform oratory or, at the extremes to didactic literature, public address now came to stand for any communication directed to the general public without regard for the medium or channel used. Thus such studies as Kathleen Jamieson on the papal encyclical was a study in public address.[79] So, too, were studies of film, or magazines, or public letters, or prayer, or any form of public symbolic inducement.[80] To be sure there were still a few studies in the old mold of neo-Aristotelianism, but they were few indeed. One

[75]Michael C. Leff and G.P. Mohrmann, "Lincoln at Cooper Union: A Rhetorical Analysis of the Text," *The Quarterly Journal of Speech 60* (1974): 346-358; G.P. Mohrmann and Michael C. Leff, "Lincoln at Cooper Union: A Rationale for Neo-Classical Criticism," *The Quarterly Journal of Speech 60* (1974): 459-467.

[76]Philip Wander and Steven Jenkins, "Rhetoric, Society, and the Critical Response," *The Quarterly Journal of Speech 58* (1972): 441-450; Wayne Brockriede, "Rhetorical Criticism as Argument," *The Quarterly Journal of Speech 60* (1974): 165-174.

[77]See Stephen E. Lucas, "The Man with the Muck Rake: A Reinterpretation," *The Quarterly Journal of Speech 59* (1973): 452-462; Richard B. Gregg, "A Rhetorical Re-examination of Arthur Vandenberg's 'Dramatic Conversion', January 10, 1945," *The Quarterly Journal of Speech 61* (1975): 154-168; Stephen E. Lucas, *Portents of Rebellion: Rhetoric and Revolution in Philadelphia, 1765-76* (Philadelphia: Temple University Press, 1976); Halford Ross Ryan, "Roosevelt's First Inaugural: A Study of Technique," *The Quarterly Journal of Speech 65* (1979): 137-149.

[78]In addition to Arnold, textbooks of note during this period include Robert L. Scott and Bernard L. Brock, eds., *Methods of Rhetorical Criticism* (New York: Harper & Row, 1972); Karlyn Kohrs Campbell, *Critiques of Contemporary Rhetoric* (Belmont, CA: Wadsworth, 1972); G.P. Mohrmann, Charles J. Stewart, and Donovan J. Ochs, eds., *Explorations in Rhetorical Criticism* (University Park: Pennsylvania State University Press, 1973); Donald C. Bryant, *Rhetorical Dimensions in Criticism* (Baton Rouge: Louisiana State University Press, 1973); James R. Andrews, *A Choice of Worlds: The Practice and Criticism of Public Discourse* (New York: Harper & Row, 1973); and Karlyn Kohrs Campbell and Kathleen Hall Jamieson, eds., *Form and Genre: Shaping Rhetorical Action* (Falls Church, VA: Speech Communication Association, 1978).

[79]Kathleen Hall Jamieson, "Interpretation of Natural Law in the Conflict Over *Humanae Vitae*," *The Quarterly Journal of Speech 60* (1974): 201-211.

[80]These studies are far too numerous to list, but a good overview is provided in Richard B. Gregg, "The Criticism of Symbolic Inducement: A Critical-Theoretical Connection," in *Speech Communication in the 20th Century*, ed. Thomas W. Benson (Carbondale: Southern Illinois University Press, 1985), 41-62.

of the more noteworthy efforts in this regard was the award-winning monograph on *The American Ideology* by Kurt Ritter and James R. Andrews (1978). For scholars trained in the older tradition of public address this explosion of pluralism in both objects of study and methodology seemed to leave little room for rhetorical history or biography—the mainstays of the traditional paradigm. Barnet Baskerville spoke for many scholars trained in the earlier tradition when, in 1977, he asked, "Must We All Be 'Rhetorical Critics?'" Baskerville's point was that scholarship in rhetoric and public address had always been broader than criticism per se and that the recent enthusiasm for criticism and critical methods risked the loss of those other aspects of public address scholarship. "What then is my concern?," asked Baskerville:

> It is that in our enthusiasm for rhetorical criticism . . . we may neglect important scholarly responsibilities. As the literary scholar has made himself custodian of a body of imaginative writings, so should we be the custodians of a body of purposive, public discourse in which the literary man for various reasons has not shown much interest.[81]

In short, Baskerville asked the field to take seriously the study of rhetorical history, the history of oratory, rhetorical biography, and other aspects of the public address tradition that were seemingly being overwhelmed by the new-found focus on criticism. "Histories of literature, of religion, of music, of journalism, we have," he wrote, "but no completely satisfactory history of American oratory."[82] He was, of course, correct in this assessment inasmuch as the *only* history of American oratory was Robert T. Oliver's *History of Public Speaking in America*, published in 1965. But implicit in Baskerville's argument was the long-held distinction between rhetorical history and rhetorical criticism, a distinction that can be traced to the 1930s and which had been articulated anew in 1975 by Bruce E. Gronbeck.

According to Gronbeck, rhetorical history was to refer to

> any examination of discourse or rhetors which essentially or primarily is *extrinsic*, to any analysis which finds most of its confirming materials *outside a rhetorical artifact*. Such traditional studies as those of a speaker's background, methods of speech preparation, examinations of psycholinguistic bases for a given message, recreations of situations demanding certain sorts of discourse, measurements of speeches' effects upon immediate and long-range audiences, campaigns' and institutions' effects upon the course of social-political history, and so on, fall into this general category of rhetorical analysis.[83]

---

[81] Barnet Baskerville, "Must We All Be 'Rhetorical Critics'?" *The Quarterly Journal of Speech 63* (1977): 112. [See p. 123, here.]
[82] Baskerville, 124.
[83] Bruce E. Gronbeck, "Rhetorical History and Rhetorical Criticism: A Distinction," *The Speech Teacher 24* (1975): 310-311.

Rhetorical criticism, on the other hand, Gronbeck defined as

> including any examination of discourse and rhetors which essentially
> or primarily is intrinsic, any analysis which finds most of its
> confirming materials inside a rhetorical artifact. Such traditional
> studies as those of rhetorical structure, typologies of strategies, most
> generic classifications, linguistic categories of analysis, the integrity
> of ideas, and discourses as cultural phenomena fall into this general
> category of rhetorical analysis.[84]

Both Gronbeck and Baskerville were merely articulating a distinction which
had long held sway among many scholars of rhetoric and public address. That
scholars had, from time to time, tried to join history with criticism under the
banner of historical-critical method—often with less than stellar results—
should not obscure the fact that in practice many scholars conceived
themselves to be either rhetorical historians or rhetorical critics, and that by
the late 1970s the critics clearly had the upper hand.

The Study of Speeches

Baskerville's plea was primarily for tolerance and openness to all sorts of
rhetorical and oratorical studies. Three years later, in 1980, G.P. Mohrmann
launched an assault on the whole business of contemporary rhetorical
criticism which he titled, appropriately enough, "Elegy in a Critical Grave-
Yard." Mohrmann, a connoisseur of language, was well aware of the multiple
meanings of "Grave." He took criticism to be a grave or serious undertaking,
thought it to be in grave or serious trouble, and sought to rescue it from the
grave of death into which it had, in his judgment, fallen. His was an elegy—
a mournful poem of lament for a field gone badly astray. The problem, as he
saw it, was that the study of oratory—the centerpiece of classical rhetorical
education—no longer occupied the hearts and minds of contemporary
rhetorical critics. Worse still, such critics seemed to be woefully ignorant of
the classical tradition which they had so blithely, in his view, overthrown
upon publication of Black's *Rhetorical Criticism: A Study in Method.* For
Mohrmann, rhetoric and public address was central to a liberal and humane
education. He noted:

> Whatever the role of education in introducing students to new ideas
> and to ways of dealing with them, the enterprise unquestionably has
> conservative dimensions. To preserve and continue the cultural
> heritage is a primary function, and speakers and speeches can tell us
> more than a little about Western Civilization, even when the Great
> Man theory has been abandoned.[85]

---

[84]Gronbeck, 314.
[85]G.P. Mohrmann, "Elegy in a Critical Grave-Yard," *Western Journal of Speech Communication 44*
(1980): 271. [See p. 136, here.]

Mohrmann well understood that the traditional paradigm had not always provided the best entree into critical understanding or appreciation, yet he was not willing to give up the vision of a rhetorical approach to texts that was both historically informed and critically engaged. While admitting that "many of us have been too often detained with th Old Dead Orators in quaint and archane ways," Mohrmann nevertheless held that "that does not mean that a rhetorical orientation to history and biography cannot be a wholesome and stimulating venture."[86] Unfortunately, what was being practiced under the label of rhetorical criticism, Mohrmann found to be neither wholesome nor very stimulating. He charged contemporary criticism with being evey bit as blind to its weaknesses as the traditional paradigm ever had been, with critics merely substituting new vocabularies for old concepts and riding a favorite "hobby horse," blissfully unaware that the steed was going nowhere. For ohrmann, the rhetorical tradition in its fullness was a necessary, perhaps even sufficient reservoir for critical practice. Unfortunately, few critics ever bothered to learn the full tradition nor to apply that wisdom to the study of speech texts. As Mohrmann observed:

> Used with intelligence and imagination, the available topics may help us trly to understand and to appreciate the text and texture of messages. That will never happen, of course, until the effort is made, and in spite of the conventional wisdom, it never has been attempted with any sustained vigor and rigor.[87]

Mohrmann was prticularly appalled at how little scholars of rhetoric and public address had studied speeches. So, too, was Stephen E. Lucas.

Writing in 1981, Lucas noted the "keen sense of schism" that had developed "between history and criticism."[88] Such a schism, he felt, was based on a mistaken notion that a rhetorical text could somehow be studied apart from the context into which it entered and of which it was a constituent part. Lucas pointed out that

> To explicte satisfactorily what a rhetorical text means or how it functions, we need to comprehend the very identity of that text as inextricably interwoven with its world. And that comprehension demands historical understanding and inescapably involves the rhetorician directly and earnestly with forces, persons, and documents extrinsic to the text under scrutiny.[89]

In short, the intrinsic/extrinsic distinction that Gronbeck had proposed in 1975 was irreparably flawed. Lucas went on to note that "many notable

---

[86]Mohramnn, 136.
[87]Mohrmann, 137.
[88]Stephen E. Lucas, "The Schism in Rhetorical Scholarship," *The Quarterly Journal of Speech 67* (1981): 1. [See p. 139, here.]
[89]Lucas, 6.

rhetorical studies so thoroughly blend description, interpretation, and evaluation as to make efforts to categorize them discreetly as either 'history' or 'criticism' nugatory and misleading."[90] Far from leading the critic away from history, a proper immersion in the speech text would necessarily lead the researcher deeper into the context, for "historical understanding is not simply a prolegomenon to critical understanding, but an organic element of the whole process of rhetorical analysis."[91] Thus Lucas issued a call for a fully rounded criticism, a criticism that was neither text-centered nor context-centered, but which implicated each with the other.

While the precise cause-effect relationships cannot be established, it is an empirical fact that following the Mohrmann-Lucas counteroffensive there was a remarkable renaissance in the traditional study of public address.[92] This renaissance was marked by several factors unique in the history of American public address: books started to be written on a regular, rather than occasional, basis; journals started to reflect a growing interest in the study of speeches—something the field had long professed but never actually done; book series were launched devoted largely or entirely to rhetoric and public address; rhetorical biographies that took seriously the interrelationships between history and criticism were published; anthologies devoted to practical criticism became commonplace; and a rotating conference devoted to the theory and criticism of public address was established. All of this happened in the 1980s.

Parallel to these events and part of the driving force behind some of them was the articulation of a theory of public address criticism that came to be known as "close reading." The chief sponsor of this theory was Michael C. Leff. Starting with a 1980 essay on "Interpretation and the Art of the Rhetorical Critic," Leff identified the central problem in public address criticism as "a thorough preoccupation with abstract theories and methods . . . [that] dulls the critic's sensitivity to the problem of interpretation. Thus, we obtain a proliferation of critical methods, without any of these methods solving the problem that lies at their collective origin—the neo-Aristotelian tendency to impose mechanical categories on texts."[93] Because "we have erred so long in the direction of the abstract," Leff argued, "it now seems reasonable to encourage efforts that begin with the particular."[94] In short, Leff proposed that the field start to give serious study to speeches and other rhetorical texts as sites of rhetorical action. The fullest

---

[90]Lucas, 154.

[91]Lucas, 161.

[92]See Martin J. Medhurst, "Public Address and Significant Scholarship: Four Challenges to the Rhetorical Renaissance," in *Texts in Context*, ed. Michael C. Leff and Fred J. Kauffeld (Davis, CA: Hermagoras Press, 1989), 29-42.

[93]Michael C. Leff, "Interpretation and the Art of the Rhetorical Critic," *Western Journal of Speech Communication 44* (1980): 345.

[94]Leff, 346.

explanation of this approach to public address criticism was his 1986 essay, "Textual Criticism: The Legacy of G.P. Mohrmann."

In "Textual Criticism," Leff pointed to the speech text as a complex artistic construction in need of expert analysis and evaluation, a construction involving "a formidable number of elements":

> the close reading and rereading of the text, the analysis of the historical and biographical circumstances that generate and frame its composition, the recognition of basic conceptions that establish the co-ordinates of the text, and an appreciation of the way these conceptions interact within the text and help determine its temporal movement.[95]

For Leff, the "well constructed oration possesses a high degree of artistic integrity and density, and its proper understanding requires careful interpretative work."[96] Following the logic laid out by Lucas in 1981, Leff observed that

> To rely exclusively either upon a formal/intrinsic or a representational/extrinsic criterion is to distort the rhetorical integrity of the discourse. Though critical analysis can separate these dimensions, the fact is that they occur simultaneously and work cooperatively within the fabric of the discourse.[97]

Leff then proceeded to formulate what he called a "theory of the text." Rather than bring a theory such as neo-Aristotelianism or dramatism or structuralism to bear on a text, Leff argued that the critic must discover the theory that lies hidden in the fabric of the text itself. Thus one works from text to theory rather than from theory to text. Since every text "retains an internal history of its own" to "experience the text is to be coached to experience the world as the text constructs it."[98]

This reformulation of the theory-text relationship led to two different responses: debate over Leff's "theoretical" approach; and, attempts to validate that approach in the form of practical criticism.[99] No better example of the second response exists than Stephen Lucas's 1988 essay on "The Renaissance of American Public Address: Text and Context in Rhetorical Criticism." In

---

[95]Michael Leff, "Textual Criticism: The Legacy of G.P. Mohrmann," *The Quarterly Journal of Speech* 72 (1986): 380. [See pp. 167-168, here.]

[96]Leff, "Textual Criticism," 168.

[97]Leff, 169.

[98]Leff, "Textual Criticism," 175.

[99]For the ongoing debate over the "close reading" of rhetorical texts see the special issue on rhetorical criticism of the *Western Journal of Speech Communication 54* (1990): 249-376. This special issues includes articles by Leff and Sachs, McGee, Gaonkar, Cox, Condit, and John Angus Campbell. See also the special forum section on "Text, Theory, and the Rhetorical Critic," *The Quarterly Journal of Speech 78* (1992): 219-237. This forum is a exchange among David Henry, Michael Leff, and Barbara Warnick on the subject of close reading.

this essay, Lucas illustrated many of the theoretical premises articulated by Leff. In so doing, he also provided an example of the kind of study which cannot easily be classified as history or criticism, for it was both.

Lucas began his essay by noting that the field's "persistent neglect of major texts in the history of American oratory is nothing short of astonishing."[100] He went on to argue that

> oratory is an art form with its own special criteria, constraints, and potentialities. Judgments about an oration as a literary production or an ideological pronouncement, legitimate and important as they may be, are tangential to its "rhetorical integrity" and cannot yield adequate assessment of it as a work of rhetoric. Such assessment can only be reached by radical attention to the internal dynamics of the text itself.[101]

Lucas then proceeded to demonstrate exactly what he meant by conducting a rhetorical examination of the preamble to the Declaration of Independence. He later expanded this critique to include the whole of the Declaration in a chapter for *American Rhetoric: Context and Criticism* (1989), edited by Thomas W. Benson, one of several collections of critical essays published in the late 1980s and early 1990s. Having demonstrated with practical criticism the efficacy of close reading, Lucas concluded:

> The ideal is to combine full and penetrating comprehension of the rhetorical situation with a sensitive and discerning reading of the text as an evolving, temporal phenomenon that creates its own internal context even as it is leavened by the social and linguistic context. This is a very different exercise from the kind of artful paraphrase of a speech that often passes for textual analysis in rhetorical criticism. The purpose of the critic is not simply to retell the speech in his or her own words, but to apprehend it fully from the inside out—to break down its rhetorical elements so completely as to determine how they function individually and to explain how they interact to shape the text as a strategic, artistic response to the exigencies of a particular situation.[102]

The movement which had begun in the early 1970s to reclaim oratory as a legitimate and valued site of rhetorical investigation reached a crucial milestone with the convening in June of 1988 of the First Public Address Conference at the University of Wisconsin, Madison. The results of that conference were published the next year under the title *Texts in Context: Critical Dialogues on Significant Episodes in American Political Rhetoric*

---

[100]Stephen E. Lucas, "The Renaissance of American Public Address: Text and Context in Rhetorical Criticism," *The Quarterly Journal of Speech 74* (1988): 247. [See p. 188, here.]

[101]Lucas, "Renaissance," 189.

[102]Lucas, "Renaissance," 197.

(1989), edited by Michael C. Leff and Fred J. Kauffeld. This first conference was followed by a second at Northwestern University in September of 1990, a third at the University of Minnesota in September 1992, with a fourth scheduled for Indiana University in October 1994.

It is more than a little ironic that the "renaissance" of public address studies in the 1980s and 1990s should be powered by the discovery of a basic unit of analysis—the speech text—which should, by all rights, have been discovered in the 1920s. Yet it was not. Furthermore, this historical irony has led to a seeming paradox: a theory of the case that operates within the confines of the particular textual site to generate critical understanding of issues that transcend the case. Nevertheless, the "renaissance" is in process. Studies of significant instances of public address are being published in speech communication journals. Rhetorical biography, once thought to be the province of a dead neo-Aristotelian paradigm, has been resurrected.[103] University press books on various aspects of rhetoric and public address appear regularly.[104] Even commercial publishers now welcome studies undertaken from a rhetorical perspective. Sourcebooks on orators are now available where none existed before.[105] Not all of these instances of rebirth follow the narrow definition of public address as platform oratory, nor should they. As David Zarefsky noted in 1989:

> we have enlarged the meaning of "public address" from a mode to a function of discourse. . . . By embracing a broader conception of public address and not reducing the term to formal oratory, our studies have enhanced the potential for understanding historical or rhetorical situations and for formulating theoretical generalizations.[106]

So whether the study of public address encompasses analysis of a single speech, the speeches given as part of a public campaign, the various sorts of symbolic inducement found in social movements, pamphlets, letters,

---

[103] Greenwood Publishing Group has, to date, produced nineteen volumes of rhetorical biography in its "Great American Orators" series, under the editorial direction of Bernard K. Duffy and Halford R. Ryan. Books have appeared on Henry Ward Beecher, Edward Everett, Theodore Roosevelt, Patrick Henry, Anna Howard Shaw, William Jennings Bryan, Robert M. LaFollette, Sr., Ronald Reagan, Richard Nixon, Clarence Darrow, Frances E. Willard, Abraham Lincoln, Mark Twain, Jonathan Edwards, Daniel Webster, Harry Emerson Fosdick, Eugene Talmadge, Elizabeth Cady Stanton, and Dwight D. Eisenhower.

[104] University presses with series in rhetoric and communication studies include Southern Illinois University Press, University of South Carolina Press, University of Alabama Press, State University of New York Press, Michigan State University Press, and University of Wisconsin Press. Oxford University Press, Chicago University Press, and the University of Illinois Press all have substantial lists in rhetoric and communication.

[105] See, especially, Bernard K. Duffy and Halford R. Ryan, eds., *American Orators Before 1900: Critical Studies and Sources* (Westport, Conn.: Greenwood Press, 1987); Bernard K. Duffy and Halford R. Ryan, eds., *American Orators of the Twentieth Century: Critical Studies and Sources* (Westport, Conn.: Greenwood Press, 1987); and Karlyn Kohrs Campbell, ed., *Women Public Speakers in the United States, 1800-1925: A Bio-Critical Sourcebook* (Westport, Conn.: Greenwood Press, 1993).

[106] David Zarefsky, "The State of the Art in Public Address Scholarship," in *Texts in Context*, ed. Michael C. Leff and Fred J. Kauffeld (Davis, CA: Hermagoras Press, 1989), 3-4. [See p. 205, here.]

proclamations, sermons, lectures, or various forms of cinematic or televisual experience, the effort to understand the artistic, historical, and political dimensions of human persuasion continues.

The essays in this volume represent landmarks in the literal sense of that term—they are marks on the intellectual landscape that indicate where scholars and ideas have passed, and in that passing left a mark for future generations. It is appropriate to revisit the landmarks that have set public address off as a field of study, for by so visiting we remember the struggles that have led to the current situation. Most of the authors of the following chapters are deceased, but their ideas live on—transformed, adapted, modified, rejected, reborn. The scholarly dialectic continues. What constitutes a study in public address, how best to approach rhetorical texts, which analytical tools are required for the job, how best to balance text with context, what role ought theory to play in the conduct or outcome of critical inquiry?—these questions live on. To answer them at all is to engender debate—and that is how it should be if we are to maintain the intellectual vitality of public address. Zarefsky is right: "Soundly conceived, skillfully executed studies of rhetorical practice are what will most assure the continued health of our field."[107] The essays which follow are a prolegomenon to such studies, for they mark where we have been and point the way to where we still must go.

---

[107]Zarefsky, 214.

The Literary Criticism of Oratory

by Herbert A. Wichelns

I

Samuel Johnson once projected a history of criticism "as it relates to judging of authors." Had the great eighteenth-century critic ever carried out his intention, he would have included some interesting comments on the orators and their judges. Histories of criticism, in whole or in part, we now have, and histories of orators. But that section of the history of criticism which deals with judging of orators is still unwritten. Yet the problem is an interesting one, and one which involves some important conceptions. Oratory—the waning influence of which is often discussed in current periodicals—has definitely lost the established place in literature that it once had. Demosthenes and Cicero, Bossuet and Burke, all hold their places in literary histories. But Webster inspires more than one modern critic to ponder the question whether oratory is literature; and if we may judge by the emphasis of literary historians generally, both in England and in America, oratory is either an outcast or a poor relation. What are the reasons for this change? It is a question not easily answered. Involved in it is some shift in the conception of oratory or of literature, or of both; nor can these conceptions have changed except in response to the life of which oratory, as well as literature, is part.

This essay, it should be said, is merely an attempt to spy out the land, to see what some critics have said of some orators, to discover what their mode of criticism has been. The discussion is limited in the main to Burke and a few nineteenth-century figures—Webster, Lincoln, Gladstone, Bright, Cobden—and to the verdicts on these found in the surveys of literary history, in critical essays, in histories of oratory, and in biographies.

Of course, we are not here concerned with the disparagement of oratory. With that, John Morley once dealt in a phrase: "Yet, after all, to disparage eloquence is to depreciate mankind."[1] Nor is the praise of eloquence of moment here. What interests us is the method of the critic: his standards, his categories of judgment, what he regards as important. These will show, not so much what he thinks of a great and ancient literary type, as how he thinks

---

Reprinted from *Studies in Rhetoric and Public Speaking in Honor of James Albert Winans.* Edited by A.M. Drummond. (New York: The Century Co., 1925).

[1] *Life of William Ewart Gladstone*, New York, 1903, II, 593.

in dealing with that type. The chief aim is to know how critics have spoken of orators.

We have not much serious criticism of oratory. The reasons are patent. Oratory is intimately associated with statecraft; it is bound up with the things of the moment; its occasion, its terms, its background, can often be understood only by the careful student of history. Again, the publication of orations as pamphlets leaves us free to regard any speech merely as an essay, as a literary effort deposited at the shrine of the muses in hope of being blessed with immortality. This view is encouraged by the difficulty of reconstructing the conditions under which the speech was delivered; by the doubt, often, whether the printed text of the speech represents what was actually said, or what the orator elaborated afterwards. Burke's corrections are said to have been the despair of his printers.[2] Some of Chatham's speeches, by a paradox of fate, have been reported to us by Samuel Johnson, whose style is as remote as possible from that of the Great Commoner, and who wrote without even having heard the speeches pronounced.[3] Only in comparatively recent times has parliamentary reporting pretended to give full records of what was actually said; and even now speeches are published for literary or political purposes which justify the corrector's pencil in changes both great and small. Under such conditions the historical study of speech making is far from easy.

Yet the conditions of democracy necessitate both the making of speeches and the study of the art. It is true that other ways of influencing opinion have long been practised, that oratory is no longer the chief means of communicating ideas to the masses. And the change is emphasized by the fact that the newer methods are now beginning to be investigated, sometimes from the point of view of the political student, sometimes from that of the "publicity expert." But, human nature being what it is, there is no likelihood that face to face persuasion will cease to be a principal mode of exerting influence, whether in courts, in senate-houses, or on the platform. It follows that the critical study of oratorical method is the study, not of a mode outworn, but of a permanent and important human activity.

Upon the great figures of the past who have used the art of public address, countless judgments have been given. These judgments have varied with the bias and preoccupation of the critics, who have been historians, biographers, or literary men, and have written accordingly. The context in which we find criticism of speeches, we must, for the purposes of this essay at least, both note and set aside. For though the aim of the critic conditions his approach to our more limited problem—the method of dealing with oratory—still we find that an historian may view an orator in the same light as does a biographer or an essayist. The literary form in which criticism of

---

[2] *Select Works,* ed. E. J. Payne, Oxford, 1892, I, xxxviii.
[3] Basil Williams, *Life of William Pitt,* New York, 1913, II, 335-337.

oratory is set does not afford a classification of the critics.

"There are," says a critic of literary critics, "three definite points, on one of which, or all of which, criticism must base itself. There is the date, and the author, and the work."[4] The points on which writers base their judgments of orators do afford a classification. The man, his work, his times, are the necessary common topics of criticism; no one of them can be wholly disregarded by any critic. But mere difference in emphasis on one or another of them is important enough to suggest a rough grouping. The writers with whom this essay deals give but a subordinate position to the date; they are interested chiefly in the man or in his works. Accordingly, we have as the first type of criticism that which is predominantly personal or biographical, is occupied with the character and the mind of the orator, goes behind the work to the man. The second type attempts to hold the scales even between the biographical and the literary interest. The third is occupied with the work and tends to ignore the man. These three classes, then, seem to represent the practice of modern writers in dealing with orators. Each merits a more detailed examination.

II

We may begin with that type of critic whose interest is in personality, who seeks the man behind the work. Critics of this type furnish forth the appreciative essays and the occasional addresses on the orators. They are as the sands of the sea. Lord Rosebery's two speeches on Burke, Whitelaw Reid's on Lincoln and on Burke, may stand as examples of the character sketch.[5] The second part of Birrell's essay on Burke will serve for the mental character sketch (the first half of the essay is biographical); other examples are Sir Walter Raleigh's essay on Burke and that by Robert Lynd.[6] All these emphasize the concrete nature of Burke's thought, the realism of his imagination, his peculiar combination of breadth of vision with intensity; they pass to the guiding principles of his thought: his hatred of abstraction, his love of order and of settled ways. But they do not occupy themselves with Burke as a speaker, nor even with him as a writer; their first and their last concern is with the man rather than with his works; and their method is to fuse into a single impression whatever of knowledge or opinion they may have of the orator's life and works. These critics, in dealing with the public speaker, think of him as something other than a speaker. Since this type of writing makes but an indirect contribution to our judgment of the orator, there is no need of a more extended account of the method, except as we find it combined with a discussion of the orator's works.

---

[4] D. Nichol Smith, *Functions of Criticism*, Oxford, 1909, p. 15.

[5] See Rosebery, *Appreciations and Addresses*, London, 1899, and Whitelaw Reid, *American and English Studies*, New York, 1913, II.

[6] See Augustine Birrell, *Obiter Dicta*, New York, 1887, II; Walter Raleigh, *Some Authors*, Oxford, 1923; Robert Lynd, *Books and Authors*, London, 1922.

III

Embedded in biographies and histories of literature, we find another type of criticism, that which combines the sketch of mind and character with some discussion of style. Of the general interest of such essays there can be no doubt. Nine tenths of so-called literary criticism deals with the lives and personalities of authors, and for the obvious reason, that every one is interested in them, whereas few will follow a technical study, however broadly based. At its best, the type of study that starts with the orator's mind and character is justified by the fact that nothing can better illuminate his work as a persuader of men. But when not at its best, the description of a man's general cast of mind stands utterly unrelated to his art: the critic fails to fuse his comment on the individual with his comment on the artist; and as a result we get some statements about the man, and some statements about the orator, but neither casts light on the other. Almost any of the literary histories will supply examples of the gulf that may yawn between a stylistic study and a study of personality.

The best example of the successful combination of the two strains is Grierson's essay on Burke in the *Cambridge History of English Literature.* In this, Burke's style, though in largest outline only, is seen to emerge from the essential nature of the man. Yet of this essay, too, it must be said that the analysis of the orator is incomplete, being overshadowed by the treatment of Burke as a writer, though, as we shall see, the passages on style have the rare virtue of keeping to the high road of criticism. The majority of critics who use the mixed method, however, do not make their study of personality fruitful for a study of style, do not separate literary style from oratorical style even to the extent that Grierson does, and do conceive of literary style as a matter of details. In fact, most of the critics of this group tend to supply a discussion of style by jotting down what has occurred to them about the author's management of words; and in the main, they notice the lesser strokes of literary art, but not its broader aspects. They have an eye for tactics, but not for strategy. This is the more strange, as these same writers habitually take large views of the orator himself, considered as a personality, and because they often remark the speaker's great themes and his leading ideas. The management of ideas—what the Romans called invention and disposition—the critics do not observe; their practice is the *salto mortale* from the largest to the smallest considerations. And it needs no mention that a critic who does not observe the management of ideas even from the point of view of structure and arrangement can have nothing to say of the adaptation of ideas to the orator's audience.

It is thus with Professor McLaughlin in his chapter in the *Cambridge History of American Literature* on Clay and Calhoun and some lesser lights. The pages are covered with such expressions as diffuse, florid, diction restrained and strong, neatly phrased, power of attack, invective, gracious persuasiveness. Of the structure of the speeches by which Clay and Calhoun exercised their influence—nothing. The drive of ideas is not represented. The background of habitual feeling which the orators at times appealed to and at times modified, is hinted at in a passage about Clay's awakening the spirit of nationalism, and in another passage contrasting the full-blooded oratory of Benton with the more polished speech of Quincy and Everett; but these are the merest hints. In the main, style for McLaughlin is neither the expression of personality nor the order and movement given to thought, but a thing of shreds and patches. It is thus, too, with Morley's pages on Burke's style in his life of the orator, and with Lodge's treatment of Webster in his life of the great American. A rather better analysis, though on the same plane of detail, may be used as an example. Oliver Elton says of Burke:

> He embodies, more powerfully than any one, the mental tendencies and changes that are seen gathering force through the eighteenth century. A volume of positive knowledge, critically sifted and ascertained: a constructive vision of the past and its institutions; the imagination, under this guidance, everywhere at play; all these elements unite in Burke. His main field is political philosophy. . . . His favorite form is oratory, uttered or written. His medium is prose, and the work of his later years, alone, outweighs all contemporary prose in power. . . . His whole body of production has the unity of some large cathedral, whose successive accretions reveal the natural growth of a single mind, without any change or essential break. . . .
>
> Already [in the *Thoughts* and in the *Observations*] the characteristics of Burke's thought and style appear, as well as his profound conversance with constitutional history, finance, and affairs. There is a constant reference to general principles, as in the famous defence of Party. The maxims that come into play go far beyond the occasion. There is a perpetual ground-swell of passion, embanked and held in check, but ever breaking out into sombre irony and sometimes into figure: but metaphors and other tropes are not yet very frequent. . . .
>
> In the art of unfolding and amplifying, Burke is the rival of the ancients. . . .
>
> In the speech on Conciliation the [oft-repeated] key-word is peace. . . . This iteration makes us see the stubborn faces on the opposite benches. There is contempt in it; their ears must be dinned, they must remember the word peace through the long intricate survey that is to follow. . . .
>
> Often he has a turn that would have aroused the fervor of the great appreciator known to us by the name of Longinus. In his speech on Economical Reform (1780) Burke risks an appeal, in the face of the Commons, to the example of the enemy. He has described . . . the reforms of the French revenue. He says: "The French have imitated us; let us, through them, imitate ourselves, ourselves in our better and happier days." A speaker who was willing to offend

for the sake of startling, and to defeat his purpose, would simply have said, "The French have imitated us: let us imitate them." Burke comes to the verge of this imprudence, but he sees the outcry on the lips of the adversary, and silences them by the word *ourselves;* and then, seizing the moment of bewilderment, repeats it and explains it by the noble past; he does not say when those days were; the days of Elizabeth or of Cromwell? Let the House choose! This is true oratory, honest diplomacy.[7]

Here, in some twenty pages, we have but two hints that Burke had to put his ideas in a form adapted to his audience: only the reiterated *peace* in all Burke's writings reminds the critic of Burke's hearers: only one stroke of tact draws his attention. Most of his account is devoted to Burke's style in the limited use of the term: to his power of amplification—his conduct of the paragraph, his use of clauses now long, now short—to his figures, comparisons, and metaphors, to his management of the sentence pattern, and to his rhythms. For Professor Elton, evidently, Burke was a man, and a mind, and an artist in prose; but he was not an orator. Interest in the minutae of style has kept Elton from bringing his view of Burke the man to bear on his view of Burke's writings. The fusing point evidently is in the strategic purpose of the works, in their function as speeches. By holding steadily to the conception of Burke as a public man, one could make the analysis of mind and the analysis of art more illuminating for each other than Elton does.

It cannot be said that in all respects Stephenson's chapter on Lincoln in the *Cambridge History of American Literature* is more successful than Elton's treatment of Burke; but it is a better interweaving of the biographical and the literary strands of interest. Stephenson's study of the personality of Lincoln is directly and persistently used in the study of Lincoln's style.

> Is it fanciful to find a connection between the way in which his mysticism develops—its atmospheric, non-dogmatic pervasiveness—and the way in which his style develops? Certainly the literary part of him works into all the portions of his utterance with the gradualness of daylight through a shadowy wood. . . . And it is to be noted that the literary quality . . . is of the whole, not of the detail. It does not appear as a gift of phrases. Rather it is the slow unfolding of those two original characteristics, taste and rhythm. What is growing is the degree of both things. The man is becoming deeper, and as he does so he imposes himself, in this atmospheric way, more steadily on his language.[8]

The psychology of mystical experience may appear a poor support for the study of style. It is but one factor of many, and Stephenson may justly be

---

[7] Oliver Elton, *Survey of English Literature, 1780-1830,* I, 234-53.
[8] *Cambridge History of American Literature,* New York, 1921, III, 374-5.

reproached for leaning too heavily upon it. Compared to Grierson's subtler analysis of Burke's mind and art, the essay of Stephenson seems forced and one-sided. Yet he illuminates his subject more than many of the writers so far mentioned, because he begins with a vigorous effort to bring his knowledge of the man to bear upon his interpretation of the work. But though we find in Stephenson's pages a suggestive study of Lincoln as literary man, we find no special regard for Lincoln as orator. The qualities of style that Stephenson mentions are the qualities of prose generally:

> At last he has his second manner, a manner quite his own. It is not his final manner, the one that was to give him his assured place in literature. However, In a wonderful blend of simplicity, directness, candor, joined with a clearness beyond praise. and a delightful cadence, it has outstripped every other politician of the hour. And back of its words, subtly affecting its phrases, . . . is that brooding sadness which was to be with him to the end.[9]

The final manner, it appears, is a sublimation of the qualities of the earlier, which was "keen, powerful, full of character, melodious, impressive";[10] and it is a sublimation which has the power to awaken the imagination by its flexibility, directness, pregnancy, wealth.

In this we have nothing new, unless it be the choice of stylistic categories that emphasize the larger pattern of ideas rather than the minute pattern of grammatical units, such as we have found in Elton and to some extent shall find in Saintsbury; it must be granted, too. that Stephenson has dispensed with detail and gained his larger view at the cost of no little vagueness. "Two things," says Stephenson of the Lincoln of 1849-1858, "grew upon him. The first was his understanding of men, the generality of men. . . . The other thing that grew upon him was his power to reach and influence them through words."[11] We have here the text for any study of Lincoln as orator; but the study itself this critic does not give us.

Elton's characterization of Burke's style stands out from the usual run of superficial comment by the closeness of its analysis and its regard for the architectonic element. Stephenson's characterization of Lincoln's style is distinguished by a vigorous if forced effort to unite the study of the man and of the work. With both we may contrast a better essay. by a critic of greater insight. Grierson says of Burke:

> What Burke has of the deeper spirit of that movement [the romantic revival] is seen not so much in the poetic imagery of his finest prose as in the philosophical imagination which informs his conception of the state, in virtue of which he transcends the

---

[9] *Cambridge History of American Literature*, III, 378.
[10] *Ibid.*, pp. 381-2.
[11] *Ibid.*, p. 377.

rationalism of the century. . . . This temper of Burke's mind is reflected in his prose. . . . To the direct, conversational prose of Dryden and Swift, changed social circumstances and the influence of Johnson had given a more oratorical cast, more dignity and weight, but, also, more of heaviness and conventional elegance. From the latter faults, Burke is saved by his passionate temperament, his ardent imagination, and the fact that he was a speaker conscious always of his audience. . . . [Burke] could delight, astound, and convince an audience. He did not easily conciliate and win them over. He lacked the first essential and index of the conciliatory speaker, *lenitas vocis;* his voice was harsh and unmusical, his gesture un-gainly. . . . And, even in the text of his speeches there is a strain of irony and scorn which is not well fitted to conciliate. . . . We have evidence that he could do both things on which Cicero lays stress—move his audience to tears and delight them by his wit. . . . Yet, neither pathos nor humor is Burke's *forte.* . . . Burke's unique power as an orator lies in the peculiar interpenetration of thought and passion. Like the poet and the prophet, he thinks most profoundly when he thinks most passionately. When he is not deeply moved, his oratory verges toward the turgid; when he indulges feeling for his own sake, as in parts of *Letters on a Regicide Peace,* it becomes hysterical. But, in his greatest speeches and pamphlets, the passion of Burke's mind shows itself in the luminous thoughts which it emits, in the imagery which at once moves *and* teaches, throwing a flood of light not only on the point in question, but on the whole neighboring sphere of man's moral and political nature.[12]

The most notable feature of these passages is not their recognition that Burke was a speaker, but their recognition that his being a speaker conditioned his style, and that he is to be judged in part at least as one who attempted to influence men by the spoken word. Grierson, like Elton, attends to the element of structure and has something to say of the nature of Burke's prose; but, unlike Elton, he distinguishes this from the description of Burke's oratory—although without maintaining the distinction: he illustrates Burke's peculiar oratorical power from a pamphlet as readily as from a speech. His categories seem less mechanical than those of Elton, who is more concerned with the development of the paragraph than with the general cast of Burke's style: nor is his judgment warped, as is Stephenson's, by having a theory to market. Each has suffered from the necessity of compression. Yet, all told, Grierson realizes better than the others that Burke's task was not merely to express his thoughts and his feelings in distinguished prose, but to communicate his thoughts and his feelings effectively. It is hardly true, however, that Grierson has in mind the actual audience of Burke; the audience of

---

[12] *Cambridge History of English Literature,* New York, 1914, XI, 30-5.

Grierson's vision seems to be universalized, to consist of the judicious listeners or readers of any age. Those judicious listeners have no practical interest in the situation; they have only a philosophical and aesthetic interest.

Of Taine in his description of Burke it cannot be said that he descends to the minutiae of style. He deals with his author's character and ideas, as do all the critics of this group, but his comments on style are simply a single impression, vivid and picturesque:

> Burke had one of those fertile and precise imaginations which believe that finished knowledge is an inner view, which never quits a subject without having clothed it in its colors and forms. . . .To all these powers of mind, which constitute a man of system, he added all those energies of heart which constitute an enthusiast. . . . He brought to politics a horror of crime, a vivacity and sincerity of conscience, a sensibility, which seem suitable only to a young man.
>
> . . .The vast amount of his works rolls impetuously in a current of eloquence. Sometimes a spoken or written discourse needs a whole volume to unfold the train of his multiplied proofs and courageous anger. It is either the exposé of a ministry, or the whole history of British India, or the complete theory of revolutions . . . which comes down like a vast overflowing stream . . . Doubtless there is foam on its eddies, mud in its bed; thousands of strange creatures sport wildly on its surface: he does not select, he lavishes. . . . Nothing strikes him as in excess. . . . He continues half a barbarian, battening in exaggeration and violence: but his fire is so sustained, his conviction so strong, his emotion so warm and abundant, that we suffer him to go on, forget our repugnance, see in his irregularities and his trespasses only the outpourings of a great heart and a deep mind. too open and too full.[13]

This is brilliant writing, unencumbered by the subaltern's interest in tactics, but it is strategy as described by a war-correspondent, not by a general. We get from it little light on how Burke solved the problem that confronts every orator: so to present ideas as to bring them into the consciousness of his hearers.

Where the critic divides his interest between the man and the work, without allowing either interest to predominate, he is often compelled to consider the work *in toto,* and we get only observations so generalized as not to include consideration of the form of the work. The speech is not thought of as essentially a means of influence; it is regarded as a specimen of prose, or as an example of philosophic thought. The date, the historical interest, the orator's own intention, are often lost from view; and criticism suffers in consequence.

---

[13]H. A. Taine, *History of English Literature*, tr. H. Van Laun, London, 1878, II, 81-3.

IV

We have seen that the critic who is occupied chiefly with the orator as a man can contribute, although indirectly, to the study of the orator as such, and that the critic who divides his attention between the man and the work must effect a fusion of the two interests if he is to help materially in the understanding of the orator. We come now to critics more distinctly literary in aim. Within this group several classes may be discriminated: the first comprises the judicial critics; the second includes the interpretative critics who take the point of view of literary style generally, regarding the speech as an essay, or as a specimen of prose; the third and last group is composed of the writers who tend to regard the speech as a special literary form.

The type of criticism that attempts a judicial evaluation of the literary merits of the work—of the orator's "literary remains"—tends to center the inquiry on the question: Is this literature? The futility of the question appears equally in the affirmative and in the negative replies to it. The fault is less with the query. however, than with the hastiness of the answers generally given. For the most part, the critics who raise this problem are not disposed really to consider it: they formulate no conception either of literature or of oratory; they will not consider their own literary standards critically and comprehensively. In short, the question is employed as a way to dispose briefly of the subject of a lecture or of a short essay in a survey of a national literature.

Thus Phelps, in his treatment of Webster and Lincoln in *Some Makers of American Literature*,[14] tells us that they have a place in literature by virtue of their style, gives us some excerpts from Lincoln and some comments on Webster's politics, but offers no reasoned criticism. St. Peter swings wide the gates of the literary heaven, but does not explain his action. We may suspect that the solemn award of a "place in literature" sometimes conceals the absence of any real principle of judgment.

Professor Trent is less easily satisfied that Webster deserves a "place in literature." He grants Webster's power to stimulate patriotism, his sonorous dignity and massiveness, his clearness and strength of style, his powers of dramatic description. But he finds only occasional splendor of imagination, discovers no soaring quality of intelligence, and is not dazzled by his philosophy or his grasp of history. Mr. Trent would like more vivacity and humor and color in Webster's style.[15] This mode of deciding Webster's place in or out of literature is important to us only as it reveals the critic's method of judging. Trent looks for clearness and strength, imagination, philosophic grasp, vivacity, humor, color in style. This is excellent so far as it goes, but goes no further than to suggest some qualities which are to be sought in any

---

[14]Boston, 1923.

[15]W. P. Trent, *History of American Literature, 1607-1865*, New York, 1917, pp. 576-7.

and all works of literary art: in dramas, in essays, in lyric poems, as well as in speeches.

Let us take a third judge. Gosse will not allow Burke to be a complete master of English prose: "Notwithstanding all its magnificence, it appears to me that the prose of Burke lacks the variety, the delicacy, the modulated music of the very finest writers."[16] Gosse adds that Burke lacks flexibility, humor, and pathos. As critical method, this is one with that of Trent.

Gosse, with his question about mastery of prose, does not directly ask, "is this literature?" Henry Cabot Lodge does, and his treatment of Webster (in the *Cambridge History of American Literature*) is curious. Lodge is concerned to show that Webster belongs to literature, and to explain the quality in his work that gives him a place among the best makers of literature. The test applied is permanence: Is Webster still read? The answer is, yes, for he is part of every schoolboy's education, and is the most quoted author in Congress. The sight of a literary critic resigning the judicial bench to the schoolmaster and the Congressman is an enjoyable one; as enjoyable as Mr. H. L. Mencken's reaction to it would be; but one could wish for grounds more relative than this. Mr. Lodge goes on to account for Webster's permanence: it lies in his power to impart to rhetoric the literary touch. The distinction between rhetoric and literature is not explained, but apparently the matter lies thus: rhetorical verse may be poetry; Byron is an example. Rhetorical prose is not literature until there is added the literary touch. We get a clue as to how the literary touch may be added: put in something imaginative, something that strikes the hearer at once. The example chosen by Lodge is a passage from Webster in which the imaginative or literary touch is given by the single word "mildew."[17] This method of criticism, too, we may reduce to that of Trent, with the exception that only one quality— imagination—is requisite for admission to the literary Valhalla.

Whether the critic's standards be imagination, or this together with other qualities such as intelligence, vivacity, humor, or whether it be merely "style," undefined and unexplained, the point of view is always that of the printed page. The oration is lost from view, and becomes an exercise in prose, musical, colorful, varied, and delicate, but, so far as the critic is concerned. formless and purposeless. Distinctions of literary type or kind are erased; the architectonic element is neglected: and the speech is regarded as a musical meditation might be regarded: as a kind of harmonious musing that drifts pleasantly along, with little of inner form and nothing of objective purpose. This, it should be recognized, is not the result of judicial criticism so much as the result of the attempt to decide too hastily whether a given work is to be admitted into the canon of literature.

---

[16]Edmund Gosse, *History of Eighteenth Century English Literature, 1660-1780,* London, 1889, pp. 365-6.

[17]*Cambridge History of American Literature,* New York, 1918, II, 101.

V

It is, perhaps, natural for the historian of literature to reduce all literary production to one standard, and thus to discuss only the common elements in all prose. One can understand also that the biographer, when in the course of his task he must turn literary critic, finds himself often inadequately equipped and his judgment of little value, except on the scale of literature generally rather than of oratory or of any given type. More is to be expected, however, of those who set up as literary critics in the first instance: those who deal directly with Webster's style, or with Lincoln as man of letters. We shall find such critics as Whipple, Hazlitt, and Saintsbury devoting themselves to the description of literary style in the orators whom they discuss. Like the summary judicial critics we have mentioned, their center of interest is the work; but they are less hurried than Gosse and Lodge and Phelps and Trent; and their aim is not judgment so much as understanding. Yet their interpretations, in the main, take the point of view of the printed page, of the prose essay. Only to a slight degree is there a shift to another point of view, that of the orator in relation to the audience on whom he exerts his influence; the immediate public begins to loom a little larger; the essential nature of the oration as a type begins to be suggested.

Saintsbury has a procedure which much resembles that of Elton, though we must note the fact that the former omits consideration of Burke as a personality and centers attention on his work. We saw that Elton, in his passages on Burke's style, attends both to the larger elements of structure and to such relatively minute points as the management of the sentence and the clause. In Saintsbury the range of considerations is the same. At times, indeed, the juxtaposition of large and small ideas is ludicrous, as when one sentence ends by awarding to Burke literary immortality, and the next describes the sentences of an early work as "short and crisp, arranged with succinct antithetic parallels, which seldom exceed a single pair of clauses."[18] The award of immortality is not, it should be said, based entirely on the shortness of Burke's sentences in his earliest works. Indeed much of Saintsbury's comment is of decided interest:

> The style of Burke is necessarily to be considered throughout as conditioned by oratory. . . . In other words, he was first of all a rhetorician. and probably the greatest that modern times have ever produced. But his rhetoric always inclined much more to the written than to the spoken form, with results annoying perhaps to him at the time, but even to him satisfactory afterwards. and an inestimable gain to the world. . . .
>
> The most important of these properties of Burke's style, in so far as it is possible to enumerate them here, are as follows. First of all,

---

[18]G. E. B. Saintsbury, *Short History of English Literature,* New York, 1915, p. 630.

and most distinctive, so much so as to have escaped no competent critic, is a very curious and, until his example made it imitable, nearly unique faculty of building up an argument or a picture by a succession of complementary strokes, not added at haphazard but growing out of and onto one another. No one has ever been such a master of the best and grandest kind of the figure called . . . Amplification, and this . . . is the direct implement by which he achieves his greatest effects.

. . . The piece [*Present Discontents*] may be said to consist of a certain number of specially labored paragraphs in which the arguments or pictures just spoken of are put as forcibly as the author can put them, and as a rule in a succession of shortish sentences, built up and glued together with the strength and flexibility of a newly fashioned fishing-rod. In the intervals the texts thus given are turned about, commented on justified, or discussed in detail, in a rhetoric for the most part, though not always, rather less serried, less evidently burnished, and in less full dress. And this general arrangement proceeds through the rest of his works.[19]

After a number of comments on Burke's skill in handling various kinds of ornament, such as humor, epigram, simile, Saintsbury returns to the idea that Burke's special and definite weapon was "imaginative argument, and the marshalling of vast masses of complicated detail into properly rhetorical battalions or (to alter the image) mosaic pictures of enduring beauty."[20] Saintsbury's attitude toward the communicative, impulsive nature of the orator's task is indicated in a passage on the well-known description of Windsor Castle. This description the critic terms "at once . . . a perfect harmonic chord, a complete visual picture, and a forcible argument."[21] It is significant that he adds, "The minor rhetoric, the suasive purpose [presumably the argumentative intent] must be kept in view; if it be left out the thing loses"; and holds Burke "far below Browne, who had no need of purpose."[22] It is less important that a critic think well of the suasive purpose than that he reckon with it, and of Saintsbury at least it must be said that he recognizes it, although grudgingly; but it cannot be said that Saintsbury has a clear conception of rhetoric as the art of communication: sometimes it means the art of prose, sometimes that of suasion.

Hazlitt's method of dealing with Burke resembles Taine's as Saintsbury's resembles that of Elton. In Hazlitt we have a critic who deals with style in the large; details of rhythm, of sentence pattern, of imagery, are ignored. His principal criticism of Burke as orator is contained in the well-known contrast

---

[19]*Ibid.*, pp. 629-30.
[20]*Ibid.*, p. 631.
[21]*Ibid.*
[22]*Ibid.*

with Chatham, really a contrast of mind and temperament in relation to
oratorical style. He follows this with some excellent comment on Burke's
prose style; nothing more is said of his oratory; only in a few passages do we
get a flash of light on the relation of Burke to his audience, as in the remark
about his eagerness to impress his reader, and in the description of his
conversational quality. It is notable too that Hazlitt finds those works which
never had the form of speeches the most significant and most typical of
Burke's style.

> Burke was so far from being a gaudy or flowery writer, that he
> was one of the severest writers we have. His words are the most like
> things: his style is the most strictly limited to the subject. He unites
> every extreme and every variety of composition: the lowest and the
> meanest words and descriptions with the highest. . . . He had no other
> object but to produce the strongest impression on his reader, by
> giving the truest, the most characteristic, the fullest, and most
> forcible description of things. trusting to the power of his own mind
> to mold them into grace and beauty. . . . Burke most frequently pro-
> duced an effect by the remoteness and novelty of his combinations,
> by the force of contrast, by the striking manner in which the most
> opposite and unpromising materials were harmoniously blended
> together; not by laying his hands on all the fine things he could think
> of, but by bringing together those things which he knew would blaze
> out into glorious light by their collision.[23]

Twelve years after writing the essay from which we have quoted, Hazlitt
had occasion to revise his estimate of Burke as a statesman; but his sketch of
Burke's style is essentially unaltered.[24] In Hazlitt we find a sense of style as
an instrument of communication; that sense is no stronger in dealing with
Burke's speeches than in dealing with his pamphlets, but it gives to Hazlitt's
criticisms a reality not often found. What is lacking is a clear sense of
Burke's communicative impulse, of his persuasive purpose, as operating in a
concrete situation. Hazlitt does not suggest the background of Burke's
speeches, ignores the events that called them forth. He views his subject, in a
sense, as Grierson does: as speaking to the judicious but disinterested hearer
of any age other than Burke's own. But the problem of the speaker, as well
as of the pamphleteer, is to interest men here and now; the understanding of
that problem requires, on the part of the critic, a strong historical sense for
the ideas and attitudes of the people (not merely of their leaders), and a full
knowledge of the public opinion of the times in which the orator spoke. This
we do not find in Hazlitt.

---

[23] *Sketches and Essays,* ed. W. C. Hazlitt, London, 1872, II, 420-1.
[24] *Political Essays with Sketches of Public Characters,* London, 1819, pp. 264-79.

Two recent writers on Lincoln commit the opposite error: they devote themselves so completely to description of the situation in which Lincoln wrote as to leave no room for criticism. L. E. Robinson's *Lincoln as Man of Letters*[25] is a biography rewritten around Lincoln's writings. It is nothing more. Instead of giving us a criticism, Professor Robinson has furnished us with some of the materials of the critic; his own judgments are too largely laudatory to cast much light. The book, therefore, is not all that its title implies. A single chapter of accurate summary and evaluation would do much to increase our understanding of Lincoln as man of letters, even though it said nothing of Lincoln as speaker. A chapter or two on Lincoln's work in various kinds—letters. state papers, speeches—would help us to a finer discrimination than Professor Robinson's book offers. Again, the proper estimate of style in any satisfactory sense requires us to do more than to weigh the soundness of an author's thought and to notice the isolated beauties of his expression. Something should be said of structure, something of adaptation to the immediate audience, whose convictions and habits of thought, whose literary usages, and whose general cultural background all condition the work both of writer and speaker. Mr. Robinson has given us the political situation as a problem in controlling political forces, with little regard to the force even of public opinion, and with almost none to the cultural background. Lincoln's works, therefore, emerge as items in a political sequence, but not as resultants of the life of his time.

Some of the deficiencies of Robinson's volume are supplied by Dodge's essay, *Lincoln as Master of Words.*[26] Dodge considers, more definitely than Robinson, the types in which Lincoln worked: he separates messages from campaign speeches, letters from occasional addresses. He has an eye on Lincoln's relation to his audience, but this manifests itself chiefly in an account of the immediate reception of a work. Reports of newspaper comments on the speeches may be a notable addition to Lincolniana; supported by more political information and more insight than Mr. Dodge's short book reveals, they might become an aid to the critical evaluation of the speeches. But in themselves they are neither a criticism nor an interpretation of Lincoln's mastery of words.

Robinson and Dodge, then, stand at opposite poles to Saintsbury and Hazlitt. The date is put in opposition to the work as a center of critical interest. If the two writers on Lincoln lack a full perception of their author's background, they do not lack a sense of its importance. If the critics of Burke do not produce a complete and rounded criticism, neither do they lose themselves in preparatory studies. Each method is incomplete; each should supplement the other.

---

[25]New York, 1923.
[26]New York, 1924.

We turn now to a critic who neglects the contribution of history to the study of oratory, but who has two compensating merits: the merit of recognizing the types in which his subject worked, and the merit of remembering that an orator has as his audience, not posterity, but certain classes of his own contemporaries. Whipple's essay on Webster is open to attack from various directions: It is padded, it "dates," it is overlaudatory, it is over-patriotic, it lacks distinction of style. But there is wheat in the chaff. Scattered through the customary discussion of Webster's choice of words, his power of epithet, his compactness of statement, his images, the development of his style, are definite suggestions of a new point of view. It is the point of view of the actual audience. To Whipple, at times at least, Webster was not a writer, but a speaker: the critic tries to imagine the man, and also his hearers: he thinks of the speech as a communication to a certain body of auditors. A phrase often betrays a mental attitude; Whipple alone of the critics we have mentioned would have written of "the eloquence, the moral power, he infused into his reasoning, so as to make the dullest citation of legal authority *tell* on the minds he addressed."[27] Nor would any other writer of this group have attempted to distinguish the types of audience Webster met. That Whipple's effort is a rambling and incoherent one, is not here in point. Nor is it pertinent that the critic goes completely astray in explaining why Webster's speeches have the nature of "organic formations, or at least of skilful engineering or architectural constructions"; though to say that the art of giving objective reality to a speech consists only of "a happy collocation and combination of words"[28] is certainly as far as possible from explaining Webster's sense of structure. What is significant in Whipple's essay is the occasional indication of a point of view that includes the audience. Such an indication is the passage in which the critic explains the source of Webster's influence:

> What gave Webster his immense influence over the opinions of the people of New England, was first, his power of so "putting things" that everybody could understand his statements; secondly, his power of so framing his arguments that all the steps, from one point to another, in a logical series, could be clearly apprehended by every intelligent farmer or mechanic who had a thoughtful interest in the affairs of the country: and thirdly, his power of inflaming the sentiment of patriotism In all honest and well-intentioned men by overwhelming appeals to that sentiment, so that after convincing their understandings, he clinched the matter by sweeping away their wills.
>
> Perhaps to these sources of influence may be added . . . a genuine respect for the intellect, as well as for the manhood, of average men.[29]

---

[27]E. P. Whipple, "Daniel Webster as a Master of English Style," in *American Literature,* Boston, 1887, p. 157.
[28]*Ibid.,* p. 208.
[29]*Ibid.,* p. 144.

In various ways the descriptive critics recognize the orator's function. In some, that recognition takes the form of a regard to the background of the speeches; in others, it takes the form of a regard to the effectiveness of the work, though that effectiveness is often construed as for the reader rather than for the listener. The "minor rhetoric, the suasive purpose" is beginning to be felt, though not always recognized and never fully taken into account.

VI

The distinction involved in the presence of a persuasive purpose is clearly recognized by some of those who have written on oratory, and by some biographers and historians. The writers now to be mentioned are aware, more keenly than any of those we have so far met, of the speech as a literary form—or if not as a literary form, then as a form of power: they tend accordingly to deal with the orator's work as limited by the conditions of the platform and the occasion, and to summon history to the aid of criticism.

The method of approach of the critics of oratory as oratory is well put by Lord Curzon at the beginning of his essay, *Modern Parliamentary Eloquence:*

> In dealing with the Parliamentary speakers of our time I shall, accordingly, confine myself to those whom I have myself heard, or for whom I can quote the testimony of others who heard them; and I shall not regard them as prose writers or literary men, still less as purveyors of instruction to their own or to future generations, but as men who produced, by the exercise of certain talents of speech, a definite impression upon contemporary audiences, and whose reputation for eloquence must be judged by that test, and that test alone.[30]

The last phrase, "that test alone," would be scanned; the judgment of orators is not solely to be determined by the impression of contemporary audiences. For the present it will be enough to note the topics touched in Curzon's anecdotes and reminiscences—his lecture is far from a systematic or searching inquiry into the subject, and is of interest rather for its method of approach than for any considered study of an orator or of a period. We value him for his promises rather than for his performance. Curzon deals with the relative rank of speakers, with the comparative value of various speeches by a single man, with the orator's appearance and demeanor, with his mode of preparation and of delivery, with his mastery of epigram or image. Skill in seizing upon the dominant characteristics of each of his subjects saves the author from the worst triviality of reminiscence. Throughout, the point of view is that of the man experienced in public life discussing the eloquence of other public men, most of whom he had known and actually

---

[30]London, 1914, p. 7.

heard. That this is not the point of view of criticism in any strict sense, is of course true; but the *naïveté* and directness of this observer correct forcibly some of the extravagances we have been examining.

The lecture on Chatham as an orator by H. M. Butler exemplifies a very different method arising from a different subject and purpose. The lecturer is thinking, he tells us, "of Oratory partly as an art, partly as a branch of literature, partly as a power of making history."[31] His method is first to touch lightly upon Chatham's early training and upon his mode of preparing and delivering his speeches; next, to present some of the general judgments upon the Great Commoner, whether of contemporaries or of later historians; then to re-create a few of the most important speeches, partly by picturing the historical setting, partly by quotation, partly by the comments of contemporary writers. The purpose of the essay is "to reawaken, however faintly, some echoes of the kingly voice of a genuine Patriot, of whom his country is still justly proud."[32] The patriotic purpose we may ignore, but the wish to reconstruct the *mise en scène* of Chatham's speeches, to put the modern Oxford audience at the point of view of those who listened to the voice of Pitt, saw the flash of his eye and felt the force of his noble bearing. This is a purpose different from that of the critics whom we have examined. It may be objected that Butler's lecture has the defects of its method: the amenities observed by a Cambridge don delivering a formal lecture at Oxford keep us from getting on with the subject; the brevity of the discourse prevents anything like a full treatment; the aim, revivification of the past, must be very broadly interpreted if it is to be really critical. Let us admit these things; it still is true that in a few pages the essential features of Pitt's eloquence are brought vividly before us, and that this is accomplished by thinking of the speech as originally delivered to its first audience rather than as read by the modern reader.

The same sense of the speaker in his relation to his audience appears in Lecky's account of Burke. This account, too, is marked by the use of contemporary witnesses, and of comparisons with Burke's great rivals. But let Lecky's method speak in part for itself:

> He spoke too often, too vehemently, and much too long; and his eloquence, though in the highest degree intellectual, powerful, various, and original, was not well adapted to a popular audience. He had little or nothing of that fire and majesty of declamation with which Chatham thrilled his hearers, and often almost overawed opposition; and as a parliamentary debater he was far inferior to Charles Fox. . . . Burke was not inferior to Fox in readiness, and in the power of clear and cogent reasoning. His wit, though not of the highest order, was only equalled by that of Townshend, Sheridan, and

---

[31]*Lord Chatham as an Orator,* Oxford, 1912, p. 5.
[32]*Ibid.,* pp. 39-40.

perhaps North, and it rarely failed in its effect upon the House. He far surpassed every other speaker in the copiousness and correctness of his diction, in the range of knowledge he brought to bear on every subject of debate, in the richness and variety of his imagination, in the gorgeous beauty of his descriptive passages. In the depth of the philosophical reflections and the felicity of the personal sketches which he delighted in scattering over his speeches. But these gifts were frequently marred by a strange want of judgment, measure. and self-control. His speeches were full of episodes and digressions, of excessive ornamentation and illustration, of dissertations on general principles of politics, which were invaluable in themselves, but very unpalatable to a tired or excited House waiting eagerly for a division.[33]

These sentences suggest, and the pages from which they are excerpted show, that historical imagination has led Lecky to regard Burke as primarily a speaker, both limited and formed by the conditions of his platform; and they exemplify, too, a happier use of stylistic categories than do the essays of Curzon and Butler. The requirements of the historian's art have fused the character sketch and the literary criticism; the fusing agent has been the conception of Burke as a public man, and of his work as public address. Both Lecky's biographical interpretation and his literary criticism are less subtle than that of Grierson; but Lecky is more definitely guided in his treatment of Burke by the conception of oratory as a special form of the literature of power and as a form molded always by the pressure of the time.

The merits of Lecky are contained, in ampler form, in Morley's biography of Gladstone. The long and varied career of the great parliamentarian makes a general summary and final judgment difficult and perhaps inadvisable; Morley does not attempt them. But his running account of Gladstone as orator, if assembled from his thousand pages, is an admirable example of what can be done by one who has the point of view of the public man, sympathy with his subject, and understanding of the speaker's art. Morley gives us much contemporary reporting: the descriptions and judgments of journalists at various stages in Gladstone's career, the impression made by the speeches upon delivery, comparison with other speakers of the time. Here history is contemporary: the biographer was himself the witness of much that he describes, and has the experienced parliamentarian's flair for the scene and the situation. Gladstone's temperament and physical equipment for the platform, his training in the art of speaking, the nature of his chief appeals, the factor of character and personality, these are some of the topics repeatedly touched. There is added a sense for the permanent results of Gladstone's speaking: not the votes in the House merely but the changed

---

[33]W. E. H. Lecky, *History of England in the Eighteenth Century*, New York, 1888, III, 2033-4.

state of public opinion brought about by the speeches.

Mr. Gladstone conquered the House, because he was saturated with a subject and its arguments; because he could state and enforce his case; because he plainly believed every word he said, and earnestly wished to press the same belief into the minds of his hearers; finally because he was from the first an eager and a powerful athlete. . . . Yet with this inborn readiness for combat, nobody was less addicted to aggression or provocation. . . .

In finance, the most important of all the many fields of his activity, Mr. Gladstone had the signal distinction of creating the public opinion by which he worked, and warming the climate in which his projects throve. . . . Nobody denies that he was often declamatory and discursive, that he often overargued and overrefined; [but] he nowhere exerted greater influence than in that department of affairs where words out of relation to fact are most surely exposed. If he often carried the proper rhetorical arts of amplification and develop-ment to excess, yet the basis of fact was both sound and clear. . . . Just as Macaulay made thousands read history, who before had turned from it as dry and repulsive, so Mr. Gladstone made thou-sands eager to follow the public balance-sheet, and the whole nation became his audience. . . .

[In the Midlothian campaign] it was the orator of concrete detail, of inductive instances, of energetic and immediate object; the orator confidently and by sure touch startling into watchfulness the whole spirit of civil duty in man; elastic and supple, pressing fact and figure with a fervid insistence that was known from his career and character to be neither forced nor feigned but to be himself. In a word, it was a man—a man impressing himself upon the kindled throngs by the breadth of his survey of great affairs of life and nations, by the depth of his vision, by the power of his stroke.[34]

Objections may be made to Morley's method chiefly on the ground of omissions. Though much is done to re-create the scene, though ample use is made of the date and the man, there is little formal analysis of the work. It is as if one had come from the House of Commons after hearing the speeches, stirred to enthusiasm but a little confused by the wealth of argument; not as if one came from a calm study of the speeches; not even as if one had corrected personal impressions by such a study. Of the structure of the speeches, little is said; but a few perorations are quoted; the details of style, one feels, although noticed at too great length by some critics, might well receive a modicum of attention here.

Although these deficiencies of Morley's treatment are not supplied by

---

[34]*Life of William Ewart Gladstone*, I, 193-4: II, 54-5, 593.

Bryce in his short and popular sketch of Gladstone, there is a summary which well supplements the running account offered by Morley. It has the merit of dealing explicitly with the orator as orator, and it offers more analysis and an adequate judgment by a qualified critic.

> Twenty years hence Mr. Gladstone's [speeches] will not be read, except of course by historians. They are too long, too diffuse, too minute in their handling of details, too elaborately qualified in their enunciation of general principles. They contain few epigrams and few. . . weighty thoughts put into telling phrases. . . . The style, in short, is not sufficiently rich or finished to give a perpetual interest to matters whose practical importance has vanished. . . .
>
> If, on the other hand, Mr. Gladstone be judged by the impression he made on his own time, his place will be high in the front rank. . . . His oratory had many conspicuous merits. There was a lively imagination, which enabled him to relieve even dull matter by pleasing figures, together with a large command of quotations and illustrations. . . . There was admirable lucidity and accuracy in exposition. There was great skill in the disposition and marshalling of his arguments and finally. . . there was a wonderful variety and grace of appropriate gesture. But above and beyond everything else which enthralled the listener, there were four qualities, two specially conspicuous in the substance of his eloquence—inventiveness and elevation: two not less remarkable in his manner—force in the delivery, expressive modulation in the voice.[35]

One is tempted to say that Morley has provided the historical setting, Bryce the critical verdict. The statement would be only partially true, for Morley does much more than set the scene. He enacts the drama; and thus he conveys his judgment—not, it is true, in the form of a critical estimate, but in the course of his narrative. The difference between these two excellent accounts is a difference in emphasis. The one lays stress on the setting: the other takes it for granted. The one tries to suggest his judgment by description; the other employs the formal categories of criticism.

Less full and rounded than either of these descriptions of an orator's style is Trevelyan's estimate of Bright. Yet in a few pages the biographer has indicated clearly the two distinguishing features of Bright's eloquence—the moral weight he carried with his audience, the persuasiveness of his visible earnestness and of his reputation for integrity, and his "sense for the value of words and for the rhythm of words and sentences";[36] has drawn a contrast between Bright and Gladstone; and has added a description of Bright's mode of work, together with some comments on the performance of the speeches

---

[35] *Gladstone, his Characteristics as Man and Statesman*, New York, 1898, pp. 41-4.
[36] G. M. Trevelyan, *Life of John Bright*, Boston, 1913, p. 384.

and various examples of details of his style. Only the mass and weight of that style are not represented.

If we leave the biographers and return to those who, like Curzon and Butler, have written directly upon eloquence, we find little of importance. Of the two general histories of oratory that we have in English, Hardwicke's[37] is so ill organized and so ill written as to be negligible; that by Sears[38] may deserve mention. It is uneven and inaccurate. It is rather a popular handbook which strings together the great names than a history: the author does not seriously consider the evolution of oratory. His sketches are of unequal merit; some give way to the interest in mere anecdote; some yield too large a place to biographical detail; others are given over to moralizing. Sears touches most of the topics of rhetorical criticism without making the point of view of public address dominant; his work is too episodic for that. And any given criticism shows marked defects in execution. It would not be fair to compare Sears's show-piece, his chapter on Webster with Morley or Bryce on Gladstone; but compare it with Trevelyan's few pages on Bright. With far greater economy, Trevelyan tells us more of Bright as a speaker than Sears can of Webster. The *History of Oratory* gives us little more than hints and suggestions of a good method.

With a single exception, the collections of eloquence have no critical significance. The exception is *Select British Eloquence,*[39] edited by Chauncey A. Goodrich, who prefaced the works of each of his orators with a sketch partly biographical and partly critical. The criticisms of Goodrich, like those of Sears, are of unequal value; some are slight, yet none descends to mere anecdote, and at his best, as in the characterizations of the eloquence of Chatham, Fox, and Burke, Goodrich reveals a more powerful grasp and a more comprehensive view of his problem than does Sears, as well as a more consistent view of his subject as a speaker. Sears at times takes the point of view of the printed page; Goodrich consistently thinks of the speeches he discusses as intended for oral delivery.

Goodrich's topics of criticism are: the orator's training, mode of work personal [physical] qualifications character as known to his audience, range of powers, dominant traits as a speaker. He deals too, of course, with those topics to which certain of the critics we have noticed confine themselves: illustration, ornament, gift of phrase, diction, wit, imagination, arrangement. But these he does not over-emphasize, nor view as independent of their effect upon an audience. Thus he can say of Chatham's sentence structure: "The sentences are not rounded or balanced periods, but are made up of short clauses, which flash themselves upon the mind with all the vividness of distinct ideas, and yet are closely connected together as tending to the same

---

[37]Henry Hardwicke, *History of Oratory and Orators,* New York, 1896.
[38]Lorenzo Sears, *History of Oratory,* Chicago, 1896.
[39]New York, 1852.

point and uniting to form larger masses of thought."[40] Perhaps the best brief indication of Goodrich's quality is his statement of Fox's "leading peculiarities."[41] According to Goodrich, Fox had a luminous simplicity, which combined unity of impression with irregular arrangement; he took everything in the concrete; he struck instantly at the heart of his subject, going to the issue at once; he did not amplify, he repeated; he rarely employed pre-conceived order of argument; reasoning was his *forte,* but it was the reasoning of the debater; he abounded in *hits*—abrupt and startling turns of thought—and in sideblows delivered in passing; he was often dramatic; he had astonishing skill in turning the course of debate to his own advantage. Here is the point of view of public address expressed as clearly as in Morley or in Curzon, though in a different idiom and without the biographer's fulness of treatment.

But probably the best single specimen of the kind of criticism now under discussion is Morley's chapter on Cobden as an agitator. This is as admirable a summary sketch as the same writer's account of Gladstone is a detailed historical picture. Bryce's brief essay on Gladstone is inferior to it both in the range of its technical criticisms and in the extent to which the critic realizes the situation in which his subject was an actor. In a few pages Morley has drawn the physical characteristics of his subject, his bent of mind, tempera-ment, idiosyncrasies; has compared and contrasted Cobden with his great associate, Bright; has given us contemporary judgments; has sketched out the dominant quality of his style, its variety and range; has noted Cobden's attitude to his hearers, his view of human nature; and has dealt with the impression given by Cobden's printed speeches and the total impression of his personality on the platform. The method, the angle of approach, the categories of description or of criticism, are the same as those employed in the great life of Gladstone; but we find them here condensed into twenty pages. It will be worth while to present the most interesting parts of Morley's criticism, if only for comparison with some of the passages already given:

> I have asked many scores of those who knew him, Conservatives as well as Liberals, what this secret [of his oratorical success] was, and in no single case did my interlocutor fail to begin, and in nearly every case he ended as he had begun, with the word *persuasiveness.* Cobden made his way to men's hearts by the union which they saw in him of simplicity, earnestness, and conviction, with a singular facility of exposition. This facility consisted in a remarkable power of apt and homely illustration, and a curious ingenuity in framing the argument that happened to be wanted. Besides his skill in thus hitting on the right argument, Cobden had the oratorical art of presenting it in the way that made its admission to the understanding of a listener

---

[40]P. 75.
[41]P. 461.

easy and undenied. He always seemed to have made exactly the right degree of allowance for the difficulty with which men follow a speech, as compared with the ease of following the same argument on a printed page. . . .

Though he abounded in matter, Cobden can hardly be described as copious. He is neat and pointed, nor is his argument ever left unclinched; but he permits himself no large excursions. What he was thinking of was the matter immediately in hand, the audience before his eyes, the point that would tell best then and there, and would be most likely to remain in men's recollections. . . . What is remarkable is, that while he kept close to the matter and substance of his case, and resorted comparatively little to sarcasm, humor, invective, pathos, or the other elements that are catalogued in manuals of rhetoric, yet no speaker was ever further removed from prosiness, or came into more real and sympathetic contact with his audience. . . .

After all, it is not tropes and perorations that make the popular speaker; it is the whole impression of his personality. We who only read them can discern certain admirable qualities in Cobden's speeches; aptness in choosing topics, lucidity in presenting them, buoyant confidence in pressing them home. But those who listened to them felt much more than all this. They were delighted by mingled vivacity and ease, by directness, by spontaneousness and reality, by the charm . . . of personal friendliness and undisguised cordiality.[42]

These passages are written in the spirit of the critic of public speaking. They have the point of view that is but faintly suggested in Elton and Grierson, that Saintsbury recognizes but does not use, and Hazlitt uses but does not recognize, and that Whipple, however irregularly, both understands and employs. But such critics as Curzon and Butler, Sears and Goodrich, Trevelyan and Bryce, think differently of their problem; they take the point of view of public address consistently and without question Morley's superiority is not in conception, but in execution, in all the writers of this group, whether historians, biographers, or professed students of oratory, there is a consciousness that oratory is partly an art, partly a power of making history, and occasionally a branch of literature. Style is less considered for its own sake than for its effect in a given situation. The question of literary immortality is regarded as beside the mark, or else, as in Bryce, as a separate question requiring separate consideration. There are, of course, differences of emphasis. Some of the biographers may be thought to deal too lightly with style. Sears perhaps thinks too little of the time, of the drama of the situation and, too much of style. But we have arrived ata different attitude towards the orator; his function is recognized for what it is: the art of influencing men in some concrete situation. Neither the personal nor the literary evaluation is the

---

[42]*Life of Richard Cobden,* Boston, 1881, pp. 130-2.

primary object. The critic speaks of the orator as a public man whose function it is to exert his influence by speech.

VII

Any attempt to sum up the results of this casual survey of what some writers have said of some public speakers must deal with the differences between literary criticism as represented by Gosse and Trent, by Elton and Grierson, and rhetorical criticism as represented by Curzon, Morley, Bryce, and Treveyan. The literary criics seem a first to have no common point of view and no agreement as to the categories of judgment or description. But by reading between their lines and searching for the main endeavor of these critics, one can discover at least a unity of purpose. Different in method as are Gosse, Elton, Saintsbury, Whipple, Hazlitt, the ends they have in view are not different.

Coupled with almost every decription of the excellences of prose and with every attempt to describe the man in connection with his work is the same effort as we find clearly and even arbitrarily expressed by those whom we have termed judicial critics. All the literary critics unite in the attempt to interpret the permanent value that they find in the work under consideration. That permanent value is not precisely indicated by the term beauty, but the two strands of aesthetic excellence and permanence are clearly found not only in the avowed judicial criticism but in those writers who emphasize description rather than judgment. Thus Grierson says of Burke:

> His preoccupation at every juncture with the fundamental issues of wise government, and the splendor of the eloquence in which he set forth these principles, an eloquence in which the wisdom of his thought and the felicity of his language and imagery seem inseparable from one another... have made his speeches and pamphlets a source of perennial freshness and interest.[43]

Perhaps a critic of temper different from Grierson's—Saintsbury, for example—would turn from the wisdom of Burke's thought to the felicity of his language and imagery. But aways there is implicit in the critic's mind the absolue standard of a timeless world: the wisdom of Burke's thought (found in the principles to which his mind always gravitates rather than in his decisions on points of policy) and the felicity of his language are not considered as of an age, but for all time. Whether the critic considers the technical excellence merely, or both technique and substance, his preoccupation is with that which age cannot wither nor custom stale. (From this point of view, the distinction between the speech and the pamphlet is of no moment, and Elton wisely speaks of Burke's favorite form as "oratory,

---

[43]*Cambridge History of English Literature,* New York, 1914, XI, 8.

uttered or written",[44] for a speech cannot be the subject of a permanent evaluation unless it is preserved in print.)

This is the implied attitude of all the literary critics. On this common ground their differences disappear or become merely differences of method or of competence. They are all, in various ways, interpreters of the permanent and universal values they find in the works of which they treat. Nor can there be any quarrel with this attitude—unless all standards be swept away. The impressionist and the historian of the evolution of literature as a self-contained activity may deny the utility or the possibility of a truly judicial criticism. But the human mind insists upon judgment *sub specie aeternitatis*. The motive often appears as a merely practical one: the reader wishes to be apprised of the best that has been said and thought in all ages; he is less concerned with the descent of literary species or with the critic's adventures among masterpieces than with the perennial freshness and interest those masterpieces may hold for him. There is, of course, much more than a practical motive to justify the interest in permanent values; but this is not the place to raise a moot question of general critical theory. We wished only to note the common ground of literary criticism in its preoccupation with the thought and the eloquence which is permanent.

If now we turn to rhetorical criticism as we found it exemplified in the preceding section, we find that its point of view is patently single. It is not concerned with permanence, nor yet with beauty. It is concerned with effect. It regards a speech as a communication to a specific audience, and holds its business to be the analysis and appreciation of the orator's method of imparting his ideas to his hearers.

Rhetoric, however, is a word that requires explanation; its use in connection with criticism is neither general nor consistent. The merely depreciatory sense in which it is often applied to bombast or false ornament need not delay us. The limited meaning which confines the term to the devices of a correct and even of an elegant prose style—in the sense of manner of writing and speaking—may also be eliminated, as likewise the broad interpretation which makes rhetoric inclusive of all style whether in prose or in poetry. There remain some definitions which have greater promise. We may mention first that of Aristotle: "the faculty of observing in any given case the available means of persuasion";[45] this readily turns into the art of persuasion as the editors of the *New English Dictionary* recognize when they define rhetoric as "the art of using language so as to persuade or influence others." The gloss on "persuade" afforded by the additional term "influence" is worthy of note. Jebb achieves the same result by defining rhetoric as "the art of using language in such a way as to produce a desired impression upon the hearer or reader."[46] There is yet a fourth definition, one which serves to

---

[44]Oliver Elton, *Survey of English Literature, 1780-1830*, London, 1912, I, 234.
[45]*Rhetoric*, ii, 2, tr. W. Rhys Roberts in *The Works of Aristotle*, XI, Oxford, 1924.
[46]Article "Rhetoric" in the *Encyclopaedia Britannica*, 9th and 11th editions.

illuminate the others as well as to emphasize their essential agreement: "taken broadly [rhetoric is] the science and art of communication in language";[47] the framers of this definition add that to throw the emphasis on communication is to emphasize prose, poetry being regarded as more distinctly expressive than communicative. A German writer has made a similar distinction between poetic as the art of poetry and rhetoric as the art of prose, but rather on the basis that prose is of the intellect, poetry of the imagination.[48] Wackernagel's basis for the distinction will hardly stand in face of the attitude of modern psychology to the "faculties"; yet the distinction itself is suggestive, and it does not contravene the more significant opposition of expression and communication. That opposition has been well stated, though with some exaggeration, by Professor Hudson:

> The writer in pure literature has his eye on his subject; his subject has filled his mind and engaged his interest, and he must tell about it; his task is expression; his form and style are organic with his subject. The writer of rhetorical discourse has his eye upon the audience and occasion; his task is persuasion; his form and style are organic with the occasion.[49]

The element of the author's personality should not be lost from sight in the case of the writer of pure literature; nor may the critic think of the audience and the occasion as alone conditioning the work of the composer of rhetorical discourse, unless indeed he include in the occasion both the personality of the speaker and the subject. The distinction is better put by Professor Baldwin:

> Rhetoric meant to the ancient world the art of instructing and moving men in their affairs; poetic the art of sharpening and expanding their vision. . . . The one is composition of ideas; the other, composition of images. In the one field life is discussed; in the other it is presented. The type of the one is a public address, moving us to assent and action; the type of the other is a play, showing us [an] action moving to an end of character. The one argues and urges; the other represents. Though both appeal to imagination, the method of rhetoric is logical; the method of poetic, as well as its detail, is imaginative.[50]

It is noteworthy that in this passage there is nothing to oppose poetry, in its common acceptation of verse, to prose. Indeed, in discussing the four forms of discourse usually treated in textbooks. Baldwin explicitly classes exposition and argument under rhetoric, leaving narrative and description to

---

[47]J. L. Gerig and F. N. Scott, article "Rhetoric" in the *New International Encyclopaedia.*
[48]K. H. W. Wackernagel, *Poetik, Rhetorik und Stilistik,* ed. L. Sieber, Halle, 1873, p. II.
[49]H. H. Hudson, "The Field of Rhetoric," *Quarterly Journal of Speech Education,* IX (1923), 177. See also the same writer's "Rhetoric and Poetry," *ibid.,* X (1924), 143 ff.
[50]C. S. Baldwin, *Ancient Rhetoric and Poetic,* New York, 1924, p. 134.

the other field. But rhetoric has been applied to the art of prose by some who include under the term even nonmetrical works of fiction. This is the attitude of Wackernagel, already mentioned, and of Saintsbury, who observes that Aristotle's *Rhetoric* holds, "if not intentionally, yet actually, something of the same posiion towards Prose as that which the *Poetics* holds towards verse."[51] In Saintsbury's view, the *Rhetoric* achieves this position in virtue of its third book, that on style and arrangement: the frst two books contain "a great deal of matter which has either the faintest connection with literary criticism or else no connection with it at all."[52] Saintsbury finds it objectionable in Aristotle that to him, "prose as prose is merely and avowedly a secondary consideraton: it is always in the main, and sometimes wholly, a mere necessary instrument of divers practical purposes,"[53] and that "he does not *wish* to consider a piece of prose as a work of art destined, first of all, if not finally, to fulfil its own laws on the one hand, and to give pleasure on the other."[54] The distinction between verse and prose has often troubled the writers of criticism. The explanation is probably that the outer form of a work is more easily understood and more constantly present to the mind than is the real form. Yet it is strange that those who find the distinction between verse and prose important should parallel this with a distinction between imagination and intellect, as if a novel had more affinities with a speech than with an epic. It is strange, too, that Saintsbury's own phrase about the right way to consider a "piece of prose"—as a work of art destined "to fulfil its own laws"—did not suggest to him the fundamental importance of a distinction between what he terms the minor or suasive rhetoric on the one hand and on the other poetic, whether or not in verse. For poetry always is free to fulfil its own law, but the writer of rhetorical discourse is, in a sense, perpetually in bondage to the occasion and the audience; and in that fact we find the line of cleavage between rhetoric and poetic.

The distinction between rhetoric as theory of public address and poetic as theory of pure literature, says Professor Baldwin, "seems not to have controlled any consecutive movement of modern criticism."[55] That it has not controlled the prcedure of critics in dealing with orators is indicated in the foregoing pages; yet we have found, too, many suggestions of a better method, and some few critical performances against which the only charge is overcondensation.

Rhetorical criticism is necessarily analytical. The scheme of a rhetorical study includes the element of the speaker's personality as a conditioning factor; it includes also the public character of the man—not what he was but

---

[51]C. E. B. Saintsbury, *History of Criticism and Literary Taste in Europe*, New York, 1900, I, 39.
[52]*Ibid.*, p. 42.
[53]*History of Criticism and Literary Taste in Europe*, p. 48.
[54]*Ibid.*, p. 52.
[55]*Op. cit.*, p. 4.

what he was thought to be. It requires a description of the speaker's audience, and of the leading ideas with which he plied his hearers—his topics the motives to which he appealed the nature of the proofs he offered. These will reveal his own judgment of human nature in his audiences, and also his judgment on the questions which he discussed. Attention must be paid, too, to the relation of the surviving texts to what was actually uttered: in case the nature of the changes is known there may be occasion to consider adaptation to two audiences—that which heard and that which read. Nor can rhetorical criticism omit the speaker's mode of arrangement and his mode of expression, nor his habit of preparation and his manner of delivery from the platform; though the last two are perhaps less significant. "Style"—in the sense which corresponds to diction and sentence movement—must receive atten-tion, but only as one among various means that secure for the speaker ready access to the minds of his auditors. Finally, the effect of the discourse on its immediate hearers is not to be ignored, either in the testimony of witnesses, nor in the record of events. And throughout such a study one must conceive of the public man as influencing the men of his own times by the power of his discourse.

VIII

What is the relation of rhetorical criticism, so understood, to literary criticism? The latter is at once broader and more limited than rhetorical criticism. It is broader because of its concern with permanent values: because it takes no account of special purpose nor of immediate effect; because it views a literary work as the voice of a human spirit addressing itself to men of all ages and times; because the critic speaks as the spectator of all time and all existence. But this universalizing of attitude brings its own limits with it: the influence of the period is necessarily relegated to the background; interpretation in the light of the writer's intention and of his situation may be ignored or slighted; and the speaker who directed his words to a definite and limited group of hearers may be made to address a universal audience. The result can only be confusion. In short, the point of view of literary criticism is proper only to its own objects, the permanent works. Upon such as are found to lie without the pale, the verdict of literary criticism is of negative value merely, and its interpretation is false and misleading because it proceeds upon a wrong assumption. If Henry Clay and Charles Fox are to be dealt with at all, it must not be on the assumption that their works, in respect of wisdom and eloquence, are or ought to be sources of perennial freshness and interest. Morley has put the matter well:

> The statesman who makes or dominates a crisis, who has to rouse and mold the mind of senate or nation, has something else to think about than the production of literary masterpieces. The great political speech, which for that matter is a sort of drama, is not made by passages for elegant extract or anthologies, but by personality,

movement, climax, spectacle, and the action of the time.[56]

But we cannot always divorce rhetorical criticism from literary. In the case of Fox or Clay or Cobden, as opposed to Fielding or Addison or De Quincey, it is proper to do so; the fact that language is a common medium to the writer of rhetorical discourse and to the writer in pure literature will give to the critics of each a common vocabulary of stylistic terms, but not a common standard. In the case of Burke the relation of the two points of view is more complex. Burke belongs to literature: but in all his important works he was a practitioner of public address written or uttered. Since his approach to *belles-lettres* was through rhetoric, it follows that rhetorical criticism is at least a preliminary to literary criticism, for it will erect the factual basis for the understanding of the works: will not merely explain allusions and establish dates, but recall the setting, reconstruct the author's own intention, and analyze his method. But the rhetorical inquiry is more than a mere preliminary; it permeates and governs all subsequent interpretation and criticism. For the statesman in letters is a statesman still: compare Burke to Charles Lamb, or even to Montaigne, and it is clear that the public man is in a sense inseparable from his audience. A statesman's wisdom and eloquence are not to be read without some share of his own sense of the body politic, and of the body politic not merely as a construct of thought, but as a living human society. A speech, like a satire, like a comedy of manners, grows directly out of a social situation; it is a man's response to a condition in human affairs. However broadly typical the situation may be when its essential elements are laid bare, it never appears without its coverings. On no plane of thought—philosophical, literary, political—is Burke to be understood without reference to the great events in America, India, France, which evoked his eloquence; nor is he to be understood without reference to the state of English society. (It is this last that is lacking in Grierson's essay: the page of comment on Burke's qualities in actual debate wants its supplement in some account of the House of Commons and the national life it represented. Perhaps the latter is the more needful to a full understanding of the abiding excellence in Burke's pages.) Something of the spirit of Morley's chapter on Cobden, and more of the spirit of the social historian (which Morley has in other parts of the biography) is necessary to the literary critic in dealing with the statesman who is also a man of letters.

In the case of Burke, then, one of the functions of rhetorical criticism is as a preliminary, but an essential and governing, preliminary, to the literary criticism which occupies itself with the permanent values of wisdom and of eloquence, of thought and of beauty, that are found in the works of the orator.

Rhetorical criticism may also be regarded as an end in itself. Even Burke may be studied from that point of view alone. Fox and Cobden and the

---

[56]*Life of William Ewart Gladstone*, II, 589-90.

majority of public speakers are not to be regarded from any other. No one will offer Cobden's works a place in pure literature. Yet the method of the great agitator has a place in the history of his times. That place is not in the history of *belles-lettres;* nor is it in the literary history which is a "survey of the life of a people as expressed in their writings." The idea of "writings" is a merely mechanical one; it does not really provide a point of view or a method; it is a book-maker's cloak for many and diverse points of view. Such a compilation as the *Cambridge History of American Literature,* for example, in spite of the excellence of single essays, may not unjustly be characterized as an uneven commentary on the literary life of the country and as a still more uneven commentary on its social and political life. It may be questioned whether the scant treatment of public men in such a compilation throws light either on the creators of pure literature, or on the makers of rhetorical discourse, or on the life of the times.

Rhetorical criticism lies at the boundary of politics (in the broadest sense) and literature; its atmosphere is that of the public life,[57] its tools are those of literature, its concern is with the ideas of the people as influenced by their leaders. The effective wielder of public discourse, like the military man, belongs to social and political history because he is one of its makers. Like the soldier, he has an art of his own which is the source of his power; but the soldier's art is distinct from the life which his conquests affect. The rhetorician's art represents a natural and normal process within that life. It includes the work of the speaker, of the pamphleteer, of the writer of editorials, and of the sermon maker. It is to be thought of as the art of popularization. Its practitioners are the Huxleys, not the Darwins, of science; the Jeffersons, not the Lockes and the Rousseaus, of politics.

Of late years the art of popularization has received a degree of attention: propaganda and publicity have been words much used; the influence of the press has been discussed; there have been some studies of public opinion. Professor Robinson's *Humanizing of Knowledge*[58] is a cogent statement of the need for popularization by the instructed element in the state, and of the need for a technique in doing so. But the book indicates, too, how little is known of the methods its author so earnestly desires to see put to use. Yet ever since Homer's day men have woven the web of words and counsel in the face of all. And ever since Aristotle's day there has been a mode of analysis of public address. Perhaps the preoccupation of literary criticism with "style" rather than with composition in the large has diverted interest from the more significant problem. Perhaps the conventional categories of historical thought have helped to obscure the problem: the history of thought, for example, is generally interpreted as the history of invention and discovery, both physical and intellectual. Yet the history of the thought of the people is at least as

---

[57]For a popular but suggestive presentation of the background of rhetorical discourse, see J. A. Spender, *The Public Life,* New York, 1925.
[58]New York, 1923.

potent a factor in the progress of the race. True, the popular thought may often represent a resisting force, and we need not marvel that the many movements of a poet's mind more readily capture the critic's attention than the few and uncertain movements of that Leviathan, the public mind. Nor is it surprising that the historians tend to be occupied with the acts and the motives of leaders. But those historians who find the spirit of an age in the total mass of its literary productions, as well as all who would tame Leviathan to the end that he shall not threaten civilization, must examine more thoroughly than they as yet have done the interactions of the inventive genius, the popularizing talent, and the public mind.

Some Problems of Scope and Method in Rhetorical Scholarship

by Donald C. Bryant

The important work in the history and criticism of American public address now being undertaken in the NATIONAL ASSOCIATION OF TEACHERS OF SPEECH is a strong reminder that our scholarship is maintaining its confident advance. Even so, the question must ever stand before us: What are we about, and how are we to go about it? If we rest content with established methods and conceptions only, and do not from time to time question our assumptions, we blind ourselves to much useful knowledge and many possibilities of fruitful interpretation.

Our problems of scope and method are shared by students of literature generally, though they have their special implications and complications for us. We must, therefore, consider them as they affect the literary scholars especially, for their methods and ours are largely parallel.

Both we and they have for materials documents in the art of communication, composed by men great and small, important and unimportant, who wrote or spoke first and foremost for their own times and societies, though always with the likelihood of exerting influences which should out-live them. There can be little doubt, furthermore, if one recalls not only Demosthenes and Cicero. but moderns like Bossuet, Burke, and Abraham Lincoln, that speeches *may* be literature. But these names are few, and speeches and speakers are many. If, nevertheless, we turn from the great orators who undoubtedly spoke literature, to the run-of-the-mill effective speakers, we find close analogies to the same sort of local topography in letters. This parallel suggests that methods and materials in literary history and critical scholarship apply likewise in oratory and rhetoric. Some modifications and adaptations, of course, are necessary; but we always have an overlapping so great that method in literary history is almost the same as in rhetorical history.

In this our common lot, two general problems seem to me urgent at the present time. They may be briefly stated as questions (1) of criticism and interpretation versus historical fact finding or reconstructing the past, and (2) of the individual point of view versus the social.

Reprinted from *The Quartery Journal of Speech* 23 (1937), with permission of the Speech Communication Association.

First we must answer those apostles of the contemporaneous who would have us adapt and interpret and criticize poems and plays, speeches and pamphlets, for today in terms of today, and leave off digging into the far corners and obscure recesses of the past for information about the authors of these works. What we need, they say, is *Hamlet* in modern dress, "Who Is to Blame" rewritten in terms of contemporary life, *Emerson and How to Know Him.* A study, we are reminded, of "Rhetorical Exercises in Tudor Education"[1] is all very well, and may be interesting; but Tudor days are gone, today is with us; and what we want to know, if anything, is what Tudor education can signify in twentieth century American society.

To this sort of argument I should answer, you are right as far as you go, but you don't go far enough. Ultimately, of course, the justification of scholarship will be its use in enabling the voices of the past to be heard effectively in the present. If this can be accomplished without literary history, well and good. To be sure, barring difficulties of language, much literature, even from the remote past, can be understood, appreciated, and enjoyed to a reasonable extent in the light of the present day. But such enjoyment and understanding are partial and incomplete. Literature is definitely impoverished without literary history. Without the background, the setting, the historical comparison and contrast which literary history provides, even the great works, the mountain peaks of letters, are but dimly known, and the lesser works, the level plain and the mounds and knolls, not at all.

The case for *rhetorical* history is still stronger. Rhetorical criticism must depend almost entirely upon historical knowledge for its effectiveness, because, in the first place, rhetorical history, as compared with literary history, is concerned with a lesser proportion of those men whose voices, unassisted, continue still to be heard. There are fewer practitioners of public address than men of letters who speak directly from one age to later ages. This is only to say that numerically and proportionately there are more Ovids than Ciceros, more Washington Irvings than Thomas Paines. If, therefore, materials for rhetorical criticism of the past are to be had, they must come largely through the agency of rhetorical history.

There is another factor which enhances the importance of the history of public address, the difference of object between literary and rhetorical criticism. For several years now, we have had in the writings on our subject a plain statement of the legal separation, if not the divorce, of literary and rhetorical criticism. Rhetorical criticism, we understand, is concerned only secondarily with permanent esthetic canons. It gains its value from its primary concern with considerations of audience-speaker-occasion—of background, surroundings, contemporary effectiveness. The criticism of oratory, while never ignoring the place and significance which a speech or a man may have at present, independent of his own age, will be mainly and emphatically

---

[1] Karl R. Wallace, QUARTERLY JOURNAL OF SPEECH (Feb., 1936), 22:28-51.

interested in what that speech and that man were, or more especially what they seemed to be, to their contemporaries in their contemporary settings. Hence it is that rhetorical criticism, unless it be criticism of current speeches, cannot do without rhetorical history, and full and accurate history at that. Studies like Professor C. Harold King's paper on Whitefield[2] are essential to rhetorical criticism. And when I say this, I am not forgetting that formal canons for rhetorical analysis can be applied with more or less profit as *exercises* to almost any speech whose language is understood. It is very useful to make a "Structural Analysis of the Sermons of Dr. Harry Emerson Fosdick,"[3] or to apply the Aristotelian categories to Burke's speech on *American Taxation*. Furthermore, the sort of objective psychological analysis derived from counting the first and second personal pronouns in Woodrow Wilson's speeches provides a do-able job and certain definite information. These analyses, however, must remain only exercises until historical study has provided, and criticism has learned to use rather complete knowledge of the setting in all of its significant aspects. We conclude, therefore, that historical study must go on, and that rhetorical criticism will be sound only when it uses the results of historical study both in judging the past in terms of the past and in judging the past for the present.

Now, if we try to answer the question, What sort of history are we to have, what is its scope to be, what its emphasis? we at once face the second large problem which I mentioned earlier, the problem of the individual point of view versus the social.

This problem is brought to us in the form of accusation. We are told that we busy ourselves with sterile, stagnant scholarship and minute dehumanized research. By our preoccupation with great figures, it is said that we convey the false impression that the past is made of great men and that anything we can find out about them justifies the search. We are chided for blinding ourselves with the constant sight of individuals and of treating them as single and self-accounting phenomena. The recommended alternative is the one which the historian of society has gradually chosen during the past quarter century. We are enjoined to study the social scope, of which individuals, even great writers and great orators, are merely phases and not such very significant phases at that. We are warned to bring our eyes down from the hills to the plain and concentrate our gaze on the great level lands and the streams and floods there. We are advised to adapt and use in our histories of literature and oratory the philosophy of movements and forces as exemplified in the work of Turner, of Parrington, of the Beards, and give up once and for all the notion that "Lives of great men all remind us . . ."

Whatever may be our ultimate decision, this is a challenge we must fairly face, a point of view whose possibilities we must study thoughtfully. It is the

---

[2] "George Whitefield: Dramatic Evangelist," QUARTERLY JOURNAL OF SPEECH (April, 1933), 19:165-175.
[3] G. S. Macvaugh, QUARTERLY JOURNAL OF SPEECH (Nov., 1932), 18:531-546.

point of view which is presented, for example, in the volume called *The Re-interpretation of American Literature,*[4] edited by Norman Foerster. Of particular importance to students of public address are the papers in this volume by Professor A. M. Schlesinger on "American History and American Literary History," and by Professor H. H. Clark on "American Literary History and American Literature," where the issues are precisely and clearly drawn.

The contention of Foerster and his associates is that the interaction of forces and tendencies is significant, while biographical and episodical information are merely curious. Therefore, they argue, the emphasis of literary history is to be shifted from figures to society: to forces, influences, and the general state of popular culture and of social organization. Literary history, they say, like political and social history, and the history of public address like both of them, are to be studied in the light of more socially significant conceptions than great figures, personal gossip, and chronology.

Professor Schlesinger's statement of the social historian's case is positive and uncompromising. To him the history of letters, and of course of public address, must be one of the social sciences, "with the main attention always fixed on what is broadly diffused rather than on what is unusual or special."[5] It is doubtless true, as he says, that

> The literary historian [and as I have shown, we may read as well the historian of the rhetorical faculty] of the future will have to widen his vision and take into proper account such factors as the invention of the rotary press, the state of general education and enlightenment, the constant cheapening of the process of printing, the increasing ease of travel and communication, the distribution of surplus wealth and leisure, the distribution of bookstores and circulating libraries, the popularization of the telephone, the motor car, movie and radio, the legislative attitudes toward such questions as censorship, international copyright, and a tariff on foreign books.[6]

The student of public address can add others of his own, *ad lib.;* but we shall still have books and men to study, great and small, and the influences which operated on these books and men and on their audiences.

This attempt to circumscribe the universe and the human soul provides useful suggestions, but tends to overshoot its mark. Granted that the ideal literary historian should be one, like Plato's philosopher king, who knows all things past and present, understands them and realizes their relations in all their social, esthetic, literary, and scientific manifestations—granted this ideal, can a man comprehend it, can a man fulfill it? Who can comprehend the *whole* of social history and all its parts?

---

[4] Harcourt, Brace and Company (1928).
[5] *Op. cit.,* 162.
[6] *Op. cit.,* 171.

Life is lived in time, and history is true only when the time-element is clearly visible in it. But when time is introduced into a picture of society to make it real and dynamic, we must see forces moving, and moving in directions: parallel, contrary, transverse—currents and cross-currents. Thus there appear many influences and movements, affecting and altering each other, sometimes coming together, sometimes diffusing, sometimes mutually deflecting each other.

To carry a whole cross-section of society forward at once is manifestly impossible, and is probably not even desirable. The days of a man's life, even a scholar's, are short, and his ability to resist the powers of confusion is not limitless. It seems to me that any student must make choices, choices of currents which seem to him worth following, men and works which seem worth studying. He must select points of concentration or departure. His focus must be narrowed to the specific phenomena to be studied, the men, or the examples of public address or the social influences to be explained. He will not attempt to set forth the whole background or the whole aftermath of the subject of his study. All social influences are important in general, but some have much bearing, some little, on any specific man or work or movement at any particular time. For the sake of comprehensibility in study and exposition, the scholar must look at the background of specific material through what H. H. Clark calls the "windows" of the foreground.

Furthermore, the whole of most fields of research by no means needs redoing. Even the most socially-minded scholar must find much already done which he would be foolish indeed not to use. Perhaps only one or two specific and limited studies need to be made, to give order and movement to a whole series of forces and influences. Perhaps a study of the contents and vogue of the McGuffey *Readers* would be sufficient to provide the necessary connection between what is already known and understood of American literature in the mid-nineteenth century and the knowledge we seek of the state of popular culture at that time. A study of the number and kind of public gatherings which people attended in a few American cities and towns prior to the rise of the itinerant lecturer may, perhaps, add enough significance to what we know now about the lecturing careers of such persons as Emerson and Harriet Beecher Stowe. And of course, competent studies of rhetorics and rhetoricians, of speeches and speakers, will be as much the proper scope of our scholarship as heretofore. Many problems as restricted and as narrow as these wait to be done and to be done in much the same way and with the same care as has been the practice of good scholars as long as there have been good scholars. The unified whole of any study may be the work of several, not one scholar. The larger conceptions of the history of public address must still depend upon the co-operative efforts of many scholars for their realization. The individual studies chosen will be as special and as exact as heretofore, but they will be chosen on a more significant plan. A sense of the whole pattern, the whole social pattern in as wide a significance as possible, should control the selection and scope of work to be done, and the scholar should realize the function in social history that his study is to serve.

The two main factors in history have always been to some extent realized—that is, figures and forces. Probably it has been the fault of history in the past, and especially the fault of the history of literature and oratory, to let the study of figures obscure or blot out the study of forces and social movements. A corrective balance unquestionably needs to be established. Figures and forces must be studied together, and perhaps in a proportion that will definitely give the predominance to forces. No one man, furthermore, can afford to devote himself entirely to figures. It is a logical fallacy— scholarly myopia. Possibly if men like Schlesinger can be taken as speaking for the main trend in history, we should for the future, a collectivist future, pursue forces exclusively and let figures take care of themselves. This extremity I for one cannot admit. That the interesting facts of human biography can be ignored, even in a picture of the great society, I am unable to believe. For one thing, how are forces to be known except largely by generalization from the study of figures? Furthermore, incarnation seems congenial to the mind. For most of us, forces are symbolized by men. The danger comes when we forget the fact of the symbolism. As Professor Grierson says, "Poems are not written by influences or movements or sources, but come from the living hearts of men."[7] And the same fact, it seems to me, must continue to be held true of specimens of public address as well.

If now the question be fairly put: Does this imply that most of our previous scholarship, which has tended to feature the individual great man, the unusual and the special (though never quite so much as its critics assume), must be thrown overboard, and that we must begin anew after we have learned the lesson which presumably some political historians learned a quarter of a century ago? If this question be asked, the answer, it appears to me, is definitely No; and I think that when the social point of view is properly diffused, it will be discovered that many of us who have labored in darkness have, nevertheless, helped in the diffusion of the light.

The ideal of all knowledge in its whole significance may well stand before our scholarship, as before education; but it must not become a will-o'-the-wisp. We must not accept an economic history, a sociological history as the whole history of literature or of oratory, any more than a political history, a scientific history, or a Marxist history. None is history; all are history. We must recognize them for what they are worth—for parts, for points of view; and we must struggle for proportion, for perspective, as well as we may, with the aid of as much sound information, as much true judgment, and as much power of synthesis as each of us is capable of mustering. And we must admit that the story is never finally done.

---

[7] "Introduction" to *The Poems of John Donne* (1929).

The Perils of Rhetorical Criticism
by Loren D. Reid

The last twenty years have noted several events of importance to those interested in the study of public address. The year 1925 saw the publication of the *Studies in Rhetoric and Public Speaking in Honor of James A. Winans;* 1928 saw the first doctorates in rhetoric and public speaking, the beginning of a group of studies which by 1943 had reached a total of more than fifty, awarded by eight different graduate schools;[1] 1939 saw the publication of Thonssen and Fatherson's *Bibliography of Speech Education,* with its more than 200 pages of entries in rhetoric and public speaking. Last year brought *A History and Criticism of American Public Address,* with its studies of the speech backgrounds of the Colonial, Early National, and Later National periods; of special topics like the teaching of rhetoric and the speaking of famous women and of twenty-eight outstanding American speakers.[2] The October, 1943, issue of the QUARTERLY JOURNAL OF SPEECH, which announced and reviewed these two volumes, also contained articles on re-search in American public speaking by Dickey,[3] Baird,[4] and Aly.[5] Committees on contemporary and on regional public address have already begun work.

Perhaps now is a good time to look over what has been done, and to make certain observations, chiefly to draw from the practice of the last twenty years principles which may be useful during the next twenty.

I

Any concept of criticism is unfolded by considering what it is not. For example:

1. *Rhetorical criticism*[6] *is not simply a discussion of the speaker's ideas.*

Reprinted from *The Quarterly Journal of Speech* 30 (1944), with permission of the Speech Communication Association.

[1] Columbia, Cornell, Iowa, Louisiana State University, Michigan, Northwestern, Southern California, Wisconsin. (From data reported annually by Franklin D. Knower in *Speech Monographs.*)

[2] Two volumes (1943) published under the auspices of the National Association of Teachers of Speech.

[3] Dallas C. Dickey, "What Directions Should Future Research in American Public Address Take?" pp. 300-304.

[4] A. Craig Baird, "Opportunities for Rasearch in State and Sectional Public Speaking," pp. 304-308.

[5] Bower Aly, "The History of American Public Address as a Research Field," pp. 308-314.

[6] The term is used from habit; some prefer "oratorial criticism." Either is liable to be misunderstood by students in other fields. For general use the more accurate (though longer) term "criticism of public address" is no doubt the one which meets with the approval of most scholars.

In its most elemental form this procedure is merely a summary: the speaker's first point was that Greek resistance delayed the advance of the Axis, his second point that the time saved made it possible to strengthen the British army. Such a discussion is slightly more critical when the writer adds a few rhetorical labels: The speaker used "emotional appeal" in his conclusion when he pictured the wounded Evzone returning to the smoking ruins of his village. A still more useful variety of criticism results when the critic analyzes a series of speeches and ferrets out the assumptions and the principal lines of argument. Even then, however, the critical task is incomplete.

Although the reader needs to know what the speaker *said,* he really seeks a critical judgment *about* the ideas of the speech. The critic should study not alone the result of invention, but the inventive process; not alone the result of arrangement and composition, but the speaker at work: what Thomas Wolfe calls "the whole stroke, catch, flow, stop, and ending, the ten thousand fittings, changings, triumphs, and surrenders."[7] It is the job that Lowes undertook for Coleridge, and that DeVoto is undertaking for Mark Twain. It is shown, in briefer scale, in several instances in the *History and Criticism:* for example, Wallace's analysis[8] of the ideas of Booker T. Washington and his methods of adaptation to his audiences; Wiley's study[9] of the composition of Lincoln's First Inaugural; Whan's picture[10] of Douglas analyzing his Illinois audiences. A really thorough execution of this aspect of rhetorical criticism can be made only about a speaker who is interested both in the art and the practice of oratory, who keeps copious journals showing the development of his ideas, who saves all of the notes and preliminary drafts of his speeches, and who bequeaths to his rhetorical executors a super-Hyde Park library, containing the above plus a set of electrical transcriptions of all his speeches.

2. *Rhetorical criticism is not simply a narrative of the circumstances under which a speech is delivered.* As a profession we declare that the speech must be related to what we term "the speech situation." This requirement of rhetorical criticism is apparently satisfied by writing an "historical background." If, however, this introductory narrative is of the perfunctory sort readily gleaned from secondary sources, it serves no real critical function. Although it is helpful to be reminded of the dates of wars or the names of opposing candidates, such statements are only an approach to the analysis of the occasion, not the analysis itself.

The kind of setting in which to place a speech might better be conceived of as a "rhetorical" rather than as an "historical" background. After making a few general statements to refresh the memory of the reader about certain historical landmarks, the critic should develop details which serve to interpret the circumstances leading up to the delivery of the speech. These details are

---

[7] *The Story of a Novel* (New York and London, 1936), p 1.
[8] *Op. cit.,* I, 410 ff.
[9] *Ibid.,* II, 866-869.
[10]*Ibid.,* II, 807 ff.

not likely to come from a college history textbook, but from letters, diaries, memoirs, and periodicals, and sometimes from specialized monographs.

To be specific, in analyzing the occasion of Churchill's address to Congress on December 26, 1941, it is only a part of the problem to review the state of the war on that date. The critic should also attempt to answer these questions: Why was Churchill invited to speak? when? and by whom? What was his prestige at that time? What information did he have about the American national temper? Did Churchill discuss with Roosevelt, or with others, what he might say to Congress? Do earlier drafts of his speech throw any light upon his thinking? What advance publicity was given to the speech? Who was in the audience? and so on. Not all the answers to these questions may prove relevant, but most of them should reveal facts which would place the speech in its true setting. And such a treatment would take the research out of the dubious category of second-rate history and put it under the heading of first-rate criticism.

3. *Rhetorical criticism is not simply a classification or tabulation of rhetorical devices.* The use of quantitative measurements has been tried, but generally abandoned. As John W. Black points out briefly in his discussion of the sentence structure of Rufus Choate, tabulations do not describe style.[11] Or, as Brigance suggests in his discussion of Jeremiah S. Black, the power of the speaker's arguments is not to be measured by the number of spittoons the speaker fills during speech delivery.[12]

Statistical methods may be of some assistance in measuring a speaker's influence. The Whan study, previously cited, attempts to judge the comparative effectiveness of Lincoln and Douglas by a study of the election returns. Gleckler's study of Willkie's Presidential campaign speeches utilizes much poll information in search of an answer to the question of whether Willkie's speaking cost him the presidency.[13] Radio indexes and public opinion polls will continue to be helpful. The principal caution to be observed in using numerical devices is that no combination of tables, polls, or spittoons can tell the whole story about the effectiveness of a speech, though they may objectify certain aspects of the problem of criticism.

4. *Rhetorical criticism is not primarily an excursion into other fields of learning.* The critic is easily tempted to abandon criticism and instead to produce treatises upon politics, religion, historical movements, military strategy, and what not. He begins with the honorable intention of giving the reader a background of eighteenth-century naval theory in order to support his analysis of a speech about a certain naval disaster, but before long he has

---

[11]*Ibid.,* I, 456.

[12]*Ibid.,* I 462. Says the observer quoted: "A small and easily surmountable case takes two spittoons; a good tough argument requires four; for a great feat of legal gymnastics he requires as many as nine successive spittoons."

[13]Marion Gleckler, *The 1940 Campaign Speeches of Wendell Willkie* (Syracuse, unpublished master's thesis, 1943).

out-Mahaned Mahan, and is offering, under the guise of background, a long discussion somewhat removed from the field of criticism. It is easy to move from rhetoric into another field. Aristotle pointed out the danger: "People fail to notice that the more correctly they handle their particular subject the further they are getting away from pure rhetoric or dialectic."[14]

II

By now the first peril of rhetorical criticism has been pointed out: the strong possibility that the critic may produce something that is not criticism at all. This is the first and greatest peril. The minor perils are numerous; a few of them are worth noting for whatever light they may shed on the critical process.

1. *Choosing a subject for study.* The problem of choosing a subject has already been authoritatively discussed, and need not be recapitulated here.[15] Generally speaking, the choices are as follows:

a. *Choose an eminent speaker.* The advice is frequently given to "study the biggest man you can find" and make a more or less definitive criticism of his speechmaking, but as the field develops, this advice diminishes in practical usefulness.[16] A related possibility is to study some aspect of the speeches of an outstanding speaker: the *History and Criticism* suggests, among others, the legal addresses of Ingersoll, the occasional speaking of Black. Furthermore, there may be an excellent speaker who is not generally known—men who, like "Private John" Allen of Mississippi, wielded considerable influence in their regions while alive, but who, because they were not associated with great historical events, are easily forgotten.

Conservative scholarly opinion generally supports the advice to pick a big man. The sources of material about him are richer, and the investigator may adapt any of half a dozen patterns of study, already worked out, for the proper presentation of his data. Conservative scholarly opinion also advises that the big man be safely dead and buried, the principal reason being the prime necessity of critical perspective. The caution is especially observed in the writing of doctoral dissertations, though the writers of masters' essays are allowed to browse at will in contemporary fields of material. Recently some dwellers in the lunatic fringe have begun to question the scholarly prohibition upon contemporary speakers as sources of doctoral material. Historians are already writing about World War II, they point out, and biographers are turning out volumes on contemporary lead-

---

[14]*Rhetoric*, translated by W. Rhys Roberts, 1358a.
[15]See the articles referred to in footnotes 3, 4, and 5.
[16]As Dickey suggests; *op. cit.,* p. 301.

ers. Although these works may contain some generalizations that will not be supported by later evidence, they will at least preserve a certain amount of contemporary data which otherwise would be lost. The career of former senator James A. Reed is an instance in point. No doubt a few were dissuaded from studying this Missouri orator while he was alive. On Friday, September 8, 1944, he died. On Saturday, September 9, according to the conservative thinkers, he acquired a partial eligibility for scholarly investigation. Yet now the critics will have to dig out of his papers answers to many questions they could have asked him personally.

   b. *Study the everyday speaking of some region.* Anyone electing to study the speech of the man in the street is liable to meet the objection of some scholars that the only type of speechmaking worth studying is the speech of some literary or historical significance: Webster at Faneuil Hall, Wilson before Congress. How trivial these items seem:

   Deliberative: George Stinson's speech at District No. 11 school house, opening his campaign ("Well, boys, we've got to get some efficiency in the sheriff's office . . .").

   Forensic: The jury address of Attorney Tom LeBiquet, in the case of Hennessey v. Hamilton Motor Company ("Now as to the half-pound of emery dust which the said defendant is alleged to have put into the said plaintiff's crankcase . . .").

   Occasional: The sermon of the Reverend Thomas Porter at the last rites of Harmon L ("Slick") Morgan ("To be sure, there was some ways in which Harmon's life was not entirely exemplary . . .")[17]

Yet scholars who look down at these examples might give much to know about the everyday speaking that went on in New Salem, Illinois, in the 1830's, in the hearing of young Abe Lincoln. Since it is difficult to know what in the contemporary speechmaking scene is worth preserving, the problem is to predict what will be of scholarly usefulness years hence.

   In short, so far as the problems of choosing a subject are concerned, once the investigator leaves the well-traveled road he must assume, in the military phrase, a certain amount of calculated risk.

   2. *Use of speech texts.* The only assuredly accurate text is one taken from an electrical transcription and carefully checked with the original recording. A stenographic report is fair, but if it has been revised by the speaker or his editor, it has undergone an unknown amount of alteration.[18] Newspaper summaries are uneven in quality. At the worst, they have been written by a reporter who got his ideas second-hand; at the best, they are summaries of a

---

[17]Gathered from observations made in Clarke County, Iowa.
[18]This topic has been discussed previously by this writer. See "Factors Contributing to Inaccuracy in the Texts of Speeches," in *Papers in Rhetoric,* edited by Donald C. Bryant (St. Louis, 1940), pp. 39-45.

press copy sent out in advance, though reporters sometimes sit attentively through long speeches.

3. *Use of various methods of supporting a critical judgment.* Eventually the critic makes a judgment about the effectiveness of a speech. This judgment may be supported by at least three different types of material:

a. *Testimony: comments of the hearers.* Although every one who hears a speech is entitled to his opinion about it, the critic should not overlook the customary tests of authority: competence, honesty, lack of prejudice, propinquity. When John Finley says of Edwin Alderman, "I am sure that Pericles would not have spoken with a more melodious voice,"[19] or when Dean Briggs calls President Eliot "the finest speaker I have ever heard,"[20] or when Lord Brougham calls Charles Fox "the most accomplished debater that ever appeared upon the theatre of public affairs in any age of the world,"[21] criticism, like a free balloon, has cut loose from terra firma. The comments are colorful, but must be—and usually are—balanced against more accurate judgments.

b. *Precept: accepted rhetorical principles.* Many critics assume that if a speaker adheres to the precepts laid down by the great rhetoricians, chiefly Aristotle, he is an effective performer. Yet as the critic studies a speech text, glancing from the text to Aristotle and back again, he should be aware of some of the objections to this procedure. One is the objection that Aristotelian rhetoric stresses persuasion rather than clear and accurate statement. The argument has too many implications to be discussed here; perhaps we need first a body of criticism employing the semantic refinements of rhetoric in order to illustrate concretely what the semanticists have in mind.[22] Another is that the Aristotelian classification of speeches is incomplete. Certainly one more suited to modern speech occasions is that suggested by Gilman: *deliberative, professional, social, ceremonial,* and *invective,* each category having a number of subheadings.[23] Another is that the classification of the methods of persuasion as *ethical, logical,* and *pathetic* leads to confused thinking. Baldwin anticipated this objection, in part, twenty years ago, when he wrote: "That the three are not mutually exclusive is evident and must have been deliberate. Aristotle is telling us that rhetoric as an art is to be

---

[19]Quoted by Charles A. Fritz in *A History and Criticism of American Public Address,* II, 553.

[20]Quoted by Louis M. Eich, *ibid.,* II, 526.

[21]Quoted by Loren D. Reid, *Charles James Fox: A Study of an Eighteenth Century Parliamentary Speaker* (Iowa City, 1932), p. 98.

[22]See Elwood Murray, "The Semantics of Rhetoric," QUARTERLY JOURNAL OF SPEECH, XXX (February, 1944), 31-41.

[23]This classification originally appeared in Gilman, Aly, and Reid, *A Course Book in Public Speaking* (Columbia, Missouri, 1937), revised edition, pp. 23-25, but has since been further revised and mimeographed.

approached from these three directions and in this order."[24] The terms themselves are not too satisfactory. The term "pathetic proof" is awkward, especially when the critic speaks of "pathetic arguments" and "pathetic appeals." Some writers in the *History and Criticism* preferred "emotional appeals" or the equivalent.[25] The term "ethical proof" is sometimes broadened to include not only the ways in which the speech itself persuades the listener to think well of the speaker, but also to embrace other sources of facts about his character and reputation.[26]

Aristotelian rhetoric cannot be made to cover every aspect of all types of speaking. Some modern treatises are more helpful in presenting the principles of exposition. Adequate standards are still being developed for the criticism of humor. The Aristotelian ideals of deliberative speaking do not seem to apply invariably to campaign speaking; here the goal is inoffensiveness of statement rather than persuasion or exact demonstration.[27] Often the most "competent" speakers are defeated for office. In fact, we may be entering a new era in American politics when the best way to be nominated may be to deny being a candidate, and the best way to be elected may be to make a small number of speeches. Moreover, students of discussion and of radio speaking are developing new terminology and techniques not to be found in the *Rhetoric*. Finally, Aristotle's comments on style, delivery, types of logical arguments, and classification of emotions are less useful than some of the terms, definitions, and classifications to be found in contemporary works. As these developments lead the critic away from Aristotle at many points, it is folly to think that the *Rhetoric* is the only book on the shelf.

c. *Comparison with other speeches.* A point of view which the critic must keep in mind is that of asking what a better speaker might have done under the same circumstances. This comparison yields two sorts of observations. First, it suggests that some ideas might have been presented more effectively; second, it reveals that some ideas, or some methods of treatment, might have been overlooked altogether.

The use of comparison has probably not yet been adequately exploited by the rhetorician, though it is a common device of literary and dramatic critics. In a recent study the judgment is expressed that Willkie's use of repetition, humor, epigram, and imagery was only mediocre. The examples cited are

---

[24]*Ancient Rhetoric and Poetic* (1924), p. 11.

[25]Bower Aly uses the term "emotional proof" in *The Rhetoric of Alexander Hamilton* (1941), pp. 32, 142, and elsewhere.

[26]The term "rhetoric" itself needs some explanation and "rhetorical" is generally considered synonymous with "grandiloquent, aureate, flowery, bombastic." (See *Webster's Dictionary of Synonyms.*)

[27]As one contemporary puts it: "The task of maintaining an adequately non-committal position while appearing to assume a definite position on each issue is an extremely difficult one."

reasonably self-evident, but the conclusion seems even more forceful when comparisons are made with touchstones from Roosevelt and Churchill.[28]

The general procedure, strikingly illustrated by Matthew Arnold, demands a knowledge of what is undeniably good in the literature of public address. The approach seems especially meritorious in that it enables the critic to demonstrate pointedly excellences as well as shortcomings, particularly in relation to speech composition. Improperly used, it could become merely "the literary criticism of oratory" of the most subjective sort. Even when properly used, it demands verbatim accuracy of the texts being compared; and the problem of securing verbatim texts is a dismal business.

III

The conclusion is obvious: Rhetorical criticism is an exacting type of research. The critic must know what is commonly called rhetoric, but to know rhetoric is not enough. He must know historical methods, but to know historical methods is not enough. He must have infinite patience in the search for details, a patience that Job might have envied. He must have the imagination to recreate events and movements long since passed into time. And he must take to heart his primary and inescapable responsibility as a critic: to interpret, to appraise, to evaluate; to say here the speaker missed, here he hit the mark; sometimes to speak with restraint when others applaud, sometimes to bestow praise when others have passed by. The many perils of rhetorical criticism have not deterred scholars of the last twenty years from producing a highly respectable body of writing about speech making, but perhaps they explain why rhetorical criticism in America remained a neglected field for three-quarters of a century after Chauncey A. Goodrich plowed the opening furrow.

---

[28]An Illustration of *repetition* from Willkie: "And the *victims* of its failure are the very persons whom it professes to represent and champion. The little business men are *victims* because their chances are more restricted than ever before. The farmers are *victims* because many of them are forced to subsist on what is virtually a dole. . . ." Compare this use of repetition—the only one in his Acceptance Speech—with a quotation illustrating Roosevelt's use of repetition: "A *nation* intact, a *nation* at peace, a *nation* prosperous, a *nation* clear in its knowledge of what powers it has to serve its own citizens, a *nation* that is in a position . . . , a *nation* which has thus proved . . ."—Gleckler, *op cit.,* p. 187. (Italics are Miss Gleckler's.)
This critic is audacious enough to rewrite some of the Willkie illustrations to show how they may be better adapted to a specific audience—a procedure which suggests that the critic himself may suggest improvements in order to validate a critical judgment. Obviously he does this gratuitously, as it is not a part of the function of criticism to rewrite speeches.

Methodology in the Criticism of Public Address

by A. Craig Baird
and
Lester Thonssen

During the past twenty years the critics of public address have been active in our universities. Their production has been impressive in quantity and acceptable in quality. Many of these scholarly contributions have found their way into university libraries as master's studies or doctoral dissertations, while others appeared as articles in learned journals, or as monographs or books. Representative of the recent output has been the collection of critical opinion on American speakers, sponsored by the SPEECH ASSOCIATION OF AMERICA.[1]

The criticism of orators, to be sure, was freely practiced by Greek and Roman scholars. Plato, Cicero, and Quintilian not only formulated principles of composition and of presentation, but recorded at length their judgment of contemporary speechmakers. As a research technique, however, the art is a contribution chiefly of twentieth century scholars. Only in the latest decades have investigators systematically developed and formulated working principles and techniques of rhetorical evaluation.

This renaissance of the criticism of public address has been accompanied by sharp scrutiny of the methods of appraisal. Has such criticism scholarly maturity? Is it chiefly history or biography? Is it analytical rather than critical? Does it suffer from undue avoidance of experimental techniques?

The thesis of this article is that the purpose of rhetorical criticism is to express a judgment on a public speech; that such judicial appraisal is a derivative of composite judgments formulated by reference to the methodologies of rhetoric, history, sociology and social psychology, logic and philosophy; and that the materials and techniques of experimental science require these other evaluative agencies in any satisfactory appraisal of public address.

Reprinted from *The Quarterly Journal of Speech* 33 (1947), with permission of the Speech Communication Association.
[1] W. N. Brigance, ed. *The History and Criticism of American Public Address*, 2 vols., 1943.

I

What is the goal of the rhetorical investigator? It is chiefly criticism. The critic may do commendable research in speech training of an orator; in the theories of speaking; in bibliographical problems; in oral language; in problems of structure; in forms of proof. These are legitimate lines of inquiry. The chief business of the rhetorical scholar, nevertheless, is the evaluation of a speech or speeches. His questions are, "Is this a good speech? If so, why?" The answers are the essence of his primary research task.

This critical judgment may limit itself to a single speech, one that was delivered either last week or last century. Or the critic may enlarge the scope of his inquiry to encompass the entire speaking career of the orator; to evaluate a speaking movement, such as temperance reform; or to interpret a period of the history of public speaking. The problem, in any case, is that of pronouncing judgment.

What is the character of this appraisal? What guiding principles and specific standards govern the judge of public speaking? According to the critical philosophy and specific methods, this appraisal of speeches usually falls into one of four categories: (1) intuitionism, (2) analysis, (3) a synthesis, or (4) an interpretation and evaluation.

Intuitionism or impressionism disavows the handicaps of science. The judge of speeches like some drama critics attends as one of the audience and registers his individual reaction to what he sees and hears. His comments are individual, impulsive, uncontrolled by clearly formulated criteria. Mainly he condemns or extols in the light of his sentiments toward the speaker or his bias toward the subject. He is a romanticist, a subjectivist, an advocate of unfettered reason. His product is usually interesting but hardly scholarly.

The second school of rhetorical criticism lies at the other end of the scale. Its approach is avowedly "inductive" and "scientific." It attempts to conform to objectivity, careful collection and interpretation of data, limited generalizations. It is analytical. It breaks down the speaking performance into elements of subject matter, forms of support, organization, and delivery. It further subdivides one of these components, counts items, and makes comparative computations. Statistical treatment is applied to figures of speech, sentence length, authorities, specific instances, or other details of language, structure, logic, or delivery. The nature of the gestures, the vocal pauses, and audience responses are tabulated. Such research produces interesting facts related to a given speech. No attempt, however, is made to pass judgment on the validity of the total speaking performance.

A third category of criticism adds synthesis to analysis. Obviously, since the speaking performance includes what the speaker does in relation to his audicnce at a given time, an estimate of the speaker's worth must involve consideration of the significant factors of the social situation. Hence the researcher, without ignoring the minutiae of speech analysis, explores the social background of audience and occasion, and dips back into the experience of the speaker himself. The rhetorical end is thus a synthesis of delivery, speech, speaker, audience, and specific occasion. The quality of such description, according to such critic, best affords proper measure of the address under examination. Synthesis logically completes analysis. But this broader treatment, however much it corrects the limitations of analysis, often ignores or obscures interpretation. If the critical function is uppermost, the pronouncement of judgment must be a central consideration.

A fourth type of criticism, then, is evaluative or interpretative. Such approach rejects subjectivism as a principle; searches out the facts and relationships brought to light by the analytic and synthetic procedures; and accepts responsibility for estimating the worth of the production. This judgment should be a significant one, in that it is carefully calculated; it retains the disinterested spirit of the analytical investigator and appropriates the techniques of the philosopher-logician-judge.

II

What of the scope and specific methodology of this judgment? What is involved in interpreting worth or value? The judgment here is essentially like that of other art forms. The critic of speeches is confronted with an art, just as is the evaluator of a novel or play. The judgment in every case is a qualitative one, a well-defined reflective pattern. The observer in every case collects the available data involved in the speech; formulates the evidence into a related series of units; systematizes criteria by which to measure the art; and establishes a conclusion derived from the application of these measures of excellence. Because the observer of speeches is concerned with an art, he almost invariably finds himself dealing with materials different from those of the "pure" scientist.

Note that the judgment of the speech-critic is based upon a comparison of performances. Part of his task is to set up standards and these are relative rather than absolute. Where shall he find them? He may turn to Aristotle, whose principles are adequate for most scholars. Or the critic may adopt the tenets of a group of rhetoricians and logicians. As an alternative, he may erect standards of worth based upon the united wisdom of his colleagues. Together the "experts" may listen to many speakers, classify them as superior, excellent, good, fair, or poor, cast the performances into comparable columns, and describe statistically and in detail the characterstics of the "superior" performers. Whatever yardstick is used, the critic will wisely refuse to succumb to the rigidities of any formula; he will define clearly his critical referents but will exercise reasonable independence and flexibility in the application of his "norms"; he will proceed with full recognition of the limitations of his materials; he will recognize, for example, that speeches have their birth and end in a situation that cannot be repeated, that no two speeches are exactly alike, that the same measuring device can hardly be indiscriminately applied.

The clue to a proper understanding of rhetorical criticism is to be found in the recognition that the canons of judgment are a synthesis of the individual constituents of the speaking situation.

The judgment concerns the effect of the discourse, or response. To what degree does the audience react favorably to the purpose of the speaker? Such question, whatever may be the difficulty of interpreting the terms *audience* and *response,* is the heart of the problem. What are the factors that unite to make possible the experience? They include, as has been repeatedly affirmed, the reactor-audience, the speaker, the speech itself as part of the communicating agency, and the time-space conditions that touch off the speaking event. The rhetorical appraisal, a synthesis of data and interpretation of these factors, seeks to gauge the immediate and larger effects of a given oral discourse.

III

How, may we ask, do we arrive at this composite judgment? What are the principles by which rhetoric expresses itself, by which speakers, audiences, and speeches are dissected and interpreted? At least four or five representative techniques are involved: those of rhetoric itself, of history, of logic, and of philosophy.

The critical judgment rests first of all upon an understanding of the concepts of rhetoric (chiefly oral discourse) and upon techniques applicable to the framework of such principles. Rhetoric, therefore, is analyzed and evaluated as communication. Its efficiency is estimated in terms of its aim of social control. The speaker's activity in initiating communication, the transfer of meaning through phonetic and gestural symbols, the activity of the auditor in converting the symbols into thought units that closely duplicate the original pattern of thinking—these fundamentals of the speaking situation are carefully checked and appraised.

The rhetorician, moreover, especially concerns himself with invention, the propositions and materials that comprise the speech; the supports and details of amplification; the logical, personal, and emotional modes of substantiation; the arrangement of ideas in the overall structure and in the smaller units; the oral language in its denotative and connotative aspects; the delivery as vocal expression as well as mental and emotional behavior; the audience adaptation as it determines or modifies each of these processes. The field of rhetoric is closely identified with written composition and with literature. But the time limitations on the speaker, the reciprocal social situation, the audience adjustments, the personal appeals through the speaker himself combine to reshape the essentials. To work with this oral configuration, to discern at once the principles and details involved in each of these divisions of the rhetorical activity, and to interpret them unitedly as the coefficient of the personal, social, and compositional factors in the speech situation are basic in the methodology of the critic of speeches.

This critical judgment, moreover, demands the utilization of the historical technique. Adequate insight into a speaker's methods of thinking and into his modes of expression is better assured if based upon complete information concerning his speech and other training, his experiences, and the source and direction of his ideas. The speech investigator, although not a biographer, will summon and test the facts concerning this orator's entire career; will have sufficient grasp of the immediate and surrounding data to interpret authoritatively that speaker's personality. The historiographer's skills in weighing the original documents, his caution in accepting hypotheses, his objectivity in fashioning complicated facts into relevancy, his maturity as a historian in interpreting the materials—these are the necessary equipment of the critic of speeches.

What is true concerning the historical techniques in application to the speaker applies even more obviously to the analysis of audience and occasion. The speech cannot be isolated from its social milieu. A reconstruction of the social background is therefore necessary. All adequate explanation of the complex economic, social, political, literary, religious, and other movements must be made. The conflicting testimony must be tested, and the interrelationship of events established. The critic, then, is a social historian as well as a biographer. He is more than an annalist or reporter of biographical externals. Out of his investigative competency he creates a pattern into which the details of proof, language, structure, and delivery find their logical relationships and explanations. His penetration into the details of occasion and audience and his analysis of the speech itself result in a genuine contribution.

This focusing of interest on the audience and the social situation suggests occasional application of some of the techniques of the social sciences. The critic may concern himself, for example, with the speech-making of a social, political, or economic movement, such as the Ku Klux Klan or Knights of Labor. He analyzes the genesis and development of the program as motivated by a sponsoring organization or institution, the situations that high light the campaign, the stereotypes that govern the pattern, the ideologies, slogans, prestige appeals, and other propagandistic features, and the trends of public opinion. At every turn the critic is alert to the speaking in his case history of social control. His rhetorical historical analysis and criticism are enriched by his discerning enumeration of these group phenomena and the persuasive influences affecting them.[2]

A fourth component of the critical process is the logical judgment based on the methods of logic. The application of the principles and techniques of logic appears both when the critic views the content and other features of the speech before him and when he analyzes and evaluates his own logical procedures in such view.

"What intellectual methods does this speaker follow? And to what extent are these methods intellectually justified?" is his inquiry. The investigation calls for a systematic examination and testing by logical principles of the chief propositions advanced (expressed directly or not) by the orator; the

---

[2] See, for example. S. Judson Crandell, "The Beginnings of a Methodology for Social Control Studies in Public Address," *Quarterly Journal of Speech*, XXXIII (1946), 36-39.

reflective pattern as revealed throughout the address; definitions and extended explanational methods of divisions of central and sub ideas; chains of reasoning; use of statistics, specific instances, analogy, causality; hypotheses or assumptions; fallacies of language, of argument in a circle, of ignoring the question; in short, the representative modes of thinking. The critic, then, if he is to interpret the ideas with more than casual judgment must familiarize himself with these logical concepts.

The critic, moreover, at every point, will apply the tests of logic to his own evaluative techniques. What of his assumptions? His collection and interpretation of evidence? His definitions and divisions? His generalizations on the basis of specific comparisons, causal references? His broad applications of induction and deduction?

Finally the criticism of a speech implies a philosophic judgment. The critic must be something of a philosopher. As historian, logician, rhetorician, he delves successfully into the minutiae of the speaking situation. He interprets the data relevant to the speaker's personality; those delineating the attitudes and other marks of the audience; those related to the larger articulation of events and personalities; those revealing purpose and interaction between the community and national trends. His is the added responsibility for ultimate synthesis. These aspects and details, as he makes clear, constitute an articulate whole. He must to some degree transform particular categories into general concepts. His is a synoptic view. His generalizations concerning speaker, speech, audience, occasion must in turn be completed by a comprehensive view of the speaking event. Unlike the subjectivist, he rests his interpretation squarely on the disciplines of history, logic, rhetoric. His catholicity is tempered by insight into his own individual attitudes and handicaps. His philosophical methods, then, apply both to his materials and to his own methods of evaluating those materials.

IV

What, then, is the role of the worker in the rhetorical field? What are his methods? In the utilization of knowledge related to the speaking situation he may concentrate on factors of delivery, the characteristics of the audience, or upon details of the speech. In doing so, he may resort to the literary, experimental, historical, normative, case-history, or other techniques. If he is to assume the role of critic, however, he will employ judgments partly rhetorical, partly historical and sociological, partly logical and partly philosophical. To derive judicial conclusions from such approaches calls for techniques other than purely or mainly experimental.

Public Address: A Study in Social and Intellectual History

by Ernest J. Wrage

In the title of a book, *Ideas Are Weapons,* Max Lerner gives to ideas a twentieth century connotation, for in this century all of the resources of man have twice comprised actual or potential materiel of warfare. The merit of the title lies in the emphasis it places upon function, although one must read beyond it to grasp the diversity of function which ideas perform. Man's capacities for thought somewhat resemble modern industrial plants which are capable of converting raw materials into either soap or bullets, of refining sugar into nutritive food or into alcohol for the manufacture of explosives. Similarly, from the biochemical processes of individual minds responding to environment may emerge ideas which serve to promote social conflict, while there are yet others fortunately, which contribute to resolution of differences. Man's intellectual activities may result in ideas which clarify his relationships with his fellow men and to the cosmos, or in ideas which close minds against further exploration in favor of blind conformity to tradition and authority. It is axiomatic that the extant records of man's responses to the social and physical world as expressed in formulations of thought provide one approach to a study of the history of his culture. Whether we seek explanations for an overt act of human behavior in the genesis and moral compulsion of an idea, or whether we accept the view that men seek out ideas which promote their interests and justify their activities, the illuminating fact is that in either case the study of ideas provides an index to the history of man's values and goals, his hopes and fears, his aspirations and negations, to what he considers expedient or inapplicable.

The word *ideas,* therefore, is not restricted here to a description of the great and noble thoughts uttered by accredited spokesmen for the edification of old and young. It is employed in a more inclusive sense and refers widely to formulations of thought as the product and expression of social incentives, which give rise and importance now to one idea, then to another. They are viewed as the product of social environment, as arising from many levels of life, and as possessing social utility. Ideas are not here treated as entities

Reprinted from *The Quarterly Journal of Speech* 33 (1947), with permission of the Speech Communication Association.

which enjoy an independent existence and which serve as objects of contemplation by the self-avowed or occasional ascetic. While the history of ideas is undeniably concerned with major works in systematized thought, and with the influence of thinker upon thinker, exclusive devotion to monumental works is hopelessly inadequate as a way of discovering and assessing those ideas which find expression in the market place. Subtle intellectual fare may be very well for stomachs accustomed to large helpings of ideational substances rich in concentration; but there also is nutritional value in the aphoristic crumbs which fall into stomachs unaccustomed and unconditioned to large helpings of such fare, and the life sustained by the crumbs is not without historical interest. The force of Emerson's ideas upon the popular mind of his time, and even later, derives less from his intricate elaborations upon man and the cosmos than from his dicta on self-reliance. Moreover, ideas arise at many levels of human life and find expression in and attain force through casual opinion as well as learned discourse; and while the life span of many popularly-held ideas is admittedly short, often these "out-of-the-way" ideas thrive and emerge at higher levels of development. This extension in the conception of the history of ideas which includes more than monumental distillations of thought in philosophy, religion, literature, and science may be offensive to those of fastidious intellectual tastes, but there is increasing awareness that adequate social and intellectual history cannot be written without accounting for popular opinions, beliefs, constellations of attitudes, and the like.

I

Ideas attain history in process, which includes transmission. The reach of an idea, its viability within a setting of time and place, and its modifications are expressed in a vast quantity of documentary sources. Man's conscious declarations of thought are embodied in a mosaic of documents, in constitutions and laws, literature and song, scientific treatises and folklore, in lectures, sermons, and speeches. Of these, not the least either in quantity or value, as Curti points out, are the lectures, sermons, and speeches:

> Historians of ideas in America have too largely based their conclusions on the study of formal treatises. But formal treatises do not tell the whole story. In fact, they sometimes give a quite false impression, for such writings are only a fraction of the records of intellectual history. For every person who laboriously wrote a systematic treatise, dozens touched the subject in a more or less casual fashion. Sometimes the fugitive essays of relatively obscure writers influenced the systematizers and formal writers quite as much as the works of better-known men. The influence of a thinker does not pass from one major writer to another without frequently being transformed or dissipated, or compressed in the hands of a whole series of people who responded to the thinker and his ideas. It is reasonably certain, moreover, that in the America of the early nineteenth century ephemeral

writings, widely scattered as they were in pamphlets, tracts, and essays, reached a much wider audience and are often more reliable evidence of the climate of opinion than the more familiar work to which historians of ideas have naturally turned. The student of the vitality and modification of ideas may well direct his attention, then, toward out-of-the-way sermons, academic addresses, Fourth of July orations, and casual guides and essays.[1]

As a parenthetical comment, one recent study which makes extensive use of fugitive literature, particularly speeches, is Merle Curti's *The Roots of American Loyalty,* published in 1946. But in the main, the rich vein of literature in speaking has hardly been tapped for this purpose except by the occasional prospector.

Curti's observations have germinal significance for the student of public address. They suggest an approach which is interesting for its freshness and fruitful in intellectual promise. If American life, to adopt his point of reference, is viewed through ideas historically viable, then ideas are to be studied as a body of intricate tissues, of differentiated yet related thought. While the establishment of macroscopic relationships provides the ultimate reasons for tracing out an American intellectual pattern, explorations of the parts is a necessary preliminary to this achievement. As an enterprise in scholarship, then, the first operation is one of collecting and classifying data within limited areas amenable to description and analysis. This accomplished, generalizations from the data become at once permissible and desirable, and provide a basis from which further exploration may be conducted.

It is at once apparent that the delineation of an American intellectual tradition calls for division of labor. It is not only the magnitude in task but diversity in data and in media of expression which invites specialization and varied technical skills in scholarship. There are, after all, appreciable and striking differences between the materials of hymnology and constitutional law. While students of philosophy, history, and literature are traditionally accredited as the official custodians and interpreters of intellectual history, it is the thesis of this paper that students of public address may contribute in substantial ways to the history of ideas. They possess credentials worthy of acknowledgment and interest in a type of materials germane to the object.

It has been amply treated and clearly said by others that the rhetoric of public address does not exist for its own sake, that its value is instrumental, and that its meaning apart from an application to something is sterile. An endorsement of this doctrine leads us to an immediate recognition that the basic ingredient of a speech is its content. The transmission of this content is its legitimate function. It is a vehicle for the conveyance of ideas. It is a

---

[1] Merle Curti, "The Great Mr. Locke: America's Philosopher, 1783-1861," *The Huntington Library Bulletin,* April, 1937, pp. 108-109.

mode of communication by means of which something of the thought of the speaker is incorporated and expressed in language in ways which make for ready comprehension and acceptance by one or more audiences. It is for the very reason that public speeches and lectures are prepared with a listening audience in mind that they serve so admirably in a study of social thought. The full import of this point is disclosed by some comparisons.

When reporting the results of work to members of his guild, the physical scientist may confine himself to an exclusive concern with data, intricate operations, and complex thought. In preparation and presentation neither detail nor comprehensiveness needs to be sacrificed, for his discourse is not prepared with an eye to the limiting factors present in the differentiated audience. As distinguished from this highly specialized form of reporting, a public speech is a more distinctly popular medium which is useful for explaining the essence of an idea, for explaining the applicability of a particular, for establishing impressions and evoking attitudes, for direction in the more or less common affairs of men. Because speeches are instruments of utility designed in the main for the popular mind, conversely and in significant ways they bear the impress of the popular mind. It is because they are pitched to levels of information, to take account of prevalent beliefs, and to mirror tone and temper of audiences that they serve as useful indices to the popular mind.

This interaction between the individual mind of the speaker and the collective mind of the audience has long been appreciated, but for the most part this interaction has been considered in terms of its relationship to the speaker's techniques. What has happened to the ideas themselves under the impact of this interaction remains a field which is relatively unexplored in any systematic sense by students of public address. The techniques of the speakers are often highly individualized and perish with their bones; their ideas live after them. From the study of speeches may be gained additional knowledge about the growth of ideas, their currency and vitality, their modifications under the impress of social requirements, and their eclipse by other ideas with different values. Such a study of speeches belongs to what Max Lerner calls the "naturalistic approach" to the history of ideas, one which includes "not only the conditions of the creation of ideas but also the conditions of their reception, not only the impulsions behind the ideas, but also the uses to which they are put, not only the thinkers but also the popularizers, the propagandists, the opinion skill-groups, the final audience that believes or disbelieves and acts accordingly."[2]

Is not such scholarship properly confined to the professional historian? The question is dated and should be so treated. Squabbles over contested rights are hangovers from an age of academic primogeniture. A study is to be judged by its merits, not by the writer's union card. But a more convincing

---

[2] Max Lerner, *Ideas Are Weapons* (1940), p. 6.

argument for participation in scholarship of the history of ideas by students of public address is made apparent when we take another step in our thinking. The very nature and character of ideas in transmission is dependent upon configurations of language. The interpretation of a speech calls for complete understanding of what goes into a speech, the purpose of the speech and the interplay of factors which comprise the public speaking situation, of nuances of meaning which emerge only from the reading of a speech in the light of its setting. At this juncture a special kind of skill becomes useful, for the problem now relates directly to the craftsmanship of the rhetorican. The student who is sensitized to rhetoric, who is schooled in its principles and techniques, brings an interest, insight, discernment, and essential skill which are assets for sholarship in the history of ideas, as that history is portrayed in public speeches.

II

The prevailing approach to the history and criticism of public address appears to consist of a study of individual speakers for their influence upon history. If one may judge from studies available through publication, they fall short of that ambitious goal for reasons which are painfully apparent to anyone who has attempted to assess influence in history. Nevertheless, they do provide a defensible pattern in research which has yielded highly interesting data about prominent speakers, their speechmaking and speaking careers. Reference is made to this standard approach to public address simply as a means of establishing and clarifying some distinctions between it and the proposed method of study which concentrates upon the ideas in speeches. The differences are those of focus, of knowledge to be gained, and of procedure to be followed in investigation. While one approach is "speaker centered," the other is "idea centered." One focuses mainly upon the speaker and the speaking activity, the other upon the speech and its content. One seeks to explain factors which contributed to personal persuasion; the other yields knowledge of more general interest in terms of man's cultural strivings and heritage.

In point of procedure it should be at once apparent that there are differences involved in a study which centers, let us say, upon Henry Clay as an orator and in a study which centers upon the ideas embodied in his speeches on the American System. To pursue the example, a study of the ideas in Clay's speeches is not committed to searching out the sources of his personal power with an audience, but is concerned with the doctrine of a self-contained economy as portrayed in his speeches in the perspective of that doctrine's history, from Hamilton to Matthew Carey's *Olive Branch,* to the congenial, nascent nationalism of Clay and contemporary speakers. Inasmuch as the American System is compounded of political and economic ideas, competence in handling the data of history is necessary; but it is also to be remembered that inasmuch as the ideas are projected through speeches, they are also the province of the rhetorician; that inasmuch as they are employed in speeches with the object of reaching and affecting a wide audience, the ideas are framed in a context of rhetorical necessities and possibilities. To adopt the rhetorical perspective is actually to approximate more closely a genuinely historical point of view when analyzing and interpreting speeches as documents of ideas in social history.

The possibilities for analysis in the rhetoric of ideas is illustrated in Roy P. Basler's essay on "Lincoln's Development As A Writer." The title of the essay should properly have included "And Speaker," for much of the brilliance of Basler's commentary arises from the treatment he gives the speeches.[3] Basler sets forth the basic ideas which are the essence of Lincoln's philosophy and links them to the dominant intellectual currents of Lincoln's age. He analyzes the rhetoric of Lincoln, not because he is interested in rhetoric *per se*, but because Lincoln's ideas were framed by his rhetoric, which, in turn, was profoundly affected by the exigencies present in the totality of social factors bearing upon the speaking situation. From an analysis of his rhetoric in this relationship, it is possible to come into a closer understanding of Lincoln's thought patterns and of the ideas he sought to lodge in the minds of his audiences. For instance, Basler recounts how the theme in the "House Divided" speech was carried through many stages of inference, that it underwent many modifications in order to achieve the nuances and implications which Lincoln desired. Basler concludes that "It would be difficult to find in all history a precise instance in which rhetoric played a more important role in human destiny than it did in Lincoln's speeches of 1858."[4] He speaks, of course, of the instrumental role of rhetoric as it served to crystallize the meanings which Lincoln sought to convey. Through a masterful analysis of the rhetoric in the Gettysburg Address, Basler presents the underlying pattern of Lincoln's thought, as is suggested by a short excerpt from his treatment:

> Lincoln's problem at Gettysburg was to do two things: to commemorate the past and to prophesy for the future. To do these things he took the theme dearest to his audience, honor for the heroic dead sons and fathers, and combined it with the theme nearest to his own heart, the preservation of democracy. Out of this double theme grew his poetic metaphor of birth, death, and spiritual rebirth, of the life of man and the life of the nation. To it he brought the fervor of devoutly religious belief. Democracy was to Lincoln a religion. and he wanted it to be in a real sense the religion of his audience. Thus he combined an elegiac theme with a patriotic theme, skillfully blending the hope of eternal life with the hope of eternal democracy.[5]

---

[3] Roy P. Basler, *Abraham Lincoln: His Speeches and Writings* (Cleveland and New York, 1946), pp. 1-49.

[4] *Ibid.*, p. 28.

[5] *Ibid.*, p. 42.

A speech is an agency of its time, one whose surviving record provides a repository of themes and their elaborations from which we may gain insight into the life of an era as well as into the mind of a man. From the study of speeches given by many men, then, it is possible to observe the reflections of prevailing social ideas and attitudes. Just as the speeches of Schwab and Barton, of Coolidge and Dawes (accompanied by the latter's broom-sweeping histrionics) portray the ethos of business and a negative view toward government intervention in social affairs, so do the speeches of Roosevelt and other New Dealers mark the break from the attitudes and conceptions which dominated the twenties. Both schools of thought express the social and economic values of the times. Both mirror the dominant moods of their respective audiences. The very structure, idiom, and tone of the speeches, moreover, play their parts in the delineation of those ideas. For example, the full import of Roosevelt's First Inaugural Address is not perceived without reference to the many nuances and imperatives of his rhetoric. It is in the metaphor of war and the image of the religious crusade, as well as in argument and statements of intention, that the speech articulates the inchoate feelings of the people on government's social responsibility. Similarly, from a wide investigation of sermons, lectures, and speeches related to issues, movements, and periods, might we not extend and refine our knowledge of social ideas portrayed in history? Such an attempt would constitute a kind of anthropological approach to a segment of cultural history.

III

Let the final argument be a practical one. Specifically, what applications may be made of this approach to public address in a university classroom? Experience has made it apparent to the writer that a course consisting only of successive case histories of individual speakers and speech-making leaves much to be desired. It certainly is open to question if an accidental chronology or arbitrary selection of orators provides a satisfactory focus and basic framework to warrant the label, "history of public address," or if it provides adequate intellectual and educational outcomes for the time expended. Interesting in its way as may be the study for its own sake of the personality, platform virtuosity, and career of an individual speaker, a mere progression of such more or less independent treatments is likely to be without secure linkage to historical processes. It is likely to result in an assortment of isolated, episodical, or even esoteric information which can make little claim to the advancement of the student's general culture.

There is more than a suggestion of antiquarianism in the whole business. We need, therefore, to provide a more solid intellectual residual. This may be realized when the focus of a course consists in the ideas communicated, in the ascertainable sources of those ideas, the historical vitality and force of the ideas, and of demonstrable refractions, modifications, or substitutions. As an adjunct to the materials of such a course, the study of the speaking careers and skills of individual speakers makes a valuable contribution. Such studies have supplementary value; but even more important is the study of the speeches themselves against a backdrop of history. Naturally, the exclusive study of speeches would result in historical distortion unless related to a larger framework of life and thought, to allied and competing ideas in the intellectual market place.

Seen against a broad and organized body of materials in intellectual and social history, the study of speeches both gives and takes on meaning in ways which contribute substantially to educational experience. Especially helpful as leads in providing background are such familiar works as Vernon L. Parrington, *Main Currents in American Thought;* Merle Curti, *The Growth of American Thought;* and Ralph H. Gabriel, *The Course of American Democratic Thought,* to mention but a few. Such literature supplies references and guidance to the main lines of thought which underlie movements and problems in American life; it brings into view not only tributaries which fed the main streams, but also rivulets of ideas which had a kind of independent existence. Speeches may be studied in relation to these movements. For example, intellectual turmoil and diluvial expression were provoked by the slavery controversy. Antislavery appeals, historians tell us, were couched in the language of personal liberty and Christian humanitarianism. Proslavery speakers, forced to compete upon an equally elevated plane, advanced arguments which derived from similar or equivalent ethical bases but which were interpreted in ways congenial to Southern institutional life and practice. True, the rhetoric of ideas fails to account for all the forces at work; yet a wide reading in sermons, lectures, and speeches does bring one into a deeper understanding of the basic ideational themes, variations upon the themes, and the dissonance which were a part of the controversy and contributed to ultimate settlement. When seen against a contextual backdrop, speeches become at once a means of illustrating and testing, of verifying or revising generalizations offered by other workers in social and intellectual history.

There is an implied recognition in what has been said, of a deficiency in the scholarship of public address. There is need for an organized body of literature which places speeches and speaking in proper relationship to the history of ideas. Quite apart from reasons of classroom utility, research in the ideas communicated through speeches needs doing as a means of contributing to knowledge and understanding generally. Adequate social and intellectual history cannot be written without reference to public speaking as it contributed to the ideas injected into public consciousness. But if research is to move forward, perhaps the time has arrived to explore in our individual and joint capacities the rationale, procedures, and materials by which it may be carried on. To this end, a symposium of papers which deals with these problems would help to clarify and stimulate research in public address in its relation to social and intellectual history.

The Study of Speeches
by Wayland Maxfield Parrish

Why do we study the speeches of the past?

What values do we seek in exhuming the long-silent utterances of dead orators on issues that are equally dead? Questions of burning interest in the time of Webster or of Lincoln have long since lost their heat, and an attempt to rekindle their embers may seem impertinent now when the whole world trembles before the problems of controlling atomic energy and containing communist Russia. And in any age what can be learned from orators that could not be better learned from the study of state papers, government reports, editorials, and scholarly essays in politics, economics, and philosophy?

When Socrates once referred to himself as "a pining man who was frantic to hear speeches," he defined a human trait which, in greater or lesser degree, is present in all of us. If, as Emerson said, "every man is an orator, how long soever he may have been a mute," perhaps we study speeches to find vicarious expression of our own unuttered eloquence. And both the lover of speeches for their own sake and the frustrated orator may find in their study something of "practical" value, for it is true of our age as it was of Aristotle's that "all men attempt to discuss statements and to maintain them, to defend themselves and to attack others,"[1] and whether we do this in formal addresses or in informal discussions we may expect to learn from a study of the notable addresses of the past some lessons that we can apply to the preparation of our own speeches, for though the subjects of controversy that concern us may be quite different from those that exercised the talents of earlier speakers, yet the *methods* of discussion and argument remain very much the same from age to age.

If we have progressed far enough in our study of rhetoric to have developed a coherent theory of speech construction we may wish to test it by applying it to the recorded speeches of the past. And if we do not have a method of our own and wish to develop one, it is surely the part of wisdom to observe carefully and analytically the practices of earlier speakers instead of depending entirely upon our own fumbling trials and errors. Any sound theory of speech-making must be derived from observation of the practices of

---

Reprinted from *American Speeches*. Edited by Wayland Maxfield Parrish and Marie Hochmuth. (New York: Longmans, Green, and Co., 1954.)
[1] *Rhetoric*, I, i.

the best speakers. In this book are recorded some of the best efforts of some of the best speakers in American history. They can be studied with profit by any aspiring rhetorician.

This suggests another reason for the study of public addresses that applies especially to more mature students of rhetoric. It is not always wise to accept uncritically the precepts of some standard textbook, whether by Aristotle, Cicero, or a modern writer, and assume its soundness and validity. The careful student will wish to compare these theories with the actual practice of masters of public address. If our textbook says, for instance, that a speaker should begin by conciliating his audience, let us examine the beginnings of a dozen or two representative addresses to see whether the theorist is supported by practice. And when Aristotle says we may argue that what is rare is a greater good than what is plentiful we may well examine a number of speeches to discover whether such an argument has actually been used.

The student who is interested in history will not lack a motive for the study of public address. He cannot be indifferent to the utterances of important men on important questions of the period he is studying. He will study speeches for the light they throw on contemporary events, and he will study events for the light they throw upon speeches. And he may discover that speeches have often been instrumental in shaping the course of history, in defining and strengthening a people's ideals, and in determining its culture.

Taking a deeper and more philosophical view, we may say that the study of speeches is worthwhile because all of man's activities are of interest to us and we assume that "in some sense human experience is worth while."[2] The Greeks believed that one of man's greatest pleasures lay in learning new things. Such a doctrine can hardly be questioned when we contemplate the insatiable modern drive for learning and discovery. In the physical sciences it has led to the quest for the innermost secrets of the atom, and in the philological sciences to the attempt to relearn all that was once known. To recover the great speeches of the past, to reconstruct the circumstances under which they were given, to discover the motives that prompted the orator to speak and the motives that prompted the audience to respond—these may surely be counted among interesting and worthy studies.

In recovering or in exploring the great thought currents of earlier times the speech may or may not be a more useful instrument than other writings, in prose or verse, but it is from its very nature likely to be more interesting and more vital. And this leads us to a consideration of the nature of public address.

What Is a Speech?

Typically, a speech is an utterance meant to be heard and intended to

---

[2] David Daiches, *A Study of Literature* (Ithaca, N.Y.: Cornell University Press, 1948), p. 228.

exert an influence of some kind on those who hear it. Typically, also the kind of influence intended may be described as persuasion. The hearer is to be moved to action or argued into the acceptance of some belief. The aim of the speaker is, in the words of William Caxton "to cause another man . . . to believe or to do that thing which thou wouldst have him for to do."[3]

Such a purpose is plainly enough discerned in Webster's Reply to Hayne or in Patrick Henry's plea for war against England. But in some presidential addresses, public lectures, and eulogies it is not so clear. In such addresses the speaker's aim may incline toward pure exposition or pure self-expression, and certainly these are legitimate aims in public address. But even so, a persuasive purpose is pretty sure to be present, for the expositor wishes to have his ideas approved and accepted, and even the plowboy who declaims his own sentiments or another's while following the furrows may have an imaginary audience in his eye. A very popular and successful modern preacher once confessed that the chief appeal of the ministry for him was in its opportunity for self-expression, but it is not on record that he ever delivered his sermons in an empty church. The orator may say, and may believe, that he is merely giving vent to his inmost convictions, and this would seem to be true of some orations and parts of orations. "I know not what course others may take, but as for me—" cried Patrick Henry. Just so, many artists assert that their work is purely personal and deny that they have any intention to communicate with others. But Professor I. A. Richards contends that the artist's "conscious neglect of communication does not in the least diminish the importance of the communicative aspect. . . . Denial that he is at all influenced in his work by a desire to affect other people, is no evidence that communication is not actually his principal object."[4] Just so, a speech may have a persuasive efficacy even though the speaker denies any intention to persuade.

It should be noted, however, that lectures or addresses that are designed solely to give the hearer information or instruction,[5] to furnish him with facts, must, from their very lack of urgency, fall short of the highest eloquence. It is the essential nature of oratory that it be moving, that it be persuasive. All of the notable speeches in American history have, directly or indirectly, this persuasive purpose. All of those included in this volume have it.

It should be noted also that typically, but not always, a speech is designed to meet a specific situation, to affect a given audience, as when a United States Senator argues for the passage of a bill, or a prosecutor pleads before a jury for the conviction of a culprit. It follows, as we shall find later, that there can be no adequate judgment of the effectiveness of an address unless we understand fully the situation which it was designed to meet.

---

[3] *Myrrour & Dyscrypcyon of the Worlde*, 1481.

[4] See his chapter on Communication and the Artist in *Principles* of *Literary Criticism* (New York: Harcourt Brace & Co., 1952).

[5] W. M. Parrish, *Speaking in Public* (New York: Charles Scribner's Sons, 1947), pp. 308-16.

Many speeches, however, do not have such an immediate specific purpose or a sharply defined audience. A public lecture may be intended for repeated delivery to many audiences, and a president's address, though delivered before an immediate audience, may be intended for the whole nation or for the whole world. And such speeches may not be directed to any specific occasion but may aim generally at winning good will, creating confidence, allaying fears, strengthening loyalties and beliefs, warning of impending dangers, preparing the public mind for measures to come, or building a more tolerant or favorable attitude toward some person or proposal or institution. But whether the audience is specific or general, present or remote, a speech is likely to have more urgency, more directness of address, and more simplicity in vocabulary, style, and structure than compositions intended to be read in private.

Keeping in mind the exceptions and reservations and modifications discussed above, we may say, then, that a speech is a spoken discourse intended to work some kind of persuasive effect upon a given audience.

The Nature of Criticism

"Let us say that the task of literary criticism is to put the reader in possession of the work of art," says Cleanth Brooks.[6] He continues, "Is this a mere reading of the work or is it a judgment of it? Frankly, I do not see how the two activities can be separated. . . . The attempt to drive a wedge between close reading of the text and evaluation of the work seems to me confused and confusing." Let us say the same of rhetorical criticism. We are concerned with the interpretation of speeches, with analysis of their content, structure, and method; and we are concerned at the same time with judgment or evaluation of their excellences and defects.

It will be apparent from the definition above that putting a reader in possession of a speech involves more than analysis of its content and form. Since the purpose of a speech is to work persuasion upon an audience, we cannot properly explain or evaluate it until we have learned a great deal about the occasion which called it forth, the speaker's relation to the occasion, the resources available to him, and the climate of opinion and current of events amidst which he operated. Particularly do we need to know the nature of the audience for whom the speech was intended so that we may understand why certain things were said and certain others omitted, and so that we may judge whether the speaker has wisely and skillfully adapted his ideas and methods to those for whom they are intended. It will help also to know something of the speaker's character, education, and experience, for these are important conditioners of what he says. And when we have formed an impression of the

---

[6] Foreword to R. W. Stallman, *Critiques and Essays in Criticism, 1920-1948* (New York: The Ronald Press Co., 1949), p. xx.

speech we may wish to test its validity by examining whatever evidence is available concerning its actual effect upon those who heard or read it.

If we study, for example, the First Inaugural Address of Franklin D. Roosevelt, how are we to understand and evaluate such phrases as "the only thing we have to fear is fear itself," "the money changers have fled from their high seats in the temple of our civilization," "a stricken nation in the midst of a stricken world"? We will have to make a careful examination of contemporary events and conditions as we find them recorded in newspapers, magazines, surveys, and histories of the period. Through similar sources we will need to examine the life and character of the speaker to discover why this kind of man was likely to say the kind of thing he did say. We will wish to know what advisers he consulted while preparing the address and how their advice influenced him. The composition of the immediate audience scattered over the Capitol Plaza is not of great importance, for the speech was addressed not to them primarily but to the nation at large, indeed to the whole world. Analysis of such an audience is a formidable task, but the critic must learn what he can of the fears and hopes of the people of the world at that time.

It is obvious that an attempt to discover and to analyze *all* the factors in the historical situation, in the consciousness of the audience, and in the baffling personality of the speaker on this occasion would require a lifetime of study and could never be complete. The critic must be selective. He must distinguish what is relevant to his purpose from what is merely interesting, and he must be limited by the prescribed scope of his study.

It is all the more important that he should not get lost in such studies, since they are, strictly speaking, extraneous to rhetoric. They are useful only insofar as they help in the rhetorical analysis of the speech itself. Properly speaking, they are excursions into the fields of history, sociology, or biography which furnish a background against which the speech itself may be studied.

It is even more important that the critic should not be diverted into an attempt to assess the *result* of a speech except as its effect may help us to judge the quality of the speech itself. Rhetoric, strictly speaking, is not concerned with the *effect* of a speech, but with its *quality,* and its quality can be determined quite apart from its effect. This is apparent when we consider that a properly qualified rhetorician should be able to analyze and to judge a written speech before it is delivered, and so before it can have had any effect. So also he should be able to criticize it after it is delivered without paying any attention to its effect.

It cannot be too often repeated that the effect of a speech *may* bear little relation to its intrinsic worth. A speaker's success in achieving a desired response from his audience is not necessarily proof that he has spoken well, or his failure, that he has spoken ill. His objective may have been too easy, or his audience may have responded as he wished despite the fact that they were actually repelled by his plea. Or, on the other hand, their votes may have been bought up in advance, or they may have had a stubborn prejudice against him or his proposal that nothing could dispel. Many of the great speeches of history have been made in lost causes. Some have been called forth by the speaker's very consciousness that his case was hopeless. Under such circumstances an orator may speak merely to put his views on record, or he may speak in defiant challenge to an opposition which he knows is invincible. Witness John Brown's moving defense when about to receive a sentence of death. One may say in such cases that the orator is speaking to posterity, or to the larger audience who will read his plea, and often that is true. But who can assess the effect of a speech on posterity? Who can determine today the effect of Woodrow Wilson's pleas for the League of Nations? How can one determine the actual influence of Lincoln's plea for malice toward none and charity for all? Indeed how can we be sure that a speech that "gets the votes" or "wins a verdict" is really the cause of the alleged results? The real reasons for a man's vote may lie hidden in his own mind. In most cases, all we know is that a plea was made, and the vote was so and so. The relation between the two is seldom discoverable.

Let us not be too confident, then, that we are measuring the effect of a speech. And in any case the totting up of such responses as are discernible is a task for a historian, a clerk, or a comptometer, not for a rhetorician. If the results of a speech are measurable, it is the job of the rhetorician to analyze the *causes* of its alleged success or failure as these are discoverable in the speech itself.

The Critic's Qualifications

It is true that anyone can pronounce judgment on speeches, and most everyone does, but only a judgment that comes from a qualified critic is worthy of respect. One of the first qualifications we look for in seeking a competent critic is a judicious temperament. Many of us are prone to make decisions before we have examined all the factors involved in a situation and weighed each in its relation to others. In judging speeches we must not hastily jump to conclusions merely because we have found something that pleases or displeases us. We must school ourselves to examine patiently all the factors relevant to a sound judgment and not to depend upon whim, prejudice, or individual preference. It is not opinion we seek, but truth.

But how can one speak of truth in a field so incapable of scientific certitude as rhetoric? We have no calipers or test tubes or mathematical formulas to help us. How can one be sure of the quality of a speech, or of its value? Sir William Osler's advice to young doctors is pertinent here. "At the outset," he said, "do not be worried about this big question—Truth. It is a very simple matter if each one of you starts with the desire to get as much as possible. No human being is constituted to know the truth, and nothing but the truth; and even the best of men must be content with fragments, with partial glimpses, never the full fruition. In this unsatisfied quest the attitude of mind, the desire, the thirst . . . the fervent longing, are the be-all and the end-all. . . . The truth is the best you can get with your best endeavor, *the best that the best men accept*—with this you must learn to be satisfied, retaining at the same time with due humility an earnest desire for an ever larger portion."[7]

Besides a thirst for truth and a judicious temperament in dealing with it, the critic of rhetoric must have special education for his task. He must have, first, a wide general education in history, politics, literature, and all the liberal studies. The speeches he studies may range through all the fields of human knowledge, they may be rich in allusions to persons and events, and the critic must be able to follow all the workings of the orator's mind. If he comes across such phrases as "a house divided against itself," "a consummation devoutly to be wished," or "be in earnest, don't equivocate, don't excuse, don't retreat a single inch," he should be able to identify and explain them. In one paragraph of a speech by George William Curtis there are references to James Otis, Wendell Phillips, Quincy, John Quincy Adams, Whittier, Longfellow, Lowell, Emerson, Parker, Beecher, Jonathan Mayhew, Roger Williams, and William Ellery Channing, and an understanding of the para-graph requires some familiarity with their lives and achievements. In such cases one must, of course, consult encyclopedias, biographical dictionaries, histories, and so on, but with the understanding that they do not take the place of a well-furnished mind.

Second, the critic must know speeches. He must have read and heard and studied many of them if he is to know the nature of the genus, speech. Only from familiarity with a large number of representative specimens will he know what he should look for in a given speech and what its distinctive qualities and merits are. To understand or to evaluate a particular thing—a horse, a motor car, a drama, a painting—one must be familiar with many specimens of that thing. It is only thus that standards of judgment are formed. Until the student acquires such a background in public address, he is not qualified to interpret or judge speeches. One of the purposes of this book is to make available some materials for that background.

Men have been studying speeches for as long as speeches have been made, and through the ages many treatises have been written to define the principles of speech-making and to reduce them to a system. The third qualification of the modern critic is familiarity with these treatises on rhetoric. Where so many competent guides have mapped out the ground, it is folly for anyone to stumble alone over such difficult and treacherous terrain, especially so since among these writers on rhetoric are some of the most eminent minds in the history of the race. With the best of these works the modern critic of public address should become thoroughly familiar. The fact that some of them were written centuries ago does not measurably diminish their value for the criticism of speeches in the middle of the nineteenth century. Rhetoric deals in the main with man's motives and desires and, whether we like it or not, basic human nature has not changed essentially in

---

[7] *Aequanimitas* (3rd ed.; Philadelphia: The Blakiston Co., 1932), pp. 397-98.

two thousand years. The way to a man's heart in ancient Athens is still the way to a man's heart today. Styles and modes of speaking may change in different ages, but wherever the fundamental purpose of speaking is to influence human conduct its essence will remain the same.

So much has been written on rhetoric that its study might absorb a whole lifetime, but for most purposes such thorough study is not needed. It is enough if one knows the best of the treatises on the subject. It is not by swallowing whole libraries, but by repeatedly and intently contemplating a few very great works, that the mind is best disciplined. And as Lane Cooper has said, "The best-read man is the one who has oftenest read the best things."[8]

There is little disagreement among modern scholars on which are the best works on rhetoric, at least until we come to modern writings. The following list contains most, if not all, of the older works that modern scholars consider most worthy of study. They should be available in any good college library.

Standard Works on Rhetoric

Plato: *Phaedrus and Gorgias*
Aristotle: *Rhetoric*
Cicero: *De Oratore*
Quintilian: *Institutio Oratoria*
Longinus(?): *On the Sublime*
Francis Bacon: *The Advancement of Learning, Chapter III*
George Campbell: *The Philosophy of Rhetoric*
Hugh Blair: *Lectures on Rhetoric and Belles Lettres*
Richard Whately: *Elements of Rhetoric*

These will serve as a base from which to examine the flood of modern studies, criticisms, and textbooks on public speaking which issue yearly from the press. A very useful summation of rhetorical theories with many suggestions of lines of study will be found in *Speech Criticism: The Development of Standards for Rhetorical Appraisal* by Lester Thonssen and A. Craig Baird.[9] Many model studies of orators may be found in A *History and Criticism of American Public Address,* sponsored by The National Association of Teachers of Speech and edited by W. N. Brigance.[10]

A word of caution may be needed against using any one of the works listed above as a sole guide in the criticism of an address. To derive all one's criteria from Whately, for instance, or even from so comprehensive a treatise as Aristotle's, is pretty sure to result in a criticism that is only partial, with neglect of some important matters and too much attention to others. So far as is possible one should be guided by all of "the best" theories of appraisal,

---

[8] *Two Views of Education* (New Haven: Yale University Press, 1922), p. 118.
[9] New York: The Ronald Press Co., 1948.
[10] New York: McGraw-Hill Book Co., 1943.

difficult as this makes the task. Jacques Barzun has well said, "The critic's role is ... to see, hear, and talk about everything in the light of *some imaginary standard set by the books with the toughest lives.*"[11] Some suggestions for forming this imaginary standard will be found in the section that follows.

The Basis of Criticism

There is general agreement among scholars that of all the books that have been written on rhetoric the one with the toughest life is Aristotle's *Rhetoric*. It has profoundly influenced nearly all subsequent writers, and its present liveliness is attested by the fact that it is available today in more English translations than probably any other ancient work. We shall lean heavily upon it in forming our "imaginary standard" of criticism.

Aristotle defined rhetoric as "the faculty of observing in any given case the available means of persuasion." Note first in this definition that rhetoric is a *faculty.* That is, it is not a definite technique with fixed rules of procedure, but merely the ability to find the elements of persuasion in a given speech. Note also that the rhetorician is not to limit his attention to the means of persuasion actually used, but is to consider all the means *available* to the speaker whether he used them or not. He should discover what the speaker *might* have said, what the situation called for, what resources were accessible to him. This, of course, points toward a careful analysis of the situation that called forth the address, the environment in which it was made, the problem that it was intended to solve. It suggests also that the critic's concern is not with the literal result of the speech, but with the speaker's use of a correct method; not with the speech's effect, but with its effectiveness. Persuasive always means persuasive to someone—a judge in a case at law, a prospective voter in an election, a listener in a popular audience. But the judge or listener as Aristotle conceives him is always a *qualified* judge—a person of good education, sound sense, and judicious temper. This is the kind of audience we must assume in assessing the effectiveness of a speech, for it is the kind of audience aimed at in the best efforts of all our orators. We admire Burke's great addresses, not because they were well adapted to the boozy country squires who sometimes sat in Parliament, but because they were designed for a better audience. In speech-making, as in life, not failure, but low aim, is crime. And so in criticism we interpret and evaluate a speech in terms of its effect upon an audience of qualified listeners.

The Means of Persuasion

With rhetorical criticism thus defined we proceed to consider some of the

---

[11]*Harper's Magazine* (July, 1949), p. 105. (Italics ours.)

most important means by which a speech works persuasion in those who hear and judge it.

One of the most important elements in persuasiveness is the impression made by the speaker's character and personality. Much of this impression is made, of course, by his appearance, voice, manner, and delivery, and cannot be recovered from study of the printed speech. Many indications of his trustworthiness *can,* however, be found in the printed text. We can learn whether he possesses those personal qualities that Aristotle thought most persuasive—virtue, intelligence, and good will. When Theodore Roosevelt said, "There should be relentless exposure of and attack upon every evil man, whether politician or business man," and when Franklin D. Roosevelt said, "Happiness lies not in the mere possession of money; it lies in the joy of achievement, in the thrill of creative effort," they were revealing a moral bent that should have stimulated their hearers to greater confidence in their integrity. Most speeches are full of such indicators of the speaker's trustworthiness, and the critic must note them and assess their value. He may note such things as whether the speaker establishes his own authority with the audience, whether he has a sympathetic understanding of their way of life, their thoughts, and their problems, whether he impresses them as being well informed on his subject, whether he is given to dogmatism, exaggeration, and overstatement, whether he has a sense of humor, whether he seems sincere, friendly, fair-minded, modest, self-respecting, respectful, courteous, and tactful.[12] The presence or absence of one or more of these qualities may dispose the hearers so favorably or so unfavorably toward the speaker that they pay little attention to what he says.

This, however, is not always true, and the second element of effectiveness we must consider is the *content* of the speech. The essential question to ask here is: Did the speaker choose the right things to say? It is desirable to separate *what* was said from how it was said—often a difficult task—and this may best be done by making a summary or précis of the speaker's thought which avoids the wording of the original. We must consider whether he seems to be acquainted with all the pertinent facts bearing on his subject and whether he uses those that are most significant or persuasive. We must determine also whether they really are facts, or only guesses, opinions, or hearsay, whether he has drawn valid inferences from them, and whether he has combined them into a coherent logical structure that will satisfy the understanding and win conviction.

It is helpful to separate the structure of the speech from the structure of the reasoning that supports it, and to outline both. Rarely will they coincide, for rarely do experienced speakers put their thoughts into the mechanical form favored by schoolboy debaters: "I will prove so and so, and my reasons

---

[12]See the chapter, "The Speaker Himself," in James A. Winans, *Speech-Making* (New York: D. Appleton-Century Co., 1938).

are, first, second, third, etc." A chronological outline will reveal the order of the speaker's thoughts; a logical outline will reveal the structure and validity of his thinking. The main proposition (or propositions) may nowhere be specifically stated, but it should be ferreted out by the critic and clearly formulated, and the supporting arguments should be marshaled under it to form a logical brief. He should ask: Just what is this speaker trying to prove, and what does he adduce to support his thesis? By this means he will best discover the essential substance of the speech—or its lack of substance.

The critic should assess also the depth and weight of the ideas presented. A great speech cannot consist of mere eloquent nothings. It must deal with great issues, not with trivial ephemera. And the critic must consider whether the orator is actuated by lofty ideals of justice, honor, liberty, and the like, or whether he is concerned with such local and temporary matters as balancing this year's budget or getting a subsidy for farmers. It is true that persuasion may be as skillful in small matters as in great, but we cannot divorce the value of a speech from the value of the ideas with which it deals.

When the plan and structure of a speech are clearly perceived, the critic may note whether there is any persuasive effect in the *order* in which ideas are presented. In the given situation is there any advantage in presenting this idea first and that one second? The notion is as old as Plato that a speech should have a beginning, a middle, and an end, and the disposition of materials, *dispositio,* was a main consideration of Roman rhetoricians. In most speeches the threefold division—introduction, discussion, conclusion— is easily discernible. And in general it will be found that the introduction is designed to win an intelligent, sympathetic, and attentive hearing, and the conclusion to sum up what has been said and to make a final appeal. These are their time-honored functions. But what the critic should note is not merely whether the speech follows this classical pattern, but whether it proceeds step by step in conformity with the need, the mood, and the expectation of the audience. The hearers may require an analysis of a problem before they will attend to its solution. They may want certain objections answered before they will listen to a proposal. Or they may entertain certain doubts or suspicions that the speaker will have to remove before he can get a fair hearing. The situation may be such that he will need to establish a common ground of interest, of feeling, or of belief with his audience before he presents his proposal. And it may be that the presentation of an unpopular theme calls for a strategy whereby the hearers are led to agree with the speaker on several non-controversial matters so that they will continue to agree when a less acceptable matter is presented. That is, the critic must look not only to the *chronological* order of materials and their logical structure, but also to the *psychological* order of presentation if one exists.

Another means of persuasion, and perhaps the most important of all, is by appeal to certain *motives* to which an audience can be expected to respond. The most persuasive speaker is he who most effectively directs his appeal to the basic interests, desires, wants, instincts, and emotions of his hearers. A complete catalogue of such motives has never been made, but the critic may get most help in this matter from Aristotle's discussion of the "Constituents of Happiness" and "Goods," and his analysis of the emotions.[13] He will be helped also, by the analyses of audiences by the Reverend George Campbell[14] and James A. Winans.[15]

Sometimes the "motivation" of a speech will be immediately clear. Patrick Henry's "Liberty or Death," for instance, is obviously an appeal to our love of liberty, though it contains many other appeals also. Curtis's "Public Duty of Educated Men" appeals, of course, to the sense of duty of the young graduates to whom it was addressed. But often the motive to which the orator appeals is hidden or obscure. It may nowhere be mentioned, and the emotions he seeks to arouse may not be named. One of the most rewarding tasks of the critic is to search them out and to determine from a study of them what kind of audience the orator presumes himself to be addressing. Does he assume that his hearers will respond to such motives as group loyalty, honor, courage, fair play, altruism, or does he appeal only to self-interest and personal security? Does he assume that they are progressive and forward-looking, or that they are timid, conservative, and fearful of anything new? Does he rely more on challenges to reason than on appeals to emotion? Does he attempt to arouse fear, anger, hatred, jealousy, or confidence, temperance, and love? And so on.

When the nature of the appeal is understood one must consider the manner in which it is presented. A speaker may scold an audience for its failure in duty, or he may ridicule its negligence, or try to shame it into action. He may present an unpopular proposal with challenging bluntness, or skillfully identify it with accepted beliefs and habitual conduct. He may rely upon effective repetition to drum in an idea and get it accepted. He may arouse emotion by effective play upon the imagination. By moving examples and illustrations he may fix responsibility upon his hearers and compel them to face the truth. And he may win them to a favorable response, as Franklin D. Roosevelt so often did, by a serene and cheerful confidence that they *will* respond favorably. All such methods of presenting a proposal the critic will note and assess.

Style

Another important means of persuasion lies in the speaker's *style*. It is style, the choice and arrangement of words, that determines in the main the value of a speech as enduring literature. And it is style that more than any other factor gives a speaker the uniqueness by which he is distinguished from

---

[13]*Rhetoric,* I, v, vi, vii; II, ii-xii.
[14]*Philosophy of Rhetoric* (New York: Funk and Wagnalls Co., 1911), Book I, Chap. VII.
[15]*Op. cit.,* Chap. XV.

other speakers. Here the authenticity of the text of the speech becomes especially important, though the critic may be more interested in what the speaker *meant* to say than in what he *did* say. But he will want to know whether the words he is studying are the speaker's own or contributed by some adviser or ghost writer.

It has been a truism since Aristotle that the first virtue of style is to be clear. But clarity is a relative matter, and the critic must ask always: Clear to whom? The brilliant academic addresses of Curtis and Phillips with their wealth of allusions to literature and history make difficult reading today. Were they clear to the erudite audiences before whom they were spoken? In its effect on its audience a speech must, of course, be *immediately* clear since, once uttered, it cannot be called back for a rehearing (unless it was recorded). In its vocabulary, its allusions, its illustrations, and its sentence structure it must be suited to the intelligence of those for whom it is intended. These are the principal considerations in criticising the clarity of a speech.

Because audiences may be dull, indifferent, and subject to many distractions, we expect a speech to have a vividness and vivacity that will win and hold attention. This is the quality that Aristotle well described as "setting a thing before the eyes." Such an effect may be obtained by concrete wording, effective descriptions, flights of imagination and fancy, the use of metaphors, examples, illustrations, analogies, by vivid narratives and dramatic dialogues and rhetorical questions. Such devices may be used in connection with parallelism of phrase and antithesis. Vivacity is obtained also by conciseness of statement, economy of style, brevity of utterance, though in this respect audiences and periods vary in their taste. Apparently the audiences of Webster's day tolerated an elaborateness of amplification that may impress us as mere flatulence and bombast. In this, as in other matters, the critic must consider the peculiar nature of the audience addressed. Finally, the vividness of a speech will depend largely upon whether the various oratorical elements are presented with appropriate variety, for any device if endlessly repeated loses its power to hold attention.

A third characteristic of a good style is its appropriateness. It should be suited to the speaker, to the audience, and to the occasion. Factors to be considered are vocabulary, the nature of the materials—facts, arguments, illustrations, and the like—the mood and temper of the speaker and of the audience, the gravity of the subject, the nature of the occasion, and so on. Here again, the validity of the criticism will depend upon how effectively the occasion has been analyzed.

Another quality to be considered is the orality or "speak-ability" of the style. There should be indications that it was meant to be spoken to an audience rather than read silently and privately by an individual reader. The factors that distinguish an oral from a written style have never been definitely set forth, but the critic will look for such things as directness of address, as revealed by personal pronouns and questions; simplicity of sentence structure; heat and vitality of expression demanded by the need for holding the attention of an audience; and a choice of words and phrases that allow for ease, smoothness, and force of utterance.[16]

In studying style one should look also for those occasional passages of sustained nobility and beauty which sometimes lift oratory into the realm of poetry. The ideas and sentiments that inspired them may no longer be meaningful, but still they live and move us by their intrinsic aptness and beauty. Sometimes, as occasionally with Ingersoll, they seem to be merely "purple patches" sewed onto the fabric of the discourse to attract attention, but often they are developed authentically from the orator's feeling and imagination. A thorough study of oratory cannot fail to take account of them.

There are other aspects of style, but those we have just discussed are perhaps the most important. For additional criteria and suggestions we recommend especially the works cited above by Aristotle, Campbell, and Blair.

Conclusion

These, then, are the principal means of persuasion that the critic of speeches will consider—character, content, logic, arrangement, motivation, and style. He will be interested also in the speaker's delivery and will learn what he can about it from available reports of the speech, but the text itself will seldom offer any suggestions about how the address was spoken. Students of classical rhetoric will note that this classification cuts across the Aristotelian three-fold division into ethical, pathetic, and logical proofs, and the five-fold Roman division of speech preparation into invention, disposition, style, delivery, and memorization. However, it will be found that all of these are accounted for, except the last.

We have been concerned chiefly with the analysis of single speeches, but it should be obvious that such analyses will prepare the student for other critical adventures. He may wish to attempt a comparative study of two or more orators, noting whether they appeal to the same or different motives, whether they arrange their materials in similar ways, how obtrusively each speaker's ego appears, how they compare in the use of illustrations and examples, how they differ or resemble each other in imagery, in vitality, in sentence form, in vocabulary, or in style. From such studies the critic will prepare himself for a sound judgment of what is unique and distinctive about a given orator. He may concern himself with the varying styles and methods that seemed to prevail in different periods of history. Or he may become interested in discovering certain recurring themes in oratory and changes in attitude toward them—such themes as liberty, democracy, human welfare, the function of government, the concept of honor, the hope of peace, the function of leadership.

These and many other lines of study may prove to be interesting and

---

[16]J. M. Clapp, "Oratorical Style and Structure," in S. B. Harding, *Select Orations Illustrating American Political History* (New York: The Macmillan Co,. 1909).

rewarding. The avenues of research are so various, and the possibility of getting lost in a blind alley is so great, that we feel impelled to warn that a rhetorical criticism is likely to be the less valuable the farther it strays from the central core of our discipline, which is the determination of whether the speaker has discovered and employed in the given case the available means of persuasion.

The Criticism of Rhetoric

by Marie Hochmuth

"Show me," Walter Savage Landor makes Pericles remark, "how great projects were executed, great advantages gained, and great calamities averted. Show me the generals and the statesmen who stood foremost, that I may bend to them in reverence; tell me their names, that I may repeat them to my children...place History on her rightful throne, and, at the sides of her, Eloquence and war."[1] Pericles hoped that when the history of Athens from the invasion of Xerxes should be written, it would give "a fair and full criticism on the orations of Antiphon,"[2] even at the expense of a narrative of the battle of Salamis.

Orators, of course, have been agents in history and, like all agents, must be supposed to have effects. Greece without Demosthenes, Rome without Cicero, England without Burke and Churchill, Germany without Hitler, and the United States without Patrick Henry and Lincoln would have been different. To believe otherwise is to succumb to the notion that human effort counts for little or nothing. Along with the other arts—painting, sculpture, drama, poetry—oratory has sometimes transformed abstractions into meaningful patterns and directives in our lives, has projected and given impetus to ideas that have become the values by which we live.

Ancient as an art form, the public speech in our age has gained new prominence as more and more public men appear on the television screen and in great public halls to "appeal directly to the people." One may legitimately question, I think, whether new prominence is accompanied by improved quality. Is there a promise of a new Golden Age of public speaking, or a threat of further deterioration in an art which once held a significant position among the arts? Will the somewhat casual ability to "say a few words" emerge in the form of a disciplined art, comparable to Athenian and Roman eloquence, the eloquence of eighteenth-century England, and the eloquence of the first half of nineteenth-century America?

I propose to deal here with the problem of evaluating human effort as it manifests itself in the making of speeches. Although I propose to deal chiefly

Reprinted from *A History and Criticism of American Public Address*. Vol. 3. Edited by Marie Hochmuth. (New York: Longmans, Green, and Co., 1955).

[1] *Selections from the Writings of Walter Savage Landor*, arr. and ed., Sidney Colvin (London: Macmillan & Co., 1882), p. 277.

[2] *Ibid.*, p. 276.

with American speeches, I assume that the basic principles may be applied to the evaluation of speeches anywhere. I am concerned not merely with evaluating the speaking of present-day speakers, but also with the evaluation of past efforts of individuals whose lifework is best reflected in the body of speeches with which they are identified.

A sense of critical awareness is, I believe, a necessary prerequisite to achieving or maintaining high quality in any art. The degree of perfection manifested in any age is a response to ideals insistently proclaimed, recalled, or restated. Furthermore, it is through critical awareness that one discovers the implications of his art for his times.

Systematic criticism of any sort has no long and well-established heritage in America. In truth, it can hardly be said to have existed at all before the nineteenth-century. As the literary critic, Van Wyck Brooks, once remarked, "There is nothing else in all modern history like the unanimity of praise and confidence with which, by its passengers, the American Ship of State was launched and manned. In all our long nineteenth-century past, there was scarcely a breath of dissent, doubt or censure. . . ."[3] In the field of literary criticism the poverty of the nineteenth century has given way to the riches of the twentieth-century, with critical warfare being one of its most distinctive features.

If one turns specifically to the records of speech-making, one finds little systematic criticism of the millions of words that have been uttered in the building of civilization. Early Colonial ministers, of course, sometimes examined the sermons of their fellows to find out if the sentiments were "correct," or for evidences of defection from generally accepted creeds. In the early part of the nineteenth century, in politics and religion, men like Everett, Webster, and Channing were praised for "great efforts" in the courts, town meetings, Congress, and the pulpit. British travelers in America surveyed the scene and placed our oratorical efforts against their great tradition of Parliamentary speaking.[4] People spoke of speech-making because it interested them. But as Wichelns observed as late as 1925, "We have not much serious criticism of oratory."[5]

The problem of criticism was sometimes complicated by literary men. They were uncertain of their genre, yet faced with a body of material that required consideration. Biographers and historians, with their own tools and preoccupations, likewise looked into the literature of speeches with some concern about how to use it. Surveying the body of critical comment on speeches for the last half of the nineteenth century, Barnet Baskerville has observed: "There is an absence of any prevailing critical temper in most of the literature. It is often eulogistic; it abounds in superlatives; it is impres-

---

[3] Van Wyck Brooks, *Sketches in Criticism* (New York: E. P. Dutton & Co., Inc., 1932), p. 11.
[4] Glenn Eugene Reddick, "Criticisms and Observations on American Public Address by British Travelers, 1785-1860" (Ph.D. dissertation, University of Illinois, 1954), pp. 40-87.
[5] Herbert A. Wichelns, "The Literary Criticism of Oratory," in *Studies in Rhetoric and Public Speaking in Honor of James Albert Winans* (New York: The Century Co., 1925), p. 182.

sionistic; it lacks system; it is personal rather than objective; it is frequently written in a style which manifests the same faults of verbosity, ostentatious erudition and gratuitous ornamentation which are attributed to the orators themselves."[6] A few exceptions may be noted in the critical commentaries of Channing, Emerson, Whipple, Godkin, and Goodrich.[7] Baskerville notes not only a lack of critical comment, but also apathy in regard to the need for systematic criticism, and concludes that such a "lack of speculation as to what criticism should be seems to indicate that critics of speaking had not yet become self-conscious. . . . Formulation of specific criteria, conscious efforts to establish a science of rhetorical criticism in America, were to come in a later period."[8]

In the criticism of speeches as in the criticism of literature generally, the twentieth-century has yielded richer harvests. Wichelns in 1925,[9] Brigance in 1943,[10] and Thonssen and Baird in 1948[11] focused attention on standards and methods for the evaluation of speeches as special genre. Spurred by the urgency of the world scene from the beginning of World War I through the period of present conflict, when misunderstanding is of the greatest concern, psychologists, linguists, aestheticians, semeioticians have been trying in good faith to advance our knowledge of the structure and use of language.

In the light of contemporary knowledge the problem of "giving fair and full criticism" to oratory may become somewhat more systematic. Our function here is not to write off previous attempts with a fine sense of superiority, but to set down in some brief form elements which must be considered when the speech as an art is being appraised.

What Is Criticism?

"Criticism, I hardly need point out," said John Dewey, "is not fault finding. It is not pointing out evils to be reformed. It is judgment engaged in discriminating among values. It is taking thought as to what is better and worse in any field at any time, with some consciousness of *why* the better is better and *why* the worse is worse."[12] Most of us will find little to disagree with in a concept of criticism whose minimal expectation is that of separation and division. Its biblical forebear is to be found in the New Testament: "But he said unto Him, Man, who made me a judge or a divider over you?"[13]

---

[6] Barnet Baskerville, "A Study of American Criticism of Public Address, 1850-1900" (Ph.D. dissertation, Northwestern University, August, 1948), p. 314.

[7] *Ibid.,* p. 315.

[8] *Ibid.,* pp. 317, 318.

[9] *Loc. cit.*

[10] William Norwood Brigance (ed.), *A History and Criticism of American Public Address* (New York: McGraw-Hill Book Co., 1943).

[11] Lester Thonssen and A. Craig Baird, *Speech Criticism* (New York: Ronald Press, 1948).

[12] *Construction and Criticism* (The First Davies Memorial Lecture, delivered February 25, 1930, for the Institute of Arts and Sciences [New York: Columbia University Press, 1930]), p. 12.

[13] Luke 12:14.

We need not haggle long over whether criticism arises because critics are frustrated speakers or writers. Nor need we add to the thousands of words already written on whether it is a science or an art. That it has not reached a standard of predictability common to the natural sciences should be obvious to all of us. Criticism, like anything else well-made, can achieve and sometimes has achieved artistic distinction. Of this much we are clearly aware: it is a universal practice, presumably fulfilling certain functions, and having values.

If we examine the critical process clearly, we may discern at least three aspects. It involves identification of what is to be evaluated; it recognizes what is to be evaluated as a cultural product of a particular time; it finally involves a judicial act of determining what is better or worse. In other words, a critic must necessarily be concerned with answering such questions as: What are we dealing with? When did the thing occur? In what relation does it stand to other similar cultural phenomena?

Let us note, for example, a typical case of identifying what one is dealing with. In it we may observe the precision with which Aristotle went about the process of naming his object, classifying, and differentiating:

> Rhetoric may be defined as the faculty of observing in any given case the available means of persuasion. This is not a function of any other art. Every other art can instruct or persuade about its own particular subject-matter; for instance, medicine about what is healthy and unhealthy, geometry about the properties of magnitudes, arithmetic about numbers, and the same is true of the other arts and sciences. But rhetoric we look upon as the power of observing the means of persuasion on almost any subject presented to us; and that is why we say that, in its technical character, it is not concerned with any special or definite class of subjects.[14]

Any critic, trained or untrained, goes through this process of identification in some way or other. Suppose a traveler walks into London's Hyde Park on Sunday afternoon and encounters a group of people surrounding a speaker uttering sounds to those who have stopped. Our traveler may previously have encountered someone quietly reclining on the grass, another absorbed in the Sunday paper, still another with brush and easel sketching the trees along the avenue. He may observe that the constituents which finally arrested his attention include the following: someone is speaking; others are listening; the event is taking place in a specific time; it is taking place in a particular locale; presumably there is some purpose; the utterance has some form; and the whole entity rests upon the natural condition that sound can be transmitted and received. If the traveler concludes that he is witnessing a

---

[14]*Rhetorica*, tr. W. Rhys Roberts, *The Works of Aristotle*, ed. W. D. Ross (Oxford: The Clarendon Press), XI, iii.2.1355ᵇ.

unified whole different from any other unified whole which he has en-countered, he will have performed the first analytic step in a total critical act, that of identifying his object and separating it from other cultural phenomena.

The traveler may go a step further. He may observe that what he is witnessing is an act bearing the marks of a culture at a particular time; the person doing the talking will have been conditioned by the culture of which he is a part; in purpose, matter, and manner the act will be a manifestation of the period of which it is a product. In fact, it will be the speaker's peculiar way of responding to the times. He will realize that time is not merely a physical fact, but a social fact. If the traveler recognizes the relations of the organic whole of which he is a witness to the cultural milieu of which it is a part, he will have performed a second analytic aspect of a critical act.

Our traveler may pass on and encounter similar behavior near by in the park. Unless he has encountered situations of a similar nature previously, or has an opportunity to witness at this time similar acts, he is in no position to perform the final aspect of judgment, for obviously what is "better or worse" involves an act of comparison. It is an act, in the main involving synthesis, in which the observer sees his object as a whole, and sees it in relation to similar cultural objects at the same or different times or places.

From time to time, critics have tended to single out for emphasis one or another aspect of the critical act. In the literary arts, we have tended at times to throw the emphasis on the person performing the act, and thus have written biography; at other times, we have tended to emphasize the cultural milieu of which the act was a part, almost to the exclusion of the act itself. In this respect, we have been sociological or historical. A concern with history or sociology, indispensable as preliminary aspects of criticism, sometimes obscures the fact that history and criticism serve different purposes. Whereas a concern for all these things is necessary, it does not represent criticism. As Edmund Wilson has enjoined the literary critics: "No matter how thorough and complete our explanation of works of literature may be from the historical and biographical points of view, we must be ready to try to estimate the relative degree of success attained by the products of the various periods and the various personalities. . . . We shall not otherwise write literary criticism at all, but merely social or political history . . . or psychological case histories from past eras, or . . . merely chronologies of books that have been published."[15]

The criticism of speeches, like the criticism of all art, involves both analysis and synthesis. It is concerned with naming and identifying its object, locating its connections with the culture of which it is a part, and seeing it in relation to other similar phenomena. It is "discriminating among values."

---

[15]"The Historical Interpretation of Literature," in *The Intent of the Critic,* ed. Donald A. Stauffer (Princeton: Princeton University Press, 1941), p. 57.

The Constituents of the Rhetorical Act

The criticism of speeches must proceed from a clear conception of the nature of a speech. Whereas a speech may be easily differentiated from the graphic and visual arts on the basis of media and means, it is less easily differentiated from other verbal arts like poetry and prose writing generally. Traditionally the speech has functioned both as an end in itself and as a means to other ends. Thus, Greek and Roman orators perfected the speech as a verbal form serving its own ends. On the other hand, the historian Thucydides, employed written forms of speeches in recording the political opinions of the day. Homer, Milton, Shakespeare, and numerous others have employed speeches as techniques for achieving particular effects within larger frameworks of verbal activity. Historically, the prose of the public speech was earliest to achieve artistic perfection; hence, the methods of the speech could be and sometimes were carried over into other forms of literary activity. All of this has been a source of confusion among critics who, at times, have mistaken the verbal record of the speaking event for the speech itself, and who just as often have applied the criteria of poetic to the evaluation of verbal activity demanding other criteria.

Two broad questions pertaining to the speech as a form have been traditional: Is the speech an art form? Is the verbal record of a speech to be considered literature? To the first question we may apply the ancient explanation that things come into being by luck, by nature, by spontaneity, or by art.[16] The records of speech-making indicate that principles and practices have entered into the making of speeches; speeches do not come into being by nature; nor are they typically the results of chance. More akin to architecture than to music as an art, the speech is primarily a practical art form. Just as the architect usually has functional ends primarily in mind in the construction of houses, office buildings, and even churches, occasionally he achieves far more than merely functional ends in a Cathedral of Chartres or of Cologne.

To the question: Are speeches literature? the answer, of course, depends on the breadth of definition. If we define literature as a "nation's mind in writing," obviously all verbal activity which is recorded is literature. If we define it as a qualitative factor in verbal activity, then the speech may or may not be literature. If we restrict the term to verbal activity whose primary purpose is to induce immediate pleasurable response, then the speech is clearly not primarily a literary form, although as an incidental aspect it may produce pleasurable response. In our age, the committee for awarding the Nobel Prize for literature chose Sir Winston Churchill in preference to Ernest Hemingway, Graham Greene, and other contenders for the award in literature for his "historical and biographical presentations and for the scintillating oratory in which he has stood forth as a defender of eternal human values."[17]

---

[16] Aristotle, *Metaphysica* in *The Works of Aristotle*, VIII, A. 3. 1070*.
[17] *The New York Times*, October 16, 1953, p. 25, cols. 2, 3, 4.

Thus, he takes his place beside Kipling, Shaw, Galsworthy, T. S. Eliot, and others as a "literary" figure.

I am concerned here with evaluating that which the Greeks called rhetoric. One need be under no illusion about the difficulties involved in using the term. Modern critics use it in a variety of ways.[18] Some use it to refer chiefly to the blandishments in a prose piece. Others use it to refer only to the "purple patches." Its use often does not reflect any clear effort to come to grips with the term. Thus, the literary historian, Vernon L. Parrington, writes of Lincoln: "Matter he judged to be of greater significance than manner. Few men who have risen to enduring eloquence have been so little indebted to rhetoric. Very likely his plainness of style was the result of deliberate restraint, in keeping with the simplicity of his nature."[19] Here rhetoric seems to be correlated with "manner," particularly with a style which is not plain. It presupposes a clean division between matter and manner, as if thought and the manner of expressing it were completely separate entities. On the other hand, the literary scholar and editor of Lincoln's speeches, Roy Basler, writes of Lincoln: "It would be difficult to find in all history a precise instance in which rhetoric played a more important role in human destiny than it did in Lincoln's speeches of 1858."[20] The meaning of the term here is not clear. It appears to mean something "in" the speeches—but not necessarily the speeches themselves. Such a confusion leads two critics to come to completely opposite conclusions in evaluating Lincoln's indebtedness to rhetoric. At a pole opposite from many attempts to correlate rhetoric with style, lies the recent observation of Duhamel: "Cicero's style was influenced by his rhetoric."[21] Here rhetoric is a cause of style, not correlative with it.

Because of this troublesomeness, I. A. Richards has recommended that we "would do better just to dismiss it to Limbo,"[22] unless the term can be revived to mean a "study of verbal understanding and misunderstanding. . . ."[23] Kenneth Burke, on the other hand, recommends that a strong arm be used to reclaim a traditional province, once perfectly clear, but usurped by other disciplines.[24]

Doubtless no contemporary interpretation of the term throws more light on its proper use than that of the classical systematizers of the art. "Rhetoric may be defined as the faculty of observing in any given case the available means of persuasion," observed Aristotle. The ancients included in the term

---

[18]Donald C. Bryant, "Rhetoric: Its Functions and Its Scope," *The Quarterly Journal of Speech,* XXXIX (December, 1953), 402-7.

[19]Vernon Lee Parrington, *The Romantic Revolution in America* in *Main Currents in American Thought* (New York: Harcourt, Brace & Co., 1927-30), p. 158.

[20]*Abraham Lincoln: His Speeches and His Writings* (Cleveland: The World Publishing Co., 1946), p. 28.

[21]P. Albert Duhamel, "The Function of Rhetoric as Effective Expression," *Journal of the History of Ideas,* X (1949), 346.

[22]I. A. Richards, *The Philosophy of Rhetoric* (New York: Oxford University Press, 1936), p. 3.

[23]*Ibid.,* p. 23.

[24]Kenneth Burke, *A Rhetoric of Motives* (New York: Prentice-Hall Inc., 1950), Introduction, xiii.

means of persuasion," observed Aristotle. The ancients included in the term all the ingredients of persuasion, the impelling fact, the reasoned argument, the strategic ordering of details, no less than the well-wrought phrase. The art of rhetoric was the art of discovering arguments, adapting them, ordering them, expressing them in clear and proper words, and of using one's personal qualities to enhance the whole to the end of achieving persuasion in an audience. It was the whole rationale of persuasive discourse.[25] The term was so used by Cicero, and Quintilian, and by vigorous eighteenth- and nineteenth-century theorists, George Campbell, Richard Whately, and others. It is also used in this way by the contemporary critic, Burke, by the Chicago school of critics, and generally by critics whose writings regularly appear in the *Quarterly Journal of Speech* and in *Speech Monographs*.

I use the term "rhetoric," then, to apply to verbal activity primarily concerned with affecting persuasion, whether it be done by writing or speaking. Rhetoric operates in the area of the contingent, where choice is to be made among alternative courses of action. Its concern is with substance as well as with form, if any arbitrary distinction is to be made. In this essay I am concerned with evaluating persuasive efficacy as it manifests itself in *oral* verbal activity, the speech. "Typically, a speech is an utterance meant to be heard and intended to exert an influence of some kind on those who hear it," remarks Wayland M. Parrish. "Typically, also the kind of influence intended may be described as persuasion."[26]

If we do not press the analogy too far, we may compare the speech with a multi-celled organism, whose units consist of speaker, audience, place, purpose, time, and form. In order to evaluate the speech, all these elements, verbal and nonverbal, must be examined.

First, consider the position of a speaker in the persuasive situation. In every instance, some specific "I" is doing the speaking. He may be familiar to us or quite unknown. If he is known, he may be known favorably or unfavorably. To the South during the Civil War, Lincoln was a "guerrilla"; to the North, in part, at least, he was "Honest Abe." Let us note for a moment the significance of the specific "I" in the speaking situation by referring to Emerson's characterization of Disraeli:

> Disraeli, the chiffonier, wastes all his talent on the House of Commons, for the want of character. He makes a smart cutting speech, really introduces new and important distinctions. . . . But he makes at last no impression, because the hearer asks, Who are you? What is dear to you? What do you stand for? And the speech and the speaker are silent, and silence is confession. A man who has been a man has foreground and background. His speech, be it never so good,

---

[25]See Donald C. Bryant, "Rhetoric: Its Functions and Its Scope," *op. cit.*, 401-24.
[26]Wayland M. Parrish and Marie Hochmuth, *American Speeches* (New York: Longmans, Green & Co., 1954), p. 3.

is subordinate and the least part of him, and as this man has no planet under him, but only his shoes, the hearer infers that the ground of the present argument may be no wider.[27]

Whether Emerson's judgment of Disraeli is or is not vindicated by history is not in question. The point is that when one listens to speeches, the individual "I" is an element in the situation. It may matter little in the judgment of "The Last Supper" who painted it, or of the "Moonlight Sonata," who composed it, or of *Pisan Cantos* whether the poet was or was not a traitor, but there is no gainsaying the fact that when speeches are being evaluated the speaker is of paramount importance. One asks the question, then: What are the predispositions, if any, toward the man who is giving the speech? This is a cell in the organism; it may be healthy or in some way defective. Either because of previous acquaintance or because of signs during the speech itself, the audience comes to some conclusion about the speaker, and this plays a part in the judgment. In the political campaign of 1952, Adlai Stevenson, scarcely known at all at the beginning of the campaign, was being compared with a rival candidate whose name was favorably known to millions. This could hardly fail to be a factor in the ultimate decision. Not only the speaking, but the *man* who spoke was a factor. The critic needs to note and assess the persuasive effect of "echoes and values" attaching to the person and character of the speaker. Rarely is this a simple matter, for the man is not always to be seen as a single individual having his own merits only. Men and women derive force from the symbolic relations in which they stand among others. Thus, Eisenhower became the "man of action" speaking for a nation proud of its ability to "get things done"; Clarence Darrow, according to Maloney in a study in this volume, became a champion for the downtrodden, the underdog, and spoke as the representative of a class. Thus, the impetus given to ideas set in motion by the speaker is not merely the impetus deriving from the force of one man's character, but often from the whole class which he images.

Next, let us consider the audience as a cell in this complex organism. Audiences neither come from a vacuum nor assemble in one. They come with pre-established systems of value, conditioning their perceptions. As Susanne Langer has observed, "Every society meets a new idea with its own concepts, its own tacit, fundamental way of seeing things; that is to say, *with its own questions, its peculiar curiosity.*"[28] We are not without knowledge in regard to the role of perception. We know that perception is selective; we both see and hear with a previously established set of values, theoretical, economic,

---

[27]*Journals of Ralph Waldo Emerson,* eds. Edward Waldo Emerson and Waldo Emerson Forbes (Boston: Houghton Mifflin Co., 1912), VII, 503.

[28]Susanne K Langer, *Philosophy in a New Key* (Mentor Books; New York: The New American Library, 1948), p. 4.

[29]Charles E. Osgood, *Method and Theory in Experimental Psychology* (New York: Oxford University Press, 1953), p. 292 ff.

aesthetic, social, political, and religious.[29] Not only do we have general sets of values that predetermine our responses, we often also have specific predispositions regarding the subject being discussed. The rhetorician discovers his potentials for persuasion in a wise regard for the prevailing attitudes in the audience. Although he need neither compromise his integrity, nor bow in subservience to an audience, he does need to understand the operating forces in the audience and select arguments that induce persuasion. He must remember that his choices are conditioned by the audience. The poem may be written with the audience thrice-removed from the creator, for the poet creates from his experience with his subject. But the speech-maker must compose his speech from the available potentials in his audience. He aims to link his propositions to their value systems, and value systems differ with age, sex, educational development, economic class, social strata, political heritage, specialized interest, and so on. The speaker is a selecter. He must exclude certain arguments and include others. He must decide how to order details and the thought patterns into which material is to be cast. All this is determined by the audience for which the speech is designed. The critic who attempts to discriminate among values without reference to the audience is doing what a rhetorical critic really cannot do. Since the audience conditioned the speaker's choices in selecting the arguments, ordering them, and expressing them, the critic must inevitably consider whether the speaker chose wisely or ill in relation to the audience. The critic's necessary tool, then, is not personal whim but clear perception of the role of choice. He must know the mood of the audience. Was it hostile, neutral, or partisan? What tensions, if any, were to be released? Was it keyed up for any particular occasion? Daniel Webster long ago called attention to the significance of occasion and audience-tone in persuasion: "True eloquence, indeed, does not consist in speech. It cannot be brought from far. Labor and learning may toil for it, but they will toil in vain. Words and phrases may be marshalled in every way, but they cannot compass it. It must exist in the man, in the subject, and in the occasion."[30] Let the critic know, then, the audience for which the speech was intended.

Third, we must consider the function of *place*. Place, of course, is not merely a physical condition. It is also a metaphysical condition, an ideological environment. We hear much of the "industrial" East, the "conservative" Midwest, the "progressive" Far West, "rumor-ridden" Washington. Speeches take place in halls, to be sure, but halls are "sacred halls," "smoke-filled rooms," places "hallowed by the memory of the sacred dead." The church is an "atmosphere" as well as a place. Place conditions both the speaker's method and the audience's reaction. People do not react in a smoke-filled room the way they do in the restrained atmosphere of the Senate gallery.

---

[30]*A Discourse in Commemoration of the Lives and Services of John Adams & Thomas Jefferson, Delivered in Faneuil Hall, Boston, August 2, 1826* (Boston: Cummings, Hilliard & Co., 1826), p. 34.

I do not intend to minimize the purely physical aspect of place, for this is sometimes important, of course. Comfort and discomfort, audibility or inaudibility may take on considerable proportions. Webster, with 100,000 people milling over Bunker Hill could not have been expected to be talking to all of them, and an inaugural crowd in a chill wind is not likely to be giving itself completely to the speaker no matter how superlative his genius. No one would expect the playing of a concerto to produce the same effect in a run-down basement room of an apartment-hotel as it does in Carnegie Hall. And no one believes that a painting hung on just any wall will look well. In evaluating speeches, the aspect of place must be recognized as a conditioning factor. "The world will little note, nor long remember what we say here, but it can never forget what they did here," Lincoln observed at Gettysburg, and generations have murmured the words as they have explored the grounds.

Fourth, is the consideration of purpose. After examining the debates in the Constitutional Convention of 1787, the historians Samuel Eliot Morison and Henry Steele Commager concluded that "the main, central and determining consideration that appears throughout the debates, is to erect a government that would be neither too strong nor too shocking to popular prejudices for adoption, and yet be sufficiently strong and well-contrived to work."[31] This analysis highlights the significant role that *purpose* plays in evaluating speech-making. At the outset, it indicates that the finished Constitutional product did not represent anyone's notion of the perfect constitution, but what the Constitutional fathers thought they could get accepted. Presumably all language is uttered with some purpose, whether it be the salutation, "Good morning," or the frankly evangelistic sermon on Sunday. These purposes control choices of materials. Whatever the end the speaker has in mind, his specific purpose is to speak with persuasive effect toward that end; his available resources for persuasion are those which can be directed toward fulfillment of purpose.

The consideration of purpose undoubtedly misleads the critics more often than any other aspect of speaking. In an age oriented toward quick and tangible evidences of success, the critic has tended to make the specific accomplishment of ends the test of rhetorical effectiveness. The number of votes in the ballot box, the amount of money collected as a result of a promotion campaign are taken to be the measure of effectiveness. They are taken to represent the fulfillment of purpose. James Hadley noted the trend in the nineteenth century and expressed concern: "Some have a simple test, and that is persuasiveness; the best oration is the most persuasive, and *vice versa,* the most persuasive is the best; for it best fulfils the end of eloquence, which is persuasion." With shrewd good sense and discrimination, Hadley continued: "The eloquence of Mike Walsh has an effect as persuasive on the

---

[31]Samuel Eliot Morison and Henry Steele Commager, *The Growth of the American Republic* (3rd ed.; New York: Oxford University Press, 1942), I, 281.

collective blackguardism of New York as the eloquence of Daniel Webster has on the collective dignity and learning of the Senate or the Supreme Court. Should we therefore decide that one is no higher than the other? Now persuasiveness ... is indeed an indispensable element in true eloquence. But there is another element ... and that is artistic perfection. ..."[32] In other words, the purpose of the speaker is to discover the available means of persuasion and the appropriate questions are: Did he discover them? What is their quality?

The critic who makes the fulfillment of specific purpose the only test of eloquence is not merely misguided, he is indeed attempting the impossible. As Leonard Bloomfield has observed, "persuasive and ... powerful [as] ... effect may be, it is nearly always uncertain."[33] He further observes: "In the long run, anything which adds to the viability of language has also an indirect but more pervasive effect. Even acts of speech that do not prompt any particular immediate response, may change the predisposition of the hearer for further responses: a beautiful poem, for instance, may make the hearer more sensitive to later stimuli. The general refinement and intensification of human response requires a great deal of linguistic interaction. Education or culture, or whatever name we choose to give it, depends upon the repetition and publication of a vast amount of speech."[34]

Clearly, the speaker should not be judged by the fulfillment of specific purpose alone. Who can know how many sinners were "almost" saved as a result of a revival service of Billy Graham? The function of the preacher is to use his talents toward this end, and it is by the talents, not by the accomplishment of the end merely that he should be judged. The odds against the accomplishment of a specific end may be insurmountable. Was Lincoln's First Inaugural rhetorically inferior because it did not prevent the Civil War? The eye of the critic must be focused on the methods used by the speaker and not merely on the ends achieved. It is reason and judgment, not a comptometer, that make a man a critic.

Fifth, is the factor of time and timing. Just as civilizations rise, develop, and decline, so too problems rise, grow in dimension, yield to solution, and eventually give way to other problems. Time represents a stage in the life of problems. It reflects itself in both the proposition of the speaker and in his mode of handling the problem. It likewise represents a stage in the life of feelings toward a proposition. Anyone knows that he is more susceptible to argument and discussion at one time than at another. A man who has just had lunch is not likely to become excited over the promise of release from hunger. A solution presented either prematurely or tardily will be found

---

[32]James Hadley, "Is Ancient Eloquence Superior to Modern?" *Essays, Philosophical and Critical* (New York: Holt & Williams, 1873), p. 349.

[33]Leonard Bloomfield, "Linguistic Aspects of Science," *International Encyclopedia of Unified Science,* Vol. I, No. 4, pp. 16, 17.

[34]Leonard Bloomfield, *Language* (New York: Henry Holt & Co., 1938), p. 41.

wanting. The man with an answer at the time when people are searching for an answer is in a much more effective position rhetorically than the man who gives an answer after doubt has already been resolved, or who offers one before the problem has become acute.

But not only are the substance of a speech and the feelings of an audience conditioned by *time,* the mode of handling data is likewise conditioned. Mode of handling is a product of a culture at a given time. The critic who tends to write off the florid style of the nineteenth-century is in effect saying that according to his "more enlightened" twentieth-century taste, the nineteenth-century mode of handling was inferior. Not many of us look with undimmed eyes upon the glories of nature and describe what we see. We look with eyes conditioned to see in terms of the language habits we have inherited. The ornate language of the nineteenth-century was shared by a multitude of people in the century, and there is little reason to suppose that it was not as persuasive as the language of the twentieth-century. Tastes vary with the times. The real question for the critic is: Does the mode of handling represent the tastes of the time? Is it adjusted to the intellectual development and the habits of the hearer? Is it in harmony with aesthetic values of the time? In the poetic age of the translators of the King James Version of the Bible, the translators wrote in God's description of the battle horse to Job:

> Hast thou given the horse strength? Hast thou clothed his neck with thunder?...The glory of his nostrils is terrible. . . . He saith among the trumpets, Ha, Ha.

Twentieth-century translators, heeding the injunction to produce a Bible "written in language direct and clear and meaningful to people today" write as follows:

> Do you give the horse his might? Do you clothe his neck with strength?...His majestic snorting is terrible. . . .When the trumpet sounds, he says, 'Aha![35]

In both cases, presumably, we have the language of the people, designed to have an impact on the readers in their own centuries. Does anyone really believe the new rendering of the passage is superior? A rhetorical critic may note differences in quality, to be sure, but the scale by which one determines persuasive effect must be a scale adjusted to the time in which the product was made.

In our discussion so far we have, in the main, been concerned with consideration of the extra-verbal aspects of persuasion. We come now to the verbal instrument itself. According to George Campbell, astute eighteenth-century rhetorical theorist and practitioner of the art of rhetoric, "there are

---

[35]See Dwight MacDonald, "The Bible in Modern Undress," *The New Yorker* (November 14, 1953), pp. 179, 187.

two things in every discourse which principally claim our attention, the sense and the expression; or in other words, the thought and the symbol by which it is communicated. These may be said to constitute the soul and the body of an oration. . . ."[36]

Both ancient and contemporary thought might question the dichotomy between "the sense and the expression" as indicated by Campbell. From Aristotle to modern times competent critics have recognized that "there can be no distinction drawn, save in reflection, between form and substance. The work itself *is* matter formed. . . ."[37] The contemporary philosopher, Jordan, notes that "At the point of the abstract ultimate what is said . . . and the way it is said . . . may be the same thing. . . ."[38] Experience, of course, reveals that so united are matter and form that when a speaker struggles to make his thoughts clear but fails, he in fact says something else.

Recognizing the inseparability of matter and form in any art, we may, nevertheless, in "reflection," consider the work in terms of constituents, arguments, broad structural pattern, and particular stylistic features.

Let us first look at the substance of a speech. Persuasion requires choices among alternatives. The speech presumably wlll consist of persuasions to induce acceptance of the speaker's point of view. Presumably this point of view is directed toward some ultimate Good. Hence, the speaker's persuasions represent directly or by implication his philosophic outlook and commitment. These persuasions will be revealed verbally in statements of fact and of opinion. "Facts cannot be selected without some personal conviction as to what is truth,"[39] observes the historian, Allan Nevins. Likewise, Karl Wallace notes: "Truth is a word I shall use to describe the moment of certainty, or commitment, or decision which signals the resolution of doubt. The decision is revealed verbally as a statement of opinion or value, or as a statement of fact."[40] Accordingly, Richard Weaver remarks: "there is no honest rhetoric without a preceding dialectic,"[41] that is, without an attempt to discover truth. Thus, the critic is brought face to face with the necessity of understanding and discriminating among the ideas or the truths to which the speaker has committed himself. But to evaluate the speaker's philosophy involves the critic in a discrimination of ethical values. The warning of Baskerville is well taken: ". . . today's critic often side-steps inquiry into the basic soundness of the speaker's position, offering the excuse that truth is relative, that everyone is entitled to his own opinion, and that the rhetorical

---

[36]*The Philosophy of Rhetoric* (New ed, with the Author's Last Additions and Corrections; Edinburgh: Neill & Co., for Archibald Constable & Co., and John Fairbairn, Edinburgh; and T. Cadwell & W. Davies, London, 1816), I, 82, 83.

[37]John Dewey, *Art as Experience* (New York: Minton, Balch & Co., ©1934), p. 109.

[38]E. Jordan, *Essays in Criticism* (Chicago: University of Chicago Press, 1952), p. 193.

[39]Allan Nevins, *The Gateway to History* (Boston: D. C. Heath & Co., 1938), p. 38.

[40]Karl R. Wallace, "The Field of Speech, 1953: An Overview" (A Speech, Delivered July 17, 1953, Summer Speech Conference, University of Michigan, Ann Arbor, Michigan [MS University of Illinois, Department of Speech]), p. 10.

[41]Richard M. Weaver, *The Ethics of Rhetoric* (Chicago: Henry Regnery Co., 1953), p. 25.

critic's task is to describe and evaluate the orator's skill in his craft and not to become entangled in complex ethical considerations."[42]

The simple fact is that audiences do not respond alike to any and every opinion, that whereas the critic may think it not his function to tangle with the problem of truth and the weight of ideas, audiences which determine the degree of persuasion do so involve themselves with these matters. Ideas are means of persuasion. Emerson responding to Webster's 7th of March speech was keenly aware of Webster's philosophic position: "Nobody doubts that there were good and plausible things to be said on the part of the South. But this is not a question of ingenuity, not a question of syllogisms, but of sides."[43] For Emerson there was always "the previous question: How came you on that side? Your argument is ingenious, your language copious, your illustrations brilliant, but your major proposition palpably absurd. Will you establish a lie?"[44] In evaluating a sermon of an American churchman, a critic recently observed: "His arguments were specious, but his rhetoric was good." That rhetoric can consist of specious arguments as well as sound ones no one will question. But that the validity and the truth of the argument has nothing to do with pronouncing the rhetoric "good" is, indeed, dubious.

The critic's function is to examine the speaker's premises, stated or implied, and to examine the truth of those premises. Inevitably he must ask such questions as: Does the orator argue from an abiding concept of the "nature of things"? from a conception of expediency? from the authority of history? from similitude? from transcendental grounds?

There are conventional means for evaluating the quality of premises. Does the premise presented "correspond" to data which may be revealed to the senses of observers? Does the truth of a premise yield to a pragmatic test? Is the truth of a premise "believed" by the many? Is the truth of a premise "self-evident"?[45] However much the critic may wish to escape discriminating among values, as an effective rhetorical critic he cannot do so.

This may not be the place to argue for any of the particular criteria of truth used through the ages. One may say that great and good men have from time to time used all of these tests, depending upon their general philosophic position. We do not ask too much when we ask a critic to reveal his philosophic position by his choice of criteria for evaluating premises. In fact, we may be paving the way for critical commentary vastly richer and more cogent than if the bases of evaluation were ignored.

Nor is the argumentative substance of the speech the critic's only concern. Persuasion represents deliberate manipulation of symbols. Symbols

---

[42]Barnet Baskerville, "Emerson as a Critic of Oratory," *The Southern Speech Journal,* XVIII (March, 1953), 161.

[43]*The Complete Works of Ralph Waldo Emerson,* ed. Edward Waldo Emerson (Centenary ed.; Boston: Houghton Mifflin & Co., 1903), XII, 225.

[44]"Eloquence," *ibid.,* VIII, 131.

[45]See C. J. Ducasse, "Propositions, Truth, and the Ultimate Criterion of Truth," *Philosophy and Phenomenological Research,* V (September-June, 1943, 1944), 317-40.

contain not only rational meanings. They contain experience also and represent attempts to create and release emotional tensions. Woven into the substance of argument are directives to action, terms of interpretation and valuation. Persuasion recognizes men to be creatures of desire; it also recognizes that desire provides a basis for action. Hence, the speaker's persuasions represent techniques for awakening and satisfying desire. Furthermore, within every culture are values that have authority. Thus, "virtue" was the ultimate Good for the Greeks; "courage," an ultimate Good for the Romans; "duty," an ultimate Good in early American Christian civilization. The critic examines the texture of persuasive compositions for those symbols of authority designed to evoke response. The perceptive critic must observe that since motives are not fixed, these authoritative symbols change from age to age. Whereas an early Christian civilization responded to appeals to action, presented in the name of "duty," a later civilization is activated to a greater degree by the promise of earthly "progress." On an ethical scale, we may find considerable difference between the lowest motive and the highest motive to which men wlll respond. The discerning critic must not only assess both extremes but he must locate the center of gravity. He need not deny the persuasive value of low motives, but he has no moral obligation to sanction the use of such motives under the label of "good" rhetoric.

"The most minute study, the widest experience in the investigation of human actions and their motives," says Gamaliel Bradford, "only make us feel more and more the shifting, terrible uncertainty of the ground under our feet."[46] The difficulty of the task gives no warrant to the critic to shirk his responsibility. Surveying the rhetoric of Hitler's *Mein Kampf,* Kenneth Burke notes: "Here is the testament of a man who swung a great people into his wake. Let us watch it carefully, and let us watch it, not merely to discover some grounds for prophesying what political move is to follow Munich, and what move to follow that move, etc.; let us try also to discover what kind of 'medicine' this medicine-man has concocted, that we may know, with greater accuracy, exactly what to guard against, if we are to forestall the concocting of similar medicine in America."[47] Such an observation suggests the responsibility of the critic. His place should be in the vanguard, not in the rear—wise-after-the-fact. He should be ready to alert a people, to warn what devices of exploitation are being exercised, by what skillful manipulations of motives men are being directed to or dissuaded from courses of action. James G. Randall asks: Was the willful manipulation of men's minds by the wily a factor in the cause of the Civil War? Is it a factor in most wars?[48] The careful examination of motives must not merely furnish an amusing pastime for the

---

[46]Cited in Allan Nevins, *op. cit.,* p. 327.
[47]"The Rhetoric of Hitler's 'Battle,' " in his *The Philosophy of Literary Form* (Baton Rouge, Louisiana: Louisiana State University Press, 1941), p. 191.
[48]J. G. Randall, "A Blundering Generation," in his *Lincoln, The Liberal Statesman* (New York: Dodd, Mead & Co., 1947), pp. 36-64.

critic; it is his urgent responsibility.

Pursuing our examination of aspects of form, we turn "in reflection" to the aspect of structure. Literary art, like all art, observes Daiches, "communicates significance through patterns."[49] A tragedy unravels through a pattern of exposition, complicating circumstances, climax, and denouement. A detective story lays down premises and takes its deductive course. The speech also is a structured organism and this structure must be a concern of the critic. By structure we mean, as Whitehead has suggested, "that eye for the whole chessboard, for the bearing of one set of ideas on another."[50] In speechmaking this has traditionally been called *dispositio*. Aristotle defined it as "the arrangement of that which has parts, in respect of place, or of potency or of kind."[51]

Probably all people need forms, for "We take delight in recognition."[52] Whether we speak a word, a sentence, or a whole speech, intelligibility depends on form. To borrow an ancient illustration, we recognize a bronze pitcher only after it has taken form from a mass of bronze and *become* a bronze pitcher.[53] In the laboratory, speech takes on a visual shape, as is shown by spectograph readings. In ordinary communication, meanings are in part determined by organization. Thus, "an rhetoric art is" yields intelligibility by assembling the elements: Rhetoric is an art.

The critic must observe the contribution made by thought pattern to the effectiveness of the whole. A thought pattern is something more than external manifestation of a beginning, a middle, and an end. It is a functional balancing of parts against each other, a determination of the relative strength of arguments. It is reflected in proportion and placing. The speaker who sandwiches weak arguments between strong arguments has at least considered force as a factor in persuasion. Structure reveals the speaker's assessment of his audience in the placement of parts, whether they are partisans, neutrals, or opponents, or are a significant mixture of two or more. To that extent, at least, it represents the psychology of the audience rather than the psychology of the speaker.[54]

We come finally to that most elusive of all aspects of the speaking act— style, still another aspect of form. Thonssen and Baird, referring to a rhetorical critic of the last century, have remarked, "Jebb is more deeply concerned with the orator's style than are most present-day critics. In this

---

[49]David Daiches, *A Study of Literature for Readers and Critics* (Ithaca, New York: Cornell University Press, 1948), p. 77.
[50]A. N. Whitehead, *The Aims of Education & Other Essays* (New York: The Macmillan Co., 1929), p. 18.
[51]*Metaphysica, op. cit.,* D. 19, 1022ᵇ.
[52]Donald A. Stauffer, "Introduction: The Intent of the Critic," *op. cit.,* p. 24.
[53]Aristotle *Metaphysica,* D. 3. 1070ᵃ.
[54]See Kenneth Burke, "Psychology and Form," in *Counter-Statement* (2nd ed.; Los Altos, California: Hermes Publications, 1953), p. 31.
[55]Lester Thonssen and A. Craig Baird, *op. cit.,* p. 257.

regard, he is perhaps, less the rhetorical and more the literary critic."[55] Rhetorical critics unfortunately tend to be less interested in style than they ought to be, for, as Lasswell has noted, "style is an indispensable feature of every configuration of meaning in any process of communication."[56]

Partly because of the difficulty, and partly because of confusion with the function of literary critics, contemporary rhetorical critics have given the matter little attention. Preoccupation with trying to distinguish written from oral style has often yielded results both fruitless and misleading. "Not only are contemporary critics . . . unable to distinguish oral from written style," observes Schrader, "but they are also confused as to the nature of style itself."[57] "Their statements are often based on untenable assumptions, and their conclusions are even contradictory."[58]

If, as Wichelns has remarked, the problem of the orator is "so to present ideas as to bring them into the consciousness of his hearers,"[59] the neglect of style becomes serious, and mistaken notions about it equally hazardous.

It is significant that the two living orators who have achieved greatest distinction for their oratory are both sensitive stylists. Churchill has a feeling for the nobility of the English sentence, and Stevenson's style became a campaign issue in the election of 1952. In general, the style of our orators has been so undistinguished as to escape the notice of listeners, but this may in part account for the lack of impact that many speakers have had on their age. It does not justify the neglect of style by rhetorical critics. If the testimony of the centuries to the importance of style needed support, we could find it in an unsuspected source—from one of the great atomic scientists of the twentieth-century. Said J. Robert Oppenheimer:

> The problem of doing justice to the implicit, the imponderable and the unknown is, of course, not unique to politics. It is always with us in science, it is with us in the most trivial of personal affairs, and it is one of the great problems of writing and of all forms of art. The means by which it is solved is sometimes called style. It is style which complements affirmation with limitation and with humility; it is style which makes it possible to act effectively, but not absolutely; it is style which, in the domain of foreign policy, enables us to find a harmony between the pursuit of ends essential to us and the regard for the views, the sensibilities, the aspirations of those to whom the problem may appear in another light; it is above all style through which power defers to reason.[60]

[56]Harold Lasswell, Nathan Leites, and Associates, *Language of Politics* (New York: George W. Stewart, Publishers, Inc., 1949), p. 38.

[57]Helen Wheatley Schrader, "A Linguistic Approach to the Study of Rhetorical Style" (Ph.D. dissertation, Northwestern University, 1949), p. 17.

[58]*Ibid.,* p. 15.

[59]"The Literary Criticism of Oratory," *op. cit.,* p. 190.

[60]"The Open Mind," *The Bulletin of the Atomic Scientists,* V, No. 1 (January, 1949), 5.

Thus, in its simplest manifestation, style is a mode of "ingratiation";[61] in its most complex aspect it is the "ultimate morality of mind."[62] It is an "aesthetic sense" says Whitehead, "based on admiration for the direct attainment of a foreseen end, simply and without waste." It is an index of a preference for "good work."[63]

That audiences have value systems pertaining to style is well known. Two thousand years ago Aristotle called attention to reaction tendencies of listeners in regard to stylistic matters: "The effect which lectures produce on a hearer depends on his habits; for we demand the language we are accustomed to, and that which is different from this seems not in keeping but somewhat unintelligible and foreign because of its unwontedness. . . . Thus some people do not listen to a speaker unless he speaks mathematically, others unless he gives instances, while others expect him to cite a poet as a witness. And some want to have everything done accurately, while others are annoyed with accuracy, either because they cannot follow the connexion of thoughts or because they regard it as pettifoggery."[64]

Aristotle's statement has been proved valid by the test of centuries. The language of persuasion must be conditioned by the needs of the audience, and the needs of the audience differ considerably. As we remarked earlier, the ideals of any age, regarding style, may differ. The late John Livingston Lowes said of the King James Version of the Bible: "Its phraseology has become part and parcel of our common tongue—bone of its bone and flesh of its flesh. Its rhythms and cadences, its turns of speech, its familiar imagery, its very words, are woven into the texture of our literature, prose and poetry alike. . . . The English of the Bible . . . is characterized not merely by a homely vigour and pithiness of phrase, but also by a singular nobility of diction and by a rhythmic quality which is, I think, unrivalled in its beauty."[65] The twentieth-century revisers of the Bible were enjoined to "combine accuracy with the simplicity, directness, and spiritual power" of the King James Version, as well as to make it "more readable for the American public of today."[66]

Style is in no sense magic. It is rather a manifestation of a speaker's or writer's temper and outlook. It has the capacity to name objects, to evaluate them, and to incite feelings toward them. In its objective manifestations it pertains to the selection of words and the ordering of them, and in this a preference for "good work" may be shown.

"Style to be good must be clear," notes Aristotle, "as is proved by the fact

---

[61]Kenneth Burke, Permanence and Change (New York: The New Republic, 1935), p. 71.
[62]A. N. Whitehead, op. cit., p. 19.
[63]Ibid., p. 19.
[64]Metaphysica, a. 3. 995ᵃ.
[65]"The Noblest Monument of English Prose," in his Essays in Appreciation (Boston: Houghton Mifflin Co., 1936), pp. 3-5, passim.
[66]Dwight MacDonald, op. cit., p. 175.

that speech which fails to convey a plain meaning will fail to do just what a speech has to do."[67] Beyond clearness, of course, lie other properties: appropriateness, distinctive language constructions, rhythm. All of these have concern for the analyst of rhetorical style, for they are means by which the orator reaches the minds of the listener. They are means by which he seeks identification and ingratiation.

For want of better methods, the rhetorical critic sometimes satisfies himself with a simple enumeration of stylistic devices of the speaker. Unless the enumerations are particularizations of the pervasive tones and effects sought by the speaker, such enumeration probably serves little purpose. We need to ask: What is language doing to further the end of ingratiation or identification? If, for instance, the prevailing tone of a speech is "humorous," we might expect language to behave in such a way as to produce humor. Hence, the rhetorical critic would look to language constructions, the diction, the characteristics of rhythm which contribute to the prevailing tone. If style is the man himself, then a close scrutiny of the details of style should tell us what manner of man is doing the speaking, and in what relationship he conceives himself to be with his audience. If it is style which "complements affirmation with limitation and with humility"; if it is style which "makes it possible to act effectively, but not absolutely"; if it is style which "in the domain of foreign policy, enables us to find a harmony between the pursuit of ends essential to us, and the regard for the views, the sensibilities, the aspirations of those to whom the problem may appear in another light"; if it is style "through which power defers to reason"—then, to look to style for manifestations of the groundswells and tensions of our times, for manifestations of healthy states and unhealthy ones must become the imperative task of the critic concerned with the implications of his art for the nation and the world. May not the simple metaphor be the harbinger of death and destruction, or the cock's crow of an era of good feeling as well as a literary tool in the grammar books?

These are the ingredients of the rhetorical situation which must be examined for their contribution to the persuasive efficacy of the whole. As one may observe, some of them are verbal aspects, others are nonverbal. Just as in drama many elements are harmonized to give delight to an audience, so too in the rhetorical situation many elements contribute to the end of persuasion. The total organism is the concern of the critic.

Evaluating Speeches of the Past

Whether the efforts of the critic are focused on speaking events in which he is a participant or on speaking events of the past, the problem is essentially the same. His aims are to evaluate rhetorical effort or to account

---

[67]*Rhetorica*, iii, 2. 1404[b].

for effectiveness or ineffectiveness in rhetorical situations. When the critic centers his attention on events of the past, he discovers that his problem increases considerably. He is confronted with the task of trying to see the orator perfecting a strategy to encompass a situation in which he himself is an actor. Not only do the speeches of public men represent the aspirations of the nation, they foreshadow the shape of things to come. Everyone recalls the majestic peroration of Lincoln's address at Gettysburg, "that this nation, under God, shall have a new birth of freedom—and that government of the people, by the people, for the people, shall not perish from the earth." It was not only a summing-up, it was a direction for the future. "Seated on the roaring loom of time," says Nevins, "for six thousand years man has woven a seamless garment. But that garment is invisible and intangible save where the dyes of written history fall upon it, and forever preserve it as a possession of generations to come."[68]

When a student concerns himself with the speeches of the past, he tries to obtain a view of the conditions, limitations, and potentialities of the leadership of speakers in all spheres, political, economic, social, cultural. He tries to discover the ideas which have been generated, the conditions of their acceptance or rejection, the scope, dimension, and intensity of concerted action. The critic of rhetoric must endeavor to see events in terms of their yet unactualized future, free from all events which were subsequent. To recover the implications of time, place, attitudes of both speaker and audience, the symbolic fitness of the speaker, the level of cultural development and taste becomes an almost insurmountable task. Not only are the nonverbal aspects of the situation capricious, but the verbal aspects are also fraught with difficulties. What was said on any given occasion may become quite blurred by the passing of time, or by the editorial hand of publishers and relatives of speakers who often want to make the speaker appear in light other than that which glowed at the time. The critic must search for the authentic record, however stony the path which leads to its discovery. If one is not evaluating the original, he is obviously evaluating something different from the original. The crumbling ruins of the Parthenon, however suggestive they may be of the beauty of the original structure, leave the spectator with something to be desired, and the Elgin marbles in the British Museum are not a satisfying substitute.

Rhetoric being essentially a process whereby means are adapted to ends, it is imperative that the critic not only know what the ends were but what resources were available at the time to secure these ends. To the extent that the critic is able to determine this, he may function effectively.

"Our common humanity is best studied in the most eminent examples that it has produced of every type of human excellence,"[69] observed the historian

---

[68] Allan Nevins, *op. cit.*, p. 5.
[69] Cited in Morris R. Cohen, *The Meaning of Human History* (La Salle, Illinois: Open Court Publishing Co., 1947), p. 224.

H. W. C. Davis. Human excellence has sometimes manifested itself in speech-making. Human effort has sometimes been directed to the end of giving clearer vision and safer passage into an unknown future. In this, the orator has shared eminently. Sometimes asserting or reasserting human values, sometimes helping to resolve conflicts of national or international scope and dimension, the speaker has through his art attempted to point the way to a better Life. In searching for effective methods for evaluating the impact of words, we search for methods whereby we may criticize present assumptions about human behavior and the forces which have operated to produce our culture.

The Practice
of Rhetorical Criticism

by Edwin Black

What is rhetorical criticism? What constitutes its distinctiveness? How, if at all, does it differ from any other sort of criticism? To answer these questions we must examine the general practice of rhetorical criticism.

To begin with the obvious, rhetorical criticism is the criticism of rhetorical discourses. This is not the profoundest of definitions, but it is not without its overtones, and we may profit by lingering on the term "rhetorical discourse." Because rhetorical critics frequently belong to academic departments of speech, rhetorical discourses are sometimes taken to be orations. Not all critics concur in this view.

> From the beginning of publication in writing . . . essentially rhetorical performances, whether already spoken or to be spoken, have been committed to paper and circulated to be read rather than heard—from Isocrates' *Panathenaicus* or Christ's *Sermon on the Mount* to Eisenhower's message on the state of the nation. Furthermore, for centuries now, especially since the invention and cheapening of the art of printing, the agitator, the teacher, the preacher, the wielder of public opinion has used the press quite independently of the platform. Hence, obviously, rhetoric must be understood to be the rationale of informative and suasory discourse both spoken and written . . .[1]

There is in this argument a needful destruction of the too tidy distinction between spoken and written discourse. Patently, the pamphlet of the Watch Tower Society is more closely related to the sermon than to the lyric poem, though it has a mechanical medium of expression in common with the latter. Patently, the *Iliad* is more closely related to the novel than to the ceremonial oration, despite its existence in an oral tradition for some years before its having been written at last. To equate rhetorical discourse with spoken discourse produces too many paradoxes. Whatever else the nature of rhetorical discourse, it is assuredly not to be confined exclusively to the spoken

---

Reprinted from *Rhetorical Criticism*. (Madison, WS: The Univ. of Wisconsin Press, 1965). Used with permission.
[1] Donald C. Bryant, "Rhetoric: Its Functions and Its Scope," *Quarterly Journal of Speech*, XXXIX (December 1953), p. 407.

word. It is a kind of discourse, simply. The means by which the discourse is disseminated have no bearing on the definition.

Whether we can take rhetorical discourse to be that discourse which is informative and suasory is open to question. Informative discourse is not usually associated with rhetoric, either historically or at present. It is true that a high proportion of the current textbooks on public speaking contain treatments of exposition, but the subject is so uniformly absent in the rhetorical theories of the past and the rhetorical criticism of the present that its presence in textbooks can be attributed to expedient or commercial considerations.

In the tradition that can be traced from Plato and Aristotle through Campbell in the eighteenth century and Whately in the nineteenth to Kenneth Burke in our own time, only two major writers on rhetoric have involved informative as well as persuasive discourse in their definitions of rhetoric: Quintilian and Campbell.

Quintilian, in his review of the definitions of rhetoric that his Greek and Roman predecessors had expounded, found persuasion or persuasive speaking to be the explicit or implied scope of every one.[2] Though Quintilian's own definition of rhetoric—"the science of speaking well"[3]—does not confine rhetoric to persuasive discourse alone, it is only persuasive discourse that Quintilian has in mind throughout his treatise. Nowhere does he suggest that "neutral" exposition is a distinctive genre of discourse to be included within the province of rhetoric. His most systematic treatment of expository speaking makes that type of address a phase in the development of forensic appeals, always with a persuasive end in view.[4]

George Campbell opens his treatise by defining eloquence as "that art or talent by which discourse is adapted to its end,"[5] a definition which certainly leaves room for expository discourse to be a part of rhetoric. He goes on to observe: "All the ends of speaking are reducible to four; every speech intended to enlighten the understanding, to please the imagination, to move the passions, or to influence the will."[6] But Campbell soon makes it clear that he does not view these "ends of speaking" as coordinates, which would make expository discourse, designed to "enlighten the understanding," a part of rhetoric. Rather, Campbell has a hierarchical view of these ends.

> In general it may be asserted, that each preceding species in the order above exhibited, is preparatory to the subsequent; that each subsequent species is founded on the preceding; and that thus they ascend in a regular progression. Knowledge, the object of the intellect, furnisheth materials for the fancy; the fancy culls, compounds,

[2] Quintilian, *Institutio Oratoria*, H. E. Butler, trans. (London, 1953), bk. ii, ch. 15.
[3] *Ibid.*, bk. i, p. 319.
[4] *Ibid.*, bk. iv, ch. 2.
[5] George Campbell, *The Philosophy of Rhetoric* (Oxford, England, 1838), p. 1.
[6] *Ibid.*

and by herminic art, disposes these materials so as to affect the passions; the passions are the natural spurs to volition or action, and so need only to be right directed.[7]

The enlightening of the understanding is, then, a legitimate end of rhetorical discourse to Campbell, but it is an end that interests him only insofar as it obtains a persuasive effect. Campbell's interest is betrayed when he comes to consider the faculties of understanding, imagination, memory, and passion. A scant paragraph is devoted to "understanding,"[8] while the other faculties receive considerably fuller treatment.[9] Further, even this paragraph treats of exposition as a preliminary to persuasion.

> . . . the first thing to be studied by the speaker is, that his *arguments* be understood. If they be unintelligible, the cause must be either in the sense or in the expression. It lies in the sense, if the *mediums of proof* be such as the hearers are unacquainted with; that is, if the ideas introduced be either without the sphere of their knowledge, or too abstract for their apprehension and habits of thinking. It lies in the sense, likewise, if the train of reasoning (though no unusual ideas should be introduced) be longer, or more complex, or more intricate, than they are accustomed to. But as the *fitness of the arguments* in these respects, depends on the capacity, education, and attainments of the hearers, which in different orders of men are different, this properly belongs to the consideration which the speaker ought to have of his audience, not as men in general, but as such men in particular. The obscurity which ariseth from the expression will come in course to be considered in the sequel.[10]

The sequel Campbell promises is the sixth chapter of *The Philosophy of Rhetoric,* "Of Perspicuity." It is a chapter full of cogent insights into the causes of obscurity and sound advice on the attainment of clarity in style, but it is not a chapter focussed on expository discourse. Most of the examples Campbell quotes in the chapter are statements with persuasive intent. He makes it clear that he does not associate perspicuity with expository discourse, but regards it as a necessary characteristic of style in any genre,". . . whatever be the ultimate intention of the orator, to inform, to convince, to please, to move, or to persuade."[11] We have in Campbell, then, one of the very few rhetorical theorists whose conception of rhetoric is not theoretically confined to persuasive discourse, and even Campbell makes persuasion the center and overriding interest of his theory.

---

[7] *Ibid.,* p. 2.
[8] *Ibid.,* p. 75.
[9] *Ibid.,* pp. 75-84.
[10] *Ibid.,* p. 75. Italics mine.
[11] Campbell, *op. cit.,* p. 222.

When we turn from the two rhetorical theorists who seem most likely to give serious attention to expository discourse and view the practice of contemporary professional critics, we find even more marked the tendency to identify works of rhetoric as persuasive discourses. The three volumes, *A History and Criticism of American Public Address,* contain no essays on speakers whose public discourses were predominantly expository rather than persuasive.[12] The critical essays appearing in the *Quarterly Journal of Speech* reveal the same hiatus. In the decade beginning with 1950, there were no studies of expository speakers in that journal, no studies even of rhetorical situations where expository discourse could be expected to predominate, such as the classroom, the scientific meeting, the occasion of the doctrinal sermon. Essays in rhetorical criticism focus on persuasive speakers or discourses, and the weight of the rhetorical tradition too falls in that direction. Consequently, we are obliged to conclude that the subject matter of rhetorical criticism is persuasive discourse.

I. A. Richards has suggested a reason for the exclusive association of rhetoric with persuasive discourse in observing that ". . . neutral exposition is a very special limited use of language, comparatively a late development . . ."[13] Whatever the reason, the association exists, and if we are to survey accurately the practice of rhetorical criticism, we must accept it as a fact.

Of course, it is important to be clear about how rhetorical discourse is to be persuasive. Persuasive in this sense refers to intent, not necessarily to accomplishment. Rhetorical discourses are those discourses, spoken or written, which aim to influence men. Whether a given discourse actually exerts an influence has no bearing on whether it is rhetorical.

At this point we must note some objections that may be raised to defining rhetorical discourses as discourses "which aim to influence men." The concepts of aim or intent or purpose are all peculiarly anthropomorphic, and one may object that, although men can be described as having aims, intentions, or purposes, it is only figurative to ascribe them to things, such as discourses. It is true that metaphors are extraordinarily dangerous and sometimes misleading in speculative writing inasmuch as they can jeopardize the precision of an objective description. Moreover, appearances are notoriously deceptive. What may appear to be a man's intentions can turn out to be mistaken. Men often blunder, or they dissemble; they say one thing and mean something else, and consequently to read the aim or purpose of a man in the text of his writing is to be susceptible to deception. As one author has put it: "Too often we look to the *message* (speech, manuscript, play, advertisement) in order to determine communicative purpose. *From a behaviorist's point of view, it is more useful to define purpose as the goal of a creator or receiver of a message, rather than as the property of the message*

---

[12]William Norwood Brigance, ed., vols. I & II (New York, 1943); and Marie Kathryn Hochmuth, ed., vol. III, *A History and Criticism of American Public Address* (New York, 1955).
[13]I. A. Richards, *The Philosophy of Rhetoric* (New York, 1936), p. 40.

itself."[14]

These objections have a measure of validity. It is perfectly true that the critic, determining the purpose of a text from evidence the text itself provides, can be mistaken. There is a margin for error and for disagreement in this phase of criticism. The essential question, however, is not whether mistakes can be made in attributing aim or intent or purpose to a text, but whether these mistakes occur often enough to force a prudent man to abandon the attempt. Is there, in sum, any sense to finding the aim of a discourse in evidence that the discourse itself provides?

Our answer lies in a postulate that must be found at the foundation of any system of rhetorical criticism. That postulate is that there will be a correspondence among the intentions of a communicator, the characteristics of his discourse, and the reactions of his auditors to that discourse. This postulate is justified by the fact that to deny it is to deny the possibility of language, as we ordinarily understand that term.

If there is no correspondence between the intentions of a communicator and the characteristics of his discourse, then expression is impossible. We grant this relationship when, wanting to go to the left, we tell the taxi driver, "Turn left." We know that the phrase, "Turn left," will correspond to our intentions in expressing those intentions better than any other sounds we could make. If there is no correspondence between the characteristics of a discourse and the reactions of auditors to it, then communication is impossible. We commonly grant this relationship too when, having said, "Turn left," we expect the taxi driver to execute a certain, prescribed maneuver.

Undoubtedly there are occasions when parts of this correspondence break down. Perhaps a passenger will say, "Turn left," when he really wants to go to the right, but he is momentarily confused. Or perhaps the taxi driver will turn right after he has been instructed to turn left, for the same reason. The slap on the back from the used car salesman does not really express his affection, and we sometimes realize it. The friendly greeting from the politician during his campaign is not an invariable sign of his goodwill. Mistakes happen, deceptions occur; the system sometimes collapses. That is why we must grant a margin for error in the critical findings postulated on this correspondence. But the important point is that we do regard such breakdowns in the system as exceptional, and almost every waking moment of our lives is spent with faith in the postulate. It is this postulate that makes possible our definition of rhetorical discourse as discourse that aims to influence. We have every reason for seeking the aims or purposes of a discourse, because we know that in the great majority of cases the aims and purposes of the communicator will be expressed, through conventional tokens, in his discourse. And as for the minority of cases in which the communicator's aims are obscured or disguised by his discourse, we have

---

[14]David K. Berlo, *The Process of Communication* (New York, 1960), p. 10. Berlo's italics.

even learned to be alert to the circumstances in which we might be misled. Such sophistication is, indeed, a condition of survival in the twentieth century. We can see, then, that attributing a purpose or an aim to a discourse refers to no more than the expectation that the aims of a man will display their symptoms in what he says and how he says it.

While the discourse itself is the most usual source for evidence of intent, it is not the only possible source. We may encounter a discourse in which we find no evidence of persuasive intent, but we discover that the author of the discourse intended to persuade nonetheless. The evidence may be the author's own testimony, or the testimony of someone who knew his mind, or some aspect of the situation in which the discourse appeared that made persuasive intent mandatory. In those cases too we must regard the discourse as rhetorical because it has met the terms of the definition. We have discovered persuasive intent, and from this discovery we must regard the discourse as a fitting subject for rhetorical criticism, regardless of what nonrhetorical characteristics it may display.

The subject matter of rhetorical criticism, then, is usually taken to be discourse that aims to influence men. And what of its practice? The methods of rhetorical criticism, although they are embodied in an ever-growing literature, are neither so numerous nor so variegated as to be beyond reckoning. Preliminary to such reckoning we must note that not every commentary on a rhetorical discourse is a critique. Rhetorical discourses can be culled for many purposes other than understanding how they work, which is the task of criticism. The political reporter may examine the deliberative address for indications of future policy; the biographer may look for clues to a cast of mind and an inner life; the poetaster may read the oration for its passages of fire; the pilgrim may search the sermon for a faith. These are legitimate preoccupations, and there are more like them; but they are not criticism. They are not disinterested enough to be criticism. Criticism has no relationship with its subject other than to account for how that subject works; it demands nothing but full disclosure. That is an ideal, of course. In fact we do have critical essays that seek for more than how their subjects work, but insofar as the critic's motives are not disinterested, his criticism will be tainted. The standard of disinterested objectivity in criticism has stood too long and been too widely accepted to require further elaboration here.

Arnold, in his survey of rhetoric in the United States since 1900, finds virtually no systematic rhetorical criticism in this country prior to 1920.[15] Even that date is too early to mark the beginning of criticism of any sophistication, for, as Arnold remarks, ". . . the early attempts at critically appraising rhetorical practice were often crude and incomplete."[16] It is only in recent

---

[15]Carroll C. Arnold, "Rhetoric in America Since 1900," *Re-Establishing the Speech Profession. The First Fifty Years,* ed. Robert T. Oliver and Marvin G. Bauer (n.p., 1959), p. 5.
[16]*Ibid.*

years that a set of practices associated with rhetorical criticism has evolved
in this country and has become sufficiently stable to reward examination.
Three distinct approaches to the practices of rhetorical criticism can be
identified among the published critical writings in this country, with one of
these three commanding by far the greatest allegiance among professional
critics. They are (1) the movement study, in which the critic focuses on the
total dispute over a single program or policy, from the genesis of persuasion
on the issue to the time when public discussion of it finally ends; (2) the psychological study, in which the critic traces the patterns of influence between
a rhetor's inner life and his rhetorical activities; and (3) the neo-Aristotelian
study, in which the critic applies to rhetorical discourse canons derived from
classical rhetoric, particularly the *Rhetoric* of Aristotle. It is this last approach
that is the most popular. It has, moreover, influenced the other two approaches without being much influenced by them in published criticism.

The Movement Study

The movement study has received a brief theoretical statement by Griffin
in which, having sketched the characteristic development of persuasive movements, he provides advice to the critic.

> . . . the student will note the crystallization of fundamental issues, the
> successive emergence of argument, appeal, counter-argument and
> counter-appeal, and the sanctions invoked by rhetoricians of both
> sides; he will note, by a process of imaginative re-living in the age,
> by an analysis of consequences, the persuasive techniques which were
> effective and those which were ineffective; and he will note a time,
> very likely, when invention runs dry, when both aggressor and
> defendant rhetoricians tend to repeat their stock of argument and
> appeal. . . . He may note the development of organizations designed
> to facilitate the dissemination of argument, such as the lecture bureau,
> the committee of correspondence, and the political party. Finally, as
> he reads, the student will note the increasing circulation and the
> ultimate extent of the appeal; the development of audiences; and as
> the movement spreads, the geographical and social stratification of
> these audiences.[17]

Griffin's own study of the antimasonic movement of the early nineteenth
century illustrates the application of these techniques.[18] They are techniques
fashioned for the analysis of argument on a large scale, for widening the
scope of the rhetorical critic from the individual performance to the sweep of

---

[17]Leland M. Griffin, "The Rhetoric of Historical Movements," *Quarterly Journal of Speech,* XXXVIII
(April 1952), pp. 186-187.
[18]Leland M. Griffin, "The Rhetorical Structure of the Antimasonic Movement," *The Rhetorical Idiom.
Essays in Rhetoric, Oratory, Language, and Drama,* ed. Donald C. Bryant (Ithaca, N.Y., 1958).

a persuasive campaign. And to characterize these techniques in this way is to reveal their limits as well as their applicability, for it is precisely the subject matter of criticism rather than its practice that the movement study affects. The implied distinction should not be pushed too far, of course. Subject matter and practice are interdependent—or at least ought to be—and a shift in one will almost always result in an alteration of the other, but insofar as we can reasonably distinguish between the two, it is the subject matter of criticism which is more affected by the movement study. In terms of critical practice, Griffin's recommendation is that of historical relativism.

> . . . the critic must judge the discourse in terms of the theories of rhetoric and public opinion indigenous to the times. This principle means that the critic will operate within the climate of theory of rhetoric and public opinion in which the speakers and writers he judges were reared, and in which they practiced; in other words, that he will measure practice in terms of the theories available, not to himself, but to the speakers and writers whom he judges. The principle means that the student of an early nineteenth-century movement will ground his judgments in the theories of Blair and Campbell; that the critic of a movement occurring within the last thirty years, on the other hand, will operate within the theoretical atmosphere created by latter-day rheto0ricians, that he will acknowledge the presence of the propagandist, and the various devices of propaganda, in the theoretical atmosphere of the times.[19]

For many purposes there can be no quarrel with Griffin's historically relative frame of critical reference. For critics to approach the study of movements in terms of the rhetorical theories affecting the movements themselves could not fail to illuminate the history of rhetorical practice. It is, then, to the rhetorical historian that Griffin offers the greatest promise. However, another hope of Griffin's seems more doubtful of fulfillment by the movement study: "From the identification of a number of rhetorical patterns, we may discover the various configurations of public discussion, whether rhetorical patterns repeat themselves when like movements occur in the intervals of time, whether a consistent set of forms may be said to exist."[20]

It does seem that, for an accumulation of movement studies to reveal recurring "rhetorical patterns," the studies must have seen the patterns in somewhat the same way. Different rhetorical historians, investigating different periods of rhetorical history, must at least share the same concept of "pattern," the same sense of "form," before their findings can be correlative. What relationship can there be between a Ciceronian critique of a persuasive movement in Roman history and a Campbellian critique of a persuasive

---

[19]Griffin, *op. cit., Quarterly Journal of Speech,* XXXVIII (April 1952), p. 187.
[20]*Ibid.,* p. 188.

movement in nineteenth-century America? Only so much relationship as there is between Cicero and Campbell. Insofar as Ciceronian theory and Campbellian theory record rhetorical activity in similar ways, the two critiques could, indeed, discern patterns. But insofar as Cicero and Campbell are dissimilar, studies based upon them would be incommensurable, would not note recurrent "configurations of public discussion," because each would have its own view of what constitutes a configuration.

There is one other difficulty, too, in Griffin's suggestions concerning critical practice in the movement study. It is that if one appraises a historical movement in terms "indigenous to the times," one would be voluntarily sacrificing one of the distinct advantages of historical perspective, and without a compensatory gain. To demonstrate, for example, as Howell does, that the argumentation of the Declaration of Independence was influenced by the rhetoric-logical theory of William Duncan is to perform a vital task of historical reconstruction;[21] but to appraise the Declaration in terms of Duncan's theory would be to forego all that we have learned since Duncan's time. It would be for the contemporaneous critic to abandon his own theory of rhetoric for Duncan's; but why would the contemporaneous critic have a theory at all if he did not believe it to be superior to Duncan's? We can well question Griffin's suggestions on critical practice if, as it seems, those suggestions would sometimes compel us to adopt inferior theories to guide our criticism.

These reservations concerning Griffin's theoretical position in no way alter the value we must accord that position. In suggesting a reconstitution of the subject matter of rhetorical criticism from the individual speaker or the individual speech to the persuasive movement, Griffin has opened a new and exciting prospect to rhetorical criticism. His own study of the antimasonic movement is a distinguished effort that highly recommends the mode. Yet, few movement studies in rhetoric have been published besides Griffin's.[22] Certainly there is as yet no cogent and reasonably uniform methodology for the movement study beyond Griffin's suggestion of historical relativism, and it is exactly in the area of methodology that Griffin seems least satisfactory.

The Psychological Study

The rhetorical critique employing a psychological approach has received no formal methodological statement, but this approach is well illustrated by

---

[21] Wilbur Samuel Howell, "The Declaration of Independence and Eighteenth-Century Logic," *The William and Mary Quarterly*, 3rd ser., XVIII (October 1961), pp. 463-84.

[22] The *Quarterly Journal* of *Speech* has published only two in the last decade: E. James Lennon, "The Pro-Northern Movement in England, 1861-1865," XLI (February 1955), pp. 27-37; and W. David Lewis, "Three Religious Orators and the Chartist Movement," XLIII (February 1957), pp. 62-68. In the same period, *Speech Monographs* has only one: Eugene E. White, "The Protasis of the Great Awakening in New England," XXI (March 1954), pp. 10-20.

Maloney's essay on Clarence Darrow.[23] After arguing that his subject cannot be approached in a conventional manner, Maloney presents his hypothesis that Darrow's rhetorical career is to be accounted for mythically.

> We must now inquire briefly into the general structure of the Darrow myth. When Darrow, in defending himself against a charge of bribery before a Los Angeles jury in 1912, said, "I have stood for the weak and the poor. I have stood for the men who toil," he suggested the nature of the fable. It was as a defender of the underdog, a devil's advocate, a man who stood perpetually opposed to the great and powerful of the earth, that he became known. . . . The twin strands of aggressiveness and insecurity interweave in the pattern of American attitudes; and it is the major function of the "underdog" myth to rationalize and reconcile the two. Thus, an alien, a working man, a Negro, following Darrow's triumphs, could see himself, in Darrow, triumphant over the forces that pressed him in, saving the unjustly doomed victim from the hangman, speaking out for freedom and justice, and at the same time might know himself the innocent victim, saved against all expectation from his enemies.[24]

Next Maloney considers the psychological influences in Darrow's early life, and finds in them the sources of Darrow's morbid fear of death, a fear which, Maloney argues, motivated many of Darrow's rhetorical transactions. The study then proceeds to sections that chart the temper of Darrow's times, trace the development of his career, and consider his use of persuasive technique. Finally, there is a longer section on Darrow's philosophical conclusions.

Maloney's is an extraordinary study. It is sensitively conceived and written in a style that is exactly suited to its subject. The critic is less interested in Darrow's rhetorical performances than in Darrow as a creature of his times and a product of his environment, but the broader interest still illuminates the rhetorical activities. This interest leads Maloney to draw his analytic techniques from anthropology and psychoanalysis. His approach to the career of Darrow corresponds to Darrow's own approach to forensic situations. As Darrow's recurrent strategy in forensic pleading was to substitute a socio-psychological vocabulary for the standard legal-moral vocabulary of the courtroom, so Maloney's critical strategy is to apply a sociopsychological vocabulary to Darrow instead of the standard vocabulary of the critical essay. Maloney has written a "defense" of Darrow.

The critic's one lapse from his otherwise sustained psychological analysis—in the section on Darrow's persuasive techniques[25]—reveals,

---

[23]Hochmuth, *op. cit.*, III, pp. 262-312.
[24]From *A History and Criticism of American Public Address,* ed. by Marie Kathryn Hochmuth (New York, 1955), vol. III, p. 266.
[25]*Ibid.*, pp 295-300.

perhaps, the pristine state of this whole approach to rhetorical criticism. In this section, the critic appraises Darrow's speaking in the categories of logical proof, pathetic proof, and, though not called so in the essay, ethos. These categories, together with the isolation of a recurrent pattern of argument in Darrow's speeches, notes on Darrow's methods of selecting jurymen, and observations on Darrow's personal appearance do not constitute an entirely satisfactory accounting for the social symbol that Darrow became through his discourse. We need not seek far for the reason; we can sense it in the abrupt shift in tone when Maloney approaches the subject of rhetorical techniques. A method for the psychological examination of rhetorical discourse was simply not available to the critic and so, though he wrote a notably successful account of the genesis and social impact of Darrow's career, the character and power of Darrow's discourse is not so well explained.

Psychological criticism, it seems, can be quite fruitful in revealing the forces engendering a discourse, but when the discourse in its turn becomes an influential force, the resources of psychological criticism are strained to account for it. The psychological critic can, as in Maloney's essay on Darrow, disclose the causal links between the rhetor and his discourse, and he can describe the way in which the discourse functions in its social setting, but his methodology does not equip him for explaining how that particular discourse came to function in that way. He is, in sum, prepared to deal with the discourse-as-symptom, but he is less able to deal with the discourse-as-communication.

There is, moreover, a danger of excessive gullibility in psy-chological criticism, a disposition to equate too simply and readily the author and his work. We can see the danger manifested even in the efforts of Kenneth Burke, who has written some of our subtlest psychological criticism. Here is Burke writing on T. S. Eliot's play, *Murder in the Cathedral:*

A work on Thomas the Saint, by Thomas the Poet, the Saint Louis boy who was too good for Saint Louis (why shouldn't he be!). Concerned with the royal road to God.

Stages: The author leaves the old locale behind to go in search of its antithesis. He will abandon the inelegancies of Missouri for the elegancies of upper-class England. By antithesis, he builds up a concept of elegance—and then he goes in search of it *geographically.* He tries to find a place here-and-now that will give sufficient bodily substance to the structure of his imagination. For a time he thinks he has found it in England. But eventually it occurs to him that England is moving towards Saint Louis. Life becomes a waste land at the thought. England is not elegant enough. And eventually the poet meditates upon God, the only symbol elegant enough. But:

Being a profound and imaginative man, being perhaps our most accomplished poet, Eliot knows very well that there is no slogan: *per elegantiam ad astra.* He questions the validity of his way. He knows that he must get to God by humbleness, so he must "transcend" his elegance, building atop it a new structure of humility. The God of elegance being the negation of Saint Louis, he must round out his development by "negating the negation." "Murder in the Cathedral" is the symbolic solution of this problem in spiritual tactics.[26]

No doubt this is lively and amusing writing, even if it is, untypical of Burke, unkind; but one can question how much it really reveals about either *Murder in the Cathedral* or T. S. Eliot. We can doubt, as a psychologist probably would, that a quest for "elegance" is ever in itself a very profound motive to action, and we can suspect that such a quest, if it exists in a particular case, is never any but the most superficial expression of motive. More broadly, we can doubt that Eliot's inner life bore quite so simple a relationship to his play as Burke alleges. We are certainly entitled to doubt, since Burke has not cited evidence for his interpretation.

We are compelled to believe in the existence of relationships between a man's deepest motives and his discourses. Such a conviction is bound up with the very ways we have of talking about human motives. The mystery lies in the identification of those characteristics of discourse which reveal motive, for we know that motive only rarely receives a full and direct expression. Usually, the motives of a man are transmuted in their linguistic expression; they are symbolized in his discourse rather than openly reported. Our difficulty, as critics, is not only that we do not fully understand how and when and why these transmutations occur, but also that these transmutations may not even follow stable and regular patterns. Thus, for example, a patient of Freud's in the early part of this century might so consistently dream and write and talk of arrows as phallic symbols that Freud, with his ingenious capacity for translation, is able to discern the motivational meaning of the symbol. Freud then publishes his findings on this patient and notes that, in the cases of other patients too, arrows are phallic symbols, so that the arrow seems to have a general symbolic value. But then—and here is where the critic is invited to disaster—someone who speaks or writes reads Freud and learns that he can disguise his true motives by writing and speaking of arrows, for he knows that his auditors, themselves having been influenced by Freud, will interpret arrow to mean phallus and not, as it means to him, something entirely different. In short, just as Freud discovered that a person who has mastered ordinary language can use it to conceal his motives, so a person who has mastered Freudian vocabulary can use it too to conceal his motives. The possibilities of deception, deliberate or unconscious, seem endless, and consequently the problems presented the psychological critic seem insoluble.

Our conclusion should assuredly not be that psychological criticism must be forever abandoned; but we are obliged to approach this enterprise with the

---

[26]Kenneth Burke, *Attitudes Toward History,* vol. I (New York, 1937), pp. 109-10.

most extreme caution. The methodology of psychological criticism is in a decidedly primitive state, and freighted with exceedingly taxing philosophical problems. In the psychological study of rhetorical discourse, as in the case of the movement study, we have little more than a promising beginning. With Maloney's essay on Darrow, the promise is high, but there is clearly no system of analysis or body of techniques available to the critic for the reliable psychological examination of argumentative strategies or discursive texture.

The Neo-Aristotelian Study

By far the dominant mode of rhetorical criticism of the presenet century in the United States has been neo-Aristotelianism. Of the forty essays on individual speakers included in the three volumes of *A History and Criticism of American Public Address,* fifteen of the studies employ techniques of criticism derived from Aristotle's *Rhetoric.*[27] The proportion of neo-Aristotelian essays becomes even more striking when we note that of the twenty-five essays that remain unaccounted for, some employ only one or two of Aristotle's canons to serve for the entire critical apparatus,[28] some are biographical essays which make little attempt at critical interpretation or appraisal,[29] and some are appreciations, eulogies, or of dubious character.[30] Only eight of the essays attempt an examination and appraisal of rhetorical discourses by the employment of techniques which are singular or which represent unconventional interpretations or applications of traditional rhetoric.[31] It is further noteworthy that the editor of the first two volumes of

[27]Brigance and Hochmuth, *op. cit.* The neo-Aristotelian essays are Orville Hitchcock, "Jonathan Edwards," I, pp. 213-237; Roy C. McCall, "Theodore Parker," I, pp. 238-264; Wayland Maxfield Parrish and Alfred Dwight Huston, "Robert G. Ingersoll," I, pp. 363-386; Karl R. Wallace, "Booker T. Washington," I, pp. 407-433; John W. Black, "Rufus Choate," I, pp. 434-458; Charles A. Fritz, "Edwin A. Alderman," II, pp. 540-556; Walter B. Emery, "Samuel Gompers," II, pp. 557-579, Ernest J. Wrage, "Henry Clay," II, pp. 603-638, Herbert L. Curry, "John C. Calhoun," II, pp. 639-664; R. Elaine Pagel and Carl Dallinger, "Charles Sumner," II, pp. 751-776, Carroll P. Lahman, "Robert M. LaFollete," II, pp. 942-967; Dayton David McKean, "Woodrow Wilson," II, pp. 968-992; Bower Aly, "Alexander Hamilton," III, pp. 24-51; Richard Murphy, "Theodore Roosevelt," III, pp. 313-364; Earnest Brandenburg and Waldo W. Braden, "Franklin Delano Roosevelt," III, pp. 458-530.

[28]*Ibid.,* Lester Thonssen, "William M. Evarts," I, pp. 483-500; Louis M. Eich, "Charles W. Eliot," 11, pp. 526-539; Forest L. Whan, "Stephen A. Douglas," II, pp. 777-827; Mildred Freburg Berry, "Abraham Lincoln: His Development in the Skills of the Platform," II, pp. 828-858; Robert D. Clark, "Harry Emerson Fosdick," III, pp. 411-457.

[29]*Ibid.,* Willard Hayes Yeager, "Wendell Phillips," I, pp. 329-362; Marvin G. Bauer, "Henry W. Grady," I, pp. 387-406; Louis A. Mallory, "Patrick Henry," II, pp. 580-602; Earl W. Wiley, "Abraham Lincoln: His Emergence as the Voice of the People," II, pp. 859-877; Henry G. Roberts, "James G. Blaine," II, pp. 878-890; Dallas C. Dickey and Donald C. Streeter, "Lucius Q. C. Lamar," III, pp. 175-221.

[30]*Ibid.,* Lionel Crocker, "Henry Ward Beecher," I, pp. 265-293; Rexford S. Mitchell, "William L. Yancy," II, pp. 734-750; Myron G. Phillips, "William Jennings Bryan," II, pp. 891-918; Herold Truslow Ross, "Albert J. Beveridge," II, pp. 919-941; Doris Yoakam Twichell, "Susan B. Anthony," III, pp. 97-132; Robert B. Huber, "Dwight L Moody," III, pp. 222-261.

[31]*Ibid.,* Marie Hochmuth and Norman Mattis, "Phillips Brooks," I, pp. 294-328; William Norwood Brigance, "Jeremiah S. Black," I, pp. 459-482; Herbert A. Wichelns, "Ralph Waldo Emerson," II, pp. 501-525; Wilbur Samuel Howell and Hoyt Hopewell Hudson, "Daniel Webster," II, pp. 665-733; Norman W. Mattis, "Thomas Hart Benton," III, pp. 52-96; Carroll C. Arnold, "George William Curtis," III, pp. 133-174; Martin Maloney, "Clarence Darrow," III, pp. 262-312; A. E. Whitehead, "William E. Borah," III, pp. 365-410.

these studies takes Aristotelian rhetoric as his point of departure in commenting upon the essays,[32] and that the editor of the third volume recommends the Aristotelian definition of rhetoric in her introductory essay,[33] and borrows several of the Aristotelian categories in the critical system she delineates.[34]

Hitchcock's essay on Jonathan Edwards will serve as a clear example of neo-Aristotelian criticism.[35] After arguing that Edwards' rhetorical biography has been neglected and is a needful study, Hitchcock has brief sections on the ethos of colonial Northampton and on Edwards' training and intellectual development. Then there follows the main critical section of the essay. In this critique Hitchcock first enumerates the "doctrines which Edwards preached."[36] He finds eight of them, and is able to convey each of the eight in a single sentence. Hitchcock then proceeds to his topics of criticism. First is organization: "Jonathan Edwards's sermons are highly organized. . . . Each is divided broadly into four large sections; the thesis is carefully stated; the discussion is developed in three or four main points; these main points are arranged according to a definite system (the order is usually logical or topical); and each tends to establish the principal thesis; the transitions from one idea to another are smoothly and easily made; frequent summaries occur."[37]

Under the heading "Organization" Hitchcock goes on to discuss the character of Edwards' introductions and conclusions, after having made some additional observations on Edwards' general practices in arranging discourse.

"Types of Proof" is the next topic. "Edwards's argumentative method" is divided into inductive and deductive methods.[38] We are told that "categorical, hypothetical, and disjunctive enthymemes appear in every sermon,"[39] that "argument from authority greatly predominates,"[40] and that "argument by explanation also becomes an important instrument of proof."[41]

Next Hitchcock examines the "emotional approach": "While Edwards uses a great many pathetic arguments, these appeals are, in general, subordinated to the logical elements."[42] "The principal appeals are to fear, shame, desire for happiness, security, and pride. Gratitude, common sense, emulation, greed, and courage receive less emphasis. In appealing to fear, Edwards frequently refers to hell."[43]

---

[32] Ibid., William Norwood Brigance, "Preface," I, p. x.
[33] Ibid., Marie Kathryn Hochmuth, "The Criticism of Rhetoric," III, pp. 4 and 8.
[34] Ibid., passim.
[35] Ibid., I, pp. 213-237.
[36] Ibid., I, p. 220.
[37] Ibid., I, p. 222.
[38] Ibid., I, p. 223.
[39] Ibid., I, p. 224.
[40] Ibid.
[41] Ibid., I, p. 225.
[42] Ibid., I, p. 227.
[43] Ibid., I, p. 227.

"Ethical proof" is examined: "Edwards . . . presented a strong ethical argument. His life was exemplary; he followed a strict moral code; his friends and neighbors thought well of him."[44]

Then style:

> Edwards wrote his sermons in a precise, plain, exact style. Nothing of fine writing or of excessive display creeps into his text. Nor are there classical allusions or other learned references. The language is the language of the audience; it is constantly toned down to the listeners' level. The analogies and comparisons are of an everyday type, apt and exact, yet often the commonest form. The quotations are Biblical and are cited with a matter-of-factness that appealed to the most unlearned listener. Even Edwards's own language has a Biblical flavor. His style can best be described as common and precise, patterned after that of the Scriptures.[45]

After further considerations of "style," Hitchcock concludes with a short section on "methods of preparation and delivery" and one on "effect." In the latter section, Hitchcock is concerned with the effects of Edwards' sermons on his immediate audience.

Enough of Hitchcock's essay has been quoted to disclose his particular merits and defects as a critic. What is important here is the general method of criticism being employed, irrespective of the skill of its particular applications. The general method is what has been designated *neo-Aristotelianism*, and Hitchcock's essay is an especially clear example of it because of the literalness with which the method is applied in this essay and the clarity with which its canons of criticism are invoked.

The primary and identifying ideas of neo-Aristotelianism that we can find recurring in the critical essays of this school are the classification of rhetorical discourses into forensic, deliberative, and epideictic; the classification of "proofs" or "means of persuasion" into logical, pathetic, and ethical; the assessment of discourse in the categories of invention, arrangement, delivery, and style; and the evaluation of rhetorical discourse in terms of its effects on its immediate audience. Each of these ideas is prominent in the Hitchcock essay except for the first. In the case of the tripartite typology of rhetorical discourses, Hitchcock was dealing with a genre—the sermon—that is post-Aristotelian and, consequently, is not easily reconciled with the traditional typology; but even in dealing with this special genre, Hitchcock scrupulously adheres to the conventions of neo-Aristotelianism.

The practice of neo-Aristotelian criticism has received formal statement in an essay first published in 1925. Wichelns' program for rhetorical criticism appeared in a significant paragraph.

---

[44]*Ibid.*, I, p. 230.
[45]*Ibid.*

Rhetorical criticism is necessarily analytic. The scheme of a rhetorical study includes the element of the speaker's personality as a conditioning factor; it includes also the public character of the man—not what he was, but what he was thought to be. It requires a description of the speaker's audience, and of the leading ideas with which he plied his hearers—his topics, the motives to which he appealed, the nature of the proofs he offered. These will reveal his own judgment of human nature in his audiences, and also his judgment on the questions which he discussed. Attention must be paid, too, to the relation of the surviving texts to what was actually uttered: in case the nature of the changes is known, there may be occasion to consider adaptation to two audiences—that which heard and that which read. Nor can rhetorical criticism omit the speaker's mode of arrangement and his mode of expression, nor his habit of preparation and his manner of delivery from the platform; though the last two are perhaps less significant. "Style"—in the sense which corresponds to diction and sentence movement—must receive attention, but only as one among various means that secure for the speaker ready access to the minds of his auditors. Finally, the effect of the discourse on its immediate hearers is not to be ignored, either in the testimony of witnesses, nor in the record of events. And throughout such a study one must conceive of the public man as influencing the men of his own times by the power of his discourse.[46]

Bryant's judgment—that this essay "set the pattern and determined the direction of rhetorical criticism for more than a quarter of a century and has had a greater and more continuous influence upon the development of the scholarship of rhetoric and public address than any other single work published in this century"[47]—suggests that one of the main sources of neo-Aristotelianism may lie in the influence of Wichelns' program of 1925. The elements of analysis recommended in the quoted paragraph could be a compendium of the topics of Aristotle or Cicero: ". . . the public character of the man . . . his topics, the motives to which he appealed, the nature of the proofs he offered . . . the speaker's mode of arrangement and his mode of expression . . . his manner of delivery from the platform . . . diction and sentence movement . . . the effect of the discourse on its immediate hearers."

The uses to which Aristotle can be interpreted as having put these topics is not the present issue. What is pertinent in clarifying neo-Aristotelianism is the fact that these are subjects for discussion in the neo-Aristotelian essay, just as they were subjects for discussion in the *Rhetoric*. Even in its most

---

[46]Herbert A. Wichelns, "The Literary Criticism of Oratory," *The Rhetorical Idiom. Essays in Rhetoric, Oratory, Language, and Drama*, ed. Donald C. Bryant (Ithaca, N.Y., 1958), pp. 38-39.
[47]Donald C. Bryant, ed., *The Rhetorical Idiom. Essays in Rhetoric, Oratory, Language, and Drama* (Ithaca, N.Y., 1958), p. 5.

faithful executions, neo-Aristotelian criticism cannot be certain of serving the purposes of Aristotle's *Rhetoric*. Aristotle has left us with no substantial body of criticism, and we can only conjecture the extent to which, had Aristotle left any, his critical writing would adhere to the principles of the *Rhetoric* or would strictly subordinate rhetorical criticism to logical analysis and political commentary. There may be little that the neo-Aristotelians have in common with Aristotle besides some recurrent topics of discussion and a vaguely derivative view of rhetorical discourse; but even so, these topics and this view may serve to define neo-Aristotelianism.

The view itself must be found behind neo-Aristotelian critiques rather than explicitly stated in them. It is a view which the neo-Aristotelian essays share. The first element of this view is the comprehension of the rhetorical discourse as tactically designed to achieve certain results with a specific audience on a specific occasion. Of the fifteen neo-Aristotelian essays in *A History and Criticism of American Public Address,* only two undertake an appraisal of rhetorical discourse in terms other than its effect on an immediate audience.[48] There is little disposition among neo-Aristotelian critics to comprehend the discourse in a larger context, to see it, as for example the movement study would, as part of a historical process of argument. To the neo-Aristotelian, the discourse is discrete and its relevant effects are immediate.[49]

Another element of the view of rhetorical discourse sustained in neo-Aristotelianism is the close relationship between rhetoric and logic. Perhaps the most striking result of this relationship is the tendency of neo-Aristotelian critics to concentrate on discourses that approach logical demonstration and to eschew the explication of discourses that do not have a demonstrative form. All the subjects of neo-Aristotelian essays in *A History and Criticism of American Public Address* are orators in the genteel tradition. Most of them

---

[48]The two exceptions are Bower Aly, "Alexander Hamilton," III, pp. 24-51; and Richard Murphy, "Theodore Roosevelt," II, pp. 313-364. Aly attempts to determine Hamilton's "place in the history of oratory" (pp. 49-50); Murphy attempts an assessment of Roosevelt's permanent value as an orator as well as his effectiveness (pp. 359-360).

[49]In this connection, it is instructive to note the series of experimental studies conducted by Hovland and his associates at Yale University: Carl I. Hovland, Irving L. Janis, and Harold H. Kelley, *Communication and Persuasion* (New Haven, 1953); Carl I. Hovland (ed.), *The Order of Presentation in Persuasion* (New Haven, 1957); Carl I. Hovland and Irving L. Janis (ed.), *Personality and Persuasibility* (New Haven, 1959). Insofar as the social scientists focus on discourses rather than on audience reactions to them, they display the same interest as neo-Aristotelian critics in the discreteness of the discourse, and in its immediate effects. Cf. *Communication and Persuasion,* pp. 56-130; and all of *The Order of Presentation in Persuasion.* Moreover, they have the same tendency as neo-Aristotelian critics to fragment the discourse and to investigate its constituents as independent variables. The approach of the Hovland group, of course, is necessitated by the technical demands of the experimental method rather than by a commitment to a critical system; however, the approaches to the rhetorical discourse are sufficiently similar so that the data unearthed by the Yale investigators could, with a minimum of mediation, directly inform neo-Aristotelianism.

The Yale studies of audiences, *Communication and Persuasion,* pp. 134-265, and all of *Personality and Persuasibility,* are in a different category. Enlisting the resources of psychology for the measurement of personality, learning, and intelligence, and relating these factors to persuasibility, these investigations have relevance to any conceivable system of rhetorical criticism and, indeed, are in the area in which rhetorical criticism must rely heavily on the findings of the social sciences.

are of the nineteenth century. The few orators treated in these volumes whose discourses are ill-suited to logical analysis—Patrick Henry, Dwight L. Moody, perhaps William Jennings Bryan—are not subjected to neo-Aristotelian criticism.

Following also from the close relationship between rhetoric and logic, which seems to characterize neo-Aristotelianism, is the tendency to assume the rationality of audiences. The very terms argument and proof are borrowed from logic and are repeatedly employed by neo-Aristotelian critics. Audiences are conceived of as responsive to arguments and proofs; and even "emotional appeals," which appears to be the rubric for persuasive discourse not susceptible to logical explanation, are often conceived of as a type of proof.

In charting the pattern of influence that flows through the rhetorical transaction, the neo-Aristotelian critic typically sees only one direction of movement: the background, training, interests, and aims of the rhetor influence his discourse, which in turn influences the audience. The neo-Aristotelians ignore the impact of the discourse on rhetorical conventions, its capacity for disposing an audience to expect certain ways of arguing and certain kinds of justifications in later discourses that they encounter, even on different subjects. Similarly, the neo-Aristotelian critics do not account for the influence of the discourse on its author: the future commitments it makes for him, rhetorically and ideologically; the choices it closes to him, rhetorically and ideologically; the public image it portrays to which he must adjust.

Our characterization of neo-Aristotelianism has been only preliminary. Because this approach to rhetorical criticism has been so dominant as to have come, in many minds, to be identified as the whole of rhetorical criticism, the pages to follow will afford it fuller treatment. It may serve as a summary statement of this preliminary definition to note again the treatment rhetorical discourse receives from each of the three practices of criticism that have been reviewed: the movement study treats of discourse as an element in a complex of historical forces shaping public opinion and public policy; the psychological study regards the rhetorical discourse as a symptom or consequence of the personal history of the rhetor, and as an element in a social configuration; neo-Aristotelianism treats rhetorical discourses as discrete communications in specific contexts, designed for specific purposes.

Our next task must be to look even more carefully at the generic nature of criticism and, with this perspective, to determine more exactly how—and if—neo-Aristotelianism works.

Must We All Be "Rhetorical Critics"?

by Barnet Baskerville

No reader of journal articles and miscellaneous publications in rhetoric and public address during the last two decades can have failed to note a mounting interest in something called "rhetorical criticism." All scholars in the field, it sometimes appears, aspire to the appellation of "critic." The publication of Edwin Black's *Rhetorical Criticism* in 1965 was especially influential in stimulating further attempts to develop and elucidate the subject; articles have appeared regularly suggesting new purposes and emphases and delineating new critical methods or approaches which are being applied to an ever widening variety of critical objects. All this is to the good, but concurrent with this glorification of the critic may be detected (or so it seems to some of us) a tacit denigration of those who are merely rhetorical "historians." Indeed, one may infer from some exceedingly censorious criticism of criticism (some of which I confess to have written myself) that when one can't quite make the grade as a critic, what he manages to come up with is "history." One book on the criticism of public address published in 1966 notes sorrowfully that "most of the so-called criticism today really is historical scholarship."[1]

A writer in one of our journals recently proposed a distinction between rhetorical history and rhetorical criticism, and went further to urge that studies of discourse should usually be "*either* exercises in rhetorical history-writing or critical ventures into interesting problematic, or insightful aspects of discourse."[2] Although I am not so sure that such a radical separation of these two kinds of study either can or should be accomplished, I do agree that there are valid distinctions to be made between a piece of writing which is essentially "historical" in intent and one which might properly be called an essay in "rhetorical criticism." I shall try to suggest such distinctions, but my primary interest in this article is in emphasizing that the work of the historian of public address and that of the rhetorical critic are complementary, that both are worthy scholarly enterprises, and that neither should be elevated above the other in our academic scale of values.

Reprinted from *The Quarterly Journal of Speech* 63 (1977), with permission of the Speech Communication Association.

[1] Anthony Hillbruner, *Critical Dimensions: The Art of Public Address Criticism* (New York: Random House, 1966), p. 6.

[2] Bruce E. Gronbeck, "Rhetorical History and Rhetorical Criticism: A Distinction," *Speech Teacher*, 24 (1975), 310.

The discussion of the relative merits of these two scholarly emphases has had a long and interesting history. Forty years ago Donald Bryant called attention to "some problems of scope and method in rhetorical scholarship," one of which was the question of whether rhetorical scholars should properly be engaging in criticism or in historical fact-finding and reconstruction of the past."[3] Expressing the opinion that "rhetorical criticism must depend almost entirely upon historical knowledge for its effectiveness," Bryant concluded that "historical study must go on . . . rhetorical criticism will be sound only when it uses the results of historical study both in judging the past in terms of the past and in judging the past for the present."

A few years later, the first two volumes of the Brigance studies appeared, significantly titled "A History *and* Criticism of American Public Address." In his preface, Professor Brigance distinguished between "the critical studies" (essays on individual speakers) and the "historical studies" (those sketching the background of various periods: Colonial, Early National, etc.). One of the charges subsequently levelled against these volumes was that the "critical studies" were often more "historical" than "critical." In his review of the Brigance volumes, Loren Reid stated that the contributors "write with a keen sense of their dual responsibility as historians and as critics of public address."[4] But he was soon warning against "The Perils of Rhetorical Criticism," the greatest of which is that "the critic may produce something that is not criticism at all."[5] This "something," we infer from the context, may be among other things "simply a narrative of the circumstances under which a speech is delivered," or "an excursion into other fields of learning."

As the study of public address continued, and as research manuals in speech began to make their appearance, the matter of history and criticism (or history *versus* criticism) surfaced again. Professor Auer in his *Introduction to Research in Speech* (1959) spoke of "the historical method, also referred to as the critical method," and later listed the critical study as a kind of historical study, one of several approaches to historical research. But Professor Bormann, in his *Theory and Research in the Communicative Arts* (1965), distinguished sharply between the historical and critical methods and warned of the difficulties of combining the two. The historian, he explained, adopts an *expository* stance. He looks for meaningful structure in past events and constructs a narrative. The critic, on the other hand, is concerned with evaluating individual works. He applies artistic standards to works of art in order to appreciate their artistry. As if commenting on the unimportance of the distinction, Professor Everett Lee Hunt asks of a passage from the third volume of *A History and Criticism of American Public Address,* "Shall we call this verdict rhetorical criticism, or shall we call it an historical, ethical, or logical

---

[3] *QJS,* 23 (1937), 183-84.
[4] *QJS,* 29 (1943), 366.
[5] *QJS,* 30 (1944), 416-22.

judgment? At any rate, it is such insight we seek . . ."[6]

The fact that a distinction, or a failure to make a distinction, can sometimes be important is seen in the case of my friend and colleague Ernest J. Wrage. In 1947, Professor Wrage's essay "Public Address: A Study in Social and Intellectual History" appeared in the *Quarterly Journal of Speech.*[7] This essay advanced the thesis that "students of public address may contribute in substantial ways to the history of ideas. They possess credentials worthy of acknowledgment and interest in a type of materials germane to the object." Because public speeches are prepared with a listening audience in mind, Wrage reasoned, "because they are pitched to levels of information, to take account of prevalent beliefs, and to mirror tone and temper of audiences . . . they serve as useful indices to the popular mind." He urged that students of public address concentrate upon the speaker's *ideas,* that a speech be regarded as "a repository of themes and their elaborations from which we may gain insight into the life of an era as well as into the mind of man." Wrage sought to challenge his fellow rhetoricians with the idea that the student of public address, like the student of music or literature or other forms of artistic expression, working in his small corner with materials that interest him most, can contribute to the writing of the more general "intellectual" history of the nation—a task in which all scholars are ultimately involved.

It is important, I think, that we remember the context of Wrage's 1947 article. He was not writing a handbook for rhetorical critics nor presenting a new critical paradigm. He was offering a rationale for the kind of historically oriented courses in American public address he was then pioneering at Northwestern University by contrasting them with the then-prevailing approach. That approach he characterized as a study of individual speakers—their personalities, platform virtuosity, and rhetorical techniques—to determine their influence on history. For this "speaker-centered" approach, with its emphasis upon personal persuasion, he proposed to substitute an "idea-centered" approach, a venture in intellectual history through public address, which he thought would yield "knowledge of more general interest in terms of man's cultural strivings and heritage."

I believe, therefore, that Professor Wrage would have been astonished to discover himself depicted in a recent textbook on *Methods of Rhetorical Criticism* as a founder of a method of criticism designated the "historical method." This approach, we are told, "assumes a causal relation between events in history and public address. It views public address "as both formed by and formative of the events of history." This "historical" approach, and another called "neo-Aristotelian," are listed as subcategories of a general type called "traditional criticism," the model for which was constructed in 1925 by

---

[6] "Thoughts on a History and Criticism of American Public Address," *QJS,* 42 (1956), 189.
[7] *QJS,* 33 (1947), 451-57.

Professor Herbert Wichelns. We are told that the salient characteristics of this so-called "traditional perspective" are that it is speaker-oriented, viewing the orator as "influencing the men of his own times by the power of his discourse;" that it is amoral, since it generously and unquestioningly grants the speaker his purpose, regardless of its ethical consequences; and that it is preoccupied with raising and answering technical questions. In view of Wrage's repeated insistence that his is an idea-centered rather than a speaker-centered approach, his close examination of the possible consequences of a speaker's purposes, and his relative lack of interest in details of technique, there would seem to be some question about this classification of him as a "traditional critic" of public address.

I have always regarded Ernest Wrage as essentially an *historian* of public address, and an uncommonly able one. I suppose it makes no great difference whether we label him historian or critic, but it *does* make a difference that he is set up as a leader of a school of criticism, and then condemned for being too much of an historian. This is what Scott and Brock seem to me to be doing when they characterize Wrage as an historical critic, and then describe "historical criticism," as being a distorted and incomplete version of "traditional criticism" because it concentrates unduly on "the historical elements."[8] Thonssen, Baird, and Braden do much the same thing. They conclude an admirably lucid discussion of the "social and intellectual history approach" by accusing its practitioners of leaning more toward being historians than speech critics, of seeking goals different from those of critics who measure artistic excellence. "This approach," they assert, "lacks sufficient dimension for adequate rhetorical criticism, for it does not judge the worth or quality of a speech or a speaker."[9] Similarly, Edwin Black, in appraising three distinct approaches to the practice of criticism, has this to say about Leland Griffin's "movement study": "It is . . . to the rhetorical historian that Griffin offers the greatest promise."[10] *Precisely.* And we might say similarly of Wrage that "It is to the intellectual historian that he offers the greatest promise." This, I am sure, would have pleased Wrage, since this is exactly the aim he affirmed. The point being made somewhat laboriously here is that it is unfair to condemn a writer for not doing well something he never set out to do, for not being what he never professed to be.

This attempt to draw a distinction between the rhetorical historian and the rhetorical critic may strike the reader as a singularly profitless endeavor. It goes without saying that the historian, like all other researchers, must be a critic in the sense that he must subject his data to critical examination. He must be able to dispel the myths which hang heavily over the "great orators." He must be able to recognize excellence when he encounters it, and to explain why it be excellence. He must select and reject materials, allocate

---

[8] *Methods of Rhetorical Criticism* (New York: Harper and Row, 1972), pp. 21-22.
[9] *Speech Criticism,* 2nd ed. (New York: Ronald Press, 1970), p. 280.
[10] *Rhetorical Criticism* (New York: Macmillan. 1965), pp. 20-21.

space, emphasize and subordinate, make judgments about the meaning and relevance of details—all on the basis of some system of values. The historian who goes beyond the production of a mere chronicle must *interpret,* and this, surely, is a critical function. Still, to insist that an historian must be "critical" is not the same as asking that he become a critic. There is a difference between adopting a critical attitude or using critical methods in one's scholarship, and evaluating individual works of art with an eye to intelligent appreciation, to discover how and why they "work," or to develop normative or predictive generalizations applicable to similar works of art. In both cases judgment is involved, but the judgments are of a different kind and in a different context. To the literary historian a novel may be essentially a document, an artifact illustrating social or intellectual history; to the literary critic, the novel is a work of art, to be evaluated for its artistry. To the rhetorical historian a speech is more than a document, for it is something that happened, rather than something written down to be read, but it too is an artifact (albeit a dynamic one) illustrating social or intellectual or political history; to the rhetorical critic it is a work of practical art, to be judged by its own artistic standards.

The above attempt to draw an analogy from the field of literature may remind some of a debate among literary scholars several decades ago. In the early 1930's, the champions of literary criticism and the champions of literary history engaged in a spirited controversy in published books, in the pages of the *English Journal,* and the meetings of the Modern Language Association. In the opinion of the critics, college departments of English were placing too much emphasis on literary history. Literary historians, it was charged, tend to look upon literature as the written record of the life of a people, "the crystallization of current political, religious, social, and economic ideals," and in so doing they ignore artistic merit and devote their attention to much writing that has no literary value. To the critics, the ultimate aim and the crowning accomplishment of literary scholarship was the appreciation and evaluation of the aesthetic qualities of the master works of literature. Not so, replied the proponents of literary history. "I do not think," wrote Howard Mumford Jones in the *English Journal,* "that it is the primary business of scholarship to produce literary criticism. We should be grateful when the scholar is also a critic, but we should not be surprised when he is not. . . . The true business of the literary scholar is, in my judgment, that he is the historian of literary culture, that is to say, *the historian of those ideas which have expressed themselves in literary form.* He is also the historian of the significant forms in which those ideas are expressed."[11] Preoccupation with criticism, Jones suggested, is apt to result in following the latest vogue in critical method or subject matter. Scholarship, he affirmed, is concerned with all times, not merely the present moment.

---

[11]"Literary Scholarship and Contemporary Criticism," *English Journal* (College Edition), 23 (1934), 755. Italics mine.

It might be supposed that those advocating the dominance of criticism would readily have acknowledged the importance of literary history to their work, but such was not always the case. Literary history, it was admitted, may be a good thing, but its values as an aid to criticism have been over-estimated. Actually, all that is needed for criticism is a body of principles, sensitivity to literature, and such learning as is necessary to an intelligent reading of the text. The paraphernalia of history—who the author was, out of what experience the literature came, why he said what he did, etc.—is largely irrelevant.[12] The other side could be equally intransigent. Arthur M. Schlesinger, coming to the aid of the literary historians, asserted that "literary criticism and literary history are two distinct branches of scholarship, each with its own point of view and technique. . . ." Grudgingly acknowledging the services rendered by aesthetic critics, he hinted that they wrote for one another rather than for posterity. Schlesinger, who admittedly favored the study of literature from "a broadly social point of view," urged the historian of letters to free himself from the domination of the literary critic![13]

I am not suggesting that the battle among rhetorical scholars, if it comes, is apt to follow similar lines. We are not likely, I think, to hear it asserted by either the historians or critics of public address that they do not need each other. In the field of imaginative literature, where the judgment to be rendered is an aesthetic one, it is understandable that some critics should take the position that extrinsic factors are irrelevant. But if the distinctions traditionally drawn between poetic and rhetoric are worth anything at all, it is clear that a consideration of "historical" data—rhetor, purpose, audience, situation—is indispensable to the critical judgment of rhetorical discourse. The dictum of Bower Aly, written in 1941, has become a commonplace: the requirement imposed by audience and occasion "determines the nature of oratory and forms the mold of its criticism." And we recall the words of Bryant quoted earlier, "rhetorical criticism must depend almost entirely upon historical knowledge for its effectiveness." An observation by literary critic David Daiches serves to highlight the contrast between the literary and the rhetorical approaches to criticism. Daiches answers the question of whether biographical or historical information is necessary to criticism by saying that it is *not* needed "in order to assess the written work as it exists, *an independent and self-existent work of art*," but he acknowledges that such information may be needed "in order to see the work properly before we begin to assess it."[14] But the artifact under scrutiny by the rhetorical critic is not "an independent and self-existent work of art"; it is discourse in context, discourse functioning in what Bitzer has described as "the rhetorical

---

[12]Ronald S. Crane, "History *vs.* Criticism in the Study of Literature," *English Journal* (College Edition), 24 (1935), 660-62.

[13]A. M. Schlesinger, "American History and American Literary History," in *Reinterpretation of American Literature,* ed. Norman Foerster (New York: Harcourt, Brace, 1928), pp. 163-64.

[14]*Critical Approaches to Literature* (Englewood Cliffs, N. J.: Prentice-Hall, 1956), p. 324.

situation." This being the case, historical information is needed both "to see the work properly" and to judge its appropriateness in modifying the situation.[15] All of which is to say that although the value of *literary* history as handmaiden to *literary* criticism may be in some doubt, there can be no such doubt regarding the close relationship between *rhetorical* history and *rhetorical* criticism.

What then is my concern? It is that in our enthusiasm for rhetorical criticism—narrowly regarded as the examination of individual works of art leading to enhanced understanding and appreciation or to normative critical statements, or broadly conceived as pronouncing a judgment upon the persuasive effects of almost anything—we may neglect important scholarly responsibilities. As the literary scholar has made himself custodian of a body of imaginative writings, so should we be the custodians of a body of purposive, public discourse in which the literary man for various reasons has not shown much interest. If, as Professor Jones asserts, the literary scholar is "the historian of literary culture," the "historian of those ideas which have expressed themselves in literary form," can it not be said that the student of public address is (among other things, perhaps) the historian of those ideas which have expressed themselves in practical public discourse?

Yet, unless I am mistaken, we are moving in a quite different direction. It is my observation, corroborated by several colleagues, that new Ph.D.'s like to regard themselves as "theorists" or "critics." Moreover, we have rushed to get courses in criticism into the undergraduate curriculum, courses which are often taken by students who can scarcely name a half-dozen American speakers or speeches, students to whom Webster, Clay, Ingersoll, Beveridge, Otis, and Everett are almost total strangers. Most of our undergraduates feel capable of writing a "criticism" of a contemporary speech by President Nixon, Father Berrigan, or Jack Anderson, but many do not see the necessity of making the acquaintance of any American speech or speaker prior to Malcolm X.

I intend no derogation of criticism, whether narrowly or broadly conceived. But I do protest the view that historical studies of orators and oratory are less important or valuable than critiques of individual speeches, that all good theses and dissertations must be titled "A Rhetorical Criticism of. . . ." Just as all scholarly writing about literature and the writing of literature is not

---

[15]Bruce Gronbeck, in the article cited earlier (n. 2), defines rhetorical history as "the study of the historical effects of rhetorical discourse." Such analysis, he affirms, is primarily e*xtrinsic,* it "finds most of its confirming materials *outside a rhetorical artifact."* Rhetorical criticism, "the analysis of rhetorical discourse and acts for a series of essentially normative or advisory purposes," is essentially *intrinsic* analysis, which "finds most of its confirming materials *inside a rhetorical artifact."* I find several difficulties in these definitions and distinctions, the most serious of which is that the rhetorical artifact is not simply an object (e.g., a speech text) as Gronbeck seems to imply, but a transaction, a dynamic process—rhetorical discourse operating in an historical context. Hence, the chief distinguishing feature of rhetorical criticism cannot be that it relies upon intrinsic rather than extrinsic analysis.

literary criticism, so all writing about orators and oratory is not rhetorical criticism. And the further point I am anxious to make is that scholarly writing which is not "criticism" is not, *ipso facto,* unworthy, nor is it necessarily an excursion into other fields of learning. Histories of literature, of religion, of music, of journalism, we have—but no completely satisfactory history of American oratory. And we shall not have one until a great many more historical (and, yes, more critical) monographs are undertaken.

If for the moment we may assume acceptance of the proposition that all students of public address need *not* be "rhetorical critics," that a need still exists for sound historical research and writing, which like all research should be "critical" in the sense we have indicated, the question remains—what kind of history? I suggest that we may profitably turn for one answer to Wrage's 1947 article. There, it will be remembered, he advanced the thesis that students of public address have the credentials and the subject matter interest to contribute substantially to the history of ideas. To the objection that to do so is to invade the sanctuary of the professional historian, he replied that "a study is to be judged by its merits, not by the writer's union card." Calling attention to the need for an academic division of labor, he pointed out that the writing of intellectual history is dependent upon contributions from scholars in a variety of fields. The same opinion was expressed a year later by historian Arthur Lovejoy, who, in an essay on "The Historiography of Ideas," noted the need for cross-fertilization among primarily distinct disciplines. The pieces to be put together in trustworthy historical synthesis, he said, "must be provided, or at least be critically inspected, by those having special training and up-to-date technical knowledge in the fields to which the pieces primarily belong."[16] And in 1946 Professor Bert Loewenberg had urged upon his colleagues in the Mississippi Valley Historical Association the importance of scholarly collaboration, and had called for "a 'Manhattan project' of learning in the social sciences and the humanities."[17]

Central to Wrage's message was the idea that speeches are *mirrors* as well as *instruments* or engines. Because speeches are prepared with listeners in mind, he said, because speeches on vital issues are "vibrant with the immediacy of life, with the sense of interaction between speaker and listeners," they are admirable indices to social thought. It appears in retrospect that Wrage's principal contribution as an historian of public address was his moderation of the overpowering emphasis upon personal persuasion, upon demonstrating the *influence* of oratory on human events. He shifted the focus to *ideas;* his was an attempt to learn what the *substance* of a speech, together with the rhetorical strategies by means of which that substance is communicated to audiences, can tell us about the times out of which the speeches grew, the audiences to whom they were addressed, and the men and women

---

[16]*Essays in the History of Ideas* (Baltimore: Johns Hopkins Press, 1948), p. 10.
[17]*The History of Ideas, 1935-1945: Retrospect and Prospect* (New York: Rinehart, 1947), pp. 21-22.

who uttered them. Professor Brigance introduced his two volumes with this sentence: "This work deals with the influence of American public address on the flow of history." Today's writers are more modest about their ability to assess influence upon history; they know that influence is an extraordinarily difficult thing to establish, much less to measure.

This change of emphasis may be seen in subsequent scholarship in the field. *American Forum* and *Contemporary Forum* made a start in selecting speeches for study which reflect the values and attitudes of their times, and later anthologies adopted a similar pattern. Idea-centered, issue-oriented courses in the history of American public address were introduced. Some of our most distinguished published volumes have been such contributions to social history as Wrage might well have applauded: Auer's *Antislavery and Disunion,* which one reviewer called "the speech profession's most imposing exercise in social and intellectual history";[18] Gunderson's *Log Cabin Campaign;* Braden's *Oratory in the Old South;* Holland's *Preaching in American History* and *America in Controversy;* Oliver's *History of Public Speaking in America,* which eschews the effusive personal eulogy of earlier histories and presents the history of American public speaking as "a central core around which to depict the general flow of the history itself."

All these scholars, and there have, of course, been others, have given credence to Wrage's observation that he "who is sensitized to rhetoric, who is schooled in its principles and techniques," possesses credentials for scholarship in the history of ideas "as that history is portrayed in public speeches." They have been engaged, as Wrage believed we should be, in illustrating, testing, verifying, and revising "generalizations offered by other workers in social and intellectual history."

Ernest Wrage, then, has provided one answer to the question, "What kind of history?" Others are not far to seek. When Howard Mumford Jones described the "true business" of the literary scholar in much the same way that Wrage counselled his fellow rhetoricians, he added: "He is also the historian of the significant forms in which those ideas are expressed." Certainly there is much to be done in recording the history of the various forms of public address. I know of no recent book which undertakes such a task, and relatively few articles. In the last century articles in the popular journals on after-dinner speaking, campaign oratory, the lecture, and various types of occasional speaking were fairly common. T. B. Reed's fifteen-volume deluxe edition of *Modern Eloquence,* published at the turn of the century, introduced each genre with a special essay. Edward E. Hale contributed a chronicle of lectures and lecturing; Lorenzo Sears described after-dinner speaking, Hamilton W. Mabie the literary address; and Senator Jonathan Dolliver wrote an excellent historical account of stump-speaking. These are modest beginnings from which genuine histories of these forms

---

[18]Wayne C. Minnick, *QJS,* 49 (1963), 85.

might be developed.

Another scholarly emphasis has been suggested by Bower Aly. Despite Wrage's warning concerning the difficulty of establishing influence, we are continually reminded that oratory *can* be a force in history. After studying the persuasive skill of Alexander Hamilton in the New York ratifying convention, Professor Aly proposes that students of public address, viewing people "engaged in the process of persuading one another to do what they want done," may formulate a "rhetorical theory of history" to replace, or at least to supplement, prevailing interpretations of history.[19]

There would also seem to be a need to make some significant beginnings toward a history of the *art* of oratory. Not a series of critical essays on individual speeches nor a collection of biographical sketches of speakers, but a history of the art, analogous to histories of the art of music or architecture. Perhaps the closest thing to the kind of approach I am suggesting here is found in Guy Carleton Lee's ten volume work on *The World's Orators* (1900). Each volume includes an essay on the period of oratory therein illustrated. These essays deal with such topics as conditions propitious to the development of an art of oratory, forces responsible for molding the art, changing conceptions of eloquence, oratorical genres and epochs, the rise and decline of oratory in various nations and periods. The claim of the editor that these essays, when taken together, comprise "a history of oratory by specialists," may be somewhat exaggerated, but they do suggest a method and a direction which twentieth-century scholars might profitably explore. What, we might ask, were the needs and expectations of audiences at different periods in our national history; how and why did these expectations and needs change, and how did oratory change with them? How was the orator regarded? What principal social functions did he perform? In what esteem was he held? How did he perceive his own role in society? What qualities in oratory were admired and applauded? What constituted oratorical excellence in a given period, and in what ways did these standards of excellence change with changing times? No doubt the completion of such a history of the art must wait upon many perceptive historical and critical monographs, but let us begin.

If it be true as Professor Homer Hockett has affirmed that "no phase of human conduct or thought is any longer regarded as closed to the historian," then it is clear that he will need considerable assistance from many who are not dignified with the title of professional historian or addressed in care of a university Department of History. There is no space here to enumerate the ways in which historians of public address may be of assistance to the general historian, but for an excellent discussion of the subject I would refer you to Marie Nichols' Louisiana State lecture on "Rhetoric, Public Address,

---

[19]*The Rhetoric of Alexander Hamilton* (New York: Columbia Univ. Press, 1941), p. 197.

and History,"[20] in which she reports conversations with professional historians who discuss the kinds of materials they look to us to provide.

Let me try in conclusion briefly to summarize some of the points I have wished to make in these speculations concerning history and criticism. First of all, it goes without saying that all scholarly research and writing must be "critical" in tone, must employ critical methods. However, "criticism" as a literary genre focuses upon the artistry of the maker; it has as its end interpretation, appreciation, elucidation, appraisal, of a work of art. Sometimes, though not necessarily, it may culminate in normative critical statements. History, on the other hand, whether primarily concerned with individuals, or with groups, movements, or eras, furnishes a record which associates works of art with background. It provides perspective. It may deal with the influence upon the art of political, economic, social, or geographical factors. Nevertheless, despite differing emphases, criticism and the history of public address are complementary studies. Historical reconstruction provides indispensable information on which judgment and appreciation may be based; it helps get straight the facts of the rhetorical situation. The critic who has the greatest familiarity with the history of his subject—its foremost practitioners, its movements, eras, forms, and changing canons of judgment—is best equipped to discern quality in individual works. And painstaking analysis of rhetorical discourse by a critic may contribute to the enrichment of subsequent historical writing about a given period, form, or movement.

Moreover, given the practical nature of rhetorical discourse, its close relationship with audience and situation, it is inevitable that "history"—the weaving of facts regarding speaker, audience, and occasion into some kind of meaningful narrative—will often constitute a part of, or a preliminary to, an essay in rhetorical criticism. Thus, the familiar concept "history and criticism" or "historical-critical studies" is particularly appropriate to public address. But all significant writing about public address need not be criticism, in the special sense of that term, nor need all scholars be rhetorical critics. The worth of a product of scholarship is determined not by the label placed upon it, but by the competence with which it is executed. A need exists for good history and biography, for meticulously researched descriptive monographs. In our field, as in most fields, there is a need for scholars who can record accurately and artistically the history of our art as it relates to more general history, to delineate its place in and contribution to the cultural history of the nation.

One would hope that this final point would be obvious, and scarcely in dispute. But perhaps it needs to be explicitly stated, if only to modify an apparent preoccupation with criticism and to defend those whose *forte* is historical writing about speakers and speaking against the repeated charge that they are guilty of excursions into other fields. Each discipline develops

---

[20]*Rhetoric and Criticism* (Baton Rouge: Louisiana State Univ. Press, 1963).

its own historians; there must be historians of public address as there are historians of literature, art, music, education, and religion. The historical method is not the sole possession of any one academic discipline.

I would suggest finally that indispensable as criticism is, and despite our remarkable success during the last decade in achieving greater artistry and sophistication in our critical writing, criticism, as it becomes more technical, becomes more parochial in its appeal; its consumers are likely to be other critics, usually in the same academic enclave. Our most effective links with the rest of the academic community are apt to be forged by scholarly writing which contributes what we are best equipped to contribute to that "'Manhattan project' of learning in the social sciences and the humanities" envisioned by Professor Loewenberg.

Elegy in a Critical Grave-Yard

by G. P. Mohrmann

It now has been fifteen years since the appearance of *Rhetorical Criticism,* and if that seems like only yesterday to some, many readers attracted to this special issue of the *Western Journal of Speech Communication* may not recall the state of the art at the time, nor will they recall reactions to the book. In the hope of giving them at least some faint hint of time and place—and especially for those who do remember—I turn to the source echoed in the title and to the first stanzas of Gray's "Elegy Written in a Country Church-Yard." Since the publication of *Rhetorical Criticism,* I have had difficulty responding to these lines as Gray might have wished, but if the images provoked are unpoetic, many seem particularly appropriate to the book and its reception.

> The curfew tolls the knell of parting day,
> The lowing herd wind slowly o'er the lea,
> The plowman homeward plods his weary way,
> And leaves the world to darkness and to me.
>
> Now fades the glimmering landscape on the sight
> And all the air a solemn stillness holds,
> Save where the beetle wheels his droning flight,
> And drowsy tinklings lull the distant folds;
>
> Save that from yonder ivy-mantled tower
> The moping owl does to the moon complain
> Of such as, wandering near her secret bower
> Molest her ancient solitary reign.

Those who do remember will recollect signs of near stampede in the lowing herd and the complaints of moping owls issuing from many ivy-mantled towers. Yet if Black tolled the knell of parting day for traditional criticism, he was not the first to molest the ancient solitary reign, for as he points out, his dissatisfaction was "not a singular emotion, if one may judge

Reprinted from *Western Journal of Speech Communication* 44 (1980), with permission of the Western Communication Association.

from the growing literature of professional protest and vocational self-analysis in the speech journals."[1] In that connection, Stewart has documented an increasing swell of protest during the thirties and forties, and for the ten years immediately preceding the publication of *Rhetorical Criticism,* he reports an "ever increasing discontent with traditional criticism."[2]

So in tolling the funeral note, Black rang Nine Taylors, but others had been ringing Major Bobs and Grandsires for years, had been ringing the changes of discontent for decades prior to 1965. Consequently, one is led to suspect that an examination of speech communication journals from 1961 through 1965 would reveal that traditional methods already were at low ebb, even though those who argued for new approaches "provided little actual methodology or illustration."[3] In any event, my assignment specified a con-temporary perspective, and while I turned to the journals when gathering materials for this report, I inspected the run of publication for the past five years in two national and four regional entries, the 1975-1979 issues of the *Quarterly Journal of Speech, Communication Monographs, Western Journal of Speech Communication, Southern Journal of Speech Communication, Central States Speech Journal,* and *Communication Quarterly* for a grand total of nine hundred articles.[4]

A seemingly safe and sane perimeter, if somewhat unimaginative. Never-theless, it no sooner had been established than my thoughts raced to Poe's narrator and his first view of that melancholy House of Usher, for "a sense of insufferable gloom pervaded my spirit. I say insufferable; for the feeling was un-relieved by any of that half-pleasurable, because poetic, sentiment with which the mind usually receives even the sternest natural images of the desolate or terrible." Unlike Prufrock, I thought I knew how to begin, but like him, I was afraid. I feared a desolate and terrible wasteland. I feared that the enterprise was predestined to end, not with a bang but a whimper. Within the established perimeter I had spent three years on the editorial board of the *Quarterly Journal of Speech,* and although it would not be fair to accuse the Editor of having been unconscionable in his demands, he did seem bent on making sure that my editorial hands would never stray to the devil's workshop. Yet I remembered having reviewed few critiques in the traditional mold, and an examination of my files confirmed the immediate impression. At best, I might just be facing an exercise in futility.

Furthermore, was it not more than a little presumptuous to undertake a postmortem at this late date? This critical hobby-horse long since had been

[1] Edwin Black, *Rhetorical Criticism: A Study in Method* (New York: Macmillan, 1965, rpt.: Madison, Wisconsin: University of Wisconsin Press, 1978), p. viii.

[2] Charles J. Stewart, "Historical Survey: Rhetorical Criticism in Twentieth Century America," in *Explorations in Rhetorical Criticism,* ed. G. P. Mohrmann, Charles J. Stewart, and Donovan J. Ochs (University Park: Pennsylvania State University Press, 1973), p. 19.

[3] Ibid.

[4] *Communication Education* occasionally features discussions of critical theory but almost no critiques.

entombed, the Reverend Edwin Black presiding, and an exhumation now seemed the depth of folly. What putrefication awaited in the dank tomb? After the damp and the worms and the termites, what could I expect to find of the poor creature's carcass? Three tiny fragments of rusting proofs? Five small mounds of sawdust, one for each of the classical offices? Or would there be nothing at all, nothing but the fetid stench of puerile biography and vacuous history?

But wait! A sudden hope curbed that disastrous line of thought. Perhaps it was not a tale told by Poe. Madeline Usher, Berenice, and Fortunato did not survive their premature burials, but maybe our steed, too, had been buried alive, and what if plodding plowman and droning beetle and moping owl had met in seance to pass some sort of miracle? It was possible. Though spavined, long in the tooth, and more than a little sway-backed, maybe our old and faithful mount still carried riders on their appointed rounds through the ranges of critical inquiry.

I can announce that it does. I have ridden the trail of the critical round-up in the pages of our journals, and if the ride had its box-canyons and dry water holes, I must report that both my hopes and fears were realized. There was some of life and some of death. To put it oxymoronically: traditional rhetorical criticism currently is in a state of moribund vitality. That figure will control the analysis here, and it seems most logical to talk first of life, then of death. A qualification, however, is necessary because the intent is not to begin by defining terms, to distinguish between and among "traditional," "neo-classical," and "neo-Aristotelian" criticism. In truth, I think I can recognize the presence of that for which I was told to look, think I can recognize the spoor of our beast.

In fact, some critics are quite content with old riding gaits and old starting gates. The walk, the trot, the canter, and the gallop are the four natural gaits, and we have the four natural gates of criticism in the four remaining classical offices, *memoria* having fallen out of the saddle-bags on the way West. The critic may not invoke Aristotle, Cicero, or Wichelns, but lines of investigation and the vocabulary may create a strong presumption; "the primary and identifying ideas" to which one must be attuned "are the classification of rhetorical discourse into forensic, deliberative and epideictic; the classification of 'proofs' or 'means of persuasion' into logical, pathetic, and ethical; the assessment of discourse in the categories of invention, arrangement, delivery, and style; and the evaluation of rhetorical discourse in terms of its effects on its immediate audience."[5]

Typical concerns and typical vocabulary exhibit a vitality in the pages of our journals, but there is an even earlier sign: the contributor. This is not to imply that riders never change horses, but most have favorite mounts they customarily ride through familiar terrain. Consequently, I have certain

---

[5] Black, p. 31.

expectations as soon as I see that Loren Reid has written "Bright's Tributes to Garrison and Field"[6] and that Cal Logue has reported on "Gubernatorial Campaign in Georgia in 1880."[7] And for good or for ill, my expectations almost always are confirmed. Of course the very titles are suggestive, and so are others: "Exploitation of Ethos: Sarah Winnemucca and Bright Eyes on the Lecture Tour,"[8] "The Seventh of March Address: A Mediating Influence,"[9] "Rhetorical Strategies in the Courtrooms of Territorial Arkansas,"[10] "Lyndon Johnson and the 'Crisis' of Tonkin Gulf: A President's Justification of War."[11] Surely titles can be misleading, but when the colon is so common, the writer usually indicates when there will be a Burkean inquiry, an application of Toulmin, a fantasy theme analysis, or some other point of departure. In the absence of an announced alternative, one expects traditional terms and bases when the object is the Convention Keynote by Dan Williams[12] or Barbara Jordan,[13] Bright as orator and teacher,[14] forensic oratory in Cicero's career,[15] rhetorical image-making,[16] or metaphors, whether archetypal or not.[17]

Again the expectation is confirmed regularly. The critics may not exhaust the available topics, but neither did the contributors to *A History and Criticism of American Public Address,* and they ordinarily were looking to an entire career and had far more space than is granted in our journals. In any event, critics look to speakers and the effects of speech-making; they explore Evan's failure to adapt to multiple audiences in 1968[18] and Jordan's success in 1978,[19] analyze a Senate speech by Arthur Vandenburg,[20] explain the rhe-

---

[6] *Quarterly Journal of Speech,* 61 (1975), 169-177.

[7] *Southern Speech Communication Journal,* 40 (1974), 12-32.

[8] Pat Creech Scholten, "Exploitation of Ethos: Sarah Winnemucca and Bright Eyes on the Lecture Tour," *Central States Speech Journal,* 41 (1977), 233-244.

[9] Paul Arntson and Craig R. Smith, "The Seventh of March Address: A Mediating Influence," *Southern Speech Communication Journal,* 40 (1975) , 288-301.

[10] Stephen A. Smith, "Rhetorical Strategies in the Courtroom of Territorial Arkansas," *Southern Speech Communication Journal,* 42 (1977), 318-333.

[11] Richard A. Cherwitz, "Lyndon Johnson and the 'Crisis' of Tonkin Gulf: A President's Justification of War," *Western Journal of Speech Communication,* 42 (1977), 93-104.

[12] Craig R. Smith, "The Republican Keynote Address of 1968: Adaptive Rhetoric for the Multiple Audience," *Western Journal of Speech Communication,* 39 (1975), 32-39.

[13] Wayne N. Thompson, "Barbara Jordan's Keynote Address: The Juxtaposition of Contradictory Values," *Southern Speech Communication Journal,* 44 (1979), 223-232.

[14] Loren Reid, "John Bright: The Orator as Teacher," *Southern Speech Communication Journal,* 41 (1975), 45-48.

[15] Richard Leo Enos, "Cicero's Forensic Oratory: The Manifestation of Power in the Roman Republic," *Southern Speech Communication Journal,* 40 (1975), 377-394.

[16] Thomas Clark, "Rhetorical Image-Making: A Case Study of the Thomas Paine-William Smith Debates," *Southern Speech Communication Journal,* 40 (1975), 248-261.

[17] William E. Richert, "Winston Churchill's Archetypal Metaphors: A Mythopoetic Translation of World War II," *Central States Speech Journal,* 28 (1977), 106-112; Hermann G. Stelzner, "Ford's War on Inflation: A Metaphor that Did Not Cross," *Communication Monographs,* 45 (1977), 284-297.

[18] Craig R. Smith, "The Republican Keynote Address of 1968."

[19] Thompson, "Barbara Jordan's Keynote Address."

[20] Richard B. Gregg, "A Rhetorical Re-examination of Arthur Vandenberg's 'Dramatic Conversion,' January 10, 1945," *Quarterly Journal of Speech,* 61 (1975), 154-168.

torical dimensions of Nazi meetings in Germany.[21] Sometimes the inheritance is patent, as it is when one encounters a summary statement that includes "delivery, law, logic, language, strategy, invective, and pathos,"[22] or the contention that "the interaction of ethos and delivery with the message elements made the value appeals seem sincere."[23] In an article on Churchill, the primary emphasis is upon his delivery;[24] language use is central in an examination of the oral argument in the Bakke case;[25] arrangement and style are fundamental in a comparison between *Common Sense* and *Cato's Letters*.[26]

So we find the familiar steed rocking in a comfortable paddock, but there is change, and if the rock is not hard rock, there are touches of modernity, traces of new tack. Examples above include the examination of non-oratorical artifacts, and critics up-date their vocabulary. In the article about Churchill, it is not delivery that detains the critic; it is "body-language."[27] Even Reid talks about Bright's "non-verbal" communication and lists "warmth, dynamism, charisma" as elements in the speaker's ethos.[28] In another critique, ethos becomes image: "The Presentation of Image in Ella T. Grasso's Campaign," the critic remarking, "Image depends upon the projected impression of the personal character of the candidate."[29] And if there is more in twentieth-century communication than is dreamed of in the Rhetoric, ethos as image plays an important part in an analysis of Wallace and the media in the Florida primary of 1972.[30]

Critics have become even more adroit at transcending logos and pathos. Inductive and deductive processes clearly are passé, as are immediate emotional connections. Now one encounters tactics and strategies and appeals to cultural or societal values. On the surface it appears quite grand, and a reader might be inclined to believe that a lively mustang now is careening the range of criticism, but when the cosmic dust of the new terminology settles, what is really seen? Why, there is our little hobby-horse rocking, rocking, rocking. And even if I did not have the testimony that I do have from contributors, I would be led to suspect that the new vocabulary simply is a way to smuggle

[21]Randall L. Bytwerk, "Rhetorical Aspects of the Nazi Meeting, 1926-1933," *Quarterly Journal of Speech,* 61 (1975), 307-318.

[22]Stephen R. Smith, 333.

[23]Thompson, 230.

[24]Manfred Weidhorn, "Churchill as Orator: Wish and Fulfillment," *Southern Speech Communication Journal,* 40 (1975) 217-227.

[25]Gayle Lewis Levison, "The Rhetoric of the Oral Argument in the Regents of the University of California V. Bakke," *Western Journal of Speech Communication,* 43 (1979), 271-277.

[26]Clark.

[27]Weidhorn.

[28]Reid, 56-57.

[29]Ardyce C. Whalen, "The Presentation of Image in Ella T. Grasso's Campaign," *Central States Speech Journal,* 27 (1976), 207-208.

[30]Michael D. Murray, "Wallace and the Media: The 1972 Florida Primary," *Southern Speech Communication Journal,* 40 (1975), 429-440.

our pony past all those editors and reviewers, those critics of critics with their olefactory lobes always sensitive to any scent of decaying horse-flesh.

Note, too, that there are times when the tradition is presented in the year-ling sales as the first foal of an entirely new breed. This has happened on more than one occasion with those riders who have climbed aboard the fantasy theme hobby. One example is to be found in Hensley's "Rhetorical Vision and the Persuasion of a Historical Movement: The Disciples of Christ in Nineteenth Century American Culture."[31] On the basis of one vision, the Disciples are millinarians;[32] in others they preach evangelization, unity, and restoration;[33] and among the fantasies are those "in which Anglo-Saxons were superior to minority races."[34] So the Disciples believed in and preached the millenium; along the way they developed three related lines of argument or appeals; they even capitalized on the myth of Anglo-Saxon superiority. It happens that Hensley's discussion strikes me as the product of an intelligent and contained mind, but I am convinced that the ground of argument is cumbered rather than clarified when all the old critical vocabulary is col-lapsed into "fantasy themes" and "rhetorical visions," the whole encom-passed in dramatism.

Another illustration appears in Kidd's "Happily Ever After and Other Relationship Styles: Advice on Interpersonal Relations in Popular Magazines, 1951-1973."[35] Although adducing no fantasy themes, she isolates two clusters of advice, each of which "included explanations for appropriate behavior in caring relationships, specific suggestions for face-to-face interaction, and provided readers modes of meaning in exchange between persons."[36] These clusters become visions. Now before Bormann published his original state-ment[37] and before she had been exposed to those notions, Kidd had executed a remarkably similar analysis of California textbooks.[38] She could not use visions then, and she really had no need for them later; once more the ground of an intelligent argument is clouded.[39]

Frost has his introspective New England farmer say, "Before I built a wall I'd ask to know/What I was walling in or walling out," and since

---

[31]Carl Wayne Hensley, "Rhetorical Vision and the Persuasion of a Historical Movement: The Disciples of Christ in Nineteenth Century America," *Quarterly Journal of Speech,* 61 (1975), 250-264.

[32]Ibid., 252-264.

[33]Ibid., 255-258.

[34]Ibid., 261.

[35]Virginia Kidd, "Happily Ever After and Other Relationship Styles: Advice on Interpersonal Relations in Popular Magazines, 1951-1973," *Quarterly Journal of Speech,* 63 (1975), 31-39.

[36]Ibid., 32.

[37]Ernest G. Bormann, "Fantasy and Rhetorical Vision: The Rhetorical Criticism of Social Reality," *Quarterly Journal of Speech,* 58 (1972), 396-407.

[38]Virginia Kidd, "The Rhetoric of the First Grade Reader," *Papers of the Conference in Rhetorical Criticism,* California State College, Hayward, California, 1970, pp. 7-10.

[39]I admit to a marked dissatisfaction with the theoretical basis that Bormann uses in his program for criticism, but I do not think that dissatisfaction distorts my interpretation of the efforts by Hensley and Kidd. And it should be noted that Kidd's discussion is far from being a traditional critique: at the same time, it demonstrates the tendency to depart from conventional and useful terminology.

fantasy theme critics wall everything in and nothing out, many do treat of topics far removed from traditional concerns and vocabulary. Nevertheless, there are those among them who seem to feel that to change brands is enough to turn a plater into a Spectacular Bid. Saying that, I surely offend both apprentices and trainer, but so be it. I would respond as Hamlet does when Gertrude complains that he has much offended her. I think, in fact, that many more of us should be much offended by the way any manner of critic has played fast and loose with the tradition. Whatever the point of departure and whether announced or not, too many have pretended that they knew not the horse, have pretended that they are virtuosos riding bareback on a show horse cavorting for the first time. They accomplish little, other than to imply that the old horse has been replaced by a more adventuresome steed, or to take self-satisfaction from the awareness that other riders are wearing the same colors. I will return to the pretense momentarily, but I have been trying to suggest that the vitality of the tradition in criticism is not all that vibrant, and it is time to turn directly to its moribund character.

For the five year run of publication in the journals and among the nine hundred articles printed, no more than fifty or sixty qualify as traditional critiques. That total obtains even when those horses decked out in novel trappings and tack are included, and a total of five or six percent smacks of the moribund. Worse, Black is right, after all, when he laments that the traditional "critic typically sees only one direction of movement: the background, training, interest, and aims of the rhetor influence his discourse which in turn influences the audience"[40] and when, after contending that this mode limits the conception of context, he complains that the approach "substitutes historical reconstruction for re-creative criticism: and it limits judicial criticism to the evaluation of immediate effects."[41] Though one may not go so far as to accept, without qualification, his contention that this "mode of rhetorical criticism is profoundly mistaken,"[42] that mode certainly did not encourage the critic to explore speech texts intensely and extensively. That is another matter to which I shall return momentarily because the earlier misuse of traditional concepts and the current pretenses regarding them eventually coalesce. To some that coalescence might be most happily resolved by utter extinction, the hooves of that sullen beast stilled forever, with a ceremonial urn containing the ashes displayed at SCA headquarters.

I have two objections to that denouement. First, Baskerville has a point when he queries, "Must We All Be 'Rhetorical Critics'?"[43] We all do not have to be, and we can use rhetorical artifacts in a variety of ways. Whatever the role of education in introducing students to new ideas and to

[40]Black, pp. 34-35.
[41]Ibid., p. 75.
[42]Ibid., p. viii.
[43]Barnet Baskerville, "Must We all Be 'Rhetorical Critics'?" *Quarterly Journal of Speech,* 63 (1977), 107-116.

ways of dealing with them, the enterprise unquestionably has conservative dimensions. To preserve and continue the cultural heritage is a primary function, and speakers and speeches can tell us more than a little about Western Civilization, even when the Great Man theory has been abandoned. One can read speeches and study speakers without engaging in close critical analysis; they can be read and studied for ideas and their configurations in a given cultural milieu. If Wrage deserved some of the credit, Baskerville taught just such a course,[44] and though there is no criticism *per se* in *The People's Voice,*[45] that hardly detracts from the quality of the book. Many of us have been too often detained with the Old Dead Orators in quaint and archane ways, but that does not mean that a rhetorical orientation to history and biography cannot be a wholesome and stimulating venture.

I have a second objection to the demise of the tradition in criticism, and to me it is vastly more important. We do not all have to be critics, but when we set up shop for a critic, we ought to know what we are about, and the farther we get from traditional matters, the greater the danger that we will forever be Willy Lomans, never knowing who we are. The Renaissance humanists made some extremely nice and curious arguments, but they knew their rhetoric and knew it well. We in the twentieth century never have established a critical identity. What does it profit us to flee from logos and pathos and ethos to strategies and values and body language, particularly when we never adequately taught ourselves and our students what logos and pathos and ethos were within the texture of the critical enterprise?

The Young Republicans who gathered at the Cooper Union Institute on the evening of February 27, 1860 surely did not stand around after Lincoln's performance and marvel among themselves about the logical bases in the first and most important movement in the speech. Nevertheless, the impact of the argument was noted and reported.[46] But suppose it had not, and suppose that Lincoln had returned to lasting obscurity in the West. His artistry remains, and if there are other profitable approaches to the text—as certainly there are—and if my co-author and I were phenomenologically naive in our analysis, I am satisfied that the uses we made of logical aspects helped explicate the text.[47]

That same co-author and I argued in a paper echoed above that in the aftermath of *Rhetorical Criticism,* critics have not done much more than achieve a nervous novelty and that "we now wander without system, without rigor, and without common points of reference, drifting farther and farther

---

[44]I would rank it very high among the courses I took as a graduate student.

[45]Barnet Baskerville, *The People's Voice* (Lexington: University Press of Kentucky, 1979).

[46]See Chicago *Tribune,* March 1, 1860, p. 1. The article includes pertinent comments from both New York *Tribune* and New York *Evening Post* reports of the speech.

[47]Michael C. Leff and G. P. Mohrmann, "Lincoln at Cooper Union: A Rhetorical Analysis of the Text," *Quarterly Journal of Speech,* 60 (1974), 346-358.

from a center that might hold together."[48] At the time, we were misunderstood because some thought we were contending that the old hobby-horse had to be resuscitated and ridden by all. That is not what we meant; that is not even what we said. We did not intend that time should be turned back four decades; we intended, instead, that critics return to common topics available in the rhetorical tradition and employ those topics to make close and careful inspection of rhetorical texts. That is something that rarely has been done, and we are convinced that the effort could well have a salutary influence upon criticism generally.

In the earlier uses of the tradition, the critic is a curcuit rider, forever circling around and about the herd, but never getting into its center. Yet if this critic seldom takes us into the text of the speech and its workings, the pretense in the contemporary adaptations and departures is no more satisfying. The casual observer may see stunning performances on spirited mounts, the glories of the equestrian world, but a closer look cuts through the noise and glamour of the Big Top. The largest of the rings is small, and it is, after all, a ring, with horse and rider going round and round. I am put in mind of the Shetland pony rides at county fairs and local picnics during the thirties, the gelded ponies plodding wearily on their treadmill to oblivion. Despite any pretense, it has not changed much since Ehninger observed that traditional critics tend to "classify certain grosser properites cast under the heads of the traditional modes and canons" and to produce "a mechanical accounting or summing up of how well the speech fits an a priori mold."[49]

New molds for old is no answer, and there is no simple cure for our malaise. The tradition, as such, hardly offers a panacea, but its components at least derive directly from the practice of rhetoric, not from anthropology, sociology, Freudian psychology, the theatre, or some other source. Used with intelligence and imagination, the available topics may help us truly to understand and to appreciate the text and texture of messages. That will never happen, of course, until the effort is made, and in spite of the conventional wisdom, it never has been attempted with any sustained vigor and rigor.[50] Until that happens, our faithful hobby-horse will rock in ever-decreasing circles, regardless of its varied guises, and by naming the parts, critics will continue to pretend they have said something about how the parts work together.

---

[48]Michael C. Leff and G. P. Mohrmann, "Old Paths and New: A Fable for Critics," Speech Communication Association convention, Washington, D.C., 1977.

[49]Douglas Ehningher, "Rhetoric and the Critic," *Western Speech*, 29 (1965), 230.

[50]To quote again from the paper cited in note 48: "We used to study speeches, right? Wrong! How about Clay, Calhoun, and Webster for openers? A total of seventeen articles in national and regional journals, but no writer has seen fit to deal with the entire text of one of their speeches. Emerson? Eight articles, none on a particular speech. Jonathan Edwards? Not one article. Acres of Diamonds? No article. The New South? One, a Hegelian analysis. Abraham Lincoln? Thirty-two articles, but only if we are generous can we say that as many as three explore the rhetoric of a given speech."

Having started by doing violence to a great poem, I conclude in the same way. I would not suggest that rhetorical artifacts hold out the attractions that compare with those Herbert Reed fashions for his unhappy recruit, but I see some sense here, though I may lack sensibility.

Naming of Parts

To-day we have naming of parts. Yesterday,
We had daily cleaning. And to-morrow morning,
We shall have what to do after firing. But to-day,
To-day we have naming of parts. Japonica
Glistens like coral in all of the neighboring gardens,
    And to-day we have naming of parts.

This is the lower sling swivel. And this
Is the upper sling swivel, whose use you will see,
When you are given your slings. And this is the piling swivel,
Which in your case you have not got. The branches
Hold in the gardens their silent, eloquent gestures,
    Which in our case we have not got.

This is the safety-catch, which is always released
With an easy flick of the thumb. And please do not let me
See anyone using his finger. You can do it quite easy
If you have any strength in your thumb. The blossoms
Are fragile and motionless, never letting anyone see
    Any of them using their finger.

And this you can see is the bolt. The purpose of this
Is to open the breech, as you see. We can slide it
Rapidly backwards and forwards: we call this
Easing the spring. And rapidly backwards and forwards
The early bees are assaulting and fumbling the flowers:
    They call it easing the Spring.

They call it easing the Spring: it is perfectly easy
If you have any strength in your thumb: like the bolt,
And the breech, and the cocking-piece, and the point of balance,
Which in our case we have not got; and the almond-blossom
Silent in all of the gardens and the bees going backwards and
forwards,
    For today we have naming of parts.

The Schism in Rhetorical Scholarship

by Stephen E. Lucas

The relationship between history and criticism in the study of public address is a perennial issue intimately connected with the nature, scope, methods, and purposes of rhetorical analysis. In recent years, thought on the issue has taken a notable turn, as both a cause and consequence of the remarkable upheaval in rhetorical scholarship since the late 1950s. There appears now to be crystallizing a keen sense of schism between history and criticism, as the two are increasingly characterized—formally and informally, in published writings and private colloquies—as conflicting rather than complementary activities.[1] Unfortunately, that characterization has neither proceeded from nor produced decisive consideration of the nature of criticism or history as scholarly enterprises. This essay seeks to explore the growing schism in rhetorical scholarship and to point the way toward a new, more discerning view of the affiliation between history and criticism in the study of public address—partly in the interest of lexical precision and conceptual refinement, partly in hopes of putting to rest a dispute that has for too long diverted attention from the substance of scholarship to its classification.[2]

1

The present disjunction between history and criticism is best seen against the traditional view that the study of history is an indispensable aspect of the process of rhetorical criticism. This view may be traced back to Herbert Wichelns' seminal essay, "The Literary Criticism of Oratory." Wichelns' task was twofold: to differentiate rhetoric from literature, and to ground rhetorical criticism in the unique nature of rhetorical discourse. How he resolved these tasks is best captured in his famous injunction that the outlook of rhetorical criticism "is patently single. It is not concerned with permanence, nor yet with beauty. It is concerned with effect. It regards a speech as a communication to a specific audience, and holds its business to be the analysis and

Reprinted from *The Quarterly Journal of Speech* 67 (1981), with permission of the Speech Communication Association.

[1] Throughout this essay I use the term "history" to refer, not to past actuality, but to study of the past. I use "public address," rhetorical communication," "public discourse," and the like to encompass the full range of verbal and nonverbal public acts of a rhetorical nature.

[2] It should be carefully noted that my concern is strictly the relationship between history and criticism in rhetorical analysis, not the relationship between history and criticism in general.

appreciation of the orator's method of imparting his ideas to his hearers." To Wichelns, the locus of rhetorical criticism was the oration itself, and the burden of the critic was to appraise the artistic proofs "that secure for the speaker ready access to the minds of his auditors." But such appraisal could not be properly conducted unless the critic comprehended thoroughly a number of extrinsic historical factors—particularly the immediate audience to whom the discourse was presented and the effect of the discourse upon that audience. Consequently, said Wichelns, it was necessary "to summon history to the aid of criticism."[3]

The inextricable connection between history and criticism adumbrated by Wichelns shortly became axiomatic. In 1933 William Brigance affirmed that it was not possible to study oratory "without studying the historical foundations on which it rests" and called for *"combined historical* and *critical* study of orators and oratorical literature." In 1937 Donald Bryant argued that since rhetorical criticism "gains its value from its primary concern with considerations of audience-speaker-occasion," it "must depend almost entirely upon historical knowledge for its effectiveness." The most detailed rendering of this position came just more than a decade later, in Thonssen and Baird's enormously influential *Speech Criticism.* This work viewed speeches as manipulative instruments that lose their vitality when considered apart from their original historical milieu. The "core of any satisfactory method of rhetorical analysis" was therefore historical, and the successful critic "must, in effect, put on the garment of the past" to explicate the origins, circumstances, and consequences of particular speeches.[4]

In short, history and criticism were seen as inseparable partners whose "union is indissoluble."[5] Studies in public address were labeled "history and criticism," while the methodology employed in such studies was identified as "historical-critical." So powerfully were the two allied that forty years after Wichelns' pathsetting essay the orthodox view remained that the rhetorical analyst "must also be a student of history... if he is to comprehend public

---

[3] Herbert Wichelns, "The Literary Criticism of Oratory," in *Studies in Rhetoric and Public Speaking in Honor of James Albert Winans,* ed. A. M. Drummond (New York: Century, 1925), pp. 209, 213, 199. In differentiating rhetoric from literature, Wichelns accepted, with some qualifications, the characterizations of each advanced during the previous two years in a brace of groundsetting essays by Hoyt H. Hudson: "The Field of Rhetoric," *Quarterly Journal of Speech Education,* 9 (1923), 167-80; "Rhetoric and Poetry," *Quarterly Journal of Speech Education,* 10 (1924), 143-54.

[4] William Norwood Brigance, "Whither Research?" *Quarterly Journal of Speech,* 19 (1933), 557-58; Donald C. Bryant, "Some Problems of Scope and Method in Rhetorical Scholarship," *Quarterly Journal of Speech,* 23 (1937), 183-84; Lester Thonssen and A. Craig Baird, *Speech Criticism: The Development of Standards for Critical Appraisal* (New York: Ronald Press, 1948), pp. 11-12. Ernest J. Wrage, "Public Address: A Study in Social and Intellectual History," *Quarterly Journal of Speech,* 33 (1947), 451-57, and Leland M. Griffin, "The Rhetoric of Historical Movements," *Quarterly Journal of Speech,* 38 (1952), 184-88, both called for departures from standard approaches to the study of public address, but neither challenged the view that such study should be firmly grounded in historical scholarship. Indeed, Wrage saw the primary responsibility of the rhetorical critic as that of contributing to the history of ideas.

[5] Thonssen and Baird, *Speech Criticism,* p. 315.

address and its role in society, and if he is to make lasting critical contributions to his discipline."[6]

Despite its durability, however, the traditional partnership had long showed signs of strain. Even in its halcyon days a handful of dissenters had warned that it was becoming more and more unequal—that criticism was all too often being subordinated to history in the study of public address. The strongest early statement came from Loren Reid. Writing in 1944, Reid declared that rhetorical criticism entailed more than simply narrating the circumstances under which a speech was delivered, recounting a speaker's ideas, or classifying a speaker's rhetorical techniques. In Reid's view, many so-called rhetorical critics were actually producing "second-rate history" rather than criticism. During the early 1950s a few other writers voiced similar concern. Among them was Marie Hochmuth, who seconded the familiar view that rhetorical criticism could not proceed apart from thorough consideration of the speaker and the historical setting. But, she held, consideration of such extrinsic matters was only a preliminary task that did not itself constitute rhetorical criticism. According to Hochmuth, history and criticism served different purposes. Students of public address should be wary of allowing their interest in purely historical matters to divert them from the responsibility to produce criticism.[7]

These early salvos prefigured what was to become an all-out fusillade. By the mid-1960s the imbalance between history and criticism had become an absorbing theme of the growing band of revisionists who sought to revitalize the study of public address, which, in the estimation of one essayist, had "reached a place where it was saying painfully little to the humanities, the social sciences, or itself." Whereas criticism and history had once been perceived as inseparable allies, the revisionists tended to portray them not only as separable but as antagonistic. Representative of this position was Anthony Hillbruner's lamentation that "much of what passes for rhetorical criticism today, unfortunately, is rhetorical history." The paramount deficiency of traditional rhetorical analysis was said to be a misguided and enfeebling

---

[6] Anthony Hillbruner, *Critical Dimensions: The Art of Public Address Criticism* (New York: Random House, 1966), p. 26. This view, of course, can still be found in recent works such as Carroll C. Arnold, *Criticism of Oral Rhetoric* (Columbus: Charles E. Merrill, 1974), and Craig R. Smith, *Orientations to Speech Criticism* (Chicago: Science Research Associates, 1976). But it no longer commands the field, as it once did.

[7] Loren D. Reid, "The Perils of Rhetorical Criticism," *Quarterly Journal of Speech,* 30 (1944), 416-22; Marie Hochmuth, "The Criticism of Rhetoric," in *A History and Criticism of American Public Address,* III, ed. Marie Hochmuth (New York: Longman's, Green, and Co., 1955), pp. 5-6. Cf. Irving J. Lee, "Four Ways of Looking at a Speech," *Quarterly Journal of Speech,* 28 (1942), 148-55; Wayne N. Thompson, "Contemporary Public Address as a Research Area," *Quarterly Journal of Speech,* 33 (1947), 274-83; Martin Maloney, "Some New Directions in Rhetorical Criticism," *Central States Speech Journal,* 4 (March 1953), 1-5; Barnet Baskerville, "The Critical Method in Speech," *Central States Speech Journal,* 4 (July 1953) 1-5; Virginia Holland, "Rhetorical Criticism: A Burkeian Method," *Quarterly Journal of Speech,* 39 (1953), 444-50; Wayland Maxfield Parrish, "The Study of Speeches," in *American Speeches,* ed. Parrish and Marie Hochmuth (New York: Longman's, Green, and Co., 1954), pp. 1-20.

preoccupation with speeches as historical artifacts. W. Charles Redding put the indictment succinctly when he bemoaned the "heavy reliance upon historical data and historical research techniques" in the study of public address. As a result, said Redding, "rhetorical scholars have too often moved out of rather than more deeply into their own subject."[8]

The dissatisfaction with conventional rhetorical analysis vitiated the traditional connection between history and criticism at almost every turn. Rejection of the customary view that the controlling aim of rhetorical criticism was to appraise a speaker's success in achieving certain effects with a particular audience on a specific occasion meant that it was no longer obligatory to ground rhetorical analysis in penetrating study of the historical setting, or to pursue the "historical" task of determining the results of a given discourse. The corresponding call for close textual analysis in the fashion of literary criticism further severed the ties between the study of rhetorical discourse and examination of its historical environment. So too did the growing interest in ideological criticism, which seemingly could be conducted with little reference to anything other than the ideas articulated by public speakers and writers. And the call to focus upon contemporary rhetorical events further encouraged belief that the long-standing junction between history and criticism was outmoded and illusory (as if contemporary history were not history at all).

Two recent essays disclose how deeply the rift between criticism and history has embedded itself in the thinking of many rhetoricians. According to Bruce Gronbeck, it is profoundly mistaken to seek to unite historical and critical approaches to public address under a uniform methodology. He argues that rhetorical history and rhetorical criticism are essentially disparate

---

[8]Malcolm O. Sillars, "Rhetoric as Act," *Quarterly Journal of Speech*, 50 (1964), 277; Anthony Hillbruner, "Criticism as Persuasion," *Southern Speech Journal*, 28 (1963), 260; W. Charles Redding, "Extrinsic and Intrinsic Criticism," in *Essays on Rhetorical Criticism*, ed. Thomas R. Nilsen (New York: Random House, 1968), p. 99. My characterization of Hillbruner as a revisionist should be seen as equivocal, given the traditional tone and orientation of his 1965 *Critical Dimensions: The Art of Public Address Criticism* (cited in note 6 above). His "Criticism as Persuasion," however, sternly disapproved of conventional ways of studying and writing about public address.

The reorientation of rhetorical scholarship during the past two decades has been accompanied by a great outpouring of works dealing with one or another aspect of rhetorical analysis. Most of these works may be classified as revisionist inasmuch as they recommend alternatives to traditional ways of comprehending public address. Among those most germane to the discussion in this and the following paragraph are Albert J. Croft, "The Functions of Rhetorical Criticism," *Quarterly Journal of Speech*, 42 (1956), 283-91; Edwin Black, *Rhetorical Criticism: A Study in Method* (New York: Macmillan, 1965); Robert L. Scott and Donald K. Smith, "The Rhetoric of Confrontation," *Quarterly Journal of Speech*, 55 (1969), 1-8; Walter R. Fisher, "Method in Rhetorical Criticism," *Southern Speech Journal*, 35 (1969), 101-9; Herbert W. Simons, "Requirements, Problems, and Strategies: A Theory of Persuasion for Social Movements," *Quarterly Journal of Speech*, 56 (1970), 1-11; Samuel L. Becker, "Rhetorical Studies for the Contemporary World," in *The Prospect of Rhetoric*, ed. Lloyd F. Bitzer and Edwin Black (Englewood Cliffs: Prentice-Hall, 1971), pp. 21-43; "Report of the Committee on the Advancement and Refinement of Rhetorical Criticism," in ibid., pp. 220-27; Karlyn Kohrs Campbell, *Critiques of Contemporary Rhetoric* (Belmont: Wadsworth, 1972); *Explorations in Rhetorical Criticism*, ed. G. P. Mohrmann, Charles J. Stewart, and Donovan J. Ochs (University Park: Pennsylvania State University Press, 1973); and the papers collected in Nilsen, *Essays on Rhetorical Criticism*.

activities that "must pursue different goals, ought to be judged by differing criteria, and usually employ varying sources of evidence." Studies of public address, therefore, ought "to be predominantly either exercises in rhetorical history-writing or critical ventures into interesting[,] problematic, or insightful aspects of discourse." Barnet Baskerville does not etch nearly as radical a division between history and criticism, although he does agree that there are fundamental distinctions "between a piece of writing which is essentially 'historical' in intent and one which might be called an essay in 'rhetorical criticism.' " More important, Baskerville bemoans what he deems a fashionable "glorification of the critic" and "tacit denigration of those who are merely rhetorical 'historians.' " Like Gronbeck, Baskerville insists that historical scholarship is a worthy undertaking and that rhetoricians should feel free to engage in exclusively historical research and writing.[9]

And so the matter stands. As rhetorical analysts have reconsidered the nature, scope, and practice of their enterprise, they have tended to destroy the accord between history and criticism effected during the formative years of rhetoric as an academic discipline. Let us now take stock of the major grounds upon which distinctions between history and criticism have been advanced.

2

One way rhetorical analysts have differentiated "history" from "criticism" is by using the former to refer to investigation of matters external to rhetorical discourse and the latter to refer to examination of discourse itself. The division, of course, parallels that between literary criticism and literary history and may be seen as implicit even in Wichelns' landmark essay of 1925. By the 1940s it was becoming explicit.[10] In the last quarter-century it has become commonplace. Even writers who insist that students of public address must attend to the full range of extrinsic factors—the speaker and his or her training, the climate of opinion and events, the audience and its attitudes, the effects of the speaker's discourse—frequently contend that all these factors, vital as they may be, are actually "excursions into the fields of history, sociology, or biography," and thus are, "strictly speaking, extraneous to rhetoric." This line of thought has reached its fullest extension in Gronbeck's definition of rhetorical criticism as "any examination of discourse and rhetors which essentially or primarily is *intrinsic*, . . . which finds most of its confirming materials *inside a rhetorical artifact.*" Rhetorical history, on

---

[9] Bruce E. Gronbeck, "Rhetorical History and Rhetorical Criticism: A Distinction," *Speech Teacher*, 24 (1975), 309-20; Barnet Baskerville, "Must We All Be 'Rhetorical Critics'?" *Quarterly Journal of Speech*, 63 (1977), 107-16.

[10] Witness the separation William N. Brigance makes, in his introduction to the first volume of *A History and Criticism of American Public Address* (New York: Longman's, Green, and Co., 1943), between "historical studies," which deal with "background," and "critical studies," which deal directly with the rhetoric of individual orators.

the other hand, he identifies as "any examination of discourse or rhetors which essentially or primarily is *extrinsic, . . .* which finds most of its confirming materials outside a *rhetorical artifact.*"[11]

Such distinctions are of meager benefit. For one thing, they raise the problem of deciding what proportion of a study must be devoted to intrinsic considerations in order to qualify for classification as "rhetorical criticism." More important, they tend to be based more on *what* rhetorical analysts look at than on *how* they look at it. If they explore the intrinsic features of rhetorical discourse, they are said to be engaged in rhetorical criticism; if they explore contextual or biographical factors extrinsic to rhetorical discourse, they are said to be engaged in rhetorical history. Obviously, the strength of such a distinction rests upon maintaining a firm separation between rhetorical discourse and elements extrinsic to it. Theoretically, such a separation may be tenable. In practice, however, it breaks down. Because rhetorical discourses are human creations that function only in particular environments, from which they can only be separated artificially, rhetorical analysts usually acquire at least "some general understanding of the author and his age."[12] Among the questions they characteristically seek to answer are: "What was the context (no matter how broadly or narrowly conceived) in which the discourse functioned?"[13] "What were the origins of the discourse?" "How did it reflect the mind of its author?" "What relationship did it bear to its audiences (contemporary or historical)?" "What kinds of consequences (immediate or long-range) did it help bring about?" "What is its standing in relation to other discourses of a like nature?" In pursuing these and similar questions, the rhetorician moves naturally and easily between the discourse and its interaction with a myriad of complex and dynamic extrinsic forces.

A variety of rhetorical analysis in the past few years has been to engage, somewhat on the model of literary criticism, in close reading of rhetorical

---

[11]Parrish, "Study of Speeches," in Parrish and Hochmuth, *American Speeches,* p. 7; Gronbeck, "Rhetorical History," 310-11, 314. Similarly, see Hochmuth, "Criticism of Rhetoric," p. 5; Ernest G. Bormann, *Theory and Research in the Communicative Arts* (New York: Holt, Rinehart and Winston, 1965), p. 234; Lawrence W. Rosenfield, "The Anatomy of Critical Discourse," *Speech Monographs,* 35 (1968), 58; Redding, "Extrinsic and Intrinsic Criticism," in Nilsen, *Essays,* pp. 98-106; J. Jeffery Auer, "Implications of the Recommendations of the New Orleans Conference from the Perspective of Historical Scholarship," in *Conceptual Frontiers in Speech-Communication,* ed. Robert J. Kibler and Larry L. Barker (New York: Speech Association of America, 1969), p. 178.
[12]R. C. Jebb, *The Attic Orators* (London: Macmillan, 1876), I, xiii.
[13]It should be noted in this connection that Black does not indict neo-Aristotelianism because it compels critics to attend to the context of rhetorical acts, but because it adopts a "restricted view of context" as confined to a specific audience and an immediate occasion. Because "the work of rhetoric is fragmentary outside its environment," says Black, "the discovery of context" acquires "an enhanced importance in rhetorical criticism." One of Black's first steps in his study of John Jay Chapman's Coatesville Address, which he offers as an antidote to neo-Aristotelianism, is to set the Address in its proper context. That context, however, "is not the vacant grocery store" in which Chapman spoke on August 18, 1912. Rather, the Address must be understood as joining in the perduring "dialogue on the moral dimensions of the American experience." Thus the context of the Coatesville Address "is less a specific place than a culture. . . . It is a context whose place must be measured by a continent and whose time must be reckoned in centuries" (*Rhetorical Criticism,* pp. 39, 83-84).

discourse—to explicate its "meaning" or to demonstrate how it "functions." Such readings, it would appear, may confidently be classified as intrinsic, since they purport to deal with the internal operations of discourse, apart from any special consideration of its author or historical milieu. In fact, however, they can seldom proceed profitably without serious attention to extrinsic matters. For rhetorical discourse invariably occurs within a particular world; and not only within a particular social, political, religious, economic, and intellectual world, but also within a special rhetorical world, with its own vocabulary, conventions, preconceptions, idioms, patois, and the like. To understand what a rhetorical document means or to ascertain how it functions, one must recapture "the full wealth of association, implication and resonance, the many levels of meaning," which a language contains in a given society at a given time.[14] This is particularly vital when dealing with texts remote from us in culture or in time. But even as we move closer to our own age, we must be exceedingly cautious about reading the likes of Webster, Lincoln, Bryan, Theodore and Franklin Roosevelt, even John Kennedy, as our contemporaries—about assuming that their languages are identical with our language, that their rhetorical praxes are also our own. To explicate satisfactorily what a rhetorical text means or how it functions, we need to comprehend the very identity of that text as inextricably interwoven with its world. And that comprehension demands historical understanding that inescapably involves the rhetorician directly and earnestly with forces, persons, and documents extrinsic to the text under scrutiny.

This interpenetration of intrinsic and extrinsic factors is pronounced even in the one area in which they have been presumed to be most distinct—the study of rhetorical effect. In traditional criticism no task was deemed more important than "to determine the immediate or delayed effect of the speeches upon specific audiences, and, ultimately, upon society."[15] In recent years, many writers have relieved the critic of this obligation, arguing that "influence is an extraordinarily difficult thing to establish, much less to measure," and that, in any event, ascertaining influence "is not a critical but an historical undertaking." This position has perhaps been put most forcefully by Wayland Parrish, who, after contending at some length that the "actual influence" of rhetoric is "seldom discoverable," concluded that "the totting up of such responses as are discernible is a task for a historian, a clerk, or a comptometer, not for a rhetorician."[16]

[14]J. G. A. Pocock, *Politics, Language and Time: Essays on Political Thought and History* (New York: Atheneum, 1973), p. 12.

[15]Thonssen and Baird, *Speech Criticism,* p. 16.

[16]Baskerville, "Must We All Be Rhetorical Critics?" 114; Donald C. Bryant, *Rhetorical Dimensions in Criticism* (Baton Rouge: Louisiana State University Press, 1973), p. 38; Parrish, "Study of Speeches," in Parrish and Hochmuth, *American Speeches,* pp. 7-8. Similarly, see Bormann, *Theory and Research,* pp. 238-42; Campbell, *Critiques,* pp. 29-30; Robert Cathcart, *Post-Communication: Critical Analysis and Evaluation* (Indianapolis: Bobbs-Merrill, 1966), pp. 21-22.

Underlying such a stark division of labor is an assumption that influence "may be identified and measured without antecedent analysis or even knowledge of the discourse" that produced it.[17] And that assumption in turn necessarily presupposes a view of rhetorical effects essentially as overt, measurable outcomes such as getting the votes or winning a verdict.[18] But such outcomes are exceptional rather than commonplace and, even when present, may not be attributable to the discourse in question. Moreover, to think of rhetorical influence as a unidimensional, linear phenomenon that can in some sense be totted up is to distort the nature of a highly convoluted process and to deter consideration of a wide range of significant consequences that cannot possibly be "measured" or determined "precisely"— such as the on-going impact of a mosaic of messages on multiple audiences; the repercussions of discourse in modulating the future rhetorical and ideological options open to its author or the cause he or she espouses; the ways of thinking, acting, and believing fostered by rhetorical communication; the self-persuasion that may accompany efforts to persuade others; the role of popular discourse in the creation, fortification, and decay of cultural norms and social identities; the influence of rhetorical acts on the evolution of conventional modes of public communication.[19]

That these and similar kinds of consequences cannot be verified with exactitude does not mean that they should remain unexplored. To attain absolute confirmation about any subject as mutable, diverse, and variegated as rhetorical influence is virtually impossible; probability, not certainty, is the best that can reasonably be expected. Claims regarding the consequences of discourse are almost unavoidably provisional and can be "proved" only by effectively marshalling the evidence and warranting the inferences upon which they are based. In assessing effect the rhetorician turns to available extrinsic evidence such as newspaper reports, election results, opinion polls, diaries, private correspondence, reminiscences, and the like. But these will not, in and of themselves, divulge what the effects were, for effects cannot be determined merely by citing the impressions of people who listened to an orator or by counting the number who read a pamphlet or voted for its author. Rather, such extrinsic data must be weighed against each other, against what was rhetorically possible in a given situation, and against the rhetorical capabilities of the discourse itself. Only in the rarest of cases is it possible to

---

[17]Bryant, *Rhetorical Dimensions,* p. 38.

[18]Cf. Parrish, "Study of Speeches," in Parrish and Hochmuth, *American Speeches,* p. 8. Although few rhetoricians forthrightly subscribe to such a presupposition, it is often implicit in their language— particularly in the images of measurement they commonly use when discussing rhetorical effect.

[19]The value of dealing with such consequences is indicated by, respectively, Becker, "Rhetorical Studies," in Bitzer and Black, *Prospect of Rhetoric,* pp. 21-43; Black, *Rhetorical Criticism,* p. 35; Thomas R. Nilsen, "Criticism and Social Consequences," *Quarterly Journal of Speech,* 42 (1956), 173-78; Don M. Burks, "Persuasion, Self-Persuasion, and Rhetorical Discourse," *Philosophy and Rhetoric,* 3 (1970), 109-19; Michael C. McGee, "In Search of 'The People': A Rhetorical Alternative," *Quarterly Journal of Speech,* 61 (1975), 235-49; Stephen E. Lucas, *Portents of Rebellion; Rhetoric and Revolution in Philadelphia, 1765-76* (Philadelphia: Temple University Press, 1976), pp. 254-62.

reach a satisfactory assessment of effect without close analysis of the discourse that contributed to it.

To take but a single example, consider Thomas Paine's *Common Sense,* first published in Philadelphia in January 1776. The extrinsic evidence attesting to the pamphlet's influence is considerable and weighty. Although there is no exact accounting of circulation figures for Paine's work, it was widely reprinted throughout America and within three months sold some 120,000 copies among a free population of less than three million persons. To reach a comparable figure today, a political tract would have to sell approximately ten million copies within 100 days. In addition to such manifest indications that *Common Sense* reached an extraordinary proportion of the politically relevant population, there are numerous testimonies from Paine's contemporaries, Whig and Tory alike, that the pamphlet was an important factor in hastening the onset of independence.[20] Given such evidence, one could reasonably conclude—without ever reading *Common Sense*—that it exerted a powerful impact upon the development of revolutionary thought and action during the first half of 1776. But the conclusion is unsatisfactory, for it leaves unanswered most of the important questions about the role of *Common Sense* in the "terrible wordy war"[21] over independence. And those questions must remain unanswered until one looks exactingly at the pamphlet itself, at its capacity within the rhetorical situation, and at its relationship to other writings on both sides of the controversy.

Once that is done, one begins to see that "the effect" of *Common Sense* was in reality a complex and multifarious phenomenon, that the pamphlet had many distinct, yet interrelated, consequences.[22] It initiated widespread public discussion of independence as a potentially acceptable alternative to continued British rule. This was particularly vital in moderate colonies such as Pennsylvania, where even the word "independence" remained opprobrious as late as the beginning of 1776. *Common Sense* removed that opprobrium, taking pro-independence Whigs off the defensive and allowing them to campaign openly and vigorously for separation. Moreover, the case for American autonomy that Paine injected into the public arena was distinguished by both its comprehensiveness and its audacity. It encompassed a

---

[20]Representative eighteenth-century judgments of the impact of *Common Sense* and historical estimates of its circulation can be found in Moses Coit Tyler, *Literary History of the American Revolution* (1897; rpnt. ed., New York: Frederick Ungar, 1957), I, 469-74; Merrill Jensen, *The Founding of a Nation: A History of the American Revolution* (New York: Oxford University Press, 1968), pp. 668-69; Winthrop D. Jordan, "Familial Politics: Thomas Paine and the Killing of the King, 1776," *Journal of American History,* 60 (1973), 295-96. A succinct record of the printing history of *Common Sense* is available in Thomas R. Adams, *American Independence, the Growth of an Idea: A Bibliographical Study of the American Political Pamphlets Printed between 1764 and 1776 Dealing with the Dispute between Great Britain and Her Colonies* (Providence: Brown University Press, 1965), pp. 164-72.

[21]Joseph Reed to Charles Pettit, March 30, 1776, in *Life and Correspondence of Joseph Reed,* ed. William B. Reed (Philadelphia: Lindsay and Blakiston, 1847), I, 182.

[22]For full treatment and documentation of the issues discussed in this and the following paragraph see Lucas, *Portents of Rebellion,* pp. 167-75, 254-62.

range of topics from the origins of government to the courage of colonial militiamen, and in the process it assailed one after another of the accepted political presuppositions which underlay the apprehension of many colonists about independence. But it did so with consummate skill. *Common Sense* was so well conceived, so soundly structured, so engagingly written, so perfectly timed that it thoroughly dominated public discussion of independence. Its shadow hung over all subsequent writings on the subject, and few authors— whether for or against severing the bond with England—strayed far from the topics introduced in Paine's pamphlet. It did not, however, single-handedly create an irresistible public surge in favor of leaving the empire. It did not convert Tories (nor was it designed to). It no doubt crystallized the thoughts of some Americans who had been leaning toward separation, and it surely helped convince a fair number of previously uncommitted and skeptical colonists that independence was necessary and possible. For other Americans it contributed to the creation of a store of public arguments that could be used to rationalize a decision for independence if and when such a decision was forced upon them.

In addition, the influence of *Common Sense* extended far beyond its immediate context, for it pioneered "a style of thinking and expression different to what had been customary" in America.[23] Unlike most pamphlets of the Revolution, *Common Sense* was not penned in the gentlemanly mode of public address that had dominated American political literature through most of the colonial period. It was, rather, the most influential precursor of the popular mode of public address that came to prevail in the new republic. That the great popularity of Paine's tract was due in some measure to its form and style was widely acknowledged at the time. Not surprisingly, it spawned imitators. Of course, few Americans—even among the gentlemanly elite— possessed Paine's remarkable verbal resources and stylistic abilities, and fewer still could match his piquant prose. But even the least talented scribbler could imitate the most obvious formal and stylistic attributes of *Common Sense*—its forthright address to ordinary citizens, its colloquial idiom, its disdain for literary convention, its direct appeal to popular emotions. Ineluctably, the pamphlet helped produce a new kind of political discourse in America—a kind of discourse that helped deepen and strengthen the democratizing aftershocks of the upheaval in British-American relations.

Much more could be said about the multifaceted nature of rhetorical effects in general and about the impact of *Common Sense* in particular.[24] But the point should be clear: in the study of influence—as in other aspects of rhetorical inquiry—the putative division between intrinsic ("critical") and

---

[23]Thomas Paine, quoted in Harry Hayden Clark, "Thomas Paine's Theories of Rhetoric," *Transactions of the Wisconsin Academy of Sciences, Arts, and Letters*, 28 (1933), 317.

[24]Indeed, the nature of rhetorical influence, the degree to which assessing such influence is a vital task for rhetorical analysis, and the most profitable approaches to such assessment are all matters in need of thorough rethinking. This brief discussion is but a step in that direction.

extrinsic ("historical") analysis is overdrawn and misleading. So too, as we shall see next, are most efforts to discriminate between history and criticism on grounds that the latter, unlike the former, entails evaluation of rhetorical works.

3

Special concern in this century about the evaluative dimension of rhetorical criticism can be dated from publication of Loren Reid's "The Perils of Rhetorical Criticism" in 1944. After reviewing the shortcomings of scholarship in public address over the preceding two decades, Reid concluded by advising that the rhetorical critic "must take to heart his primary and inescapable responsibility as a critic: to interpret, to appraise, to evaluate; to say here the speaker missed, here he hit the mark; sometimes to speak with restraint when others applaud, sometimes to bestow praise when others have passed by." During the past three decades this conception of rhetorical criticism as necessarily judicial has been reiterated by an impressive range of writers, including Thonssen and Baird ("The chief business of the rhetorical scholar . . . is the evaluation of a speech or speeches"), Barnet Baskerville ("By its very nature, all criticism is judicial"), Marie Hochmuth (criticism "involves a judicial act of determining what is better or worse"), Edwin Black ("At the culmination of the critical process is the evaluation of the discourse or of its author"), Robert Cathcart ("The end sought in criticism is a *judgment* of the work under consideration"), Anthony Hillbruner ("The highest role to which the critic can aspire is the passing of judgment"), Lawrence Rosenfield ("criticism does eventuate in, or at least has as an ultimate objective, assessment"), Karlyn Campbell ("'good' criticism . . . makes clear and unmistakable judgments about the quality, worth, and consequences of the discourse"), and Walter Fisher ("the most fundamental task of the critic is to make evaluative judgments").[25]

From this notion that criticism entails evaluation has derived a second major view of the distinction between criticism and history in the study of public address. Unlike the rhetorical historian, whose objectives are commonly described as "largely descriptive in character," the rhetorical critic is said to use history "for the more important job of judgment." This distinction has been developed most fully by Ernest Bormann. The critic, Bormann

---

[25] Reid, "Perils of Rhetorical Criticism," 422; A. Craig Baird and Lester Thonssen, "Methodology in the Criticism of Public Address," *Quarterly Journal of Speech*, 33 (1947), 134; Baskerville, "Critical Method in Speech," 1; Hochmuth, "Criticism of Rhetoric," 4; Edwin Black, "Moral Values and Rhetorical Criticism," lecture presented at University of Wisconsin, July 1965, quoted in Rosenfield, "Anatomy of Critical Discourse," 54; Cathcart, *Post-Communication*, p. 89; Hillbruner, *Critical Dimensions*, p. 149; Rosenfield, "Anatomy of Critical Discourse," 54; Campbell, *Critiques*, pp. 21-22; Walter R. Fisher, "Rhetorical Criticism as Criticism," *Western Speech*, 38 (1974), 78. Not all of the above writers agree about the kinds of evaluations rhetorical critics ought to make, or about the best ways to reach them, but they are in fundamental agreement that critics need to engage in evaluation of some sort.

observes, uses "the same tools of scholarship as the historian." Both critics
and historians develop viewpoints toward their subjects and seek structure in
the works they examine. Their ultimate goals, however, differ greatly. The
controlling aim of historians is to explain past rhetorical events, not to render
judgments about them. If an historian makes such judgments, "they will tend
to be tangential to his main concern." The critic, on the other hand, "to do
his job fully," must assess the critical object against "standards of excellence"
that have "a certain universality and permanence." The rhetorical critic recognizes the historical context of the work under scrutiny, but, says Bormann,
may well overlook that context in appraising the work "against some artistic
standard."[26]

Insistence that criticism must be evaluative is, of course, not unique to
rhetoricians. It has long recurred among literary critics and may be traced
back at least to Aristophanes, who sought to determine in what order of
excellence the poets should be ranked, and on what basis. But there is another
view of criticism, one that possesses an equally ancient and illustrious
heritage—the view that criticism does not seek to judge but to explain.[27] And
this view also has its adherents among students of rhetoric. Some may be
interpreted as adopting this view inasmuch as they do not expressly identify
evaluation as incumbent upon rhetorical critics.[28] Others unconditionally admit
to the realm of rhetorical criticism studies that are not explicitly judicial.
Wayne Brockriede, for instance, recognizes both "criticism that has explicit
evaluation as its primary purpose" and "criticism that aims primarily at
explicit analysis." Donald Bryant offers an equally inclusive conception when
he states that "all analytic, interpretive, particularizing, or generalizing examinations of the arts broadly conceived—individual works, kinds, elements,
aspects, and authors—are essays in criticism." Phillip Tompkins, moving
from Bryant's well-known definition of rhetoric, describes rhetorical criticism
as "the *process of explicating a specific attempt* (whether successful or
unsuccessful) to adjust ideas to people and people to ideas." Such explication,
Tompkins argues, is neither coequal with nor demanding of evaluation.[29]

Not only do rhetoricians disagree over the role of evaluation in criticism,
but there appears to be at least a trace of ambiguity regarding the matter

---

[26]Hillbruner, "Criticism as Persuasion," 260-61; Bormann, *Theory and Research*, pp. 227-29.

[27]*Lectures in Criticism*, ed. Huntington Cairns, (Baltimore: Johns Hopkins University Press, 1949), pp.
1-8.

[28]The report of the Committee on Rhetorical Criticism at the National Conference on Rhetoric, for
instance, makes no mention of evaluation as an obligatory aspect of rhetorical criticism. In the view of
the committee, "any critic regardless of the subject of his inquiry, becomes a rhetorical critic when his
work centers on suasory potential or persuasive effects, their source, nature, operation, and
consequences" in Bitzer and Black, *Prospect*, p. 221.

[29]Wayne Brockriede, "Rhetorical Criticism as Argument," *Quarterly Journal of Speech*, 60 (1974), 165;
Bryant, *Rhetorical Dimensions*, p. 26; Phillip K. Tompkins, "The Rhetorical Criticism of Non-
Oratorical Works," *Quarterly Journal of Speech*, 55 (1969), 431. Similarly, see *Methods of Rhetorical
Criticism: A Twentieth-Century Perspective*, ed. Robert L. Scott and Bernard L. Brock (New York:
Harper and Row, 1972), p. 341; Mark S. Klyne, "Toward a Pluralistic Rhetorical Criticism," in Nilsen,
Essays, p. 147; Gary D. Keele, "Keele on Fisher," *Western Speech*, 38 (1974), 278-80.

within the writings of some who claim that criticism must be judicial. Even Edwin Black, who is frequently cited as the leading champion of judicial criticism, seems to adopt a somewhat equivocal stance. In the opening chapter of *Rhetorical Criticism* Black explains that critics must go "beyond perception" to "appraisal"—"beyond seeing a thing" to "attaching a value to it." Later, however, he appears to adopt a view of criticism as explication, when he states that "criticism has no relationship with its subject other than to account for how that subject works; it demands nothing but full disclosure."[30]

The ambivalence of many scholars about the role of evaluation in rhetorical criticism is further evident when we turn from what rhetorical critics say they do to what they actually do in their published works. Theories of rhetorical criticism often have little to do with the way criticism is practiced. In fact, relatively few essays in "rhetorical criticism" truly entail *explicit* evaluation as either a necessary or sufficient procedure. In this respect, the apparent attitude of most rhetoricians is well stated by Redding, who, while reiterating that the *total* enterprise of criticism" is "'the full, evaluated apprehension of the critical subject," argues strongly for the value of critical studies "that frankly concentrate upon analysis."[31] In practice, if not in theory, most rhetorical critics produce scholarship that is essentially analytic rather than judicial.

To be sure, there are two senses in which all essays under the aegis of "rhetorical criticism" may be denominated as implicitly, if not explicitly, judicial, and it is precisely these senses that most writers appear to have in mind when they assert that criticism is necessarily evaluative.[32] First, it may be argued that perception itself is evaluative; that facts are never neutral and have no objective existence apart from the frame of reference of the person who apprehends them. According to this relativist theory of perception, we view the world through the distorting lenses of our individual experiences, aspirations, and values. Every perception is a construction; every observation is an interpretation; every experience is infused with value judgments. So too is ordinary language, which we use to order and communicate our perceptions. Seen from this point of view, rhetorical criticism—like any other human endeavor—is never value-free and is always "to some extent evaluative, judgmental, and subjective."[33]

A second position, consanguineous with the first, holds that there is no sharp line to be drawn between explanation and judgment, that "in most

---

[30]Black, *Rhetorical Criticism*, pp. 5, 18. Also see the shifting stances on the same issue by Barnet Baskerville in the following essays: "Critical Method in Speech," 1; "Rhetorical Criticism, 1971: Retrospect, Prospect, Introspect," *Southern Speech Journal*, 37 (1971), 119-20; "Responses, Queries, and a Few Caveats," in Bitzer and Black, *Prospect*, p. 164; "Must We All Be Rhetorical Critics?" 110, 112, 115-16.

[31]Redding, "Intrinsic and Extrinsic Criticism," in Nilsen, *Essays*, p. 107.

[32]The distinction between implicit and explicit evaluation is a vital one that has seldom been recognized by rhetoricians. Their failure to recognize it helps, I think, to account for much of the ambiguity and ambivalence evident in the long-standing debate over the role of evaluation in rhetorical analysis.

[33]Campbell, *Critiques*, p. 1.

explanations a judgment of some sort is necessarily implied." This is the stance of Scott and Brock, who hold that rhetorical critics must pass judgment "in some way or another, implicitly or explicitly." Despite the efforts of many critics "to ignore the evaluative purpose of criticism," they can never escape evaluation entirely, for "the descriptive act, in and of itself, implies that the phenomenon as described is worth attending to." Black enunciates a similar view. In his estimation, "evaluation of the discourse or of its author" should represent "the culmination of the critical process." But, he suggests, even in the absence of such overt terminal judgment, rhetorical criticism is ineluctably judicial:

> Even the purely technical objective of understanding how a discourse works carries the assumption that it *does* work, and that assumption is an assessment. Similarly, to understand why a thing has failed is at least to suspect that it has failed, and that assumption is an assessment. There is, then, no criticism without appraisal; there is no "neutral criticism." On[e] critic's judgment may be absolute and dogmatic, another's tentative and barely committal: but however faint the judicial element in criticism may become, it abides.[34]

However accurate these views of the ubiquity of evaluation, they are of little value in distinguishing between history and criticism in rhetorical scholarship.[35] There is a crucial difference between explicit evaluation in rhetorical criticism and evaluation as an inescapable part of all perception and interpretation. To say that rhetorical critics must forthrightly judge rhetorical works against some set of criteria is one thing. To say that rhetorical critics can never escape some sort of evaluative process no matter how they try is quite another. The latter position rests upon such a broad construction of "evaluation" as to rob the term of any special meaning.[36] More important for present purposes, it does not provide ground by which to separate rhetorical criticism from rhetorical history (or from any other mode of humanistic scholarship). The perception of the rhetorical historian is inherently no more pure or unmediated than that of the critic. The facts of history are always refracted through the mind of the historian, whose point of view enters irrevocably into every observation he or she makes. As Charles Beard put it, "no historian can describe the past as it actually was," for the observation, selection, and ordering of materials must inexorably be determined by each scholar's "biases, prejudices, beliefs, affections, general upbringing, and

---

[34]Cairns, *Lectures in Criticism*, p. 7; Scott and Brock, *Methods*, p. 9; Black, "Moral Values," quoted in Rosenfield, "Anatomy of Critical Discourse," 54. Also see Edwin Black, "The Second Persona," *Quarterly Journal of Speech*, 56 (1970), 109-10; Brockriede, "Criticism as Argument," 165; Baskerville, "Rhetorical Criticism, 1971," 119-20.

[35]Nor was it the aim of the writers just quoted so to distinguish.

[36]Cf. the conclusion of Morris Weitz with respect to much the same issue in literary criticism, in *Hamlet and the Philosophy of Literary Criticism* (Chicago: University of Chicago Press, 1964), p. 269.

experience." Neither can historians escape the value-laden connotations of the ordinary language they use to present their views of the past. It naturally follows that implicit evaluation is as unavoidable for historians as for critics. Friedrich Meinecke, the great German historian, pointed out that even the "mere selection" of most historical facts is "impossible without an evaluation":

> The historian selects his material not only according to general categories . . . but also according to his living interest in the concrete content of material. He lays hold of it as something having more or less of value, and in this he is evaluating it. The presentation and exposition of culturally important facts is utterly impossible without a lively sensitivity for the values they reveal. Although the historian may, in form, abstain from value-judgments of his own, they are there between the lines and act as such upon the reader.[37]

Not only is some sort of implicit evaluation as inescapable for rhetorical historians as for critics, but it may be argued that rendering more-or-less explicit verdicts about the artistry, worth, or efficacy of rhetorical acts need not be arbitrarily divorced from the province of rhetorical history—particularly since such verdicts are likely to be cursory and haphazard unless grounded in penetrating historical understanding of what was valuable or possible in any given rhetorical transaction. Before the rise of professionalized history in the late nineteenth century, the writing of history was widely regarded as a judicial enterprise that, in the words of Charles W. Eliot, "shows the young the springs of public honor and dishonor; sets before them the national failings, weaknesses, and sins; warns them against future dangers by exhibiting the losses and sufferings of the past; enshrines in their hearts the national heroes; and strengthens in them the precious love of country."[38]

---

[37]Charles Beard, review of Maurice Mendelbaum's *The Problem of Historical Knowledge*, in *The Philosophy of History in Our Own Time*, ed. Hans Meyerhoff (New York: Doubleday, 1959), p. 139; Charles Beard, "Written History as an Act of Faith," in ibid., p. 141; Friedrich Meinecke, "Values and Causalities in History," in *The Varieties of History*, 2d ed., ed. Fritz Stern (New York: Random House, 1972), p. 273. The positions encountered by Beard and Meinecke are so common among historians and philosophers of history as to constitute first principles. Notable statements include Raymond Aron, *Introduction to the Philosophy of History: An Essay on the Limits of Historical Objectivity*, trans. George J. Irwin (Boston: Beacon Press, 1961); Charles Beard, "That Noble Dream," *American Historical Review*, 41 (1935), 74-87; Carl L. Becker, "What Are Historical Facts?" *Western Political Quarterly*, 8 (1955), 327-40; Edward Hallett Carr, *What is History?* (New York: Random House, 1961); R. G. Collingwood, *The Idea of History* (New York: Oxford University Press, 1946); Benedetto Croce, *History: Its Theory and Practice*, trans. Douglas Ainslee (New York: Harcourt, Brace, and Co., 1921); John Dewey, *Logic: The Theory of Inquiry* (New York: Henry Holt and Co., 1938), pp. 230-39; Patrick Gardiner, *The Nature of Historical Explanation* (New York: Oxford University Press, 1961); Herbert Muller, *The Uses of the Past: Profiles of Former Societies* (New York: Oxford University Press, 1952), chap. 2; Murray G. Murphey, *Our Knowledge of the Historical Past* (Indianapolis: Bobbs-Merrill, 1973).

[38]Charles W. Eliot, *Educational Reform: Essays and Addresses* (New York: The Century Company, 1898), p. 105.

Today the view that a principal task of the historian is to judge the thoughts, actions, and precepts of earlier times has few adherents. Yet it has some,[39] and in certain varieties of history—most notably biography and military history—such judgment is not at all uncommon. As military historians judge the effectiveness and implications of the battlefield tactics of wartime commanders, or as biographers evaluate the standards and achievements of historical figures, so may rhetorical historians make similar assessments about the rhetorical activities of speakers and writers. Indeed, many notable rhetorical studies so thoroughly blend description, interpretation, and evaluation as to make efforts to categorize them discreetly as either "history" or "criticism" nugatory and misleading.[40]

But even if it be granted that rendering explicit assessments of the effectiveness, artistry, and ethics of public address is exclusive to rhetorical criticism, the procedures by which one reaches such terminal judgments usually require substantial historical acumen. This is most obvious of pragmatic judgments, which entail the historical tasks of placing rhetorical acts firmly in context and gauging their impact upon readers and listeners. It is less obvious of artistic judgments, which seek to assess the quality of discourse "as a self-contained unit, without regard for any particular audience."[41] But as we have seen, it is seldom possible to deal satisfactorily with the internal Operations of public address without serious attention to historical factors extrinsic to the text itself. Moreover, as Black has observed, because the standards against which critics commonly seek to assess rhetorical quality are based upon their presumed capacity to achieve desired results with audiences, passes for a formalistic judgment of artistry "is usually a pragmatic judgment at bottom."[42]

---

[39] See, for instance, A. J. P. Taylor, *Rumours of Wars* (London: Hamish Hamilton, 1952), pp. 9-13; Isaiah Berlin, *Historical Inevitability* (London: Oxford University Press, 1954); C. V. Wedgwood, *Truth and Opinion: Historical Essays* (London: Collins, 1960), pp. 42-54; John Higham, "Beyond Consensus: The Historian as Moral Critic," *American Historical Review,* 67 (1962), 609-25; Page Smith, *The Historian and History* (New York: Alfred A. Knopf, 1964), pp. 218-31; Howard Zinn, *The Politics of History* (Boston: Beacon Press, 1970).

[40] Such studies include Carroll C. Arnold, "Lord Thomas Erskine: Modern Advocate," *Quarterly Journal of Speech,* 44 (1958), 17-30; Ross Scanlan, "Adolf Hitler and the Technique of Mass Brainwashing," in *The Rhetorical Idiom,* ed. Donald C. Bryant (Ithaca: Cornell University Press, 1958), pp. 201-20; Eugene E. White, "Puritan Preaching and the Authority of God," in *Preaching in American History,* ed. DeWitte Holland (Nashville: Abingdon Press, 1969), pp. 36-73; Robert P. Newman, "Under the Veneer: Nixon's Vietnam Speech of November 3, 1969," *Quarterly Journal of Speech,* 56 (1970), 168-78; James R. Andrews, "The Passionate Negation: The Chartist Movement in Rhetorical Perspective," *Quarterly Journal of Speech,* 59 (1973), 196-208; Richard B. Gregg, "A Rhetorical Re-Examination of Arthur Vandenberg's 'Dramatic Conversion,' January 10, 1945," *Quarterly Journal of Speech,* 61 (1975), 154-68; John Agnus Campbell, "The Polemical Mr. Darwin," *Quarterly Journal of Speech,* 61 (1975), 375-90; Michael Osborn, "The Evolution of the Archetypal Sea in Rhetoric and Poetic," *Quarterly Journal of Speech,* 63 (1977), 347-63; Barnet Baskerville, *The People's Voice: The Orator in American Society* (Lexington: University Press of Kentucky, 1979); Lloyd Bitzer and Theodore Rueter, *Carter vs Ford: The Counterfeit Debates of 1976* (Madison: University of Wisconsin Press, 1980).

[41] Black, *Rhetorical Criticism,* p. 62. The standard exposition of artistic criticism in rhetoric remains Parrish's "The Study of Speeches," in Parrish and Hochmuth, *American Speeches,* pp. 1-20.

[42] Black, *Rhetorical Criticism,* p. 68.

A somewhat similar conclusion may be drawn about ethical judgments, which deal with the truth of a rhetor's claims, the propriety of a rhetor's techniques, or the moral consequences of a rhetor's discourse. Since we only hold people responsible for acts of volition, the burden of rhetorical critics is more to assess the *truthfulness* of a claimant than the truth of his or her claims. Making the former assessment is not simply a matter of comparing what a rhetor said either with what was known to be true by the rhetor's contemporaries or with what is now known to be true. Rather, it is a matter of testing a rhetor's statements against what the *rhetor* believed to be true when he or she advanced them. And this demands the same kind of historical skill utilized by the biographer. Likewise, assessing the ethics of a speaker's persuasive techniques necessitates determining what those techniques in fact were and weighing whether their use was ethical in the historical situation in which they were employed. Finally, evaluating the moral consequences of discourse requires the prior task of estimating what impact it actually had upon readers or listeners. In each case, reaching moral judgment—as with reaching pragmatic or artistic judgment—entails historical industry and understanding.

It would appear, then, that the judicial aspects of rhetorical criticism do not provide a secure purchase point for divorcing criticism from history in the study of public address. Nor does an examination of method reveal fundamental fissures between historical and critical scholarship in rhetoric.

4

Although one reads much of "historical method" and "critical method," as if there were grave differences between the two, there is typically little distinction when it comes to the study of public address. Rhetorical critics and historians employ essentially similar methods inasmuch as the central task of each is making inferences about probabilities on the basis of limited data. In this general sense, both may be said to use the critical method, and in fact historians commonly designate their method as "critical" and identify the process of interrogating and evaluating historical evidence as "historical criticism."[43] Beyond this, historians are wedded to no special method. Indeed, it may be argued that "history has no method or methods" at all if one defines method in its strict sense as a settled, systematic mode of procedure in which one step produces a specifiable result and is necessarily followed by another step, which also produces a specifiable result, and so on until the

---

[43]See, for example, Marc Bloch, *The Historian's Craft*, trans. Joseph R. Strayer (New York: Alfred A. Knopf, 1953), chap. 3; G. Kitson Clark, *The Critical Historian* (New York: Basic Books, 1967); Louis Gottschalk, *Understanding History: A Primer of Historical Method*, 2d. ed. (New York: Alfred A. Knopf, 1969), chaps. 6-7; Homer C. Hockett, *The Critical Method in Historical Research and Writing* (New York: Macmillan, 1955), part I; Gregg Phifer, "The Historical Approach," in *An Introduction to Graduate Study in Speech and Theatre*, ed. Clyde W. Dow (East Lansing, Michigan State University Press, 1961), pp. 52-80.

process is complete and yields the final product. Using the term "method" in this fashion, one can sensibly speak of, say, the open-hearth method of making steel, or the various methods of teaching children how to swim, but not the method of historical inquiry. As Jacques Barzun explains, "history resists any genuine application of method."

> The handbooks say: consult your sources, test and authenticate them, assemble the ascertained facts, write your report, and give clear references. After publication another volume is classified as history on some library shelf. But all this is hardly more than a general description of the work of intelligence, such as is performed by every student and professional, with or without a method. Method for the historian is only a metaphor to say that he is rational and resourceful, imaginative and conscientious. Nothing prescribes the actual steps of his work.

Nor should it. Historians ought to be *methodical* in selecting, ordering, and criticizing evidence, but the key to successful historical scholarship is not the rigid use of orthodox procedures, but the resourcefulness and judgment of the individual historian, who "had better keep his mental activity unrestricted" by formal methods, which only constrain the mind by dictating in advance the operation of thought upon its material.[44]

The parallels between this conception of method in history and prevailing ideas about method in rhetorical criticism should be so patent as to require little elaboration. Rhetorical critics employ the critical method broadly conceived, but, like rhetorical historians, reject the uniform application of predetermined formulas, which are most likely to produce scholarship that is dull, mechanical, unimaginative, and commonplace. "There are," Fisher notes, "as many approaches to rhetorical criticism as there are useful things to say about the rhetorical process." Indeed, so powerful is the commitment to critical pluralism that most rhetorical critics today eschew even the term "method," preferring instead to talk of critical "orientations," "approaches," and "perspectives." And whatever particular orientation, approach, or perspective an individual critic elects is not prescribed beforehand, but depends upon the purposes of the critic and the nature of the rhetorical work under scrutiny. Eventually, of course, "some schema must control the analysis" if criticism is to avoid being "totally whimsical and subjective." Yet good criticism does not result from doggedly following a set of formulary procedures, but from the full, free interplay of intelligence with the critical

---

[44]Jacques Barzun, *Clio and the Doctors: Psycho-History, Quanto-History and History* (Chicago: University of Chicago Press, 1974), pp. 39-41, 89-90. This viewpoint is well capsulized in Samuel Eliot Morison's dictum that historical method "is a product of common sense applied to circumstances" ("Faith of a Historian," *American Historical Review,* 56 [1951], 263). But cf. Lee Benson, *Toward the Scientific Study of History* (Philadelphia: Lippincott, 1972), esp. pp. 239-40, for a sharply worded contrary view.

object. The main ideal of criticism is, in Kenneth Burke's words, "to use all that is there to use." If there is a method of rhetorical criticism (or of rhetorical history), it is simply what mathematical physicist P. W. Bridgeman describes as the "scientific method"—"nothing more than doing one's damnedest with one's mind, no holds barred."[45]

Of course, "method" need not be construed only in its strict sense. Indeed, the term is commonly used more broadly—to refer to the general procedures by which various kinds of scholars go about their work. It is likely this usage that most writers have in mind when they refer to differences between historical and critical method in the study of public address. But however clear such differences may appear in the abstract, they are usually difficult to detect in practice. The procedures employed by most rhetoricians are not readily set apart as "critical" versus "historical." Critics at times offer explicit evaluations of rhetorical transactions; so at times do historians. Historians at times make causal inferences about the influence of rhetorical acts; so at times do critics. Critics at times focus intently upon the internal operations of discourse; so at times do historians. Historians at times attend closely to the context of public communication; so at times do critics. From verifying the authenticity of texts, to plumbing the intentions of their authors, to comprehending the context in which rhetoric occurs, to explicating the discursive and social processes by which it functions, to assessing its artistry, worth, or consequences, rhetorical critics and rhetorical historians employ essentially similar scholarly procedures. What differs from study to study are not so much the methods employed, but the research questions asked and the skill with which they are answered.

These resemblances in method come as no surprise when one considers the extent to which rhetorical critics and historians share common epistemological premises. Both deal with contingencies and both recognize the elusiveness of Truth. Neither are engaged in a search for universal laws. Both seek to elucidate tendencies or probabilities. Although some writers have bemoaned an objectivistic bias in historical approaches to public address,[46] most historians are fully aware that "there can be no 'pure' history—history-in-itself, recorded from nobody's point of view, for nobody's sake. The most objective history conceivable is still a selection and an inter-

---

[45]Fisher, "Method in Rhetorical Criticism," 107; G. P. Mohrmann and Michael C. Leff, "Lincoln at Cooper Union: A Rationale for Neo-Classical Criticism," *Quarterly Journal of Speech,* 60 (1974), 465; Kenneth Burke, *The Philosophy of Literary Form,* rev. ed. (New York: Vintage Press, 1957), p. 21; P. W. Bridgeman, "The Prospect for Intelligence," *Yale Review,* 34 (1945), 450, quoted in Thomas C. Cochran, "History and the Social Sciences," in *The Craft of American History: Selected Essays,* ed. A. S. Eisenstadt (New York: Harper and Row, 1966), II, 109.
[46]Linnea Ratcliff, "Rhetorical Criticism: An Alternative Perspective," *Southern Speech Journal,* 37 (1971), 125-35; Philip Wander and Steven Jenkins, "Rhetoric, Society, and the Critical Response," *Quarterly Journal of Speech,* 58 (1972), 441-50; James W. Chesebro and Caroline D. Hamsher, "Contemporary Rhetorical Theory and Criticism: Dimensions of the New Rhetoric," *Speech Monographs,* 42 (1975), 311-34.

pretation, necessarily governed by some special interests and based on some particular beliefs."[47] Historians can never recapture the past just as it was. All they can know of the past depends upon the available evidence, and the selection, interpretation, and evaluation of that evidence will inevitably be influenced by the personal values and professional skill of individual historians. Both critics and historians strive to explicate rhetorical events as wisely, as fully, and as objectively as possible. But neither can be completely value-free and neither offer absolute interpretations. Both must impose their own constructions on their material and on their readers.[48]

Given these methodological and epistemological likenesses, historical and critical studies in public address naturally share common rhetorical characteristics. Critics and historians alike typically work with at least some conception of audience in mind, and both unavoidably interpose themselves between the rhetorical event and their readers. Both strive to persuade readers to see rhetorical events in certain ways, and both confront the compositional demands of arrangement, emphasis, clarity, and vividness in writing convincing accounts of their subjects. Neither, however, deal with questions through controlled experimental investigation, and the discourse of both possesses the spread, richness, and ambiguity of ordinary language. Rhetorical critics and historians alike gain their greatest insights through the exercise of creative imagination, and the work of both is often judged by literary as well as

---

[47]Muller, *Uses of the Past*, pp. 43-44. Also see the works cited in footnote 37 above. It should be stressed that this view is also shared by so-called objectivist historians. They agree that perception is inherently value-laden, but reject what Oscar Handlin calls "the deceptive path from acknowledgment that no person . . . [is] entirely free of prejudice or capable of attaining a totally objective view of the past to the conclusion that all efforts to do so . . . [are] in vain and that, in the end, the past . . . [is] entirely a recreation emanating from the mind of the historian" (*Truth in History* [Cambridge: Harvard University Press, 1979], p. 410). Also see Ernest Nagel, *The Structure of Science* (London: Routledge and Kegan Paul, 1961), pp. 473-502, 547-606; Arthur O. Lovejoy, "Present Standpoints and Past History," *Journal of Philosophy*, 36 (1939), 477-89; Christopher Blake, "Can History Be Objective?" in *Theories of History*, ed. Patrick Gardiner (New York: Macmillan, 1959), pp. 329-43; Sidney Hook, "Objectivity and Reconstruction in History," in *Philosophy and History*, ed. Sidney Hook (New York: New York University Press, 1963), pp. 250-74; Peter Gay, *Style in History* (New York: McGraw Hill, 1974), pp. 185-217.

[48]This is not to endorse the extremely relativistic position that truth is unattainable, that every interpretation is hopelessly biased, and that every assessment is as good as another. "There is," as René Wellek points out, "a difference between the psychology of the investigator, his presumed bias, ideology, perspective, and the logical structure of his propositions. The genesis of a theory does not necessarily invalidate its truth. Men can correct their biases, criticize their presuppositions, rise above their temporal and local limitations, aim at objectivity, arrive at some knowledge and truth. . . . There are utterly fantastic interpretations, partial, distorted interpretations. . . . The concept of adequacy of interpretation leads clearly to the concept of the correctness of judgment. Evaluation grows out of understanding; correct evaluation out of correct understanding. There is a hierarchy of viewpoints implied in the very concept of adequacy of interpretation. Just as there is correct interpretation, at least as an ideal, so there is correct judgment, good judgment" (*Concepts of Criticism*, ed. Stephen G. Nichols, Jr., [New Haven: Yale University Press, 1963], pp. 14, 18). In the words of Abraham Kaplan, "everything depends on the conduct of the inquiry, on the way in which we arrive at our conclusions. Freedom from bias means having an open mind, not an empty one" (*The Conduct of Inquiry* [San Francisco: Chandler, 1964], p. 375). See also the second paragraph to follow in the present essay.

scholarly standards.[49]

Yet neither are chiefly concerned with producing works that are merely persuasive or whose distinguishing feature is high literary merit. The central, irreducible obligation of both critics and historians is to deal with subjects as faithfully, as accurately, as impartially as the limitations of human nature and ordinary language allow. Neither expected their claims to be accepted on faith, and both carry the responsibility of making reasoned assertions that are evidentially and inferentially warranted. Both are bound by the dictates of intellectual honesty and are subject to the highest imperatives of liberal scholarship. History and criticism alike are, to borrow Droysen's words, "not 'the light and the truth,' but a search therefor, a sermon thereupon, a consecration thereto."[50]

5

The acute sense of schism between history and criticism in rhetorical scholarship is relatively recent. As disenchantment with conventional approaches to the study of public address deepened and strengthened, more and more rhetoricians differentiated between criticism and history and called upon their colleagues to produce the former rather than the latter—by which they usually meant writing studies that concentrated upon intrinsic features of rhetorical discourse, evaluated rhetorical works or their authors, and/or followed critical rather than historical methods. As we have seen, however, these distinctions are far from immutable and sometimes blur to the point of disappearing altogether. Consequently, we may conclude with Everett Hunt, who once dismissed quarrels between history and criticism as akin to "the bitter complaints of Jason, who, in denouncing Medea, wished that men could get children without women."[51]

But the conclusion is a bit premature, for, like many truisms, it camouflages a tangled skein of complex issues. I do not mean to claim that

---

[49]On the rhetorical aspects of criticism consult Black, *Rhetorical Criticism,* pp. 6-9; Rosenfield, "Anatomy of Critical Discourse," 54-57; Arnold, *Criticism of Oral Rhetoric,* pp. 10-17, 278-82; Hillbruner, "Criticism as Persuasion"; Bryant, *Rhetorical Dimensions,* pp. 29-31; "Report of the Committee on . . . Rhetorical Criticism," in Bitzer and Black, *Prospect,* pp. 223-24. Among the historians who have dealt with the rhetorical nature of their craft are Gay, *Style in History;* Carl L. Becker, "The Art of Writing," in *Detachment and the Writing of History: Essays and Letters of Carl L. Becker,* ed. Phil L. Snyder, (Ithaca: Cornell University Press, 1958), pp. 121-44; Carl B. Cone, "Major Factors in the Rhetoric of Historians," *Quarterly Journal of Speech,* 33 (1947), 437-50; J. H. Hexter, "Historiography: The Rhetoric of History," in *International Encyclopedia of the Social Sciences,* ed. David L. Sills (New York: Free Press, 1968), VI, 368-73; Allan Nevins, *The Gateway to History,* rev. ed. (Chicago: Quadrangle Books, 1963), chap. 13; George M. Trevelyan, *Clio, A Muse, and Other Essays Literary and Pedestrian* (London: Longman's, Green and Co., 1914), chap. 1.

[50]Johann Gustav Droysen, *Outline of the Principles of History,* trans. E. Benjamin Andrews (Boston: Ginn and Co., 1893), p. 49.

[51]Everett Lee Hunt, "Rhetoric and Literary Criticism," *Quarterly Journal of Speech,* 21 (1935), 568.

because rhetorical history and rhetorical criticism share common characteristics there are no meaningful differences between them. Distinctions between
the two may capture somewhat disparate approaches, purposes, and intellectual viewpoints. Yet the very nature of rhetoric militates against a sharp
distinction between historical and critical inquiry. Dwelling upon the
supposed differences between them has for many years been a kind of red
herring that has fastened attention upon the categorization of scholarship
rather than upon its quality. In the study of rhetorical discourse, history and
criticism are most profitably seen as reciprocal modes of understanding. The
boundary between the two is usually so fluid and indistinct that to insist upon
a firm partition is fruitless.[52]

Nor do I wish even to intimate that we ought to return to the traditional
paradigm of "history and criticism." Although that paradigm predicated a
close working relationship between criticism and history, it was nonetheless
informed by many of the current misconceptions about the nature of critical
and historical inquiry in public address. For one thing, it portrayed the two as
fundamentally discrete kinds of intellectual activities. For another, although it
insisted that rhetorical criticism could not be written without a strong reliance
upon history, it mistakenly implied that adequate rhetorical history could
quite easily be written without regard for criticism. Moreover, the traditional
paradigm was based upon a severely restricted view of rhetoric and of rhetorical analysis. It generally posed the wrong questions about rhetorical phenomena and went about answering them in myopic and unsophisticated ways.

The breakdown of the conventional archetype of "history and criticism"
and the emergence of manifold new approaches has enriched both the
diversity and quality of rhetorical scholarship. But the durability of whatever
progress we have made is likely to be imperiled if the present breach between
criticism and history continues to widen. For that breach is much more than
terminological. As we have seen, it depends upon and reinforces an attenuated
view of the complex and interconnected ways of comprehending rhetorical
transactions. Consequently, it must ultimately straighten rhetorical analysis
and fetter the development of rhetorical theory.

What we need is not to expand further the rift between history and
criticism, but to recognize and to capitalize upon their essential similarities.
All rhetorical analysis deals with the past: the present is but a fleeting
moment that can never be fully recaptured. All subjects for rhetorical study
are inherently historical, whether they occurred one minute or one thousand
years ago. From resolving questions of textual accuracy, to charting the
evolution of rhetorical documents, to gauging the rhetorical temperament of
their authors, to penetrating the dynamics of rhetorical situations, to

---

[52]For a similar warning, though in a different context, see John Higham, "The Schism in American
Scholarship," *American Historical Review*, 72 (1966), 1-21, from which the title of the present essay
has been adapted.

explicating the formal properties and social functions of discourse, to rendering evaluative judgments, the rhetorician inescapably confronts a wide range of concerns that require rigorous historical interrogation. Seen from this point of view, historical understanding is not simply a prolegomenon to critical understanding, but an organic element of the whole process of rhetorical analysis.

At the center of that process, for historians and critics alike, is the quest to elucidate rhetorical transactions. Both share an abiding interest in the study of people as rhetorical animals, and both hold as controlling premises that language is a powerful means of social inducement and that people are, "by nature, subject to and capable of persuasion."[53] Moreover, what characterizes rhetorical criticism at its best is no less characteristic of rhetorical history at its best—a keen and penetrating focus on the functional attributes of rhetorical acts. Although accurate description is a necessary aspect of both history and criticism, it is not sufficient for signal attainment in either. Analysis, explanation, interpretation—these are the vital elements of rhetorical analysis, critical and historical alike. Rhetorical historians, like rhetorical critics, are concerned above all with what messages do rather than with what they are, and the central office of each is to explicate how rhetorical communication works.[54] To the extent that either critics or historians fulfill this office rigorously and resourcefully, they will produce scholarship essential to understanding the rhetorical dimensions of human experience.

---

[53]Karlyn Kohrs Campbell, "The Ontological Foundations of Rhetorical Theory," *Philosophy and Rhetoric*, 3 (1970), 97.

[54]Cf. Black, *Rhetorical Criticism*, p. 18; Bryant, *Rhetorical Dimensions*, p. 27; *Rhetoric: A Tradition in Transition*, ed. Walter R. Fisher (East Lansing: Michigan State University Press, 1974), pp. ix-x.

Textual Criticism:
The Legacy of G. P. Mohrmann
by Michael Leff

At the moment of his fatal heart attack last November, Jerry Mohrmann was engaged in his normal academic business. He was writing rhetorical criticism. More specifically, he was completing a close analysis of a short but important speech text—John Calhoun's oration "On the Reception of the Abolition Petitions." This study had a specific and seemingly narrow focus, but it arose from a number of complex, general issues and incorporated many of Jerry's characteristic interests. Thus, to recall the history of this project allows us to learn much not only about the man but also about the vocation he pursued.

During the last decade of his life, Jerry was greatly concerned about achieving a better and deeper understanding of that vocation. The period was one of accelerating and often bewildering change within the discipline. It spawned revisionist movements in several directions, as rhetorical critics attempted to alter and expand the traditional objects and methods of study.[1] In some measure, Jerry participated in this revisionist impulse. He found traditional speech criticism wanting; it was, he argued, narrowly and mechanically conceived, and thus it failed to take us "into the text of the speech and its workings."[2] In an effort to prove this point, he invoked an uncharacteristic method—he did some counting. But he expressed his point in characteristic prose:

> We used to study speeches, right? Wrong! How about Clay, Calhoun, and Webster for openers? A total of seventeen articles in national and regional journals, but no writer has seen fit to deal with the entire text of one of their speeches. Emerson? Eight articles, none

---

Reprinted from *The Quarterly Journal of Speech* 72 (1986), with permission of the Speech Communication Association.

[1] The report of the National Developmental Project on Rhetoric held in 1970 adumbrated this development. See Lloyd F. Bitzer and Edwin Black, eds., *The Prospect of Rhetoric* (Englewood Cliffs, NJ: Prentice Hall, 1971), especially the chapter, "Report of the Committee on the Advancement and Refinement of Rhetorical Criticism," pp. 220-27. For evidence of Mohrmann's participation in this movement, see the book he co-edited with Charles J. Stewart and Donovan J. Ochs, *Explorations in Rhetorical Criticism* (University Park and London: Pennsylvania State University Press, 1973).

[2] G. P. Mohrmann, "Elegy in a Critical Grave-Yard," *Western Journal of Speech Communication,* 44 (1980), 272.

on a particular speech text. Jonathan Edwards? Not one article. Acres of Diamonds? No article. The New South? One, a Hegelian analysis. Abraham Lincoln? Thirty-two articles, but only if we are generous can we say that as many as three explore the rhetoric of a given speech.[3]

For Jerry, this inattention to speech texts was a symptom of a more fundamental problem. It indicated a failure to engage the rhetorical process as it manifested itself in the actual conduct of discourse. Thus, in Jerry's words, the critic became a "circuit rider, forever circling the herd, but never getting to its center."[4]

Other critics shared this scepticism about the older approach, but most were inclined to abandon rather than to refurbish it. The prevailing mood called for new methods and attention to new forms of discourse. Jerry, however, feared that the stampede away from tradition might decenter and shatter an already fragile enterprise. It was important, therefore, to retain certain common objects and methods of study, and if some of our revisions worked within the tradition, we might achieve that goal. Moreover, in his view, revisionism too often concentrated entirely on methodological and terminological interests; this focus yielded only a cosmetic change, a substitution of new moulds for old ones, and the central problem of understanding the "text and texture of messages" was obscured rather than resolved.[5] Genuine progress, he concluded, depended upon closer attention to the phenomena we studied rather than the generation of abstract methods for its study.

Having adopted this position, Jerry obviously had to do more than preach about what needed doing. He had to demonstrate the value of textual studies by providing concrete models. During the last years of his life, this task occupied much of his attention, and the critique of Calhoun represented the leading edge of the project. The work, however, proceeded at a very slow rate. Part of the reason for this was Jerry's characteristic habit of mulling things over, of writing and rewriting drafts in an effort to flesh out rather than flatten interpretative problems. But, more important, the project proved to involve unexpected complications.

The motive for textual criticism, as Jerry conceived it, is to divert attention away from theoretical constructions and to focus on the rhetorical action embodied in particular discourses. Consequently, the enterprise begins with a severely empirical orientation; the critic must attend to the elements contained within the text itself. The empirical contents of a text, however, are

---

[3] The quotation comes from an unpublished paper, "Old Paths and New: A Fable for Critics," presented at the Speech Communication Association convention held at Washington D. C. in 1977. Mohrmann and I co-authored that paper, but those familiar with Mohrmann's style will recognize that he is the author of the passage cited in the text.
[4] Mohrmann, 272.
[5] Mohrmann, 273.

in no way equivalent to the symbolic action that marks a work as a rhetorical discourse. Texts simply do not yield up their own rhetorical interpretation. Critics must move from what is given in the text to something that they themselves produce—an account of the rhetorical dynamics implicit within it. At minimum, this act of interpretation requires a means to justify the identification of significant features in the text and to explain the interactions among these features. Since this process necessarily entails principles or categories "not native to the original," it requires an exercise of judgment at some level of abstraction, and it eventuates in something we might call theoretical understanding of the particular case.[6]

Paradoxically, then, the effort to displace theory with action leads from action back to theory. Of course, the new perspective alters the placement and status of theory; to paraphrase Clifford Geertz, theory functions not to generalize to or from cases but within them.[7] But, judged by the prevailing standards in our discipline, this formulation seems odd, if not unintelligible. And in the absence of already established models, the critic striving to advance from the text to a theoretical account of its particular rhetorical action confronts a number of bewildering problems. The features in the text seem to knot and unravel in an almost constant motion and attention to the particular strains against the requirements of theoretical understanding. The difficulties involved are so complex and so intimately connected with the study of specific texts that they are virtually impossible to describe in abstract terms. Fortunately, however, Jerry's effort to explain Calhoun's "Speech on the Reception of the Abolition Petitions" offers a useful and well documented case history. The story of his tribulations provides the best mechanism for locating the problems I have just suggested.

The project originated almost a decade ago, when Jerry and I jointly taught a course devoted to the masterpieces of oratorical literature. As we approached the unit on deliberative rhetoric, I suggested that we begin with Calhoun's speech. It probably did not merit the title of "masterpiece," but it had a number of virtues for pedagogical purposes. The speech was short, easy for students to read and comprehend, and easy for us to analyze, since, like Calhoun's oratory in general, it moved in a straightforward linear and logical direction. Although not very subtle or interesting in and of itself, the speech, I thought, might gently introduce students to the complexities they would confront in Demosthenes or Edmund Burke. Jerry listened to my argument, grunted assent, and departed carrying the text of the speech home with him.

When I arrived at the office the next morning, Jerry was already prowling the halls, his eyes twinkling with cantankerous delight. There was no phatic communication that morning—no greeting, no prefatory remarks. Instead, there was a whirling half turn toward me, the pointing of a well exercised

---

[6] E. D. Hirsch, Jr., *Validity in Interpretation* (New Haven: Yale University Press, 1976), p. 170.
[7] Clifford Geertz, *The Interpretation of Cultures* (New York: Basic Books, 1973), p. 26.

index finger in my direction, and the simple announcement: "Young man, you're wrong." And I was.

Beneath the progression of Calhoun's overt assertions and arguments, Jerry had uncovered a rather subtle conceptual pattern layered within the text. This pattern, occluded by the seemingly dead metaphors used in its expression, consisted in a related pair of spatial images. The first of these worked along a horizontal axis and depicted the union as a container. Its contents were parts or sections arranged in discrete compartments which occupied positions of absolute parity. The container, moreover, was less important than the divided parts it contained. The second image turned the spatial axis in a vertical direction as Calhoun constructed a theory of social hierarchy. Civilized nations, Calhoun imagined, rested upon a structure of class relations that moved from bottom to top. This vertical arrangement arose out of historical necessity, and both the material and moral progress of society required a stable stratification of the various orders within the population.

Once recognized, these two spatial orientations seemed to explain the order and movement of the text. The speech, that is, apparently pivoted from the horizontal to the vertical axis. In the first part of his argument, Calhoun invoked the horizontal image of separate but equal sections contained within the union. Congress was not a fit place to entertain petitions advocating an end to slavery, since such abolitionist rhetoric constituted an assault on the autonomous space occupied by the Southern states. Toward the middle of the speech, however, Calhoun rather abruptly shifted his orientation, announcing that he would assume "the higher ground" and defend slavery as "a positive good." It was here that he clearly invoked the vertical image of separate and unequal classes in the social order. All societies, he asserted, relegated the laboring class to the bottom of the heap. The existence of an under-class, therefore, was not grounds for passing moral judgment. The real issue depended upon the treatment accorded those who held this position, and by that standard, the South's peculiar institution proved beneficent, a point underscored by contrast to the "wage slavery" oppressing laborers in the industrial North.

This scheme of alternating spatial and argumentative directions offered an attractive and promising interpretative hypothesis, but it did not tell the whole story, since it could not account for much of the detail in the text. As Jerry returned to the text, he discovered some fascinating complications. In the first place, vertical dimensions insinuated themselves into the dominantly horizontal emphasis of the opening argument. Early in the speech, for example, Calhoun identified abolitionism as a contagion which was spreading and working its way *upward* through the fabric of Northern society. Left unchecked, it would infect those in the *highest stations* in the North, and under that circumstance, the abolitionist spirit would break across territorial boundaries as one section attempted to impose its moral predilections on another. Thus, a kind of vertical lift was conceived as a force moving to disrupt the properly static, horizontal relations among the parts of the union.

Likewise, the horizontal dimension intruded into the dominantly vertical imagery of the concluding argument. As Calhoun described the vertical symmetry of Southern society, he provided a motive for its defense against incursions from without. In the face of the impending abolitionist threat, the South must close ranks and take concerted action. It must defend every inch of its territory. In this instance, images of sectional conflict suggested a movement across space that endangered a stable, vertical structure. And once again, the intersection between spatial axes delineated a course of movement.

These observations not only complicated assessment of the external structure of the text, but they also raised general questions about the function of spatial metaphors. These questions prompted a study of the literature on the subject, and what Jerry found there confirmed what he had seen operating in Calhoun's discourse. "Spatial images," Jerry concluded, "are very far from being static entities. Certainly they may suggest a security born of stability, but at the same time, few are not freighted with ramifications nourished in a potential for movement. . . . When we talk of metaphorical space and place, we are not talking of passive constructs, are talking instead about constructs alive with the potential for action."[8] This conclusion is interesting in its own right, but within the economy of Jerry's project, it was only a preliminary, a guideline to help direct further encounters with the text. The crucial task was to understand how the potential in such constructs became actualized.

Furthermore, since the discourse was an oration presented under the pressure of specific circumstances, interpretation could not rest content with isolated judgments about the text itself. The demands of the situation had to be entered into the equation. Thus, examining the text from yet another angle, Jerry viewed it in the context of the debates of the period and of Calhoun's place within them, noting especially his effort both to speak as the voice of his section and to play a decisive role in national politics. These historical and biographic data did more than illuminate details in the text; they were essential to an informed judgment of its general configuration. Without reference to them, no one could hope to comprehend the pattern Calhoun saw in the events he recounted; no one could explain the fragmented and tortured logic that such a skilled logician wove into the text and attempted to project onto the world. This was a logic that demanded preservation of slavery and social inequality as the only secure means of maintaining free and equal institutions. The segmented images of space and place ranging through the text must have reflected a context that promoted an analytic psychosis—a habit of mind so preoccupied with the division of parts as to preclude synthetic reflection about the whole.

In short, the history of this exercise in textual criticism reveals the formidable number of elements involved in the enterprise: the close reading

---

[8] The quotation is from p. 5 of the unfinished manuscript of the Calhoun study. It bears the title, "Place and Space: Calhoun's Fatal Security." I want to thank Marilyn Mohrmann for allowing me access to this manuscript as well as some or Jerry's other papers.

and rereading of the text, the analysis of the historical and biographical circumstances that generate and frame its composition, the recognition of basic conceptions that establish the co-ordinates of the text, and an appreciation of the way these conceptions interact within the text and help determine its temporal movement. Unfortunately, Jerry did not complete the project. The last and best draft of his essay breaks off just as he began to integrate the elements of his analysis. Nevertheless, the work he did accomplish is sufficient to alert us to the importance of his effort and to allow us to outline a program for carrying his objectives forward.

In the remainder of this paper, I want to pursue the implications in Jerry's work—to generalize, expand, and, in some respects, to reinterpret the basic assumptions that animated his critical practice. I would emphasize, however, that the whole formulation is tentative. This is necessarily true, since the approach under consideration aims toward the understanding of practice rather than the articulation of a method. The ultimate test of its value, therefore, must refer to case studies. Nevertheless, Jerry and I have used this approach for some time, and it now seems appropriate to reflect on its general features. My objective is simply to clarify some implicit principles, and in keeping with Jerry's commitment to tradition, I shall try to so do within the context of the literature in our field.

The critique of Calhoun clearly reveals the most fundamental premise in Jerry's critical program: *Oratory is an art form.* A well constructed oration possesses a high degree of artistic integrity and density, and its proper understanding requires careful interpretative work. This position might seem to call forth a truism, but, for reasons I will soon explain, to entertain it seriously involves a significant departure from much of the existing rhetorical scholarship. Moreover, on reflection, this stance seems to entail some crucial issues. Unlike poetry and other "purer" forms of verbal art, the oration does not call attention to its own status as an art form. Oratory succeeds best when it appears to blend into the context of ordinary experience. It is a genre of discourse that effaces its own constructions. Placed at the margins of art and ordinary experience, oratorical discourse strains simultaneously toward autonomous coherence and transparent reference to the world in which it appears. The referential dimension is the more obvious, and its prominence often blinds the observer to the embedded artistic strategy that makes its referential surface appear plausible and natural. In fact, when the artistic imagination engages the public world, when the discourse cannot invoke suspension of disbelief, artistic strategy and referential content become virtually consubstantial. As a consequence, if the critic is to remain faithful to the object of study, the grounds for artistic judgment appear ambiguous and fragile.

To clarify this problem, we can again refer to Jerry's critique for concrete guidance. The critique began with the identification of two metaphoric conceptions that seemed to undergird the argument. These images, when seen in relation to other properties in the text, exerted a powerful influence on the internal, formal dimensions of the discourse. They established the conceptual space in which the discourse operated, and as the space shifted from horizontal to vertical dimensions, these conceptions also directed the temporal progression of the discourse. Thus, we can appreciate how the text developed internally through symbolically constructed relations in space and time. But, even as these symbols manifested themselves in the text, they reached outward to embrace and impart attitudes toward the things and events they symbolized. Moreover, these symbols were not fictional constructs made to be contemplated within their own self-contained horizons; they were actions on the minds of the audience bearing on its direct experience of public events. In short, Calhoun's oration was both an artistic construction and a literal representation of the public world. And, in addition, it was also an instrument designed to prompt further action in the world to which the text referred.

This teleological reading of the speech seems to afford the only adequate ground for effecting artistic rhetorical judgment. To rely exclusively either upon a formal/instrinsic or a representational/extrinsic criterion is to distort the rhetorical integrity of the discourse. Though critical analysis can separate these dimensions, the fact is that they occur simultaneously and work cooperatively within the fabric of the discourse. Attention to the purpose of the discourse, however, acts as shuttle to the threads unraveled in the analytical process. It preserves the interdependence of the intrinsic and extrinsic strands, since it refers analysis back to a synthetic judgment about the discourse in its entirety. From this perspective, the oration achieves unity as it formulates a response to circumstances and events in public consciousness and deploys its own internal resources to alter public consciousness about these circumstances and events. This rhetorical process negotiates between the symbolic action manifested by the text and the more ambiguous symbolic world based in the plurality of ordinary public experience.

Two points implied in this formulation require additional comment. First, I need to explain how and why the term "art" has shifted meaning in the course of my argument; second, I need to consider the status of rhetoric as a temporal art, a point that is crucial to but still only implicit in my argument. In fact, these two issues are very closely connected. For the sake of convenience, however, I will deal with them seriatim.

Earlier, and in keeping with conventional usage, I used the terms "art" and "artistic" to indicate formal or aesthetic properties in a text. But, just a few moments ago, in defining a standard for rhetorical judgment, I invoked notably different meanings for these terms. The art of and the artistry in oratory were identified in respect to a coordinating function, specifically the coordination between the internal and external impulses inherent in the rhetorical enterprise. The ground for unifying these impulses, moreover, was found in the end or purpose animating the particular discourse.

From this perspective, oratory assumes a rather special status as an art form, a status that allows us to appreciate Jerry's insistence on close textual analysis eventuating in generalization within cases. To put the point simply, a program of close textual analysis changes received notions about the relationship between the general and the particular, between theory and critical practice. The assessment of a rhetorical discourse must now hinge on the particulars of the case—the local circumstances that frame and motivate the work and the unique blend of formal and material elements that constitute its substance. Abstract, general principles may aid in guiding this judgment, but they do not represent the content of rhetorical theory. Theory is something that arises from an understanding of the particular, and abstract principles become important only as they are instantiated and individuated within the texture of an actual discourse. This perspective, then, stresses the motile, adaptive character of rhetorical discourse so as to identify theoretical knowledge with a complete understanding of a material case.[9]

This position may seem paradoxical—how can theoretical knowledge arise from a particular, material instance, especially when the object of study is the product of ephemeral interests and circumstances? The answer rests in the capacity that exemplars or touchstones possess for generating theoretical understanding of rhetorical action. The action in an oration is bound to the moment of its utterance, and in this sense, oratory is radically particular. Yet, a well constructed oration can encompass particulars in a way that establishes an abiding rhetorical standard I emphasize the phrase "rhetorical standard," since I do not mean that a speech may display noteworthy literary features or express great ideas capable of being appreciated outside the context of the discourse. Judgments made along these ideological and aesthetic lines constitute a legitimate and important aspect of the critical endeavor. But insofar as they must fail to account for the rhetorical integrity of a particular discourse, they cannot render an adequate assessment of the rhetorical dimensions of that work. Thus, what I am arguing is that some discourses coordinate particulars in such a striking and compelling fashion that they command attention as models of rhetorical excellence independent of our interest in these particulars *per se*. As rhetorical artifacts, their enduring significance consists in the artistic unity they display in response to specific and transitory circumstances. The critic who achieves a thorough understanding of such a discourse preserves its integrity by remaining mindful of its status as a material embodiment of rhetorical action, and the discourse, understood in this light, can serve as a paradigm or exemplary case.

Since the exemplary case instantiates a standard of excellence, it provides access to qualitative grounds for rhetorical judgment. As Edwin Black notes, reference to such cases allows the critic "to hold certain expectations of what rhetorical discourse ought to do" and to "gain certain insights into what rhetorical discourse is capable of doing."[10] These expectations and insights

---

[9] This position has some affinity with Michael Calvin McGee's argument in "A Materialist Conception of Rhetoric," in *Explorations in Rhetoric: Studies in Honor of Douglas Ehninger*, Ray E. McKerrow, ed. (Glenville Ill.: Scott, Foresman and Co., 1982), pp. 23-31, esp. pp. 28-31. Also see Barry Brummett, Rhetorical Theory as Heuristic and Moral: A Pedagogical Justification," *Communication Education*, 33 (1984), 97-105.
[10] Edwin Black, *Rhetorical Criticism: A Study in Method* (New York: Macmillan Co., 1965), p. 67.

provide a basis for judging a discourse as a unified and complete field of action, since the standard invoked is a paradigm case itself judged in its entirety. Moreover, I think it fair to regard such critical activity as theoretical, though not in the dominant contemporary sense, which refers to theory as a body of doctrine, an abstract set of principles organized in a self-contained and coherent structure. Instead, theory becomes linked with a kind of activity, and its meaning approximates the early Greek sense of *theoria,* which, as Wesley Trimpi explains, denotes "a viewing or observing of something as a whole in order to understand it."[11]

The recognition of the circumstantial, time-bound nature of rhetorical discourse leads to the second issue I must address—the status of oratory as a temporal art. Once more Jerry's study of Calhoun offers a convenient way to set our bearings. In Calhoun's speech, Jerry discovered that the rhetorical action moved along two basic co-ordinates—the temporal and the spatial. Owing to the special characteristics of the text, Jerry began with conceptions of space. In general, however, I believe that time is the more important dimension, for it holds priority both in respect to the intrinsic and extrinsic functions discharged by the oratorical art. Considered intrinsically, oratory, like the novel and other verbal forms, is a dominantly temporal art; that is, it develops in time through the progression of spoken or written words. Considered extrinsically, oratory directs itself toward what the Greeks called *kairos*—a fitting, appropriate, or timely response to a given situation. Both these dimensions of time, moreover, require careful attention if we are to develop an adequate base for textual criticism. This point becomes fully apparent when we examine the literature in our field.

Though not always recognized as such, the intersection between time and rhetoric has played a persistent and crucial role in the history of our discipline. The origin of the field traces itself back to the effort of the Cornell school to define a territory for oratorical studies. And this effort pivots on a temporal distinction between the functions of rhetoric and poetic. On this view, poetic discourse addresses a diffuse, timeless audience about matters of enduring concern. Rhetorical discourse, by contrast, addresses a well defined, immediate audience about issues of momentary concern. Hence, rhetoric is a captive of historical time, and the critic, *qua* rhetorical critic, remains bound to the circumstances that define the case at hand.[12]

As a rough and general principle, this distinction has considerable merit. Unfortunately, perhaps because of the anxiety to distance the fledgling rhetorical enterprise from its literary parent, the point was stretched out of all

---

[11] Wesley Trimpi, *Muses of One Mind: The Literary Analysis of Experience and Its Continuity* (Princeton, NJ: Princeton University Press, 1983), p. xiii.

[12] This position receives its classic formulation in Herbert Wichelns' 1925 essay, "The Literary Criticism of Oratory." The essay is reprinted in *Methods of Rhetorical Criticism,* Robert L. Scott and Bernard L. Brock, eds. (New York: Harper and Row, 1972), pp. 27-60. Also see G. P. Mohrmann and Michael C. Leff, "Lincoln at Cooper Union: A Rationale for Neo-Classical Criticism," *Quarterly Journal of Speech,* 60 (1974), 460.

proportion, and the result was inattention to the properties of the rhetorical text *per se.* The oration simply became a medium for organizing historical and biographical research or a resource for illustrating the elements contained in the abstract taxonomy that passed for a theory of rhetoric. The text offered no organic resistance of its own. It was simply there, a closed but accessible space ready to be entered whenever someone wanted to find live specimens of the fauna classified in the various rhetorical bestiaries.

Even after the scholarship had drifted away from its original moorings, the transparency of the text persisted as a general assumption. Thus, in 1957, Thomas Nilsen argued that critical interpretation must work itself out through the history of ideas, since particular oratorical texts did not pose any significant interpretative problems.[13] And twelve years later, Phillip Tompkins located the interpretative task in the study of audience reactions; textual analysis, he maintained, could not explain the interaction between the rhetorical structure of a message and its impact on receivers.[14] An undeclared allegiance to similar assumptions has colored most of the critical studies that have directly addressed time as a rhetorical consideration. In the early seventies, for example, Barbara Larson, Bruce Gronbeck, and Edwin Black wrote important essays on the subject, but all of them conceived time as an extrinsic influence on the production or reception of a rhetorical text without considering that it might function as a constituent of the text.[15]

This macroscopic, extrinsic approach perhaps receives its most sophisticated treatment in Thomas Farrell's essay "Knowledge in Time." Farrell clearly identifies rhetoric as a temporal phenomenon. He writes: "Whether any public position may prove well-founded, appropriate, even true can come to depend on its placement in the long run of unfolding moments."[16] Here again the sweep of historic time receives priority, but Farrell is not thinking simply of the text/context relationship. Among other things, he is concerned about the placement of a rhetorical act in relation to "an endless succession of discursive acts."[17] Consequently, rhetoric achieves a certain durability through a network of intertextual influences. This perspective, of course, still decenters the particular rhetorical text, since, as Farrell argues, "rhetorical

---

[13]Thomas R. Nilsen, "Interpretative Function of the Critic," *Western Journal of Speech Communication,* 21 (1976), 70-76.

[14]Phillip K. Tompkins, "The Rhetorical Criticism of Non-Oratorical Works," *Quarterly Journal of Speech,* 55 (1969), 438-439.

[15]Barbara A. Larson, "The Election Eve Address of Edmund Muskie: A Case Study of Televised Public Address," *Central States Speech Journal,* 23 (1972), 78-85; Bruce E. Gronbeck, "Rhetorical Timing in Public Communication," *Central States Speech Journal,* 25 (1974), 84-94; and Edwin Black, "Electing Time," *Quarterly Journal of Speech,* 59 (1973), 125-129. A broader conception of time, such as I am attempting to explain, may stand near the origin of artistic rhetoric in the fifth century B.C. See John Poulakos, "The Place of Time in Gorgias," paper presented at the Speech Communication Annual Convention, Louisville, Kentucky, 1982.

[16]Thomas B. Farrell, "Knowledge in Time: Toward an Extension of Rhetorical Form," in J. Robert Cox and Charles Arthur Willard, *Advances in Argumentation Theory and Research* (Carbondale and Edwardsville: Southern Illinois University Press, 1982, p. 123.

[17]Farrell, p. 128.

argument generally is not determined by any single author."[18] In short, Farrell attributes conceptual solidity to rhetoric, but it is entirely diachronic, something charted across the arc of historic change.

It is possible, however, to narrow this perspective, to punctuate the flow of historic time and to conceive a notion of "unfolding moments" that applies to particular texts. For this purpose, we need only recognize that rhetorical discourses are themselves temporal phenomena. They emerge in time; they are conditioned by other discourses and by the progression of events, but they are also constructed things that occupy a span of time. And while it is true that rhetorical "argument generally is not determined by any single author," it is also true that rhetorical argument generally is constructed by a single author. Every rhetorical text is a particular construction that unfolds in time as it is written or spoken and as it is processed by a listener or reader. The rhetorical text, then, is a historical development occurring within a broader context of historical developments. However circumscribed by extrinsic events, the text retains an internal history of its own.

The oration, therefore, engages time on at least two levels. It is constrained by and refers to the order and relation of events in the world, but it also constructs a certain order and relation of elements within its own pattern of utterance. This internal pattern, the timing in the text, determines the appearance of the discourse as an intervention in historic time, but the discourse also stretches beyond its own margins to influence the appearance of the world in which it is made. The timing in the discourse mediates our perception of time in the public world. *The central task of textual criticism is to understand how rhetorical action effects this negotiation, how the construction of a symbolic event invites a reconstruction of the events to which it refers.* The complexity of this process, moreover, reveals the artistic density of well made rhetorical texts and the reason that they demand and reward careful interpretive study.

The rhetorical significance of the ratio between time and timing is yet another matter better understood when exemplified rather than described in abstract terms. Unfortunately, the time limits for this presentation do not allow the opportunity to deal with a case study in adequate detail. Nevertheless, even though there is the risk of oversimplification, a short illustration seems necessary to clarify the issue. For this purpose, Lincoln's "House Divided Speech" offers a useful point of reference, since Lincoln coordinates this ratio in exemplary fashion.[19]

Lincoln delivered his speech immediately after receiving the Republican nomination for the Senate in 1858. His purpose was to solidify support within his own party by preventing desertion in favor of Stephen Douglas, the

---

[18]Farrell, p. 124.

[19]For a much more detailed development of the argument that follows, see my paper, "Rhetorical Timing in Lincoln's 'House Divided' Speech'," published under separate cover in the series of Van Zelst Lectures in Communication (Evanston: Northwestern University, 1983).

Democratic incumbent. For a variety of reasons, Douglas' doctrine of popular sovereignty had attracted favorable notice among Republicans, and Lincoln set out to demonstrate that Douglas' position actually was incompatible with the tenets of the Republican Party. The order of Lincoln's argument proceeded through three carefully timed main sections.

The opening section articulated the conceptual ground for the speech as a whole. Here Lincoln described the union as a house. The house was divided against itself, but it would not remain so. The currents of time and circumstance would render it all one thing or the other, all free or all slave. This image subtlely worked to undercut Douglas' position, since it imparted a moral impulse to events, a directional tendency that overwhelmed such efforts at political temporizing as the doctrine of popular sovereignty. The remainder of the speech ramified the implications compacted within this image; as Lincoln filtered recent political history through its moral lens, he constructed a narrative that drove Douglas outside the ambit of Republican principle.

This symbolic ostracism moved through two uneven steps. In the second major section of the text, Lincoln narrated the leading political events of the period between 1854 and 1858. The nuanced story he told implicated Douglas in a virulent, covert conspiracy designed to promote slavery and overturn free state constitutions. In the final section, however, Douglas emerged in a rather different light. He was a "caged and toothless" lion, rendered impotent by his own temporizing, and duped into a position that encouraged the pro-slavery tendency.

The sequence of these two steps brilliantly illustrates the artistic and persuasive force of rhetorical timing. Given the context, Lincoln could discredit Douglas either by proving that he pretended moral neutrality in order to advance the pro-slavery tendency or by proving that the stance of moral neutrality unwittingly gave impetus to that tendency. Either point was sufficient to undercut Douglas, but the first obviously was the more serious charge and the more difficult to establish. Thus, as Lincoln worked to render this charge credible, he opened the ground for his less ambitious but equally effective second point. An audience induced to consider seriously whether Douglas had directed a conspiracy to force slavery into Illinois was thoroughly prepared to receive the argument that his position simply did not measure up to the standards demanded by the Republican party.

In this way, Lincoln develops a strategy to encompass his local contest with Douglas. But, we are in the presence of a rhetorical genius, and so it is not surprising that his discourse extends to broader and more profound aspects of the context. Even as he stretches the fabric of events so as to leave Douglas comfortably outside the Republican frame, Lincoln weaves these events into a new pattern. Previously confused tendencies begin to assume choate form and to progress in ethically tilted directions, and ultimately political history is reconfigured as moral narrative. This pattern unfolds as the discourse progresses, as its ideas, images, rhythms, and allusions appear, combine, and sort themselves out. This dynamic within the text induces the auditor to follow and assent to its internal movement, and as it does so, it places the auditor in contact with the vision of the world it represents. Thus, to experience the text is to be coached to experience the world as the text constructs it.[20]

In referring to the "House Divided Speech," one further problem surfaces. Some time ago I divided the basic coordinates of rhetorical action into the categories of time and space, and then shunted conceptions of space to the side, arguing that the temporal dimension had priority. Yet, in Lincoln's speech, the whole movement of the text appears to devolve from the initial spatial metaphor. That is, when Lincoln conceives the union as a house, he establishes a conceptual frame that regulates and orders the progression of elements across the text. Moreover, it is not difficult to cite other evidence that reveals the power of metaphor to frame and localize rhetorical action. In Jerry's critique of the Calhoun speech, for example, much of the rhetorical action hinges on the two basic spatial images. More generally, Michael Osborn's study of archetypes demonstrates how powerful recurrent symbols, such as light, or elevation, or the sea, can inform and control the content of a text.[21] And recently Robert Ivie has shown how clusters of unobtrusive metaphors often reveal the basic assumptions guiding certain kinds of discourse.[22] Using a method that allows critics to track metaphoric patterns to their base, Ivie has uncovered foundational conceptions that set the direction of foreign policy debates. Thus, for example, among rhetors advocating detente with the Soviet Union, some view international relations as a "game" in which cooperation yields better results than competition. Other rhetors, however, conceive the antagonism between the two superpowers as a "disease" that must be cured. Obviously, these root conceptions are important, and they seem to operate at a level beneath the temporal flow at the surface of a discourse.

At the least, this evidence mandates some revision in my original position. If a rhetorical discourse is a field of action, it is also necessary to conceive boundaries that delimit the field. Recent studies of the tropes, metaphor in particular, clearly indicate that such boundaries normally consist in images or clusters of images that subsist below the surface action of the discourse.[23] These images, then, define the conceptual space of the discourse. The textual critic must recognize these base concepts and incorporate them into the interpretative process, and for this reason, a *purely* temporal orientation seems untenable.

---

[20]My language here, as well as the whole drift of the argument, clearly borrows from Kenneth Burke. See, for example, A *Rhetoric of Motives* (Berkeley and Los Angeles: University of California Press, 1969), p. 58.

[21]Michael Osborn, "Archetypal Metaphor in Rhetoric: The Light-Dark Family," *Quarterly Journal of Speech,* 53 (1967), 115-26, and "The Evolution of the Archetypal Sea in Rhetoric and Poetic," *Quarterly Journal of Speech,* 63 (1977), 347-63.

[22]Robert L. Ivie, "Metaphor and the Rhetorical Invention of Cold War 'Idealists'," paper presented at the Speech Communication Association convention, Denver, Colorado, November, 1985.

[23]In addition to the sources cited above, see George Lakoft and Mark Johnson, *Metaphors We Live By* (Chicago: University of Chicago Press, 1980).

It is possible, however, to press this point more aggressively. The conceptual base of the discourse, its "spatial" location, may seem to hold priority over the temporal dimension, since the base concepts apparently limit and exert some control over the movement of the other elements in the discourse. In certain respects, this arrangement of priorities is reasonable, but I am sceptical about its general application to rhetorical criticism. Insofar as we regard rhetoric as a form of action, a determination of the foundations implicit in a text seems less central than an understanding of the interactions that occur across and within its phenomenal surface. The temporal dimension, the timing in the text, conveys the rhetorical action, and thus, although critics cannot discount the force of the textual substructure, their primary attention should remain focused on the unfolding surface.

This position seems consistent with the temporal movement of the critical process itself. Even those critics bent on discovering root concepts cannot proceed until they have studied the surface structure of the text with great care. A good many conceptual tokens appear along that surface, and unless judgment is prejudiced or arbitrary, none of them can be deemed fundamental without an understanding of the movement of the whole. And so, the critic must start with the superstructure in order to locate the substructure. More important, the identification of root concepts does not represent the proper end of the critical process. From a purely rhetorical perspective at least, the interest in conceptual foundations is motivated by the desire to gain a better insight into what happens in the discourse itself. After all, to do nothing more than reduce the discourse to its conceptual bases is to convert a field of action into a set of static entities. The critic, therefore, must rise back to the surface of the text in order to understand how the rhetorical process breathes life into concepts and turns them into palpable incentives for action.

I must confess some uneasiness about this last argument, and as I wrote it, a vision of an old friend prowling the hallway came to mind. In this instance, I do not think he would say: "Young man, you're wrong." For one thing, I am no longer so young, and more to the point, I hope my argument actually is not "wrong." What Jerry Mohrmann probably would say is that I have not mulled things over long enough, have not looked carefully enough at the actual phenomena, and have allowed my thinking to stray too far in a single direction. In fact, the argument I have just sketched describes a rather narrow perspective, which might best be labelled as a "purely" or "radically" rhetorical approach to the text, an approach that single-mindedly concentrates on understanding rhetorical action for its own sake.

The long history of the tradition warns us about the dangers and difficulties involved in trying to purify the discipline. There are, in fact, almost as many conceptions of rhetoric as there are rhetoricians, and one person's "pure rhetoric" is another's sophism. Furthermore, the business of rhetorical criticism hardly can be reduced to a single set of motives. There are critics interested in rhetorical discourse as a way of understanding how we use metaphor and what its use tells us about our conceptual apparatus. And other critics seek to understand the base concepts in a kind of discourse so as to enter into rather than just observe the debate, to understand the rhetoric of the peace movement, for example, in order to make it a better and more effective agency for changing the political world. These motives are not only legitimate, but, to some degree, they always insinuate themselves into the most purely academic study of particular cases.

What I have attempted, therefore, is to clarify one critical perspective and not to discredit or displace other perspectives. In this process, I have identified certain basic conceptions implicit in a kind of critical practice, and I have tried to organize them and drive them toward coherence. At the end of the line, the project begins to come undone. An approach devoted to the theoretical understanding of particulars cannot suffer translation into a purely programmatic vision. Nevertheless, clarification of this vision serves an important purpose; it establishes a conscious base of operation, and in doing so, it not only makes a certain kind of critical practice more accessible, but it also alerts us to what we might not otherwise notice—the limitations necessarily involved whenever we adopt a perspective.

These limitations are not necessarily debilitating, since as Jerry Mohrmann's work demonstrates, a critical perspective need not close itself into a system rotten with its own perfection. The critic can invoke what Walter Fisher calls "informed innocence" and remain open to the particular object of study.[24] To achieve this end, however, we must pay heed to the human voice that resonates in all rhetorical discourse. In the face of the almost infinite abstractions we can use to analyze rhetorical performance in general, we need to find ways to approach our subject on a human scale. That, I believe, was Jerry Mohrmann's guiding concern and his surest connection with the tradition. For him, the study of rhetoric was satisfying only insofar as it remained attached to the integrity of a discourse unfolding within the drama of local circumstances and straining to encompass and alter the configuration of those circumstances. In its particular moments, rhetorical discourse brings us into intimate contact with the human condition, and critics who dwell in those moments participate in the long arc of a tradition that stretches from Isocrates to Jerry Mohrmann, for they too speak with a human voice.

---

[24]Walter R. Fisher, "Genre: Concepts and Applications in Rhetorical Criticism," *Western Journal of Speech Communication,* 44 (1980), 299.

The Renaissance of American Public Address: Text and Context in Rhetorical Criticism

by Stephen E. Lucas

The study of American public address is in the midst of a remarkable renaissance. Widely perceived a decade ago as in serious decline, it is stronger today than ever before. This is evident not only in the quality of recent journal articles and convention papers, but also in the growing number of books by scholars in public address.[1] The purpose of this essay is to take stock of these developments—to assess the present state of work in American public address and to suggest directions for future scholarship. Before turning to these matters, however, we should explore the parameters of public address as an area of scholarly inquiry.

1

Traditionally, of course, the study of public address meant the study of great speakers and speeches. Scholars in public address usually focused on the speaking careers of individual orators, and they typically employed what was known as the historical-critical method. Over the years they produced some distinguished works, including the pioneering, three-volume *History*

Reprinted from *The Quarterly Journal of Speech* 74 (1988), with permission of the Speech Communication Association.

[1] These books include Roderick P. Hart, *Verbal Style and the Presidency: A Computer-Based Analysis* (Orlando, FL.: Academic Press, 1984); Kathleen Hall Jamieson, *Packaging the Presidency: A History and Criticism of Presidential Campaign Advertising* (New York: Oxford University Press, 1984); Frederick J. Antczak, *Thought and Character: The Rhetoric of Democratic Education* (Ames: Iowa State University Press, 1985); Ernest G. Bormann, *The Force of Fantasy: Restoring the American Dream* (Carbondale: Southern Illinois University Press, 1985); Kathleen J. Turner, *Lyndon Johnson's Dual War: Vietnam and the Press* (Chicago: University of Chicago Press, 1985); J. Michael Hogan, *The Panama Canal in American Politics: Domestic Advocacy and the Evolution of Policy* (Carbondale: Southern Illinois University Press, 1986); Robert E. Denton, Jr., and Dan F. Hahn, *Presidential Communication: Description and Analysis* (New York: Praeger, 1986); David Zarefsky, *President Johnson's War on Poverty: Rhetoric and History* (University: University of Alabama Press, 1986); John C. Hammerback, Richard J. Jensen, and Jose Angel Gutierrez, *A War of Words: Chicano Protest in the 1960s and 1970s* (Westport, CT: Greenwood Press, 1986); Roderick P. Hart, *The Sound of Leadership: Presidential Communication in the Modern Age* (Chicago: University of Chicago Press, 1987); and the works cited in notes 14 and 15 below. As Robert L. Ivie noted in a recent review, more books on American public address have appeared since 1984 than during the preceding fourteen years ("The Complete Criticism of Political Rhetoric," *Quarterly Journal of Speech* 73 [1987]: 98).

and Criticism of American Public Address, Carroll Arnold's explication of Lord Thomas Erskine as a forensic pleader, Herbert Wichelns's classic essay on Ralph Waldo Emerson, Loren Reid's biography of Charles James Fox, Robert Gunderson's *The Log-Cabin Campaign,* J. Jeffrey Auer's *Antislavery and Disunion,* and Robert Oliver's *History of Public Speaking in America.*[2] So dominant was the traditional study of public address that, in its golden age of the 1930s, 40s, and 50s, it all but eliminated other approaches to rhetorical criticism. To be a rhetorical critic in those days usually meant that one was also a student of British or American public address.

As we know, however, not everyone liked the traditional paradigm, and not all studies conforming to it were distinguished. By the early 1960s it was under sustained attack, and it was dealt a lethal stroke in 1965 by Edwin Black's enormously influential *Rhetorical Criticism: A Study in Method.* Black's devastating assault on neo-Aristotelianism was at once an indictment of the prevailing method of rhetorical criticism and of the traditional paradigm of scholarship in public address. But, we should note, it was not an indictment of public address *per se* as an area of scholarship. As its subtitle announced, Black's book was a study in method. It sought to "stimulate and expand the dialogue on rhetorical criticism," to promote "variety in the methods of rhetoric," and to multiply "the options available to the critic." Although Black questioned neo-Aristotelianism's "too tidy distinction between spoken and written discourse," assailed its "restricted view of context," and decried its emphasis on immediate effect as the controlling basis for critical judgment, he did not call for the elimination—or even a diminution—of studies dealing with rhetorical discourses of historical consequence.[3] Indeed, almost all of the case studies Black developed to illustrate his alternative approach to criticism—John Jay Chapman's Coatesville speech of August 16, 1912, John Henry Newman's *Apologia pro Vita sua,* the Lincoln-Douglas debates of 1858, Jonathan Edwards's "Sinners in the Hands of an Angry God," and Lincoln's Second Inaugural—were drawn from the standard materials of Anglo-American public address.

Yet, as often happens, the tide of scholarly revisionism swept everything out to sea. Neo-Aristotelianism as a method of criticism and public address as an area of scholarship were so closely allied that as students of rhetoric

---

[2] William Norwood Brigance and Marie Hochmuth, eds., *A History and Criticism of American Public Address,* 3 vols. (New York: McGraw-Hill, 1943-1955); Carroll C. Arnold, "Lord Thomas Erskine— Modern Advocate," *Quarterly Journal of Speech* 44 (1958): 17-30; Herbert A. Wichelns, "Ralph Waldo Emerson," in Brigance and Hochmuth, *History and Criticism,* 2: 501-525; Loren Reid, *Charles James Fox: A Man for the People* (Columbia: University of Missouri Press, 1969); Robert Gray Gunderson, *The Log-Cabin Campaign* (Lexington: University of Kentucky Press, 1957); J. Jeffrey Auer, ed., *Antislavery and Disunion, 1858-1861: Studies in the Rhetoric of Compromise and Conflict* (New York: Harper & Row, 1963); Robert T. Oliver, *History of Public Speaking in America,* (Boston: Allyn and Bacon, 1965). A more recent work in the same tradition is Barnet Baskerville, *The People's Voice: The Orator in American Society* (Lexington: University Press of Kentucky, 1979).

[3] Edwin Black, *Rhetorical Criticism: A Study in Method* (New York: Macmillan, 1965), viii, 11, 39.

followed Black in rejecting the former, they also tended to reject the latter. As neo-Aristotelianism became discredited, so too did the study of public address. Indeed, the very term "public address" fell into disrepute and rhetorical scholars all but fell over one another in rushing to announce that they were "rhetorical critics" rather than students of "public address." In many schools, courses in British and American "public address" disappeared from the curriculum, to be replaced by courses in social movements, protest rhetoric, political communication, rhetorical genres, campaign rhetoric, presidential rhetoric, rhetoric and social values, the rhetoric of the New Left, the rhetoric of the far right, the rhetoric of controversy, the rhetoric of social control, and the like. Similarly, essays on such topics came to dominate the pages of our national and regional journals.

And so some writers have remarked the death of public address as a subject of rhetorical inquiry during the mid-1960s and early 1970s.[4] But did the study of public address really die? If we conceive of that study according to the traditional paradigm, the answer is probably yes. But what if we conceive of the matter differently? What if we move beyond the traditional paradigm? What if we think of public address not just as the study of historical speakers and speeches, but as study of the full range of public, discursive rhetorical acts—historical and contemporary, oral and written, considered individually or as part of a broader campaign or movement? Moreover, what if we dissociate public address from its debilitating identification with neo-Aristotelianism and affirm that studies in public address employ a wide variety of critical methods, approaches, and perspectives?

Once we take these steps, it can be argued that the study of public address did not die, though it certainly underwent a dramatic metamorphosis—especially in its increasing attention to contemporary rhetorical events, in its growing concern with such collective rhetorical phenomena as social movements and political campaign and in its shift from neo-Aristotelianism to critical pluralism.[5] The result was a burst of creative and innovative scholarship that produced such studies as Edwin Black's "The Second Persona," Richard Gregg's "The Ego-Function of the Rhetoric of Protest," James Andrews's "Confrontation at Columbia," Roderick Hart's "The Rhetoric of the True Believer," Parke Burgess's "The Rhetoric of Black Power," Robert Scott and Donald Smith's "The Rhetoric of Confrontation," Karlyn Campbell's "The Rhetoric of Women's Liberation," and Michael

---

[4] Bruce E. Gronbeck, "The Birth, Death, and Rebirth of Public Address," presented at Speech Communication Association annual convention, Denver, Colorado, November 1985.

[5] The many accounts of these changes include Charles J. Stewart, "Historical Survey: Rhetorical Criticism in Twentieth-Century America," in G. P. Mohrmann, Charles J. Stewart, and Donovan J. Ochs, eds., *Explorations in Rhetorical Criticism* (University Park: Pennsylvania State University Press, 1973), 1-31; Richard B. Gregg, "The Criticism of Symbolic Inducement: A Critical-Theoretical Connection," in Thomas W. Benson, ed., *Speech Communication in the Twentieth Century* (Carbondale: Southern Illinois University Press, 1985), 41-62.

Osborn's "Evolution of the Archetypal Sea."[6] These are all important works that look very different from studies adhering to the traditional paradigm, but I would submit that they are nevertheless studies in public address.

To be sure, one can object that such works are "critical" rather than "historical," but as I have argued elsewhere, such a distinction is overdrawn and misleading.[7] Besides, even if one grants that there is a fundamental distinction between critical and historical approaches to rhetorical analysis, on what basis should we exclude either from the ken of public address? It is time to free public address from the shackles of its past. Let us leave behind forever the parochial conception of public address that dominated the traditional paradigm and that continues to influence the way many students of communication perceive it. Let us recognize once and for all that studies in public address can focus on historical or contemporary rhetorical phenomena, can range from mere chronicle to the most audacious interpretation and assessment, can—indeed, should—adopt whatever critical posture works best to explicate the object of inquiry.

2

This recognition seems particularly important in light of two recent developments in the study of American public address. The first of these developments is a resurgence of interest in the American oratorical tradition. Such interest, which had been at the center of conventional scholarship, declined precipitously during the 1960s and 1970s as the locus of study shifted to contemporary events and as the scope of rhetoric expanded to take in every form of symbolic inducement. Living in a turbulent age of warfare abroad and upheaval at home, many rhetorical scholars were motivated by "a deep concern for the pressing problems of our time."[8] Students of public address were upbraided for being "concerned only with the discourse of the past" and were urged to broaden their work to include contemporary rhetoric as manifested in "informal conversations, group settings, public settings, mass

---

[6] Edwin Black, "The Second Persona," *Quarterly Journal of Speech* 56 (1970): 109-19; Richard B. Gregg, "The Ego-Function of the Rhetoric of Protest," *Philosophy and Rhetoric* 4 (1971): 71-91; James R. Andrews, "Confrontation at Columbia: A Case Study in Coercive Rhetoric," *Quarterly Journal of Speech* 55 (1969): 9-16, Roderick P. Hart, "The Rhetoric of the True Believer," *Speech Monographs* 38 (1971): 249-61; Parke G. Burgess, "The Rhetoric of Black Power: A Moral Demand?" *Quarterly Journal of Speech* 54 (1968): 122-33; Robert L. Scott and Donald K. Smith, "The Rhetoric of Confrontation," *Quarterly Journal of Speech* 55 (1969): 1-8; Karlyn Kohrs Campbell, "The Rhetoric of Women's Liberation: An Oxymoron," *Quarterly Journal of Speech* 59 (1973): 74-86; Michael Osborn, "The Evolution of the Archetypal Sea in Rhetoric and Poetic," *Quarterly Journal of Speech* 63 (1977): 347-63.

[7] Stephen E. Lucas, "The Schism in Rhetorical Scholarship," *Quarterly Journal of Speech* 67 (1981): 1-20.

[8] "Report of the Committee on the Advancement and Refinement of Rhetorical Criticism," in Lloyd F. Bitzer and Edwin Black, eds., *The Prospect of Rhetoric: Report of the National Developmental Project* (Englewood Cliffs, NJ: Prentice-Hall, 1971), 225.

media messages, picketing, sloganeering, chanting, singing, marching, gesturing, ritual, institutional and cultural symbols, intercultural transactions, and so forth."[9] As reasoned public discourse was overshadowed at every turn by discord and confrontation, it became clear that the study of platform speaking could not explicate the informal, fragmentary, disruptive, often non-discursive modes of rhetorical influence employed by Black Power advocates and New Left activists. Indeed, some scholars detected a conservative bias in the values of civility, rationality, and decorum underlying traditional concepts of oratory. Such values, they claimed, were in fact "masks for the preservation of injustice"—ideological weapons used by elites who, "having already a share in power, have the leisure to aestheticize and moralize rhetoric, to demand elegant style and the display of a civil, friendly, reasonable ethos."[10] Set against this backdrop, the model of the great orator standing heroically at the crossroads of history in the finest tradition of the human spirit seemed hopelessly romantic and outmoded.

But times change, and with them the goals, values, and orientations of scholars. While the Age of Aquarius was preoccupied with the rhetoric of the streets, the Age of Reagan has restored the rhetoric of the platform. Studies of the New Left are passe, scholarship in the rhetoric of social movements is moribund, and it is hard to find even a glimmer of interest in confrontation as a communication strategy. Alienation is out, consensus is in, and methods of managing consensus—including formal public speaking—are again respectable on campus.[11] Perhaps most important, the stunning rhetorical triumphs of Ronald Reagan during his first presidential administration made the study of oratory once again relevant. Not only have we seen a plethora of studies dealing with Reagan as a speaker, but we have witnessed a general revival of interest in oratory as a force in American history. Among the manifestations of this revival are a growing number of books, essays, and convention programs devoted to American speakers, publication of the first comprehensive anthology of American public address in twenty years,[12] the recent national conference on the oratory of Martin Luther King, Jr.,[13] and the appearance of the volume under review here—*American Orators of the Twentieth Century: Critical Studies and Sources,* edited by Bernard K. Duffy

---

[9] Samuel L. Becker, "Rhetorical Studies for the Contemporary World," in Bitzer and Black, *Prospect of Rhetoric,* 40; "Report of the Committee on the Advancement and Refinement of Rhetorical Criticism," in Bitzer and Black, *Prospect of Rhetoric,* 225.

[10] Scott and Smith, "Rhetoric of Confrontation," 8; Robert M. Browne, "Response to Edward P. J. Corbett, 'The Rhetoric of the Open Hand and the Rhetoric of the Closed Fist,'" in Douglas Ehninger, ed., *Contemporary Rhetoric: A Reader's Coursebook* (Glenview, IL: Scott, Foresman, 1972), 214.

[11] Indeed, not only are they respectable, but they are among the most sought-after undergraduate courses. See, for example, James W. Gibson, Michael S. Hanna, and Bill M. Huddleston, "The Basic Speech Course at U. S. College and Universities: IV," *Communication Education* 34 (1985): 281-91.

[12] Ronald F. Reid, ed., *Three Centuries of American Rhetorical Discourse: An Anthology and a Review* (Prospect Heights, IL: Waveland Press, 1988).

[13] The conference was held at the Martin Luther King, Jr., Center in Atlanta, Georgia on January 9-10, 1988.

and Halford R. Ryan.[14]

A collection of encyclopedia-style essays on fifty-eight leading political, social, and religious speakers, *American Orators of the Twentieth Century* fills an enormous void in the literature on American public address. Unlike the studies in Brigance and Hochmuth's *History and Criticism of American Public Address,* some of which ran to monograph length, the entries in this work range from six to nine pages and follow a fairly standard format. Each assesses the orator's impact on American life and delineates such aspects of his or her speaking as argumentation, style, persuasive techniques, delivery, and methods of speech preparation. Appended to each essay is a chronology of the orator's major speeches and a list of information sources that includes leading research collections, speech anthologies, critical studies, and biographies.

Given the large number of contributors, the entries are remarkably even in coverage and clarity. As one would expect in a basic reference work, there is little new information and few flights of critical fancy. Yet despite an occasional oversight (such, for example, as failing to mention either Martin Luther King's 1964 Nobel Peace Prize lecture or his speech at New York's Riverside Church on April 4, 1967, in which he broke decisively from the Johnson administration over the war in Vietnam), the book admirably fulfills its purpose. Moreover, given the constraints imposed by the encyclopedia-like format, there are a surprising number of essays that stand out for their acuity of insight, their power of synthesis, and their grace of expression. To mention only a few, they include the selections on Jimmy Carter (by Richard Leeman and Martin Slann), Dwight Eisenhower (by Richard Crable), Billy Graham (by Hal Fulmer), Billy James Hargis (by Dale Leathers), Barbara Jordan (by David Henry), Edward Kennedy (by William Pederson), Anna Howard Shaw (by Wil Linkugel), and Harry Truman (by Halford Ryan).

As with any volume of this nature, questions inevitably arise about why certain speakers are included while others are excluded. On what grounds, for example, does one treat John Jay Chapman, Herbert Hoover, and Henry Kissinger—none of whom achieved distinction as an orator—and leave out such spellbinders as Norman Vincent Peale and Stokely Carmichael? How does one cover essentially regional figures such as Samuel Ervin and Herbert Talmadge and leave out such speakers of acknowledged national importance as Henry Cabot Lodge and Norman Thomas? By what criteria does one give essays to Jesse Helms and Jerry Falwell, but not to Phyllis Schlafly? To Henry Wallace, but not to Wendell Wilkie or Eugene McCarthy? To Betty Friedan and Ti-Grace Atkinson, but not to Jane Addams or Carrie Chapman Catt?

These are difficult questions, and the answers undoubtedly lie in a combination of factors, including the length of the book, the expertise of the

---

[14]Bernard K. Duffy and Halford R. Ryan, eds., *American Orators of the Twentieth Century: Critical Studies and Sources* (Westport, CT: Greenwood Press, 1987).

contributors, and the orientations of the editors. It is impossible to satisfy everybody. One person's favorite orator will be another's *bête noire*. What one scholar regards as a minor speaker will be seen by others as a leader of the first importance. While one reader laments that too much space is devoted to current speakers, his or her colleagues will grumble that too much is given to rhetors who have long been dead and buried. On the whole, the editors have achieved a sensible balance among mainstream political leaders, religious orators, and spokesmen and spokeswomen for a variety of historical and contemporary causes. If we judge the book on the quality of the essays it contains, rather than on the alternative speakers it might have included, it deserves high marks. Scrupulously edited, superbly produced, and splendidly bound, it will be the standard reference work on its subject for years to come.

Equally important, along with its companion volume, *American Orators Before 1900,*[15] it has spawned what is surely the most ambitious publishing project in the history of rhetoric as an academic discipline. That project is a series of book-length studies of major American orators from the colonial period to the present. To be published by Greenwood Press under the general editorship of Duffy and Ryan, the series is currently projected to comprise thirty-five volumes, the first of which is slated to appear next year. Following a consistent design, each book will devote somewhat more than half of its 200 pages to critical study of the speaker's career as an orator, including key individual addresses as well as such matters as his or her emergence on the public platform, characteristic arguments and rhetorical methods, stylistic traits and manner of delivery, utilization of the mass media, patterns of speech preparation, employment of ghost writers, philosophy of public persuasion, impact upon society, and contributions to rhetorical theory. Each volume will also present authoritative texts of the orator's major speeches and a bibliographic review of research sources and scholarly literature.

While this project testifies to the vitality of American public address as an area of scholarship, it will also be a test of that vitality. Most important, we must not allow our interest in orators to eclipse our interest in oratory. The problem facing rhetorical critics in this regard was stated clearly by Herbert Wichelns in his landmark 1925 essay, "The Literary Criticism of Oratory." Biographical studies, he said, too often lose sight of the speaker as a speaker; their "first and last concern" becomes the person rather than his or her rhetorical works. Unfortunately, Wichelns's injunction has not been universally heeded. One of the major weaknesses of traditional scholarship in public address has been its inclination to get so caught up in the minutiae of a speaker's background, education, personality, and career as to all but ignore his or her discourse. Thus Donald Bryant observed thirty-five years ago that the "tendency to write biographies of speakers…rather than rhetorico-critical

[15]Bernard K. Duffy and Halford R. Ryan, eds., *American Orators Before 1900: Critical Studies and Sources* (Westport, CT: Greenwood Press, 1987).

studies must be kept in check," while Roderick Hart has more recently scored the "personality fixation" that turns many studies of public address into studies of public addressers.[16]

This is not to denigrate all biographical inquiry in public address. Given the intimate connection between thought and language, between selfhood and expression, there will always be a place for studies that move from examination of a speaker's idiocratic patterns of discourse to judgments about his or her character, personality, and habits of mind—just as there is a continuing need for rhetorical biographies of figures such as Daniel Webster, Wendell Phillips, and Robert La Follette whose public careers cannot begin to be understood apart from their careers as orators. Moreover, it is invariably true that the more we know about a speaker's life in general, the more likely we are to transcend what is obvious about his or her discourse and to reach a level of insight that produces genuine scholarly breakthroughs. But we will not reach this level of insight if we return to the kinds of plodding, pedestrian studies that typified much work in public address during the 1940s and 1950s. We need to be bold and imaginative, rigorous and resourceful—and we must ensure that rhetorical analysis takes precedence over biographical description. If we are successful, we will make a major contribution indeed to understanding the rich heritage of American oratory.

3

This brings us to the second major development in current scholarship on American public address—a growing interest in close analysis of rhetorical texts. While it would seem axiomatic that a concern for texts—their composition, their generic features, their internal workings, their cultural meanings, their social import—should be at the heart of work in public address, such has not been the case historically. The preoccupation of traditional criticism with recreating the historical milieu, describing the immediate setting, assaying the composition and attitudes of the audience, and determining the effect of the speech led to a derogation of intensive textual analysis as a mere exercise.[17] Consequently, wrote W. Charles Redding in a 1957 essay that deserves more attention than it has received, rhetorical scholars too often "moved out of rather than more deeply into their own subject." According to Redding, about three-fourths of the typical public address study was devoted to historical or biographical information, "with sometimes as little as one-

---

[16]Herbert A. Wichelns, "The Literary Criticism of Oratory," in A. M. Drummond, ed., *Studies in Rhetoric and Public Speaking in Honor of James A. Winans* (New York: Century, 1925), 184; Donald C. Bryant, "Rhetoric: Its Function and Its Scope," *Quarterly Journal of Speech* 39 (1953): 423; Roderick P. Hart, "Contemporary Scholarship in Public Address: A Research Editorial," *Western Journal of Speech Communication* 50 (1986): 286.

[17]See, for example, the view of textual criticism in Donald C. Bryant, "Some Problems or Scope and Method in Rhetorical Scholarship," *Quarterly Journal of Speech* 23 (1937): 184.

tenth allotted to rhetorical analysis of speeches." Ten years later Barnet Baskerville sounded the same refrain when he noted the proliferation of works in which "illustration of the Aristotelian topics . . . substituted for a close reading of the speeches themselves."[18]

The deficiencies of traditional criticism in this regard are well illustrated by Marie Hochmuth Nichols's well-known essay on Abraham Lincoln's first inaugural address. Although often commended as a specimen of neo-Aristotelianism at its best, the essay gives startlingly little attention to what Lincoln said on March 4, 1861. Of its fifty-one pages, only twelve deal directly with the text of Lincoln's speech. The remaining thirty-nine pages are given over to reprinting the speech and to recounting such matters as the growth of sectional conflict during the previous forty years, the secession of the deep South after Lincoln's election, the state of public opinion on the eve of Lincoln's inauguration, the weather on March 4, 1861, the physical setting of the inaugural ceremonies, Lincoln's appearance and contemporary reputation, the preparation of his inaugural address, his manner of delivery during the speech, the behavior of his immediate audience, and the response of politicians, editorialists, and citizens throughout the land. There can be no quarrel with the way Nichols treats these matters. Her account is fastidiously researched and felicitously written. Unfortunately, it is divorced from and, surprisingly, largely irrelevant to her comments about the text of Lincoln's speech. A close reading of the essay reveals that its two sections—the lengthy description of context and the brief discussion of text—could almost stand as independent essays. Moreover, as in most traditional studies, her treatment of the text is more a descriptive summary of Lincoln's speech than a probing, incisive examination of its rhetorical dynamics.[19]

The standing of close textual analysis plummeted even further during the 1960s and 1970s. As the focus of rhetorical criticism shifted to social movements, political campaigns, ideological systems, and general communication processes, most rhetorical critics concluded that the individual speech "is not an appropriate unit of analysis." The sharpest statement of this position came in Samuel Becker's influential "Rhetorical Studies for the Contemporary World," written for the 1970 Wingspread Conference of the National Developmental Project on Rhetoric. According to Becker, students of public address erred by focusing "too exclusively upon major speakers and writers, the nature of their messages, and the relatively direct impact of these messages." Even the most puissant single discourse, he argued, was "only a minute part of the communication environment" and accounted for "only a

---

[18]W. Charles Redding, "Extrinsic and Intrinsic Criticism," *Western Speech* 21 (1957): 96, 100; Barnet Baskerville, "Selected Writings on the Criticism of Public Address, Addendum 1967," in Thomas R. Nilsen, ed. *Essays on Rhetorical Criticism* (New York: Random House, 1968), 189. For a revised and expanded version of Redding's essay see Nilsen, *Essays on Rhetorical Criticism*, 98-125.

[19]In Wayland Maxfield Parrish and Marie Hochmuth, eds., *American Speeches* (New York: Longman's, Green and Co., 1954), 21-71.

small portion of the variance in human behavior." If scholarship in public address were to become more realistic in its assumptions about communication behavior and more relevant to the contemporary world, it would have to abjure "internal criticism where the major purpose is to 'explain' the way in which a message 'works.' " Given the widespread acceptance of such ideas, it is little wonder that G. P. Mohrmann despaired, as the 1980s began, that neither traditional studies of public address nor revisionist approaches to rhetorical criticism had encouraged sufficient attention to "the text of the speech and its workings."[20]

Indeed, our persistent neglect of major texts in the history of American oratory is nothing short of astonishing. How can it be that we are in our seventh decade as an academic discipline and have yet to produce a body of rich critical literature providing authoritative textual studies of such acknowledged masterpieces as Jonathan Edwards's "Sinners in the Hands of an Angry God," John Hancock's Boston massacre oration, Fisher Ames's speech on the Jay Treaty, Thomas Jefferson's first inaugural address, Daniel Webster's first Bunker Hill oration, Ralph Waldo Emerson's "The American Scholar," Wendell Phillips's "The Murder of Lovejoy," Frederick Douglass's "What To the Slave Is the Fourth of July?," Abraham Lincoln's Gettysburg Address, Henry Grady's "The New South," Booker T. Washington's Atlanta Exposition Address, William Jennings Bryan's "The Cross of Gold," Susan B. Anthony's "Is It a Crime for a U.S. Citizen to Vote?," Albert J. Beveridge's "The March of the Flag," Russell Herrman Conwell's "Acres of Diamonds," Anna Howard Shaw's "The Fundamental Principle of a Republic," Franklin Roosevelt's first inaugural address, Douglas MacArthur's "Farewell to the Cadets," John F. Kennedy's address to the Houston Ministerial Association, and Martin Luther King's "I Have a Dream."

These are unsurpassed exemplars of the rhetorician's art that deserve to be studied and appreciated in the same way students of literature study and appreciate *Hamlet* as the highest expression of Elizabethan drama or *Crime and Punishment* as the preeminent psychological novel.[21] Moreover, they are historical and cultural documents of the first order. Central to our country's mythic heritage and historical experience, they merit interrogation as quintessentially American documents on the same order as *The Scarlet Letter, Huckleberry Finn,* or *The Great Gatsby.* Just as our colleagues in English have a powerful corpus of scholarship illuminating the literary artistry of great poems, novels, and short stories, we need no less powerful a corpus of scholarship explicating the rhetorical artistry of classic speeches and orations.

---

[20]Wayne Brockriede, "Trends in the Study of Rhetoric: Toward a Blending of Criticism and Science," in Bitzer and Black, *Prospect of Rhetoric,* 126; Samuel L. Becker, "Rhetorical Studies for the Contemporary World," in Bitzer and Black, *Prospect of Rhetoric,* 25, 22; G. P. Mohrmann, "Elegy in a Critical Grave-Yard," *Western Journal of Speech Communication* 44 (1980): 272.
[21]Cf. Bormann, *Force of Fantasy,* 60.

At a time when scholars in a variety of academic disciplines have redis-covered the importance of rhetoric in general and of the American oratorical tradition in particular,[22] we should not leave to others the task of elucidating the central texts of that tradition. Indeed, such elucidation may well be the most urgent priority currently facing students of American public address.

Questions of priority aside, the time is certainly propitious for such an enterprise. Not only are we experiencing a resurgence of interest in American oratory, but students of public address are at last becoming more attuned to "the text and texture of messages"—partly because of the explosion of language studies in general, partly because of the influence of structuralism, deconstructionism, and reader-response criticism, partly because it is one way to identify the special angle of vision of the rhetorical critic in contrast to that of the historian, biographer, or sociologist. This last point has been stated most trenchantly by Michael Leff, who has been in the forefront of the turn toward textual criticism. He argues that students of rhetoric must go beyond setting a speech in context and explaining what it says to "account for what the speech does, . . . to appreciate the way it articulates and structures what is said as the discourse unfolds." Whereas other scholars may rest content with summarizing the doctrines of a speech or offering a few passing comments on its structure, style, and delivery, rhetorical critics should probe its artistic coherence by attending to "the action within the text—to the way elements condition one another within the life cycle of the performance."[23] The word "performance" is key here, for, as Leff notes, oratory is an art form with its own special criteria, constraints, and potentialities. Judgments about an oration as a literary production or an ideological pronouncement, legitimate and important as they may be, are tangential to its "rhetorical integrity" and cannot yield adequate assessment of it as a work of rhetoric. Such assessment can only be reached by radical attention to the internal dynamics of the text itself.[24]

This is not to say textual studies in public address can afford to overlook context. As Black has noted, "the work of rhetoric is fragmentary outside its environment; it functions only in a particular world. By contrast, the work of fine art is more self-sufficient and detached from any specific ambiance. This

---

[22]See, for example, James W. Ceaser, Glen E. Thurow, Jeffrey Tulis, and Joseph M. Bessette, "The Rise of the Rhetorical Presidency," *Presidential Studies Quarterly* 11 (1981): 158-71; Robert A. Ferguson, *Law and Letters in American Culture* (Cambridge: Harvard University Press, 1984); Glen E. Thurow and Jeffery D. Wallin, eds., *Rhetoric and American Statesmanship* (Durham, NC: Carolina Academic Press, 1984); Paul D. Erickson, *Reagan Speaks: The Making of an American Myth* (New York: New York University Press, 1985); Harry S. Stout, *The New England Soul: Preaching and Religious Culture in Colonial New England* (New York: Oxford University Press, 1986); Paul D. Erickson, *The Poetry of Events: Daniel Webster's Rhetoric of the Constitution and Union,* (New York: New York University Press, 1986).

[23]Mohrmann, "Elegy in a Critical Grave-Yard," 272-73; Michael C. Leff, *Rhetorical Timing in Lincoln's "House Divided" Speech* (Evanston, IL: Northwestern University School of Speech, 1984), 6-7.

[24]Michael C. Leff, "Textual Criticism: The Legacy of C. P. Mohrmann," *Quarterly Journal of Speech* 72 (1986): 378, 381, 383.

fact gives the discovery of context an enhanced importance in rhetorical criticism as opposed to criticism of the fine arts."[25] Because rhetorical discourse occurs only within a particular world, we need to comprehend the very identity of any given text as inextricably interwoven with its world. Unlike modern literary criticism, which is usually concerned with the relationship between a text and "the self considered in isolation,"[26] rhetorical criticism is concerned preeminently with the relationship between a text and its social audience, whether that audience be conceived as the immediate auditors for Charles Sumner's "The Crime against Kansas," the reading public for Angelina Grimke's *Appeal to the Christian Women of the South,* the television viewers for Richard Nixon's "Checkers" speech, or the judgment of posterity, which was part of the "opinions of mankind" appealed to in the Declaration of Independence. So, too, must textual criticism proceed with due regard for the political, religious, economic, intellectual, and institutional forces that condition both the development of the text and its internal operations.

In addition to all these factors, which can be grouped under the heading of *social context,* textual studies in public address need to give special consideration to what might be called *linguistic context.* "A living language," as H. L. Mencken remarked, "is like a man suffering incessantly from small hemorrhages."[27] Not only is it constantly modified by the introduction of neologisms, but the meaning of established words is under steady assault. No matter what the circumstances of its creation, every rhetorical text is situated within a particular linguistic context with its own vocabulary, conventions, idioms, and patois. One cannot hope to plumb what the text means or to chart its internal dynamics without recapturing "the full wealth of association, implication and resonance, the many levels of meaning," which a language possesses in a given society at a given time.[28] This is most important when dealing with texts remote from us in time or culture, but even as we move closer to our own age, we must be exceedingly cautious about reading the likes of Webster, Lincoln, Anthony, Bryan, Wilson, FDR, even John Kennedy or Martin Luther King as our contemporaries—about assuming that their languages are identical with our language, that their linguistic worlds are also our own.[29]

Once one begins to attend to linguistic context, the lines between text and context, between intrinsic and extrinsic analysis, begin to blur. But there is yet another kind of context—*textual context*—which obliterates those lines

---

[25]Black, *Rhetorical Criticism,* 39.

[26]Jane P. Tompkins, "The Reader in History: The Changing Shape of Literary Response," in Jane P. Tompkins, ed., *Reader-Response Criticism: From Formalism to Post-Structuralism* (Baltimore: Johns Hopkins University Press, 1980), 210.

[27]Quoted in Robert McCrum, William Cran, and Robert MacNeil, *The Story of English* (New York: Viking, 1986), 5.

[28]J. G. A. Pocock, *Politics, Language, and Time: Essays on Political Thought and History* (New York: Atheneum, 1973), 12.

[29]Cf. Lucas, "Schism in Rhetorical Scholarship," 6.

altogether. As oxymoronic as it may sound, the notion of textual context is crucial to the close analysis of rhetorical works. Based on the understanding that rhetorical discourses are temporal phenomena, it holds that a text creates its own internal context as it unfolds in time and is processed by a listener or reader.[30] Meaning and effect are produced, not by the text as a static entity, but by the progressive interaction of the audience with the temporal flow of ideational, dispositional, stylistic, and syntactical elements in the discourse. Each word, each phrase, each sentence conditions the response of the audience to each succeeding word, phrase, and sentence. The benefit of close textual analysis is that it allows the critic, in essence, to "slow down" the action within the text so as to keep its evolving internal context in sharp focus and to allow more precise explication of its rhetorical artistry. To borrow Stanley Fish's analogy about the methods of reader-response literary criticism, "It is as if a slow-motion camera with an automatic stop action effect were recording our linguistic experiences and presenting them to us for viewing."[31]

We can illustrate by looking briefly at the preamble of the Declaration of Independence:

> We hold these truths to be self-evident, that all men are created equal, that they are endowed by their Creator with certain unalienable Rights, that among these are Life, Liberty and the pursuit of Happiness. That to secure these rights, Governments are instituted among Men, deriving their just powers from the consent of the governed. That whenever any Form of Government becomes destructive of these ends, it is the Right of the People to alter or to abolish it, and to institute new Government, laying its foundation on such principles and organizing its powers in such form, as to them shall seem most likely to effect their Safety and Happiness. Prudence, indeed, will dictate that Governments long established should not be changed for light and transient causes; and accordingly all experience hath shown that mankind are more disposed to suffer, while evils are sufferable, than to right themselves by abolishing the forms to which they are accustomed. But when a long train of abuses and usurpations, pursuing invariably the same Object evinces a design to reduce them under absolute Despotism, it is their right, it is their duty, to throw off such Government, and to provide new Guards for their future security.[32]

These five sentences were part of a carefully crafted rhetorical text designed to persuade a "candid world" that the American colonists were justified in

---

[30]Leff, "Textual Criticism," 384.
[31]Stanley Fish, *Self-Consuming Artifacts* (Berkeley: University of California Press, 1972), 389.
[32]Julian P. Boyd, ed., *The Papers of Thomas Jefferson* (Princeton, NJ: Princeton University Press, 1950-), I: 429-30.

seeking independence of British rule. They also include some of the most admired and enduring passages of Western political prose. By close textual analysis we can illumine both their rhetorical power and their abiding esteem.[33]

The first thing to notice about the preamble is its location in the text. It is situated immediately after the eloquent opening sentence of the Declaration:

> When in the Course of human events, it becomes necessary for one people to dissolve the political bands which have connected them with another, and to assume among the powers of the earth, the separate and equal station to which the Laws of Nature and or Nature's God entitle them, a decent respect to the opinions of mankind requires that they should declare the causes which impel them to the separation.[34]

Taken out of context, this sentence is so general it could be used as the introduction to a declaration by any oppressed people. Seen within its original context, however, it is a model of subtlety, nuance, and implication. From its magisterial opening phrase, which sets the American Revolution within the whole "course of human events," to its assertion that "the Laws of Nature and of Nature's God" entitle America to a "separate and equal station among the powers of the earth," to its quest for sanction from "the opinions of mankind," this sentence elevates the quarrel with England from a petty political dispute to a major event in the grand sweep of history. It dignifies the Revolution as a contest of principle and implies that the American cause has a special claim to moral legitimacy—all without mentioning England or America by name.

In like fashion, the preamble makes no explicit mention of the British-American conflict. Its purpose is to establish a philosophy of government that makes revolution justifiable, even meritorious. The core of that philosophy is presented in the first three sentences of the preamble in a series of five propositions that are characterized as self-evident truths, truths that, in Locke's words, would command "universal and ready assent upon hearing and understanding the terms." [35]

Proposition 1: That all men are created equal.
Proposition 2: That they [all men, from proposition 1] are endowed
                  by their creator with certain unalienable rights.
Proposition 3: That among these [man's unalienable rights, from

---

[33]The analysis that follows is drawn from Stephen E. Lucas, "Justifying America: The Declaration of Independence as a Rhetorical Document," in Thomas W. Benson, ed., *American Rhetoric: Context and Criticism* (Carbondale: Southern Illinois University Press, in press).
[34]Boyd, *Papers of Jefferson,* 1: 429.
[35]John Locke, *An Essay Concerning Human Understanding,* ed. Alexander Campbell Fraser (New York: Dover, 1959), Book I, chap. II, sect. 18.

proposition 2] are life, liberty, and the pursuit of happiness.

Proposition 4: That to secure these rights [man's unalienable rights, from propositions 2 and 3] governments are instituted among men.

Proposition 5: That whenever any form of government becomes destructive of these ends [securing man's unalienable rights, from propositions 2-4], it is the right of the people to alter or abolish it.

When we look at all five propositions, we see they are meant to be read together and have been meticulously written to achieve a specific rhetorical objective. The first three lead into the fourth, which in turn leads into the fifth. And it is the fifth, proclaiming the right of revolution when a government becomes destructive of the people's unalienable rights, that is most crucial in the overall argument of the Declaration. The first four are merely preliminary steps designed to give philosophical grounding to the fifth.

At first glance, these propositions appear to comprise what was known in the eighteenth century as a sorites—"a Way of argument in which a great Number of Propositions are so linked together, that the Predicate of one becomes continually the Subject of the next following, until at last a Conclusion is formed by bringing together the Subject of the First Proposition and the Predicate of the last." In his *Elements of Logick,* William Duncan provided the following example of a sorites:

God is omnipotent.

An omnipotent Being can do every thing possible.

He that can do every thing possible, can do whatever involves not a Contradiction.

Therefore God can do whatever involves not a Contradiction.[36]

Although the section of the preamble we have been considering is not a sorites (because it does not bring together the subject of the first proposition and the predicate of the last), its propositions are written in such a way as to take on the appearance of a logical demonstration. They are so tightly interwoven linguistically that they seem to make up a sequence in which the final proposition—asserting the right of revolution—is logically derived from the first four propositions. This is accomplished partly by the mimicry of the form of a sorites and partly by the sheer number of propositions, the accumulation of which is reinforced by the slow, deliberate pace of the text and by the use of "That . . ." to introduce each proposition. There is also a step-like progression from proposition to proposition, a progression that is

---

[36]William Duncan, *The Elements of Logick* (London: R. Dodsley, 1748), 242. Also see Isaac Watts, *Logick: or, The Right Use of Reason in the Enquiry after Truth,* 8th ed. (London: T. Longman, T. Shewell, and J. Brackstone, 1745), 304; [Henry Aldrich], *A Compendium of Logic,* 3rd ed. (London: [1790]), 23.

accentuated by the skillful use of demonstrative pronouns to make each succeeding proposition appear to be an inevitable consequence of the preceding propositions.

Having created the appearance of demonstrating the right of revolution, the preamble interjects a qualifier in its fourth sentence—"that Governments long established should not be changed for light and transient causes." In so stating, the Declaration reaffirmed the basic tenet of British revolutionary theory that obedience to lawful rulers was obligatory and that forceful resistance to government was warranted only when "the Mischief be grown general" and the tyranny or "Designs of the Rulers become notorious." It also implied that the Continental Congress would never promote revolution for anything less than the most serious and abiding causes. Like the rest of mankind, Americans were "more disposed to suffer, while evils are sufferable, than to right themselves by abolishing the forms to which they are accustomed." This, too, was a standard part of the Whig tradition and contained distinct echoes of Locke's statement, "Till the mischief be grown general, and the ill designs of the Rulers become visible, or their attempts sensible to the greater part, the People, who are more disposed to suffer, than right themselves by Resistance, are not apt to stir."[37]

"But . . ." the final sentence of the preamble begins, abruptly shifting the reader away from the qualifier introduced in sentence four to the forceful reaffirmation of the people's right and duty to "throw off" their government "when a long train of abuses and usurpations, pursuing invariably the same object evinces a design to reduce them under absolute Despotism." Although nothing is said here about the controversy with England, there is no escaping the implication that the colonists had indeed suffered a "long train of abuses and usurpations" and circumstances had now made it "necessary," as the introduction of the Declaration had stated, for "one people" (the Americans) to separate from "another" people (the British). It is also worth noting that this last sentence of the preamble, like the third sentence, pronounces not just the people's obligation to resist tyranny, but also their duty to institute new government to guard their "future security." This, of course, is just what America was doing in July of 1776. At the very time the Continental Congress issued the Declaration, it was also developing the Articles of Confederation, which would result in a form of government quite different

---

[37]John, Lord Somers, *The Judgment of Whole Kingdoms and Nations, Concerning the Rights, Power and Prerogative of Kings, and the Rights, Privileges and Properties of the People* (London: T. Harrison, 1710), paras. 83, 186; John Locke, *Two Treatises of Government*, ed. Peter Laslett (Cambridge: Cambridge University Press, 1964), Book II, sect. 230. Garry Wills, *Inventing America: Jefferson's Declaration of Independence* (New York: Doubleday, 1978), argues at great length that Jefferson was indebted to the Scottish common sense philosophers rather than to Locke for the ideas expressed in the preamble. The textual parallels between Locke's *Second Treatise of Government* and the Declaration, however, are much stronger than those between the Declaration and any of the common sense writers. This point is made most emphatically by Ronald Hamowy, "Jefferson and the Scottish Enlightenment: A Critique of Garry Wills' *Inventing America: Jefferson's Declaration of Independence*," *William and Mary Quarterly* 36 (1979): 503-23.

from the constitutional monarchy of Great Britain. By stressing the right of an oppressed people to establish new forms of government, the Declaration not only justified the colonists' efforts in this regard, but also implied that the Revolution was not anarchic and that America could be regarded as a responsible member of the community of nations.

Although the preamble is the best known part of the Declaration today, it attracted considerably less attention in its own time. For most eighteenth-century readers it was an unobjectionable statement of commonplace political principles. As Jefferson stated years later, the purpose of the Declaration was "not to find out new principles, or new arguments, never before thought of . . . but to place before mankind the common sense of the subject, in terms so plain and firm as to command their assent."[38] Far from being a weakness of the preamble, however, the lack of new ideas was perhaps its greatest strength. If one overlooks the introductory opening sentence of the Declaration, the document as a whole is structured along the lines of a deductive argument that can easily be put in syllogistic form:

Major premise: When government deliberately seeks to reduce the people under absolute despotism, the people have a right, indeed a duty, to alter or abolish that form of government and to create new guards for their future security.

Minor premise: The government of Great Britain has deliberately sought to reduce the American colonists under absolute despotism.

Conclusion: Therefore, the American colonists have a right, indeed a duty, to alter or abolish their present form of government and to create new guards for their future security.[39]

As the major premise in this argument, the preamble allowed Congress to reason from self-evident principles of government accepted by almost all contemporary readers of the Declaration.

But there is more to the rhetorical artistry of the preamble than its argumentative force. Like the rest of the Declaration, the preamble is "brief, free of verbiage, a model of clear, concise, simple statement."[40] It capsulizes in five sentences—202 words—what it took John Locke thousands of words to explain in his *Second Treatise of Government*. Each word is chosen and placed to achieve maximum impact. Each clause is indispensable to the

---

[38]Thomas Jefferson to Henry Lee, May 8, 1825, in Paul Leicester Ford, ed., *The Writings of Thomas Jefferson* (New York: Putnam's, 1892-1899), X: 343.

[39]For slightly different wordings of this syllogism see Carl L. Becker, *The Declaration of Independence: A Study in the History of Political Ideas* (New York: Knopf, 1922), 203-4; Wilbur Samuel Howell, "The Declaration of Independence and Eighteenth-Century Logic," *William and Mary Quarterly* 18 (1961): 479.

[40]Becker, *Declaration of Independence*, 201.

progression of thought. Each sentence is carefully constructed internally and in relation to what precedes and follows. In its ability to compress complex ideas into a brief, clear statement, the preamble is a paradigm of eighteenth-century Enlightenment prose style, in which purity, simplicity, directness, precision, and, above all, perspicuity were the highest rhetorical and literary virtues. In keeping with Jefferson's ideas about tasteful and effective discourse, the preamble is "disfigured by no gaudy tinsel of rhetoric or declamation" and proceeds "without ever using a superfluous word."[41]

The stately and dignified tone of the preamble comes partly from what the eighteenth century called Style Periodique, in which, as Hugh Blair explained in his *Lectures on Rhetoric and Belles Lettres*, "the sentences are composed of several members linked together, and hanging upon one another, so that the sense of the whole is not brought out till the close." This, Blair said, "is the most pompous, musical, and oratorical manner of composing" and "gives an air of gravity and dignity to composition." The gravity and dignity of the preamble were reinforced by its conformance with the rhetorical precept that "when we aim at dignity or elevation, the sound [of each sentence] should be made to grow to the last; the longest members of the period, and the fullest and most sonorous words, should be reserved to the conclusion." None of the sentences of the preamble end on a single-syllable word; only one, the second (and least euphonious), ends on a two-syllable word. The other four end with three-syllable words, and in each case the closing syllable is at least a medium-length four-letter syllable, which helps bring the sentence to "a full and harmonious close."[42]

The preamble also has a powerful sense of structural unity. This is achieved, in large measure, by its resemblance to a sorites and by its intricate linkage of propositions—both of which we observed earlier. But the sense of unity is subtly reinforced by the preamble's latent chronological progression of thought, in which the reader is moved from the creation of mankind, to the institution of government, to the throwing off of government when it fails to protect the people's unalienable rights, to the creation of new government that will better secure the people's safety and happiness. This dramatic scenario, with its first act implicitly set in the Garden of Eden (where man was "created equal"), may, for some readers, have contained mythic overtones of man's fall from divine grace. At the very least, it gives an almost archetypal quality to the preamble and continues the notion, broached in the first

---

[41]Thomas Jefferson, *Autobiography*, ed. Dumas Malone (New York: Capricorn, 1959), 114; Jefferson to John Adams, October 14, 1816, in Lester J. Cappon, ed., *The Adams-Jefferson Letters* (Chapel Hill: University of North Carolina Press, 1959), II: 491. Jefferson's surviving papers contain no specific comments on the style of the Declaration and few on prose style in general. His ideas on the latter subject are examined by Stephen D. Cox, "The Literary Aesthetic of Thomas Jefferson," in J. A. Leo Lemay, ed., *Essays in Early Virginia Literature Honoring Richard Beale Davis* (New York: Franklin, 1977), 235-56.

[42]Hugh Blair, *Lectures on Rhetoric and Belles Lettres* (London: W. Strahan, T. Cadell, and W. Creech, 1783), I, 206-7, 259.

sentence of the Declaration, that the American Revolution is a major develop-ment in "the course of human events."

Although much more could be said about the preamble, this should suffice to suggest how a student of public address might get at the internal dynamics of a text without engaging in a purely formalistic, literary analysis. The ideal is to combine full and penetrating comprehension of the rhetorical situation with a sensitive and discerning reading of the text as an evolving, temporal phenomenon that creates its own internal context even as it is leavened by the social and linguistic context. This is a very different enter-prise from the kind of artful paraphrase of a speech that often passes for textual analysis in rhetorical criticism. The purpose of the critic is not simply to retell the speech in his or her own words, but to apprehend it fully from the inside out—to break down its rhetorical elements so completely as to determine how they function individually and to explain how they interact to shape the text as a strategic, artistic response to the exigencies of a particular situation.

Intensely analytic and highly interpretive, this kind of study will seldom be achieved by adhering to any single method of criticism, whether it be neo-Aristotelianism, Burkeanism, fantasy theme analysis, or whatever. Nor is it likely to be realized by rigidly interpreting the text through the lens of a single pre-existing theory. The critic is more likely to be successful when he or she approaches a rhetorical transaction "in what is hoped to be its own terms, without conscious expectations drawn from any sources other than the rhetorical transaction itself."[43] Beyond the fact that it will foreground the text, the final shape of this kind of study is unpredictable. It will depend on the interests and abilities of the individual critic and on what he or she discovers in the course of his or her investigation. It might look like my explication of the Declaration of Independence, it might look like Leff's analysis of Lincoln's House Divided speech, it might look like Stelzner's study of FDR's war message, it might look like Black's parsing of an editorial from the *New York Times,* it might look like Campbell's exploration of Elizabeth Cady Stanton's "Solitude of Self," it might look like Fulkerson's examination of King's "Letter from Birmingham Jail," it might look like Slagell's dissection of Lincoln's second inaugural address.[44]

While we have been concerned in this essay with the close analysis of individual texts with an eye toward explicating their rhetorical artistry, it is

---

[43]Edwin Black, "A Note on Theory and Practice in Rhetorical Criticism," *Western Journal of Speech Communication* 44 (1980): 331-32.

[44]Leff, *Rhetorical Timing;* Hermann G. Stelzner, " 'War Message,' December 8, 1941: An Approach to Language," *Speech Monographs* 33 (1966): 419-37; Edwin Black, "Ideological Justifications," *Quarterly Journal of Speech* 70 (1984): 144-50; Karlyn Kohrs Campbell, "Stanton's 'The Solitude of Self': A Rationale for Feminism," *Quarterly Journal of Speech* 66 (1980): 304-12; Richard P. Fulkerson, "The Public Letter as Rhetorical Form: Structure, Logic, and Style in King's 'Letter from Birmingham Jail,' " *Quarterly Journal of Speech* 65 (1979): 121-36; Amy M. Slagell, "A Textual Analysis of Abraham Lincoln's Second Inaugural Address," M. A. Thesis, University of Wisconsin, 1987.

important to stress that there are many other applications of textual study in public address. One obvious application is in assaying a speaker's purpose or meaning. How, for example, can we hope to resolve the continuing disputes over the aims of George Washington's Farewell Address or over the ideas of Booker T. Washington's Atlanta Exposition Address without close and probing study of the texts?[45] Another application lies in the area of psychological or biographical criticism, as is demonstrated by Richard Ohmann's *Shaw: The Style and the Man,* or by Richard Weaver's assessment of Abraham Lincoln's habitual use of argument from principle and Edmund Burke's preference for argument from circumstance. Indeed, as I have tried to demonstrate elsewhere, even such an apparently extrinsic matter as gauging the effects of Thomas Paine's *Common Sense* cannot proceed profitably without serious attention to intrinsic, textual features.[46] At the center of rhetorical transactions and, I would argue, properly at the center of the critic's concern, is the text itself. This is true whether the "text" in question is Jonathan Smith's speech on the federal constitution, Hitler's *Mein Kampf,* Malthus's *Essay on The Principle of Population,* Marvell's "To His Coy Mistress," a collection of Quaker sermons, the genre of apologia, the political philosophy of neo-liberalism, Norman Rockwell's "Four Freedoms" posters, or Alain Resnais's classic film *Hiroshima, Mon Amour.*[47]

Just as all textual studies should not be cast from an identical mold, so should public address studies in general be vigorously pluralistic. As important as it is that we develop a body of work based on close analysis of classic texts from the rich heritage of American public address, it is equally important that we avoid the critical monism of traditional scholarship. As Walter Fisher has written, "There are as many approaches to rhetorical criticism as there are useful things to say about the rhetorical process." Movement studies, campaign studies, genre studies, ideological studies, period studies,

---

[45]The nature and extent of the disputes over these matters can be gauged from Burton Ira Kaufman, ed., *Washington's Farewell Address: The View from the Twentieth Century* (Chicago: Quadrangle, 1969), and Robert L. Heath, "A Time for Silence: Booker T. Washington in Atlanta," *Quarterly Journal of Speech* 64 (1978): 385-99.

[46]Richard M. Ohmann, *Shaw: The Style and the Man* (Middletown, CT: Wesleyan University Press, 1962); Richard M. Weaver, *The Ethics of Rhetoric* (Chicago: Henry Regnery, 1953), 54-114; Lucas, "Schism in Rhetorical Scholarship," 8-10.

[47]For studies of these works see Carroll C. Arnold, *Criticism of Oral Rhetoric* (Columbus, OH: Charles E. Merrill, 1974), 376-84; Michael McGuire, "Mythic Rhetoric in *Mein Kampf:* A Structuralist Critique," *Quarterly Journal of Speech* 63 (1977): 1-13; Arthur E. Walzer, "Logic and Rhetoric in Malthus's *Essay on the Principle of Population,* 1798," *Quarterly Journal of Speech* 73 (1987): 1-17; Joseph J. Moldenhauer, "The Voices of Seduction in 'To His Coy Mistress': A Rhetorical Analysis," *Texas Studies in Literature and Language* 10 (1968): 189-206; Michael P. Graves, "Functions of Key Metaphors in Early Quaker Sermons, 1671-1700," *Quarterly Journal of Speech* 69 (1983): 364-78; B. L. Ware and Wil A. Linkugel, "They Spoke in Defense of Themselves: On the Generic Criticism of Apologia," *Quarterly Journal of Speech* 59 (1973): 273-83; Michael Weiler, "The Rhetoric of Neo-Liberalism," *Quarterly Journal of Speech* 70 (1984): 362-78; Lesler C. Olson, "Portraits in Praise of a People: Norman Rockwell's Icons in Franklin D. Roosevelt's 'Four Freedoms' Campaign," *Quarterly Journal of Speech* 59 (1983): 15-24; Martin J. Medhurst, *"Hiroshima, Mon Amour:* From Iconography to Rhetoric," *Quarterly Journal of Speech* 68 (1982): 345-70.

biographical studies, feminist studies, media studies—all are necessary and valuable components of scholarship in American public address. We should proceed in the spirit of Robert Penn Warren's adage that "there is no single, correct kind of criticism, no complete criticism." There are only "different kinds of perspectives, giving, when successful, different kinds of insights."[48] In the last analysis, our scholarship will be judged, not by the perspectives from which it proceeds, but by the quality of insight it produces.

4

Finally, regardless of our individual areas of specialization, the time has come to assert the intrinsic value of scholarship in American public address. For too long the study of public address has been regarded as a handmaiden of other academic disciplines or of cognate areas within our own discipline. Although still evident today, the former tendency was particularly pronounced during the reign of neo-Aristotelianism. Eager to attain intellectual respectability within the academy at large and wedded to a method of rhetorical criticism that depended "almost entirely upon historical knowledge for its effectiveness," students of public address came increasingly to identify their work with that of professional historians. Whereas Wichelns had argued that the rhetorician's obligation to assess speeches in light of their original context made it necessary "to summon history to the aid of criticism," by the 1940s scholars of public address had reversed the equation and were summoning criticism to the aid of history. Thus Ernest Wrage urged that rhetorical critics make their marks by contributing "in substantial ways to the history of ideas," while Charles Lomas defined their role as that of "filling in the gaps left by historians." This line of thought reached its fullest expression in Marie Nichols's *Rhetoric and Criticism*. Observing that in the ancient world history was never studied for its own sake but for what it could bring to oratory, Nichols argued that today "the position is reversed, and we may well ask with humility: What can the rhetorician bring to history?" In her view, students of public address should approach their work by inquiring, "What are the historians doing that may well be supplemented by the work of the rhetoricians?"[49]

Less obsequious, but no less pronounced, has been the tendency of recent years to measure the worth of scholarship in public address by its contributions to rhetorical theory. The manifesto of this development was

---

[48]Walter R. Fisher, "Method in Rhetorical Criticism," *Southern Speech Journal* 35 (1969): 107; Robert Penn Warren quoted in Malcolm Cowley, ed., *Writers at Work: The Paris Review Interviews* (New York: Knopf, 1958), 199.

[49]Bryant, "Some Problems of Scope and Method," 183; Wichelns, "Literary Criticism of Oratory," 199; Ernest J. Wrage, "Public Address: A Study in Social and Intellectual History," *Quarterly Journal of Speech* 33 (1947): 453; Charles W. Lomas, "Rhetorical Criticism and Historical Perspective," *Western Speech* 32 (1968): 198; Marie Hochmuth Nichols, *Rhetoric and Criticism* (Baton Rouge: Louisiana State University Press, 1963), 25.

John Waite Bowers's "The Pre-Scientific Function of Rhetorical Criticism." According to Bowers, rhetorical criticism had "a much nobler end" than explicating "a single piece of work in a single context." That end was "to contribute to an economical set of scientifically verifiable statements accounting for the origins and effects of *all* rhetorical discourses in *all* contexts." By the time of the Wingspread Conference in 1970, there was growing agreement that "a major concern of every . . . public address scholar is to be confident that his work is contributing to the development of systems and theories."[50] The contribution to theory could be made in one of two ways. The first, as Bowers explained, was through a "pre-scientific" function in which the critic produced "testable hypotheses which, when verified, will have the status of scientific laws." The second, as Wayne Brockriede stated, was through a post-predictive function in which the critic tested "the explanatory and predictive power of a theory in the real world of historical and contemporary rhetorical transactions." In either case, what the critic learned about individual rhetorical transactions was deemed of secondary importance to explicating "the nature of symbolic processes themselves." This position has been stated with special clarity and vigor by Roderick Hart, who laments that research in public address lacks a "visceral concern for theory" and is too often conducted "in a theoretical vacuum." In his view, students of public address have an obligation "to tease theory from their research" so as to contribute to "the development and refinement of synthetic, inclusive, and predictive theoretical statements about human persuasion."[51]

There can be no quarrel with either the notion that scholarship in American public address can contribute to historical knowledge or that it can aid in the development and refinement of rhetorical theory. The problem lies in the suggestion that such scholarship is valuable primarily to the extent that it meets the agendas of professional historians or of rhetorical theorists. While rhetorical studies of the Lincoln-Douglas debates or of Franklin Roosevelt's wartime speeches can certainly help fill in the historical record, by the same token historical studies of the political milieu of 1858 or of public attitudes toward American involvement in World War II can shed important light on the rhetorical record. Why should we regard completing the historical record as more consequential than understanding the Lincoln-Douglas debates or FDR's wartime addresses for their own sakes? Indeed, given the growing centrality of language studies to virtually every field of contemporary scholarship, it might make as much sense, if not more, to measure the value of work

---

[50] John Waite Bowers, "The Pre-Scientific Function of Rhetorical Criticism," in Nilsen, *Essays on Rhetorical Criticism,* 127; Becker, "Rhetorical Studies for the Contemporary World," in Bitzer and Black, *Prospect of Rhetoric,* 22.

[51] Bowers, "Pre-Scientific Function," in Nilsen, *Essays on Rhetorical Criticism,* 127; Brockriede, "Trends in the Study of Rhetoric," in Bitzer and Black, *Prospect of Rhetoric,* 136; Karlyn Kohrs Campbell, "Criticism: Ephemeral and Enduring," *Speech Teacher* 23 (1974):12; Roderick P. Hart, "Theory Building and Rhetorical Criticism," *Central States Speech Journal* 27 (1976): 70-71. Also see Hart, "Contemporary Scholarship in Public Address," 284-86.

in American history by the extent of its contributions to scholarship in public address.

Similarly, while research on the parent-child metaphor in the rhetoric of the American Revolution can help enrich our theoretical understanding of the social power of metaphor, it is equally true that regnant theories of metaphor can help elucidate the functioning of the parent-child metaphor in the discourse of the Revolution. Why should we necessarily privilege adding to theories of metaphor over understanding the role of metaphor in the Revolution? On what grounds, other than personal preference, does one argue that the latter is "less interesting" than the former?[52] Although one can make a case that understanding the general nature of rhetorical activity is more important than explicating individual rhetorical transactions, it can be argued with equal plausibility that rhetorical theory is less valuable for its own sake than for its ability to illuminate concrete rhetorical transactions. Indeed, given the growing recognition of the futility of seeking covering laws in any realm of human behavior as malleable and effervescent as modes of symbolic interaction, it may well be that penetrating understanding of particular cases—what Clifford Geertz calls "thick description"—is a more realistic aim than holding out the promise of developing testable, predictive, scientific laws of rhetorical behavior.[53]

This is treacherous territory, and I wish not to be misunderstood. I am not claiming work in public address is superior to that in history or in rhetorical theory. Nor am I arguing that scholarship in public address should be antihistorical or atheoretical. As we have seen, given the nature of rhetoric as situationally grounded, even textual studies in public address cannot afford to ignore the historicity of their subject. Moreover, "one cannot compose rhetorical criticism without assuming, consciously or unconsciously, some theoretical frame of reference."[54] But I can see no reason for students of American public address to take supplementing the work of professional historians or enhancing the growth of rhetorical theory as their raison d'être. The study of public address is as important a subject in its own right as the study of history or of rhetorical theory (or, for that matter, of art, or literature, or philosophy). Understanding the discursive operations of the Declaration of Independence, recovering the writings and speeches of nineteenth-century women advocates, documenting the role of television evangelists in recent political campaigns, explaining the oratorical power of Martin Luther King, investigating the day-to-day rhetorical practice of the modern presidency, assessing the ethics of Richard Nixon's "Checkers" speech—these are all worthy enterprises regardless of their relation to the work of historians or to the state of rhetorical theory.

---

[52]Hart, "Contemporary Scholarship in Public Address," 285.
[53]Clifford Geertz, The Interpretation of Cultures (New York: Basic Books, 1973), 3-30.
[54]Black, Rhetorical Criticism, 132.

This is not to say all studies in American public address are equally valuable. Some are valuable because they fill gaps in our knowledge—as, for example, Kathleen Jamieson's *Packaging the Presidency* has filled a large vacuum in what we know about the origins and evolution of presidential campaign advertising. Others are valuable because they synthesize existing knowledge or make it conveniently available—as Duffy and Ryan's *American Orators of the Twentieth Century* has done with respect to its subject. Still others are valuable because they establish the critical salience of heretofore overlooked texts or rhetors—as Black's analysis of John Jay Chapman's Coatesville Address secured a place for that speech in the canon of American public address. Finally, the largest group will be valuable because they reinterpret the artistry, methods, meaning, evolution, significance, and the like of established rhetors, texts, movements, genres, or periods—as, for example, Carl Burgchardt has compelled us to adopt a new perspective on Robert La Follette by explicating his habitual use of the melodramatic scenario, or as David Zarefsky has provided a clearer, sharper perspective on the constellations of argument in the Lincoln-Douglas debates.[55] If some of these works also command the attention of historians, hold consequential implications for rhetorical theorists, or advance our understanding of the methods and potentialities of rhetorical criticism in general, so much the better. But let us recognize these as subsidiary benefits of scholarship in American public address rather than as fundamental rationales for it.

None of this should be read as a call for intellectual insularity. Students of public address ought not see themselves as the acolytes of any other group of scholars, but they should always be willing to learn from others, whether the others be historians, rhetorical theorists, literary critics, political scientists, linguists, philosophers, sociologists, anthropologists, or whatever. Knowledge is not subject to the artificial boundaries of academic disciplines. It is, rather, like a tapestry upon which scholars of disparate backgrounds, methods, and interests weave their intricate and special designs. Let us weave with full regard for the designs of others, but also with full recognition of the intrinsic value of our own designs.

---

[55] Jamieson, *Packaging the Presidency;* Black, *Rhetorical Criticism,* 78-90; Duffy and Ryan, *American Orators of the Twentieth Century;* Carl R. Burgchardt, "Discovering Rhetorical Imprints: La Follette, 'Iago,' and the Melodramatic Scenario," *Quarterly Journal of Speech* 71 (1985): 441-56; David Zarefsky, "The Lincoln-Douglas Debates Revisited: The Evolution of Public Argument," *Quarterly Journal of Speech* 72 (1986): 162-84.

The State of the Art in
Public Address Scholarship

by David Zarefsky

The decision to publish a series of studies in public address is cause for celebration. Twenty years ago, such a venture might well have been derided as a last-ditch reactionary effort, on the part of scholars whom the field had passed by, to join in a misbegotten protest against "the tyranny of relevance." The story of the death, burial, and resurrection of public address scholarship over the past two decades is an oft-told tale.[1]

I

As the conventional wisdom would have it, public address was the dominant subject of study in the field of rhetorical scholarship during most of the 1930s, 1940s, and 1950s. Study after study accumulated, mostly biographical, mostly of dead orators. All were done in the same mold, the "cookie cutter" of neo-Aristotelianism. They appeared to lack justification save for the naive and often unexpressed belief that studying landmark orators would enable us to derive principles by which to improve our own rhetorical practice.[2] At their best, these studies were bad history and bad criticism both.

But, the story continues, all that was changed in the mid-1960s when Edwin Black exposed the pitfalls of neo-Aristotelianism.[3] In response to his clarion call, scholars abandoned public address, rushing instead to call themselves rhetorical critics or theorists. When Barnet Baskerville asked, "Must we all be 'rhetorical critics'?"[4] his inquiry seemed to many to be silly,

---

Reprinted from *Texts in Context*. Edited by Michael C. Leff and Fred J. Kauffeld. (Davis, CA: Hermagoras Press, 1989).

[1] A succinct account was given, for example, by Bruce E. Gronbeck, in a paper, "The Birth, Death, and Rebirth of Public Address," presented at the Speech Communication Association convention, Denver, Colorado, November 1985.

[2] For an example in which this rationale was stated explicitly, see Warren C. Shaw, *History of American Oratory* (Indianapolis: Bobbs-Merrill, 1928), 672.

[3] Edwin Black, *Rhetorical Criticism: A Study in Method* (New York: Macmillan, 1965).

[4] Barnet Baskerville, "Must We All Be 'Rhetorical Critics'?" *Quarterly Journal of Speech,* 63 (April, 1977): 107-116.

because the answer was so obvious—"Of course we must." But now, in the 1980s, whether because of the oratorical success of Ronald Reagan or because our varied bicentennial celebrations have sensitized us anew to our heritage and tradition, public address studies once more have come into fashion and are enjoying a remarkable renaissance.

In fact, nothing of the sort happened. Public address studies never died. The very years which were supposedly the nadir of research in public address saw the appearance in our journals of extended controversy over the analysis of a specific text—Richard Nixon's "Vietnamization" speech of November 3, 1969. The exchange among Forbes Hill, Karlyn Campbell, and Robert Newman not only focused attention on the text but raised questions about the role of the scholar of public address which are with us still.[5] Those same years witnessed new attention to the public speaking of groups traditionally excluded from the public forum, chiefly blacks and women. And they witnessed the research leading to Stephen Lucas's *Portents of Rebellion,*[6] one of the first of a generation of book-length studies of important rhetorical acts.

What has happened, however, is that there has been a change both in the respectability of public address studies within the discipline and in the self-reflexive nature of the studies themselves. Both changes are related, and both bespeak the maturation of a field of study. They recognize that the earlier conception of public address studies was unduly rigid, in at least three respects. First, it presumed one object of study—the public oration—to the exclusion of other types of public rhetorical acts. Second, it presumed a perspective—the historical. The term "historical" was used in opposition both to "contemporary" and to "critical." Public address studies did not involve people or events that were of current interest or relevance; they therefore seemed antiquarian. Moreover, they represented the worst tradition of names-and-dates history, providing little more than chronology and certainly excluding interpretation or judgment. It was not hard to see why public address was regarded as the intellectual backwater of the discipline. Third, it presumed a method—neo-Aristotelianism, not as Aristotle himself probably would have done it but as a set of categories automatically applied to any speaker or speech. The resulting studies were not theoretically interesting and often had as their primary finding that the neo-Aristotelian categories could be made to fit virtually anything.

Throughout the academy, and particularly in the human sciences, the late

---

[5] See Forbes Hill, "Conventional Wisdom—Traditional Form: The President's Message of November 3, 1969," *Quarterly Journal of Speech,* 58 (December, 1972): 373-386; Karlyn Kohrs Campbell, "An Exercise in the Rhetoric of Mythical America," *Critiques of Contemporary Rhetoric* (Belmont, Cal.: Wadsworth, 1972), 50-58; Campbell, " 'Conventional Wisdom—Traditional Form': A Rejoinder," *Quarterly Journal of Speech,* 58 (December, 1972): 451-454; Hill, "Reply to Professor Campbell," *Quarterly Journal of Speech,* 58, (December, 1972): 454-460; Robert P. Newman, "Under the Veneer, Nixon's Speech of November 3, 1969," *Quarterly Journal of Speech,* 56 (April, 1970), 168-178.
[6] Stephen E. Lucas, *Portents of Rebellion: Rhetoric and Revolution in Philadelphia, 1765-76* (Philadelphia: Temple University Press, 1976).

1960s and 1970s were marked by a self-reflexiveness about method and assumptions which called into question traditional models and paradigms. Public address studies were no exception. As scholars realized that rigidity as to the object, perspective, and method of study were constricting inquiry and producing studies that largely just replicated the assumptions, they began to probe in new directions. They examined other rhetorical forms besides the public speech, other units of study besides the individual orator, other perspectives besides the narrowly historical, and other methods besides neo-Aristotelianism. The resulting studies, now accumulating over a decade or more, make more substantial theoretical contributions, exhibit a richer array of approaches, demonstrate more methodological sophistication and awareness of assumptions, and—at least in my opinion—are more interesting. Along with the growing recognition of rhetoric's centrality to culture, they help to explain the revival of interest in public address.

II

One could point to many signs of vitality in public address. To start with, we have enlarged the meaning of "public address" from a mode to a function of discourse. It seems self-evident that any rhetorical act is "addressed" and hence evokes a "public." What we study when we study public address, then, is really rhetorical practice in all its manifestations. (In a recent review essay, Lucas takes a similar position, concluding that the phrase "public address" really identifies all public discursive rhetorical acts.[7] Although discourse certainly is at the center of the rhetorical tradition, I am not sure why only discursive sets are addressed to a public.) By embracing a broader conception of public address and not reducing the term to formal oratory, our studies have enhanced the potential for understanding historical or rhetorical situations and for formulating theoretical generalizations.

Moreover, our research exhibits a healthy pluralism of methods and approaches. These range from the microscopic analysis of individual texts to the macroscopic study of movements and campaigns. The underlying metaphor or approach may be traditional neo-Aristotelianism enlarged beyond the "cookie cutter" mold, or it may be dramatism, formism, organicism, ideology, or who knows what. This pluralism serves several valuable purposes. It enables multiple perspectives to be brought to bear on a single work, as illustrated in the recent symposium on Lincoln's Second Inaugural Address.[8] It permits a more careful articulation of the relationship between text and context. And it permits us to see public address as a social process including, for instance, media in diffusing public messages among audiences.

---

[7] Stephen E. Lucas, "The Renaissance of American Public Address: Text and Context in Rhetorical Criticism," *Quarterly Journal of Speech*, 74 (May, 1988): 243-262.
[8] The symposium appears in *Communication Reports*, 1 (Winter, 1988): 9-37.

Within the academy, public address courses are again fashionable, at-tracting healthy enrollments. My own university, Northwestern, may serve as a reasonable example. In 1970 the standard course in the history of American public address, which had been developed by Ernest Wrage, was scrapped in favor of one-quarter courses in the rhetoric of revivals, the rhetoric of demagogues, the rhetoric of social movements, and so on. In the mid-1970s the course was reintroduced, now retitled "Rhetorical history of the United States" to avoid the seemingly limiting term "public address," and it today exists alongside such generic courses as political communication, the rhetoric of war, and the rhetoric of social movements. Next fall 100 undergraduates will be reading Puritan sermons and the debate between Webster and Hayne. This experience is not atypical, and it has prompted authors and publishers to issue appropriate textual and reference materials in public address. Most of the standard anthologies are now out of print, but Waveland Press has just issued Ron Reid's *Three Centuries of American Rhetorical Discourse* and Longmans is soon to publish a two-volume anthology edited by Jim Andrews and me.[9] Under the editorship of Bernard Duffy and Halford Ross Ryan Greenwood Press has published a valuable two-volume reference work[10] and is undertaking an ambitious series of rhetorical biographies. Such a healthy publishing program is both a sign of and a stimulus for intensified scholarly activity.

Another sign of health is that scholars in other fields are discovering the role of public address. To be sure, they are not citing our work as often as we would like, and they sometimes remain oblivious to the discipline of Speech Communication. Nevertheless, there is growing work in what we like to call the cognate disciplines that reflects the importance of public address. History is the field I know best. Perhaps reflecting the influence of Charles Beard, many traditional historians seemed to assume that the primary motives in history were economic, and that rhetorical acts were at best transient and ephemeral, at worst attempts to mask true motives. One searches in vain through standard histories for extended treatments even of the Lincoln-Douglas debates as historical acts, much less as texts which offer valuable historical evidence about the culture at the time. But that is changing. Twenty years ago Bernard Bailyn published *Ideological Origins of the American Revolution,* in which he focuses on what the colonists themselves said were the causes of the struggle, taking the discourse of the revolutionary pamphlets

---

[9] Ronald F. Reid, ed., *Three Centuries of American Rhetorical Discourse* (Prospect Heights, Ill.: Waveland Press, 1987); James R. Andrews and David Zarefsky, ed., *American Voices: Significant Speeches in United States History, 1630-1945* (New York: Longmans, in press); David Zarefsky and James R. Andrews, ed. *Contemporary American Voices: Significant Speeches in United States History, 1945-Present* (New York: Longmans, in preparation).
[10] Bernard K. Duffy and Halford Ross Ryan, ed., *American Orators of the Twentieth Century* (Westport, Conn.: Greenwood Press, 1987); Duffy and Ryan, ed., *American Orators Before 1900* (Westport, Conn.: Greenwood Press, 1987).

seriously. Gordon Wood undertook a similar analysis of the early years of the republic.[11] More recently, historians have shown a strong interest in what they call "political culture," and—most importantly for our purposes—they maintain that the political culture of an age is constituted by its discourse. So, for example, Daniel Walker Howe, in his *The Political Culture of the American Whigs,* notes that the spirited debate between Whigs and Jacksonians was controlled by conventions of discourse.[12] Most recently, Jeffrey K. Tulis has published *The Rhetorical Presidency,* a particularly insightful analysis of how 19th and 20th century Presidents reflected radically different notions of the place of rhetoric in public affairs. Although the focus is limited to the Presidency, Tulis charts cultural attitudes and values about rhetoric in a manner not unlike Barnet Baskerville's *The People's Choice.*[13]

Although I emphasize the field of history, similar developments are taking place in other allied disciplines. Political scientists are focusing anew on political communication, and are examining rhetoric as a resource for power. Sociologists are finding symbolic structures as meaningful social units. Whole fields, of course, are becoming more aware of their own rhetorical practice, a phenomenon which has given rise to the Project of Rhetoric of Inquiry at the University of Iowa.[14]

There are dangers, of course, in the discovery of rhetoric by "outsiders." We could so rejoice at no longer being outcasts that we allow our own field of study to be defined by others; we could focus so much on disciplinary discourse that we forget that rhetorical practice traditionally has been associated with the public forum. But as signs of the vitality of public address, the rhetorical interests of scholars in other fields are valuable evidence.

Furthermore, our own studies have assumed greater depth and richness. With the exception of textbooks, for most of our history our discipline has been primarily a journal-article field. Whether that is because we undertook limited projects, or because publishers denied access to us for longer studies, is an unproductive question. The fact is that, particularly in the last decade, scholars in public address have produced a significant number of book-length

---

[11]Bernard Bailyn, *Ideological Origins of the American Revolution* (Cambridge, Mass.: Harvard Univ. Press, 1967); Gordon S. Wood, *The Creation of the American Republic, 1776-1787* (Chapel Hill: Univ. of North Carolina Press, 1969).

[12]Daniel Walker Howe, *The Political Culture of the American Whigs* (Chicago: Univ. of Chicago Press, 1979), esp. 23-24.

[13]Jeffrey K. Tulis, *The Rhetorical Presidency* (Princeton: Princeton Univ. Press, 1987); Barnet Baskerville, *The People's Choice: The Orator in American Society* (Lexington, Ky.: Univ. Press of Kentucky, 1979).

[14]See especially John S. Nelson, Allan Megill, and Donald N. McCloskey, ed., *The Rhetoric of the Human Sciences: Language and Argument in Scholarship and Public Affairs* (Madison: Univ. of Wisconsin Press, 1987). A series of books on this theme is being published by the University of Wisconsin Press.

manuscripts, with more on the way.[15] This is not self-evidently a sign of vitality—after all, much nonsense can be found between hard covers. But it does permit greater depth of research and exposition; it does permit scholars to undertake more ambitious inquiries which require more space in which to present the results; it does make our work more accessible to larger audiences, and it does increase the chances that it will be noticed and reviewed outside our own discipline. And, of course, the growing interest of respected university presses in publishing public address studies is itself a sign of vitality.

III

These types of evidence all point to health, intellectual ferment, and excitement about the study of public address. There is one theme which warrants discussion in more detail, however, because I believe it to be at the base of the recent renaissance. Our studies in public address are increasingly theory-driven, and cases are related directly to theories; this condition is a strength, but it also implies a possible weakness.

By "theory," I do not mean the rigor and rigidity of covering laws from which precise causal statements can be derived. Although originating in the philosophy of history, this approach sometimes characterizes theory construction in the social sciences. What I have in mind is a construct more like "explanation."[16] A study in public address is theory-driven if it is prompted by or suggestive of questions about processes or events which are broader than the given case and to whose answers the study can make a contribution. This is a justification for study quite different from the claim that it will be another study of a given type which is warranted because no one has done it before.

According to most models of the logic of inquiry, a researcher formulates a theoretically interesting question. When it is appropriate to test the question by controlled experimentation or a sample survey, the researcher does that. When it is appropriate to test the question by reference to a particular case—as, for example, in anthropology or history—that is what is done. Now, in

---

[15]Examples include Kathleen Hall Jamieson, *Packaging the Presidency: A History and Criticism of Presidential Campaign Advertising* (New York: Oxford Univ. Press, 1984); Ernest G. Bormann, *The Force of Fantasy: Restoring the American Dream* (Carbondale: Southern Ill. Univ. Press, 1985); Kathleen J. Turner, *Lyndon Johnson's Dual War: Vietnam and the Press* (Chicago: Univ. of Chicago Press, 1985); Frederick J. Antczak, *Thought and Character: The Rhetoric of Democratic Education* (Ames: Iowa State Univ. Press, 1985); J. Michael Hogan, *The Panama Canal in American Politics: Domestic Advocacy and the Evolution of Policy* (Carbondale: Southern Ill. Univ. Press, 1986); David Zarefsky, *President Johnson's War on Poverty: Rhetoric and History* (University, Ala: Univ. of Alabama Press, 1986); Roderick P. Hart, *The Sound of Leadership: Presidential Communication in the Modern Age* (Chicago: Univ. of Chicago Press, 1987); and Kathleen Hall Jamieson, *Eloquence in an Electronic Age: The Transformation of Political Speechmaking* (New York: Oxford Univ. Press, 1988).
[16]On different approaches to the meaning of "theory," see Carl G. Hempel, "The Function of General Laws in History," *Journal of Philosophy*, 39 (1942): 35-48; William Dray, *Laws and Explanation in History* (London: Oxford Univ. Press, 1957).

fact, research often does not proceed in that way. I suspect that it is an intriguing aspect of the case which often is the initial motive for the study, and that only later does one's interest in the case lead to broader questions. But it does lead there, and in presenting the results of research, the scholar typically stresses the linkage between the specific case and the questions of broader significance. In this sense the most significant feature of much of our recent public address research is that it is guided and influenced by theory.

The theory which animates a given study might come from any of several places. Most obviously, it might come from rhetorical theory or the philosophy of communication. A particular precept is either developed or tested, as the case may be, by reference to specific rhetorical practice. An example from my own work is my attempt to explain Lyndon Johnson's advocacy of affirmative action by reference to Perelman and Olbrechts-Tyteca's theory of dissociation. More generally Ernest Bormann's history of early American public discourse flows from his own symbolic convergence theory of communication and his concept of fantasy themes and rhetorical visions.[17]

Another obvious source of theoretical underpinning for public address studies lies in the nature of the rhetorical object. Form and genre studies are the clearest example. Harrell, Ware, and Linkugel analyze Nixon's public defenses concerning the Watergate scandal by reference to the generic form of apologia which Nixon is assumed to exhibit. Likewise, Rod Hart's extended study, *The Political Pulpit*, proceeds from a theory of the inaugural address as a rhetorical genre.[18]

But rhetorical sources are not the only places where one might find theory which guides public address studies. Potent studies can relate to a theory of the situation or of the context; often such theories may derive from other disciplines. Theories of the rise and fall of Presidential power, the ebb and flow of liberalism and conservatism, the dialectic of reform and reaction, the power of metaphor, or the social basis of information processing—to name but a few—can provide firm grounding and linkages.

Whatever the source of theory in the particular case, public address studies are also guided by a more general if unarticulated theory of the process of public address itself—and from it, too, interesting questions may flow. It is a theory which blends elements of symbolic interactionism with Kenneth Burke's concept of identification. It holds that reality is not "given" but that we perceive it as we define it through symbols. Definitions of situations involve choices among symbols, and the choices are not neutral. The symbols then serve as the premises for argument and appeal to others.

---

[17]David Zarefsky, "Lyndon Johnson Redefines 'Equal Opportunity': The Beginnings of Affirmative Action," *Central States Speech Journal*, 31 (Summer, 1980): 85-94; Bormann, *The Force of Fantasy*.

[18]Jackson Harrell, B. L. Ware, and Wil A. Linkugel, "Failure of Apology in American Politics: Nixon on Watergate," *Speech Monographs*, 42 (November, 1975): 245-261; Roderick P. Hart, *The Political Pulpit* (West Lafayette, Ind.: Purdue Univ. Press, 1977).

The exchange of symbols through discourse validates and modifies our views of the world, and likewise in exchanging symbols we modify others' views of the world, and in this way we influence and relate to them. This process of symbolic exchange involves identification between speakers and audiences, and to study public address is to study how, within the frame of often unrecognized ideology, speakers' central values and proposals are connected with the ideas and predispositions of the audience, and how each modifies the other. The importance of such a study is that the creation and exchange of symbols is both the glue holding society together (through evoking common bonds) and also the force which moves people toward goals (by evoking a utopian symbolic vision).

The grounding of studies theoretically has obvious benefits. It permits generalization beyond the bounds of the particular case. It furnishes the criterion for evaluating research results, whether the particular inquiry "led" anywhere. It enables a discipline to develop a cumulative body of research, and in that sense to "get better." But there also are pitfalls to be avoided. Theories drawn from rhetoric and communication philosophy may develop the same cookie-cutter problem for which neo-Aristotelianism was reviled; the studies may say more about the all-encompassing nature of the theory than about the rhetorical act being examined. Theories which presume the constancy of a rhetorical form may be insensitive to the importance of context or the role of cultural change; the Tulis book, for example, in my opinion, casts serious doubt on the allegation that there are unchanging generic requirements for the Presidential inaugural address. And theories drawn from context, situation, or other disciplines can become weak imitations of the real thing—the very charge that was invoked against earlier public address studies.

To my mind, though, there is an even greater pitfall in the assumption that theories must transcend particular cases. That assumption, of course, characterizes the perspective of the social sciences, according to which theory is a source of generalization. But we should also be sensitive to the perspective of the humanities, according to which a theory of the particular case may prompt useful study which enriches or deepens understanding of that case. This line of thinking begins with the premise that public address is an important phenomenon in its own right—not just for what a case study might contribute to rhetorical or scientific theories. It assumes that particular cases of discourse may present interesting questions, paradoxes, or anomalies, which a study of public address might answer by developing a "theory of the case." Illustrative of excellent studies in this regard are Leff's analyses of space and time in Lincoln's "House Divided" speech and his second Inaugural Address.[19] The result of each of those studies is to suggest a theory which

---

[19]Michael C. Leff, "Rhetorical Timing in Lincoln's 'House Divided' Speech," *The Van Zelst Lecture in Communication* (Evanston, Ill.: Northwestern University, 1983); "Dimensions of Temporality in Lincoln's Second Inaugural," *Communication Reports*, 1 (Winter, 1988); 26-31.

more fully encompasses the case than do the alternatives Leff's analysis of the "House Divided" speech responds to the accusations by some historians that the speech is inconsistent or that it develops farfetched charges which obviously were not believable. His study of the Second Inaugural Address speaks to the question of how Lincoln could fuse the secular and the sacred.

In summary, then, I believe the primary reason for the current greater strength of public address studies is that they are theory-driven, but we need to be clear about what that means. Theory permits drawing inferences which connect the study to something else—maybe to a broader generalization, maybe to an explanation of the specific case. Rhetorical studies need not always be driven by rhetorical theories, and in any case we need to be sure that our theories are sensitive to the richness of detail which is evident only in the study of particular cases.

IV

So far I have characterized the state of public address scholarship as mature and healthy. One sign of a mature and healthy field is that it can confront difficult issues about its own purpose and method. I should like to close by referring to several of these.

First, we need to settle the question of the relationship between history and criticism by reinventing, as it were, the "historical-critical method." Now, not all history is critical; not all criticism is historical. Granted. But any instance of public address consists of a text (using that term broadly) and hence is susceptible to critical examination. And any instance of public address occurs in some context and hence is susceptible to historical study. The emphasis between text and context will vary from one study to the next, but I find it hard to imagine a decent study of public address which does not partake of both.

Perhaps another way to say this is that any public address study should be interpretive. It should say something that makes a difference about the work with which it is concerned. What it "says" is an argument, a statement containing an inference which goes beyond the text itself yet is supported by good reasons.[20] Excluded from this definition are such modes as simple narratives of what happened, restatement of the text, recitation of the factual conditions surrounding the delivery of the speech—pure history—or formulaic studies for which the context is irrelevant—pure criticism. The middle ground, what is both historical and critical, is where interpretive studies thrive. Yes, one can posit distinctions between rhetorical history and rhetorical criticism,[21] but for public address studies it does not seem to me to be

---

[20]This view of argument is obviously influenced by Wayne Brockriede, "Where Is Argument?" *Journal of the American Forensic Association*, 11 (Spring, 1975): 179-182.
[21]See, for example, Bruce Gronbeck, "Rhetorical History and Rhetorical Criticism: A Distinction," *Speech Teacher*, 24 (November, 1975): 309-320.

useful to do so, since they embody both.

Second, having said that, it follows that public address scholars need to become more sophisticated with both historical and critical methods. I share Ronald Carpenter's concern[22] that we are not sufficiently meticulous about using the available primary sources to understand a historical situation, with the result that we may offer critical claims easily dismissed by reference to historical evidence—that we may offer, as it were, "a promising theory killed by a fact." As a discipline, we are not as skilled as we ought to be at knowing how to identify and locate the relevant primary sources, how to assess them, and how to use them as evidence for claims that we might advance. Likewise, our familiarity with theories of criticism needs to advance well beyond any of the formulaic approaches or any of the currently popular schools, such as structuralism and deconstruction, to a philosophical understanding of the act of criticism itself: What does it mean to make judgments? How can they be supported and tested? Especially in a world of critical pluralism, what distinguishes interpretation from misinterpretation?[23]

Third, we need to deal with all the same problems of canonization which confront our colleagues in literature. On the one hand, we do need to revisit what by common consent are a body of great speeches. Mohrmann is right in noting with surprise that many of these "great speeches" have never been subjected to careful rhetorical study.[24] Presumably, works acquire canonical status for some reason, and renewed attention to the "classic" texts might help us to understand those reasons. At the same time, the standard canon of public address is not neutral. Some groups of speakers are notoriously under-represented, and some topics are treated as taboo. We must be sure that our concept of a canon does not become a closed system and that we continually engage the question of what it means to say that any given instance of public address belongs in the canon.

Fourth, we need to clarify the stance from which the student of public address approaches the work. I have argued elsewhere that the analyst can be a commentator, explicating the rhetorical method in the text and making manifest what is latent in the work; or a partisan, entering the same discourse community as the rhetor and engaging his or her claims and arguments; or a judge who invokes and revises norms.[25] It is important to recognize the differences among these stances so that we do not slip from one to another. Although he does not use this language, that in effect is the charge Forbes

---

[22]See Ronald H. Carpenter, "Whatever Happened to the 'Historical' in Historical-Critical Method?" paper presented at the Southern Speech Communication Association convention, April, 1986.

[23]This is the central theme of Wayne C. Booth, *Critical Understanding: The Powers and Limits of Pluralism* (Chicago: Univ. of Chicago Press, 1979).

[24]Cited in Michael Leff, "Textual Criticism, The Legacy of G. P. Mohrmann," *Quarterly Journal of Speech,* 72 (November, 1986): 377.

[25]David Zarefsky, "Argumentation and the Politics of Criticism," *Argument and Critical Practices: Proceedings of the Fifth SCA/AFA Summer Conference on Argumentation,* ed. Joseph W. Wenzel (Annandale, Va.: SCA, 1987), 53-59.

Hill brings against Karlyn Campbell in their famous exchange: that is, that she is acting both as a partisan and as a judge, violating the ethical principle that one should not be a judge in one's own cause. It is also important to recognize that the function of commentary is primary; analysis which ignores questions such as "What is happening here?" and proceeds to refutation may be attacking a straw man, throwing volleys against a creation that might not be recognized by its own maker. Moreover, judgment risks becoming self-sealing, calcifying into prejudice, because it does not open itself to confrontation with the thing judged.

Fifth, we need more comparative studies of the same rhetorical objects, exemplified by the symposium on Lincoln's Second Inaugural in the first issue of *Communication Reports.*[26] Comparative perspectives on the same text focus our attention on how the analyst's assumptions and methods shape the impressions one has of the object itself. They also invite attention to the need for standards of judgment and choice among competing interpretations. If one regards studies as making arguments, then the standards evolve from a notion of criticism as an argument field.

Sixth, we need to revisit the idea of rhetorical biography. Many of our earliest studies were biographical, and many were conceptually weak; we risk the *post hoc* fallacy if we assume that they were weak because biographical. A pattern of rhetorical choice that develops over time, significant changes in rhetorical practice, rhetorical method that is influenced by or responsive to important events in a speaker's life—all these are fruitful subjects for investigation. The biographical series planned by Greenwood Press affords scholars the opportunity to bring to rhetorical biography the maturity and theoretical grounding for the discipline that has been observed in other studies.

Seventh, we need to play our part in helping to explicate the fundamental construct of "public" on which public address scholarship is based. This need has several dimensions. Our studies implicitly presume a culture in which there is such a thing as a "public forum"; we need to explore how rhetorical practice is affected in cultures which lack such a construct. We also need to explore more carefully how the widening and narrowing of the public forum affect rhetorical practice; my colleague Tom Goodnight has initiated a productive line of work in this respect by focusing on the public, private, and technical as spheres of argument.[27] And we need to explore how discourse constructs and responds to crises in the nature of the public, such as the tangled nature of authority in the late 1970s which my colleague Tom Farrell has explored through the discourse of President Carter.[28] The place where

---

[26]See note 8.

[27]G. Thomas Goodnight, "The Personal, Technical, and Public Spheres of Argument: A Speculative Inquiry into the Art of Public Deliberation," *Journal of the American Forensic Association,* 18 (Spring, 1982): 214-227.

[28]See Thomas B. Farrell, "Knowledge in Time: Toward an Extension of Rhetorical Form," *Advances in Argumentation Theory and Research,* ed. J. Robert Cox and Charles Arthur Willard (Carbondale: Southern Ill. Univ. Press, 1982), esp. 138-151.

studies of rhetorical theory and practice join is precisely this elemental construct of "the public", and it is at that place that case studies may make their most direct contribution to the advancement of theory.

And, finally, we need to keep discussions such as this one within their proper bounds. Assaying the state of the art is heady stuff, and the temptation to pontificate is sometimes great. Discourse such as this is useful if it helps to spot trends, focus issues, or stimulate scholarship. But it is parasitic if it fosters the extended "paradigm wars" which may substitute for the actual work of the discipline. Put simply, we do not need to spend time arguing about whether we follow a "rules" or "laws" perspective, whether we are historians or critics, whether we draw our inspiration from the humanities or the social sciences, or any of the other pseudo-issues which have plagued this and related disciplines. We should have a healthy tolerance for ambiguity about these matters, following Burke's admonition to use all that is there to use. Instead we should do what public address scholars do best: ground our theories in the data and not lose sight of the cases. Soundly conceived, skillfully executed studies of rhetorical practice are what will most assure the continued health of our field.

Bibliography

Aly, Bower. "The History of American Public Address as a Research Field." *The Quarterly Journal of Speech 29* (1943): 308-314.

Andrews, James R. *The Practice of Rhetorical Criticism.* New York: Longman, 1990.

Andrews, James R. and David Zarefsky, eds. *American Voices: Significant Speeches in American History 1640-1945.* New York: Longman, 1989.

Andrews, James R. and David Zarefsky, eds. *Contemporary American Voices: Significant Speeches in American History 1945-Present.* New York: Longman, 1992.

Arnold, Carroll C. "The Case Against Speech: An Examination of Critical Viewpoints." *The Quarterly Journal of Speech 40* (1954): 165-169.

Arnold, Carroll C. *Criticism of Oral Rhetoric.* Columbus: Charles E. Merrill, 1974.

Arnold, Carroll C. "Reflections on American Public Discourse." *Central States Speech Journal 28* (1977): 73-85.

Auer, J. Jeffery, ed. *Antislavery and Disunion, 1858-1861: Studies in the Rhetoric of Compromise and Conflict.* New York: Harper & Row, 1963.

Baskerville, Barnet. *The People's Voice: The Orator in American Society.* Lexington: University of Kentucky Press, 1979.

Benson, Thomas W., ed. *American Rhetoric: Context and Criticism.* Carbondale: Southern Illinois University Press, 1989.

Benson, Thomas W. "The Senses of Rhetoric: A Tropical System for Critics." *Central States Speech Journal 29* (1978): 237-250.

Benson, Thomas W., ed. *Speech Communication in the 20th Century.* Carbondale: Southern Illinois University Press, 1985.

Bitzer, Lloyd F. "The Rhetorical Situation." *Philosophy & Rhetoric 1* (1968): 1-18.

Bitzer, Lloyd F. and Edwin Black, eds. *The Prospect of Rhetoric.* Englewood Cliffs: Prentice-Hall, 1971.

Black, Edwin. "A Note on Theory and Practice in Rhetorical Criticism." *Western Journal of Speech Communication 44* (1980): 331-336.

Black, Edwin. *Rhetorical Criticism: A Study in Method.* New York: Macmillan, 1965.

Black, Edwin. *Rhetorical Questions: Studies of Public Discourse.* Chicago: University of Chicago Press, 1992.

Blankenship, Jane and Hermann G. Stelzner, eds. *Rhetoric and Communication: Studies in the University of Illinois Tradition.* Urbana: University of Illinois Press, 1976.

Bormann, Ernest G. *The Force of Fantasy: Restoring the American Dream.* Carbondale: Southern Illinois University Press, 1985.

Bostdorff, Denise M. *The Presidency and the Rhetoric of Foreign Crisis.* Columbia: University of South Carolina Press, 1993.

Braden, Waldo W., ed. *Oratory in the Old South.* Baton Rouge: Louisiana State University Press, 1970.

Brigance, William Norwood, ed. *A History and Criticism of American Public Address.* 2 Vol. New York: McGraw-Hill, 1943.

Brock, Bernard L., Robert L. Scott, and James W. Chesebro, eds. *Methods of Rhetorical Criticism: A Twentieth-Century Perspective.* 3rd ed. Detroit: Wayne State University Press, 1989.

Brockriede, Wayne. "Rhetorical Criticism as Argument." *The Quarterly Journal of Speech 60* (1974): 165-174.

Bryant, Donald C. *Rhetorical Dimensions in Criticism.* Baton Rouge: Louisiana State University Press, 1973.

Calloway-Thomas, Carolyn and John Louis Lucaites, eds. *Martin Luther King Jr., and the Sermonic Power of Public Discourse.* University: University of Alabama Press, 1993.

Campbell, Karlyn Kohrs. *Critiques of Contemporary Rhetoric.* Belmont: Wadsworth, 1972.

Campbell, Karlyn Kohrs and Kathleen Hall Jamieson. *Deeds Done in Words: Presidential Rhetoric and the Genres of Governance.* Chicago: University of Chicago Press, 1990.

Campbell, Karlyn Kohrs and Kathleen Hall Jamieson, eds. *Form and Genre: Shaping Rhetorical Action.* Falls Church: Speech Communication Association, 1978.

Campbell, Karlyn Kohrs. "The Nature of Criticism in Rhetorical and Communicative Studies." *Central States Speech Journal 30* (1979): 4-13.

Campbell, Karlyn Kohrs, ed. *Women Public Speakers in the United States, 1800-1925: A Bio-Critical Sourcebook.* Westport: Greenwood Press, 1993.

Cathcart, Robert. *Post Communication: Rhetorical Analysis and Evaluation.* 2nd ed. Indianapolis: Bobbs-Merrill, 1981.

Crandell, S. Judson. "The Beginnings of a Methodology for Social Control Studies in Public Address." *The Quarterly Journal of Speech 33* (1947): 36-39.

Croft, Albert J. "The Functions of Rhetorical Criticism." *The Quarterly Journal of Speech 42* (1956): 283-291.

Dickey, Dallas C. "What Directions Should Future Research in American Public Address Take?" *The Quarterly Journal of Speech 29* (1943): 300-304.

Duffy, Bernard K. and Halford R. Ryan, eds. *American Orators Before 1900: Critical Studies and Sources.* Westport: Greenwood Press, 1987.

Duffy, Bernard K. and Halford R. Ryan, eds. *American Orators of the Twentieth Century: Critical Studies and Sources.* Westport: Greenwood Press, 1987.

Fisher, Walter R. "Method in Rhetorical Criticism." *Southern Speech Journal 35* (1969): 101-109.

Fisher, Walter R., ed. *Rhetoric: A Tradition in Transition.* East Lansing: Michigan State University Press, 1974.

Foss, Sonja K. *Rhetorical Criticism: Exploration & Practice.* Prospect Heights: Waveland Press, 1989.

Gregg, Richard B. "The Criticism of Symbolic Inducement: A Critical-Theoretical Connection." In *Speech Communication in the 20th Century,* ed. Thomas W.

Benson, 41-62. Carbondale: Southern Illinois University Press, 1985.

Griffin, Leland M. "The Rhetoric of Historical Movements." *The Quarterly Journal of Speech 38* (1952): 184-188.

Gronbeck, Bruce E. "Rhetorical History and Rhetorical Criticism: A Distinction." *The Speech Teacher 24* (1975): 309-320.

Gustainis, J. Justin. *American Rhetoric and the Vietnam War.* New York: Praeger, 1993.

Harlman, Robert, ed. *Rhetoric, Mass Media, and the Law.* University of Alabama Press, 1990.

Hart, Roderick P. "Contemporary Scholarship in Public Address: A Research Editorial." *Western Journal of Speech Communication 50* (1986): 283-295.

Hart, Roderick P. *The Sound of Leadership: Presidential Communication in the Modern Age.* Chicago: University of Chicago Press, 1987.

Hart, Roderick P. "Theory Building and Rhetorical Criticism: An Informal Statement of Opinion." *Central State Speech Journal 27* (1976): 70-77.

Hillbruner, Anthony. *Critical Dimensions: The Art of Public Address Criticism.* New York: Random House, 1966.

Hitchcock, Orville, "Public Address and Liberal Education." *Central States Speech Journal 27* (1976): 169-175.

Hochmuth, Marie, ed. *A History and Criticism of American Public Address.* Vol. III. New York: Russell & Russell, 1955.

Hochmuth, Marie. *Rhetoric and Criticism.* Baton Rouge: Louisiana State University Press, 1963.

Holland, Dewitte, ed. *Preaching in American History.* Nashville: Abingdon Press, 1969.

Iltis, Robert S. and Stephen H. Browne. "Tradition and Resurgence in Public Address Studies." In *Speech Communication: Essays to Commemorate the 75th Anniversary of The Speech Communication Association,* ed. Gerald M. Phillips and Julia T. Wood, 81-93. Carbondale: Southern Illinois University Press, 1990.

Jamieson, Kathleen Hall. *Eloquence in an Electronic Age: The Transformation of Political Speechmaking.* New York: Oxford University Press, 1988.

Johannesen, Richard L., R.R. Allen, and Wil A. Linkugel, eds. *Contemporary American Speeches.* 6th ed. Dubuque: Kendall/Hunt, 1988.

Kiewe, Amos. *The Modern Presidency and Crisis Rhetoric.* New York: Praeger, 1993.

Leff, Michael C. "Interpretation and the Art of the Rhetorical Critic." *Western Journal of Speech Communication 44* (1980): 337-349.

Leff, Michael C. and Fred J. Kauffeld, eds. *Texts in Context: Critical Dialogues on Significant Episodes in American Political Rhetoric.* Davis, CA: Hermagoras Press, 1989.

Logue, Calvin M. and Howard Dorgan, eds. *A New Diversity in Contemporary Southern Rhetoric.* Baton Rouge: Louisiana State University Press, 1987.

Lucas, Stephen E. *Portents of Rebellion.* Philadelphia: Temple University Press, 1976.

Medhurst, Martin J., ed. *Eisenhower's War of Words: Rhetoric and Leadership.* East Lansing: Michigan State University Press, 1993.

Medhurst, Martin J. "Public Address and Significant Scholarship: Four Challenges to the Rhetorical Renaissance." In *Texts in Context,* ed. Michael C. Leff and Fred J. Kauffeld, 29-42. Davis, CA: Hermagoras Press, 1989.

Medhurst, Martin J., Robert L. Ivie, Phillip Wander, and Robert L. Scott. *Cold War Rhetoric: Strategy, Metaphor, and Ideology.* Westport: Greenwood Press, 1990.

Medhurst, Martin J. and Thomas W. Benson, eds. *Rhetorical Dimensions in Media: A Critical Casebook.* 2nd ed. Dubuque: Kendall/Hunt, 1991.

Mohrmann, G.P., Charles J. Stewart, and Donovan J. Ochs, eds. *Exploration in Rhetorical Criticism.* University Park: The Pennsylvania State University Press, 1973.

Nilsen, Thomas R. "Criticism and Social Consequences." *The Quarterly Journal of Speech 42* (1956): 173-178.

Nilsen, Thomas R., ed. *Essays in Rhetorical Criticism.* New York: Random House, 1968.

Oliver, Robert T. *History of Public Speaking in America.* Boston: Allyn and Bacon, 1965.

Parrish, Wayland Maxfield and Marie Hochmuch, eds. *American Speeches.* New York: Longmans, Green, 1954.

Reid, Ronald F., ed. *Three Centuries of American Political Discourse.* Prospect Heights: Waveland Press, 1988.

Ritter, Kurt and James R. Andrews. *The American Ideology.* Falls Church: Speech Communication Association, 1978.

Rohler, Lloyd and Roger Cook, eds. *Great Speeches for Criticism & Analysis.* 2nd ed. Greenwood, Ind: Educational Video Group, 1993.

Rosenfield, Lawrence W. "The Anatomy of Critical Discourse." *Speech Monographs 35* (1968): 50-69.

Ryan, Halford Ross, ed. *American Rhetoric from Roosevelt to Reagan.* Prospect Heights: Waveland Press, 1983.

Ryan, Halford R., ed. *The Inaugural Addresses of Twentieth-Century American Presidents.* New York: Praeger, 1993.

Sillars, Malcolm O. *Messages, Meanings, and Culture: Approaches to Communication Criticism.* New York: Harper/Collins, 1991.

Simons, Herbert W. and Aram Aghazarian, eds. *Form, Genre, and the Study of Political Discourse.* Columbia: University of South Carolina Press, 1986.

Thompson, Wayne N. "Contemporary Public Address: A Problem in Criticism." *The Quarterly Journal of Speech 40* (1954): 24-30.

Thompson, Wayne N. "Contemporary Public Address as a Research Area." *The Quarterly Journal of Speech 33* (1947): 274-283.

Thonssen, Lester, A. Craig Baird, and Waldo W. Braden. *Speech Criticism*. 2nd ed. New York: Ronald Press, 1970.

Wallace, Karl R., ed. *History of Speech Education in America: Background Studies*. New York: Appleton-Century-Crofts, 1954.

Wander, Philip and Steven Jenkins. "Rhetoric, Society, and the Critical Response." *The Quarterly Journal of Speech 58* (1972): 441-450.

Weiler, Michael and W. Barnett Pearce, eds. *Reagan and Public Discourse in America*. University: University of Alabama Press, 1992.

White, Eugene E. *The Context of Human Discourse: A Configurational Criticism of Rhetoric*. Columbia: University of South Carolina Press, 1992.

White, Eugene E., ed. *Rhetoric in Transition*. University Park: The Pennsylvania State University Press, 1980.

Windt, Theodore and Beth Ingold, eds. *Essays in Presidential Rhetoric*. 2nd ed. Dubuque: Kendall/Hunt, 1987.

Windt, Theodore Otto Jr. *Presidents and Protesters: Political Rhetoric in the 1960s*. University: University of Alabama Press, 1990.

Wrage, Ernest J. and Barnet Baskerville, eds. *Contemporary Forum: American Speeches on Twentieth-Century Issues*. New York: Harper & Brothers, 1962.

Zarefsky, David. "Argumentation and the Politics of Criticism." In *Argument and Critical Practices*, ed. Joseph W. Wenzel, 53-59. Annandale, VA: Speech Communication Association, 1987.

Zarefsky, David. *Lincoln, Douglas, and Slavery: In the Crucible of Public Debate*. Chicago: University of Chicago Press, 1990.

Zarefsky, David. *Lyndon Johnson's War on Poverty: Rhetoric and History*. University: University of Alabama Press, 1986.

Index